CONTENTS

Acknowledgements   vii

Introduction to the Ecohouse Design Guide   1

1 The form of the house: the building as an analogy   15
2 The environmental impact of building materials   38
   Andre Viljoen and Katrin Bohn
3 Detailing the envelope   63
4 Building-in soul   85
   Christopher Day
5 Ventilation   95
6 Health and happiness in the home   123
7 Passive solar design   148
8 Photovoltaics   165
9 Solar hot water systems   200
10 Using water wisely   216

Case study introduction: towards the new vernacular   239

Owner	*Place*	*Country*	*Designer/Architect/Team*	
1 Sue Roaf	Oxford	UK	Sue Roaf and David Woods	242
2 Inglis & Goudsmit	Findhorn	Scotland	Johan Vorster	246
3 Økologiske Hus AS, Norges Forskningstråd, statens Forurensningstilsyn	Marnardal	Norway	Bjørn Berge, Gaia, Lista AS	251
4 Krister Wiberg	Lund	Sweden	Krister Wiberg	254
5 Dr and Mrs Ramlal	Hyderabad	India	Prashant Kapoor, Saleem Akhtar, Arun Prasad, Manuel Fuentes	256
6 Syounai	Hamamatsu	Japan	OM Solar	262
7 Mr and Mrs I. Sagara	Inagi	Tokyo, Japan	Ken-ichi Kimura, Mr H Matsuoka	266
8 Jimmy Lim	Kuala Lumpur	Malaysia	Jimmy Lim, CSL Associates	268
9 Ministry of Construction, Indonesia	Surabaya	Indonesia	Prof. Silas, Dr Y Kodama	272
10 F. and F. Riedweg	Townsville	Australia	Felix Riedweg	275
11 Graham Duncan	Waiheke Island	New Zealand	Graham Duncan	279

Owner	*Place*	*Country*	*Designer/Architect/Team*	
12 Ashok and Rajiv Lall	Delhi	India	Ashok Lall Architects	282
13 M. L. Bidani	Delhi	India	Arvind Krishan	288
14 Isaac Meir	Negev Desert Highlands	Israel	Isaac Meir	291
15 Manuel Fuentes and Ana Lopez	Bariloche	Argentina	Manuel Fuentes	296
16 David Morrison and Susan Parson	Oyster Pond	St Maarten	David Morrison Associates	303
17 Jose Roberto Garcia-Chavez	Mexico City	Mexico	Jose Roberto Garcia-Chavez	308
18 Richard Levine	Lexington, KT	USA	Richard Levine	313
19 Charles Middleton	Gravenhurst, Ontario	Canada	Charles Middleton	317
20 Christopher Day	Pembrokeshire	Wales	Christopher Day	321
21 David Johnson	Monmouth	Wales	Andrew Yeats, Matthew Hill, Steve Wade	325
Glossary				328
References				336
Conversion Factors				343
Index				345

ECOHOUSE:

A DESIGN GUIDE

Sue Roaf, Manuel Fuentes, Stephanie Thomas

Architectural
Press

OXFORD AMSTERDAM BOSTON LONDON NEW YORK PARIS
SAN DIEGO SAN FRANCISCO SINGAPORE SYDNEY TOKYO

Architectural Press
An imprint of Elsevier Science
Linacre House, Jordan Hill, Oxford OX2 8DP
200 Wheeler Road, Burlington, MA 01803

First published 2001
Reprinted 2001, 2002

British Library Cataloguing in Publication Data
A catalogue record for this book is available from the British Library

Library of Congress Cataloguing in Publication Data
A catalogue record for this book is available from the Library of Congress

ISBN 0 7506 4904 6

For information on all Architectural Press publications
visit our website at www.architecturalpress.com

Composition by Scribe Design, Gillingham, Kent
Printed and bound in Italy by Printer Trento SRL

ACKNOWLEDGEMENTS

The authors would like to thank the following people for their help in compiling this book:

- for chapters of, and contributors to the book: Christopher Day, Andre Viljoen, Katrin Bohn and Robert and Brenda Vale; for the climate maps: Cherry Bonaria;
- for illustrations: Tony Garrett, Edward Mazna, Andrew Marsh, Ian Giuliani, Glasshead Films Ltd, and The Centre for Window and Cladding Technology, Bath, with a special thanks to Michael Howlett for his beautiful pencil drawings;
- for case studies: all those who have helped to make the studies so varied and interesting, many many thanks, including Puteri SC Cempaka for help with locating the Indonesian example;
- for support during the writing of the book: Ana Lopez, Ryan Rees, Mr Thomas (Stephanie's father), Christopher and Richard Roaf, and Maita Kessler;
- for contributions to the text: everyone who has helped, including Fergus Nicol, Steven Szokolay, John Willoughby, David Woods, David Olivier, Jeremy Dain, George Goudsmit, Andrew Bairstow, Vivien Walker, Michael Humpheys and Ellen Salazar;
- thanks are also due to our many students on the MSc in Energy Efficient Building at Oxford Brookes University who are just brilliant. Manuel, Stephanie, Cherry, Ellen, Prashant, Valpy, Andrew and Johann have all helped make this book happen, as have many others along the way. Keep up the good work!
- for future contributions: this is very much a work in progress, so can we thank now all those people who will be kind enough to send in advice, suggestions, information and corrections to be included in the next edition of the book;
- thanks to Nat Rea (tel: +44 2076 245063) for his photos of the Oxford Ecohouse;
- for Figures 8.12 and 8.13 © Times Newspapers Limited, 27th January 1996.

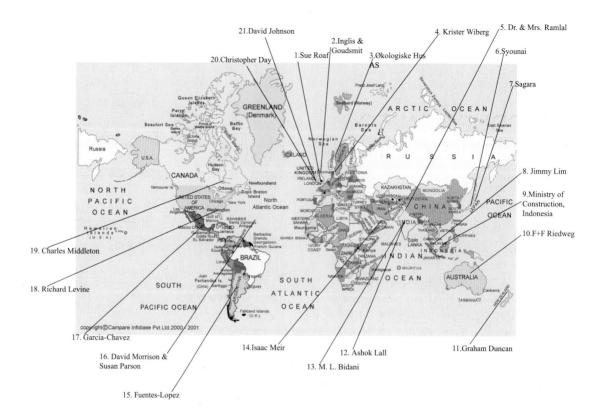

21.David Johnson

20.Christopher Day

1.Sue Roaf

2.Inglis & Goudsmit

3.Økologiske Hus AS

4. Krister Wiberg

5. Dr. & Mrs. Ramlal

6.Syounai

7.Sagara

8. Jimmy Lim

9.Ministry of Construction, Indonesia

10.F+F Riedweg

11.Graham Duncan

12. Ashok Lall

13. M. L. Bidani

14.Isaac Meir

15. Fuentes-Lopez

16. David Morrison & Susan Parson

17. Garcia-Chavez

18. Richard Levine

19. Charles Middleton

copyright©Campare Infobase Pvt.Ltd.2000 - 2001

INTRODUCTION TO
THE ECOHOUSE DESIGN GUIDE

The first question to answer should be: what is an ecohouse? Eco-architecture sees buildings as part of the larger ecology of the planet and the building as part of a living habitat. This contrasts with the more common notions of many architects, who see a building as a work of art, perhaps on exhibition in a settlement or as 'frozen music' in the people-less pictures of glossy magazines. Some architects see the process of design as a production line with the building as a product to be deposited on a site, regardless of its particular environment or qualities. You will see from the case studies at the end of the book that ecohouses are closely connected to their site, society, climate, region and the planet.

Why bother making buildings connect in this way? Because the alternative is not acceptable and 'modern buildings' are literally destroying the planet. It does not help that the numbers of people on the planet are growing so rapidly (5.3 billion in 1990; 8.1 billion by 2020; 10.7 billion in the 2080s) or that we have increasingly sophisticated technologies to exploit the Earth's natural resources. But it should be widely known that buildings are the single most damaging polluters on the planet, consuming over half of all the energy used in developed countries and producing over half of all climate-change gases.

The shift towards green design began in the 1970s and was a pragmatic response to higher oil prices. It was then that the first of the oil shocks, in 1973, sent fossil fuel prices sky high and the 'futurologists' began to look at the life history of fossil fuels on the planet and make claims about how much oil and gas were left. Their predictions were alarming and, 30 years on, we appear still to have abundant oil. However, their calculations on total reserves were fairly accurate and many of their predictions have yet to be proved wrong. From the features on gas, oil and coal below you can see that it is now estimated that we have left around 40 years

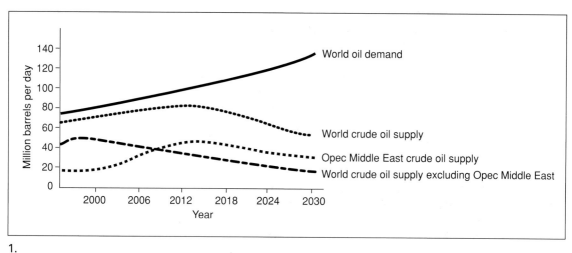

1.

World oil demand and conventional oil supply in millions of barrels per day
(*Guardian*, 17 June 2000, p. 30).

of conventional oil reserves and 65 years of gas, at current rates
of extraction. Recent studies (see Bartsh and Muller, 2000) point
to 2012 as being when the oil shortages will really begin to bite
hard and to start changing the face of society.

OIL: the estimates of total oil reserves have changed little in
20 years and the last big oil field discovered was in the North Sea
in the 1960s. The output from the southern 48 States of America
began to decline in the 1940s. The output from oil fields typically
follows a form of bell-shaped curve, rising steeply to a plateau then
falling sharply. Every day the world consumes around 70 million
barrels of crude oil. To date, we have used around half of the total
estimated oil reserves globally and it is thought that within a few
years we will reach the peak of global oil production, after which
time conventional oil production will decline.

The capacity for exploiting those reserves can be increased by
technologies that allow more of the reserves to be extracted, for
example by using pumped gas and water. Thus in the USA, UK and
Norway, for instance, reserves are intensively exploited while in
other areas, such as Saudi Arabia, Kuwait and Iraq, they are not.
The term 'reserves' indicates the long-term potential of an oil field
while 'capacity' describes what can be pumped from that field
taking into consideration constraints such as the technical efficiency
of the extraction process. An increase in the rate of recovery of oil
from a field from 30 per cent to 60 per cent is the equivalent of
doubling the proven recoverable resource.

Perhaps worst hit by the decline in oil reserves will be the fields
in the USA and the North Sea, which will be badly affected by

OIL (continued): 2020. Issues of how to sustain current lifestyles in these regions, with declining oil reserves, unpredictable global oil prices and geopolitical conditions, should prove very interesting.

There is capacity for considerable expansion in oil production over the next few years to meet increased global demands from the various oil producing countries. However, the capacity to increase supplies may well not actually meet the increasing demands. The cost of oil will depend on the match between demand and supply, the 'time lag' between synchronizing these and the size of 'buffer' supplies that are currently largely held in the Gulf. Prices will rise when governments perceive a reduction in the size of the buffer, or anticipate that demands for oil are growing faster than investment in capacity expansion. The oil crises of 1973 and 1979 were caused by such a mismatch of demand and consumption. Recently the oil price on the global market has fluctuated from under US$10 a barrel to over US$30 a barrel. Our societies are highly dependent on oil, the price of which has not proven particularly predictable in the past.

The world does hold huge reserves of non-conventional oil that will be exploited when the scarcity of conventional reserves pushes the price of a barrel above $30 for long periods.

When making long-term predictions, analysts have to balance the capacity, or production, of a field against the size of its reserves and the onset of 'oil field decline'. If, as some maintain, global production will plateau in around 2005 and we continue to increase our global demand as predicted, there is a strong likelihood of considerable volatility in oil prices in the future, as happened in the 1970s. No one is brave enough to stake their reputations on what oil will cost in 5, 10, 15 or 20 years but pundits suggest that by around 2015 global natural decline in conventional oil production will be noticeable, and may be considerable after around 2020. These declines can be compensated for by developments in non-conventional oil production but at a high cost to the consumer. One worry is that old oil fields in areas such as the Middle East and Venezuela are already showing signs of fatigue and may not yield their full potential of reserves. A rough figure given is that we may have around 40 years left of conventional oil reserves.

As Bartsch and Muller (2000) state in their recent book *Fossil Fuels in a Changing Climate*, 'It is not that we will not have enough oil to take us to 2020 but that the road is likely to be bumpy and subject to a number of economic and political shocks'.

GAS: reserves of natural gas are abundant and current estimates suggest that stocks could last for 65 years at current rates of consumption. Some countries rely on gas for over half of all the primary energy they use and the biggest increase in demand is for gas-powered electricity stations. Gas is a cleaner fuel for the generation of electricity than coal or oil and results in less CO_2 emissions per unit of delivered energy generated because gas-fired power stations are more efficient.

Two interesting characteristics of gas are that:

1 it is difficult to move over long distances without leakage and
2 most of it is located in countries where demand for it is lower. For instance, in Europe there are around 3.2 trillion (3.2 $\times 10^{12}$) cubic metres of proven reserves of natural gas and the Europeans are consuming around 0.38 trillion cubic metres per year, which gives us at this rate just under 10 years of gas left in Europe. However, more reserves may be found. In the USA the situation is more difficult with around 3.2 trillion cubic metres proven reserves left and 0.686 trillion tonnes being consumed a year. At this rate the USA has around 5 years of reserves of their own natural gas left. However, such countries are very aware of the limitations of their own reserves and import large quantities of cheap gas now, with a view to conserving their own stocks for the future. For example if the USA imports three-quarters of the gas they use every year at current rates their own stocks could last for 20 years.

Fortunately there are abundant reserves in other areas of the world of which 77 per cent are in the Middle East (39 per cent) and North Africa (38 per cent). It is estimated that globally there are reserves that will support demand for gas for the next 60 years at least. However, as local reserves of gas are depleted and countries have to buy more and more of their stocks from the global market they will have to pay the global market price. The rate of uptake of cleaner gas technologies, used to reduce CO_2 emissions, for instance, from power stations, will be influenced by the cost of gas, which will increasingly be dictated by the highest bidders. Prices will eventually rise significantly in countries where the fuel is now very cheap, such as the USA, but obviously will be less affected in countries such as Denmark where fuel prices have been kept high and energy efficiency is widely practised. The USA now consumes around 27 per cent of the world's gas (with 4 per cent of the world population) and is responsible for about 23 per cent per year of global gas production.

COAL: the main problem with coal is that it is a dirty fuel and contributes 38 per cent of CO_2 emissions from commercial fuels and is also a major source of sulphur dioxide and nitrous oxides emissions, as well as particulates and other emissions. Coal currently provides only 26 per cent of the world's primary energy consumption, very much less than in 1950 when this figure was 59 per cent. There are abundant reserves of coal in the ground estimated to be capable of lasting over 200 years. Over 50 per cent of the reserves are in the USA, China and Russia. The coal industry does have the additional problems of poor working conditions in some mines and the high costs of transport for the fuel. In France it is expected that all mines will be closed by 2005.

The costs of producing coal vary significantly. Internationally traded coal ranges in delivered price to the European Union (EU) of between US$30 and US$55 per tonne, which in terms of fuel oil is roughly equivalent to US$45–75 per tonne. This compares with the average spot price of fuel oil delivered to northwest Europe in 1997 of US$90–95 per tonne and between US$65 and US$70 per tonne in the first half of 1998. This indicates that coal is very competitively priced against oil but it does have a high environmental impact compared with fuel oil (medium impact) and gas turbines and natural gas combined-cycle power plants (low impact), which will limit its wider use globally in the future for environmental reasons.

The oil crisis of the 1970s resulted in the rise of the solar house movement: homes built to use clean renewable energy from the sun. Two such houses can be seen in the case studies in Kentucky and Tokyo. These houses used passive solar and solar hot water systems with rock bed and ground storage systems to store heat between the seasons. Such innovative houses provided the foundations on which were developed the blueprints for the ecohouses of the twenty-first century.

In the 1980s came the next big shock – climate change. It was then that the rates of depletion in the ozone layer and the increase in greenhouse gases and global warming became apparent. The predictions made by the Intergovernmental Panel on Climate Change in 1990 have been borne out by the steadily increasing global temperatures over the 1990s, the hottest decade on record.

Just as people dismiss the fossil fuel depletion claims by saying that 'they were wrong in the 1970s about oil, you see we have not run out yet', so climate change predictions are simplistically rebuffed with phrases such as 'the climate of the world has always changed'. It is obvious from Figure 2 that this is indeed correct,

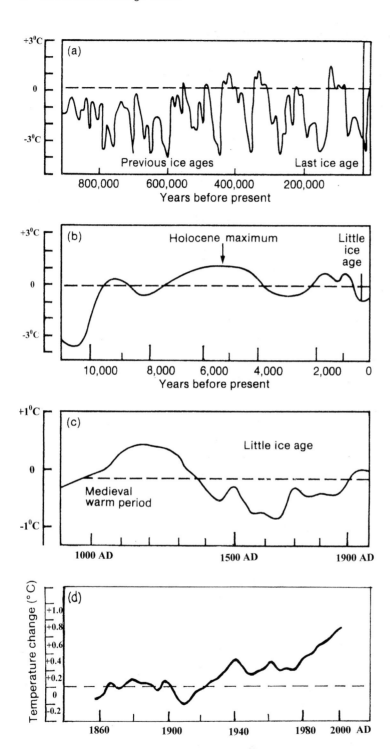

2.
Climate change over four time scales: a, the last 1 million years; b, the last 10 000 years;
c, the last 1000 years; d, the last 140 years (sources, a–c: Houghton et al.,1990; d:
http://www.met-office.gov.uk/sec5/CR_div/CoP5/obs_pred_clim_change.html).

but what is deeply worrying is the revealed rate and scale of change that is now happening.

The main greenhouse gas is CO_2 and the main source of CO_2 (ca. 50 per cent of all man-made emissions) is buildings. If we continue to produce greenhouse gases at current rates of increase in a 'business-as-usual fashion' predictions by the UK Meteorological Office indicate impacts will be substantial and by 2080 will include:

- a rise in global average temperatures of 3°C over the 1961–1990 average by 2080;
- substantial dieback of tropical forests and grasslands with resulting loss of CO_2 sink;
- substantial overall decreases in rainfall amounts in Australia, India, southern Africa and most of South America, Europe and the Middle East. Increases will be seen in North America, Asia (particularly central Asia) and central eastern Africa;
- an increase in cereal yields at high and mid-latitudes such as North America, China, Argentina and much of Europe. At the same time cereal yields in Africa, the Middle East and particularly India will decrease, leading to increases in the risk of famine in some regions;
- sea levels will be about 40 cm higher than present with an estimated increase in the annual number of people flooded from approximately 13 million today to 94 million in 2080. Of this increase 60 per cent will be in southern Asia, from Pakistan through India, Sri Lanka, Bangladesh and Burma and 20 per cent in Southeast Asia from Thailand, Vietnam, Indonesia and the Philippines. Under all scenarios sea level rises will affect coastal wetlands, low lying islands and coastal lowlands;
- health impacts will be widespread and diverse. By the 2080s an estimated 290 million more people will be at risk from malaria, with the greatest risk in China and central Asia. Fewer people will die in winter in temperate cities and more will die in summer from heat-related problems (www.met.office.gov.uk/sec5/CR_div/CoP5/obs_pred_clim_change.html). Skin cancer rates will soar. In Queensland, where UV-B radiation is the highest, it is predicted that three out of every four people will get skin cancer. In America, in 1935 the chances of getting skin cancer were 1 in 1500, in 2000 the chances are 1 in 75 (www.geocities.com/Rainforest/Vines/4030/impacts.html).

There are so many related impacts of greenhouse gas emissions that we only touch on them here. Yet we see them illustrated daily in newspaper articles on the extinction of species, the increase in number and intensity of floods and cyclones, water shortages and the starvation that results from droughts. What is certain is that we must act now to reduce CO_2 emissions globally and that one of the most effective sectors from which to achieve rapid reductions in emissions is buildings. Houses consume around half of all the energy used in buildings.

A recent Report by the Commission on Environmental Pollution in the UK states that if we are to begin to attempt to stabilize climate change we will have to introduce cuts in all CO_2 emissions of around 60 per cent. This means using 60 per cent less energy to run the home (http://www.rcep.org.uk/). This is actually not too difficult, as demonstrated in many ecohouses. For instance, the Oxford Ecohouse emits around 140 kg CO_2 per year while other, similar sized, houses in Oxford will produce around 6500 kg CO_2 per year. This is because the Oxford Ecohouse is run largely using renewable solar energy. This demonstrates how important solar technologies are for the 'Low Carbon Lifestyle'.

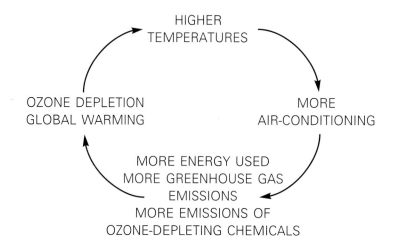

But what is the typical architectural response to the challenge of global warming? It is not to make the building do more of the work in providing better shelter against climate change, nor to use solar technologies, but to install air-conditioning, which is a key element in the vicious circle that is creating global warming.

Air-conditioning systems represent the greatest source of climate change gases of any single technology. In the USA, which has only 4 per cent of the world's population and yet produces around 25 per cent of the global CO_2 annually, over 40 per cent of electricity generated is used in air-conditioning systems. Energy efficiency is absolutely not an issue, in general, with the US architectural profession. Indeed, climate change is not an issue in the majority of architectural offices around the world who have systematically, over the last 30 years, shut the indoor climate off from the outdoor climate, so requiring air-conditioning to make the building habitable. Air-conditioning engineers have traditionally made their profits by putting as much plant as possible into a building. It is not uncommon for heating and ventilating engineers to insist on having fixed windows throughout a building, not least because the calculations for system performance are too difficult if an open-window scenario is adopted. So, many buildings have to be air-conditioned all year round while perhaps for only one, two or three months is the external climate uncomfortably hot or cold. In addition, many 'fashionable' architect-designed buildings contain excessive glass, overheat, create extreme indoor discomfort and can only be saved from becoming hellish environments by huge amounts of air-conditioning plant. When sensible engineers suggest that perhaps the building would be better without, for instance, the glass roof, architects have been heard to retort that engineers cannot understand great design ideas and they should do what they are paid to do and not express opinions about the building's aesthetics.

The world needs a new profession of ecotects, or archi-neers or engi-tects, who can design passive buildings that use minimal energy and what energy they do use comes from renewable sources if possible. It is the only way forward.

The scenario for future global energy consumption developed in the early 1990s by the Shell oil company demonstrates this well. Figure 3 shows how the demand for energy continues to grow exponentially while conventional fuel sources such as oil and gas begin to show significant reductions in output. The gap is filled by renewable energies such as wind and photovoltaic (PV, solar

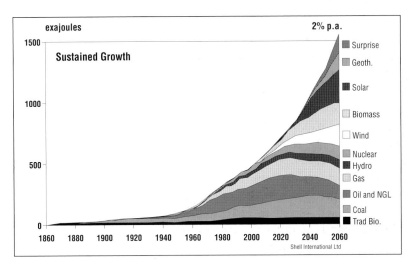

3.
A Shell prediction graph developed in the early 1990s on a 'sustained growth' scenario. It shows the gradual drop-off in fossil fuel supply, the increasing demand for energy and the growth of the renewable energy sector (Shell, UK Ltd, with thanks to Roger Booth).

electric) energy. It was on the strength of such predictions that Shell and BP have invested huge amounts of money in the development of PV production and distribution companies.

By the decisions we make on the drawing boards in our comfortable offices the global environment is changed. The world is warming and the ozone layer thinning. Some time in the not too distant future building designers will be made to take into account their own global environmental responsibilities. This will be done through building regulations, fuel price increases and carbon taxes. The sooner we start to change architecture, from an appearance-driven process to a performance-driven art, the better prepared we will be to lay the building foundations of the post-fossil-fuel age. The best place to start learning is with an ecohouse.

We have tried to bring together 'How to' information on key issues not well covered in other books. This includes developing technologies, thermal mass, ventilation, cold bridging, materials issues, passive solar design, photovoltaics, cyclone design and grey water systems. The book is not a comprehensive guide to all aspects of low-energy or ecological building. Many subjects have been very well covered in other books; for example, passive solar design (Mazria, 1979; Yannas, 1994), low-energy house design in the UK (Vale and Vale, 2000), materials (Borer and Harris, 1998; Berge, 2000) and timber-frame houses (Pitts, 1989, 2000; Talbott, 1993). We also think that house buyers can choose many elements for their house pragmatically, with a little help from their local building supplies store. For instance, what is the best glass for their windows, based on what is locally available, compared performance data and what they can afford.

We do incorporate the wisdom learnt from ecohouses around the world in the Case Study section. These are not ordinary houses. The majority are built by architects for themselves and often by themselves, not for clients. They express, in their varied forms, the local climates, resources, culture and the tastes of their designers, as well as the design ethos of the times in which they were built.

The temptation to 'innovate' can often lead us unwittingly into problems, but from them we learn. For example, the early solar houses often overheated because, in the rush to utilize free, clean solar energy, the dangers of the sun were underestimated. The best modern buildings do have excellent solar control and yet it is astounding to see how many still employ glass roofs and walls that not only can cause severe discomfort to people inside but also can result in huge bills for compensatory cooling systems. Some people never seem to learn. Clients should avoid such designers.

Today photovoltaics are already cost-effective in virtually all countries for off-grid systems. In far-sighted countries, such as Japan and Germany, there are already over 10 000 installed domestic PV systems in use. In Britain (where £900 000 000 was spent on the Millennium dome at Greenwich) there are about ten installed grid-connected PV systems on houses. To adapt an old Yorkshire expression, some people are 'all front parlour and no Sunday lunch' when it comes to sustainability and sensibly investing in the future for our children.

It is incredible to note that in many parts of the world the challenges of trying to reduce the catastrophic impacts of buildings on the environment are still left to individuals, including Britain. The challenges ahead seem so enormous that it is difficult to see what we, as individuals, can do. But it was Confucius who said that if each person solved the small problems over which they have control then the larger problems would disappear.

Why are such important issues as the impacts of climate change and fossil fuel depletion ignored by politicians when our species is so obviously at an ecological watershed? We are only one species on the planet, yet we are multiplying exponentially, every day we destroy other species and their ecological niches and, in many parts of the world, we are even destroying our own peoples and their habitats. This was historically demonstrated on Easter Island where the population destroyed all the trees on the island and had to flee to survive, or die. This is happening around us today. Will it be obvious to us that we are the cause, when the first of the Small Islands disappear altogether when sea level rises? Will we register that fact?

Species can adopt symbiotic, parasitic or predatory lifestyles, and they can also commit suicide, just as species such as lemmings do. There is potentially much to be learnt about how we can develop through the study of ecology, by comparing our behaviour with that of other species on the planet.

ECOLOGY is defined as the study of the interactions of organisms and their physical and biological environment. Organisms have the ability to control the movement of energy and material between their internal and external environments. They adapt in order to use the water, energy, heat, light and resources available in different environments and climates to sustain life in the multiplicity of ecosystems on the planet.

Competition between species is a driving force that can lead to evolutionary divergence between species, to elimination of species and also, more positively, to a co-evolution and the development of mutually supportive relationships. Evolution requires adaptation, not only to adjust to the changing circumstances of climate and environment, but also to changing populations and resources.

The theory of evolutionary ecology begins with Charles Darwin in the late nineteenth century. He regarded the environment as the key agent of 'selective mortality' without mentioning the relationship of birth rate to the survival of species. In 1930 Ronald Fisher's classic book *The Genetical Theory of Natural Selection*, dealt with the importance of population growth rates but this subject was largely marginalized until 1966 when the theory of the 'life histories' of populations became popular. This theory states that adaptation is largely the making of compromises in the allocation of time and energy to competing demands. It introduced the idea that very different 'life history' adaptations are favoured under conditions of high and low population densities in relation to the carrying capacity of the environment. At high densities, selection favours adaptations that enable populations to survive and reproduce with few resources and hence demands 'efficiency' in the way resources are used. At low densities, adaptations promoting rapid population increases are favoured, regardless of efficiency. Natural selection adjusts the amount of time and resources expended not only in accordance with changes in the environment but also with the life history of a population.

So how would this affect us? In times of ecological threat animal species respond in a variety of ways, from becoming spiteful to being altruistic. Ecologists would perhaps expect selfish behaviour to prevail to the exclusion of altruism because it is the selfish behaviours that increase the reproductive success of the dominant species or individual.

Growth, however, is a survival strategy for species with a life history at a low-density phase. At high densities, populations must employ strategies of efficiency to survive. Human beings are unique in the history of the world because of the sheer scale of the impacts we have had on the global environment and in particular on the Earth's atmosphere, and our ability to comprehend, and alter, them.

If we are to survive the challenges ahead of us in the twenty-first century, with some semblance of normality retained, we will have to effect fairly radical changes in what we, as individuals, expect from the infrastructures of our own ecological niches, our houses and settlements and society. To do this we will have to behave fairly altruistically, not only towards our own families, friends and neighbours but also to the larger family of our fellow human beings. Altruism is not unknown when bonds of loyalty are stretched to encompass larger and larger groups. Humans seldom question that, in times of war, they are asked to die for their country. This they do ultimately to protect their families, through whom their genes are perpetuated.

When faced with the twenty-first century challenges it is the global nature of human being's environmental impacts that make it imperative to see our kin as all the people of the world. If not, few of us will survive. There are no safe islands in the twenty-first century. Europe knows that if the countries of northern Africa suffer from repeated severe droughts it is to Europe that the ravaged populations of these regions will flee. The same is true of America, Mexico and Latin America. The history of humans is one of diasporas, the dispersions of peoples. If there are more people and fewer resources, such movements will surely affect each of our everyday lives?

Buildings are only part of our habitat. Buildings are intimately linked to the local, regional and global environments that are all part of our 'Ecological Niche'. It is the responsibility of our generation to begin to adapt our buildings to ensure that we can stabilize climate change, that we can live without fossil fuels and that we do not unsustainably pollute the environment. Only by so doing can we ensure the survival of our own habitats.

This cannot be so difficult because people survived on the planet for millennia without the miracle fuels of oil and gas. Traditional buildings have much to teach us about how to design regionally appropriate structures.

We can change fast enough. We can mix the wisdom of the master builders, new knowledge, materials and renewable technologies to create ecobuildings, the New Vernacular, to minimize the environmental impacts of buildings. We can now measure those impacts with the new methodologies for counting the environmental costs of buildings. We do need a new type of designer, part architect, part engineer, and to get rid of heating and cooling machines where possible or power them with renewable energy. What you will read in the first section of the book shows that all of this is possible and, in the second section, that it is already being done in many of the case study ecohouses from around the world.

1 THE FORM OF THE HOUSE: THE BUILDING AS AN ANALOGY

Twentieth-century architecture was influenced by a single analogy coined by the great French architect, Le Corbusier. He proposed that 'the building is a machine for living in'. This is very far from the truth. The mistake, at its heart, is that a machine is an inanimate object that can be turned on and off and operates only at the whim of its controller. A building is very different because, although it is true that it can be controlled by its occupants, the driving force that acts upon the building to create comfort and shelter is the climate and its weather, neither of which can be controlled, predicted or turned on and off.

Machines are fixed, static objects, amenable to scientific assessment. Buildings are part of a complex interaction between people, the buildings themselves, the climate and the environment. The view that buildings are fixed also fits well with certain types of scientific analysis, of daylight factors, energy flows, U-values, mechanical ventilation and so on. But this mechanistic view finds the more dynamic parts of the system (temperature, natural ventilation, passive cooling and all the multitude of human interactions) very difficult to model and, therefore, to understand. In houses it is often these 'difficult' parts of the system that change a house into a home, and the building into a delight.

Considerations of daylight, energy, thermal insulation and the use of machinery, of course, cannot be avoided – but because we can calculate them does not mean that they are our only concern. Figure 1.1 demonstrates, for instance, that buildings have their own thermal life beyond what we can see. If we could see heat, as the thermal imagining camera does, we would probably treat a building very differently. We would know exactly where we need to put a bit more insulation or place a sun shade, which sun shade to use or which corner of the room is cold and needs a little attention.

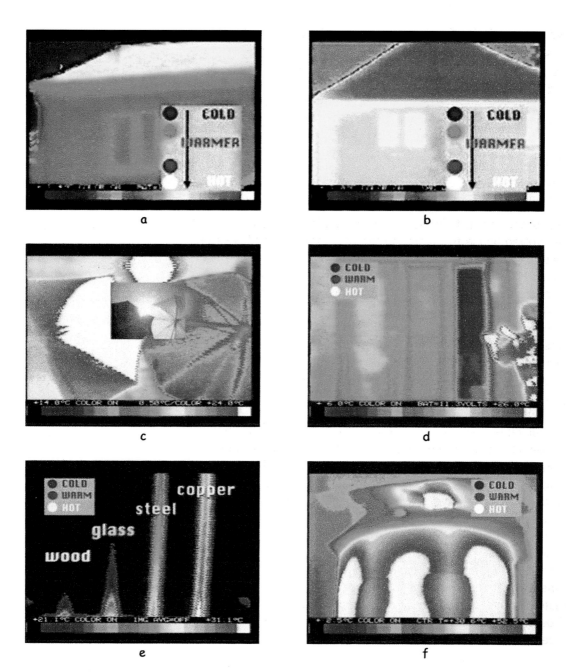

1.1.

Thermographic images: a, The Oxford Ecohouse, built in 1994, on an Autumn morning; b, the house next door built in the 1950s; c, a black umbrella (left) and a white umbrella (right) showing that the black material absorbs radiation and gets hot while the white umbrella reflects the sun from its surface and remains cooler; d, a person opening a window from the inside in the Oxford Ecohouse; e, rods of copper, steel, glass and wood demonstrating that heat is conducted more efficiently in some materials; f the Kakkleoven in the Oxford Ecohouse showing the hot ducts in the high mass stove and the hot metal flue passing into the concrete floor above and heating it locally. These images are reproduced with thanks to Glasshead Films Ltd who took the films for Channel 4, and George Jenkinson and Andy Hudson of Oxford Brookes University for their digital re-mastering and transmission of the images (Glasshead Films Ltd).

We have to design for the invisible as well as the visible and so how is this to be done? Buildings have been traditionally designed using accepted premises (propositions that are adopted after reasoning) as well as, of course, on premises (the building and adjuncts set forth at the beginning of a building deed). Three principles on which all building should be based are:

1 design for a climate;
2 design for the environment;
3 design for time, be it day or night, a season or the lifetime of a building and design a building that will adapt over time.

Humans have been building on these premises for millennia and have evolved house types around the world that are well suited to particular climates, environments and societies. This was done by learning from experience, and with the benefit of repetitive tools and processes that help designers and builders through the complex range of tasks necessary to actually put a building together.

One tool of the imagination that is often used when starting a design is the analogy. An analogy is used where two forms may not look alike but they function in the same way, just as Le Corbusier described a building as a 'machine for living in'. This book starts by considering building form, on which the most powerful influence in design should be the climate. In this chapter, analogies are used to demonstrate how different forms can relate to some of the many different climatic functions of a building. The analogies themselves may seem a little simplistic but you will find that they change the way you look at buildings. To further illustrate the relationship between buildings and climate, a number of examples of vernacular buildings are included.

Finally, at the end of the chapter, a method for evaluating the climatic requirements of a building form in a particular climate is outlined with the Nicol graph. This simply shows what the mean climate of a site is, what the comfort requirements of local people will be and gives an indication of how much heating and cooling will be needed to achieve those comfort conditions in that climate.

THE THIRD SKIN

Buildings are our third skin. To survive we need shelter from the elements using three skins. The first is provided by our own skin, the second by a layer of clothes and the third is the building. In some climates it is only with all three skins that we can provide sufficient shelter to survive, in others the first skin is enough. The more extreme the climate, the more we have to rely on the build-

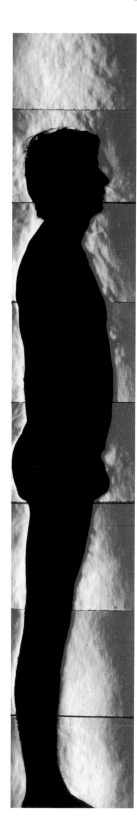

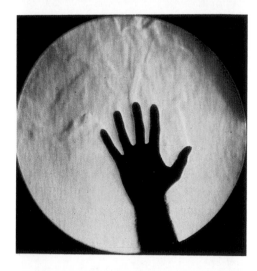

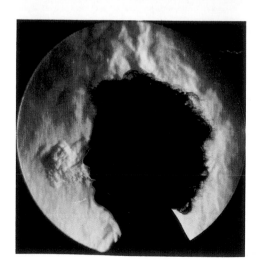

1.2.
People typically generate heat, between 70 and 120 watts each according to how much work they are doing. Figure 1.1. shows the radiant surface temperatures of a person opening a window. This figure shows a thermal image of heat plumes around people, as the heat from our skin warms the air around us it rises, driven by the buoyancy of hot air (Clark, C. and Edholme, D., 1985).

ing to protect us from the elements. Just as we take off and put on clothes as the weather and the climate changes so we can shed skins.

THE HEAT EXCHANGER

The greater the volume of the building the more surface area it has to lose, or gain, heat from. Figure 1.3 shows that different plan forms can have more or less wall area for the same plan area. The surface area:volume ratio is very important in conserving heat transfer into and out of a building. To conserve heat or cold the building must be designed with a compact form to reduce the efficiency of the building as a heat exchanger.

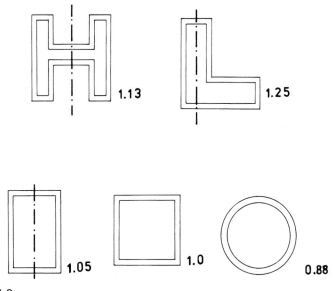

1.3.
Buildings can have very different perimeter:area ratios depending on their plan form (Krishan, 1995).

A good example of how not to lose heat because of the shape of a building is given by the ice-house (Figure 1.4). In many countries of the world, before refrigerators were invented, people used to store ice that had been harvested in winter from lakes and ponds in ice-houses. When the hot summer months came it was taken out and used to cool food, drinks and rooms. The only way that ice could be kept so long was to ensure that it had a minimum surface area:volume ratio to lose heat from. Ice-houses were designed so that as the ice slipped lower down it would retain its ball-like shape. Some ice-houses could store ice for two years without it melting (Beamon and Roaf, 1990).

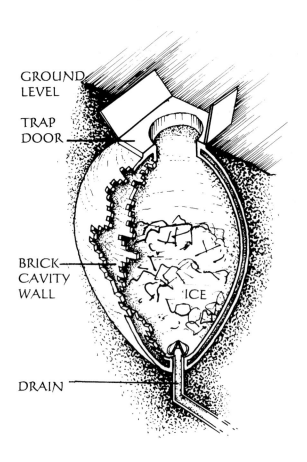

GROUND
LEVEL

TRAP
DOOR

BRICK
CAVITY
WALL

ICE

DRAIN

1.4.
The ice-house at Hooke, Chailey, Sussex. Drawn after a 1776 diagram by William Broderick Thomas. This may be the first illustrated cavity brick wall in Britain and here the cavity was used to keep the groundwater away from the ice, rather than for its insulating properties (Beamon and Roaf, 1990).

In warm or hot countries the building must become a good heat dissipater. Just as people who are hot sprawl out to lose heat, so buildings sprawl in warm and hot climates. In many hot climates buildings have a high surface area:volume ratio but the walls facing the sun are protected from direct radiation by verandas, balconies or wide eaves. The shallower floor plan of heat-dissipating buildings also promotes easy cross-ventilation of rooms for cooling, which in compact plan forms is more difficult. House forms in such climates are either long and thin or have a courtyard, or light well, in the centre of the house, to maximize the building's wall area. The relationship between ventilation and cooling is dealt with in Chapter 5.

Do not confuse a hot climate, with mean maximum temperatures below 38°C, with a very hot climate, which is even hotter. In the hottest cities of Saudi Arabia, Iraq, India and Yemen, for instance, houses are very tall with up to seven or eight storeys, each providing another layer of protection against the sun. The courtyards in the very hottest areas are replaced with light wells that allow for cross-ventilation and light penetration but are more

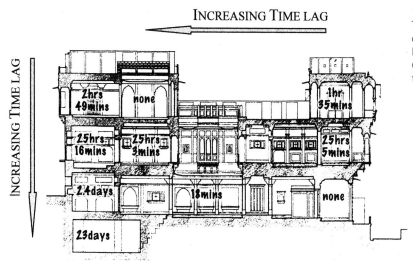

INCREASING TIME LAG

INCREASING TIME LAG

2hrs 49mins   none

1hr 35mins

2.5hrs 16mins   2.5hrs 3mins   2.5hrs 5mins

2.4days   18mins   none

23days

1.5.
Time lags between indoor and outdoor temperatures in a Havelli in Jaisalmer, India (Matthews, 2000). (South is to the right of this section.)

shaded against the sun overhead. The outer walls of such buildings are often shaded with shutters, verandas, balconies and mushrabiyah, or ventilated timber cantilevered windows. In such climates rooms can become vertical or horizontal buffers, as can shade elements that keep the sun off mass walls that would transport the heat inwards by conduction. Figure 1.5 shows how a large house, a Havelli, is coupled in the upper floors to the air temperature while in the basement room it is coupled thermally to the more stable ground temperatures.

THE TEA COSY

Well-insulated structures are like tea cosies. How quickly the tea cools will depend on how big the pot is, how thick the tea cosy is and how cold the air is outside it. The effectiveness of the insulated envelope depends on a number of variables, not least the area of the envelope in relation to the heating requirements of the occupants in it and the available internal heat sources.

For example, take the tent dwellers of the Mongolian steppes of Siberia to the deserts of Saudi Arabia. The Turkoman yurt (Figure 1.6) is a tent built on a framework of bent wood, with a felt cloth tent, in which ten or more people can live through the freezing winter months. Heavy clothes are worn, even indoors, and a single central brazier provides heat. The yurt is an airtight structure into which there is very little infiltration of cold air from the driving wind. The area of the whole floor is only in the region of 15–20 m^2 so the body heat of the people in the tent makes up a significant amount of the heat they need to warm the family.

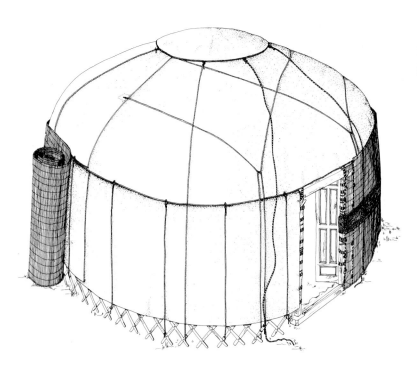

1.6.
A Yurt of the Turkoman tribe of Iran (Andrews, 1997, drawn by Susan Parker).

You would probably not survive a severe Mongolian winter in a 300 m² gher with one small brazier fire and ten people. Insulated envelope buildings need constant heating, from a heat source or from other internal gains such as machines and body heat. The yurt works well because its occupants go to bed very early to conserve heat and light, and sleep at night under thick quilts, often with more than one to a bed, saving considerably on heating. Considerations of the thermal performance of building envelopes are covered in Chapter 2.

THE GREENHOUSE

Imagine living in a greenhouse. There are no climates in which it would be comfortable. Glass lets in light and, with it, heat. Incoming solar radiation heats us to help keep our internal body temperature at 37°C. It can also overheat us. Once solar radiation has passed through glass it hits a surface in the building and is reflected or re-radiated at a changed wavelength that can no longer pass, in the same way, back out through the glass, so causing the inside of the greenhouse to heat up.

This is exactly what is happening with the world's atmosphere. The short-wave radiation can pass through the clear atmosphere relatively unimpeded. But the long-wave terrestrial radiation emitted by the warm surface of the Earth is partially absorbed by a number of the trace gases in the cooler atmosphere above. Since, on average, the outgoing long-wave radiation balances the incoming solar radiation, both the atmosphere and the surface will be warmer than they would be without greenhouse gases.

Once inside the atmosphere or the greenhouse, it is difficult for the radiation to pass back out, and this is why it is fairly pointless to use internal blinds because, although they shade people from direct sunlight, the heat cannot escape from the space. External shading would prevent this problem. Conversely, greenhouses become very cold at night, because they lose heat from the building surface by radiation and eventually become almost as cold as the outside temperature. It would take a fairly brave person to actually try to live in a 'transparent' greenhouse, or suggest to someone else that they should!

Greenhouses are direct solar gain buildings. The ways in which the sun can be captured and used in such buildings is covered in Chapter 5.

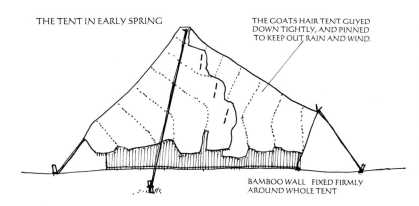

THE TENT IN EARLY SPRING

THE GOATS HAIR TENT GUYED DOWN TIGHTLY, AND PINNED TO KEEP OUT RAIN AND WIND.

BAMBOO WALL FIXED FIRMLY AROUND WHOLE TENT

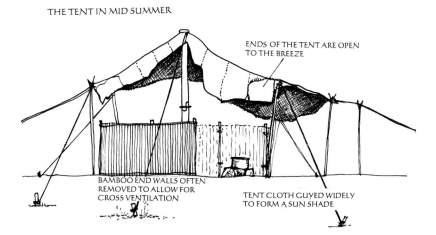

THE TENT IN MID SUMMER

ENDS OF THE TENT ARE OPEN TO THE BREEZE

BAMBOO END WALLS OFTEN REMOVED TO ALLOW FOR CROSS VENTILATION

TENT CLOTH GUYED WIDELY TO FORM A SUN SHADE

1.7.
The changing forms of the black tents of the Luri tribes of Iran over the year. Upper figure: the goatskin tent cloth is guyed and pegged down to keep out the wind and driving rain. Lower figure: as spring progresses the tent cloth is raised to let in the warm breezes and in mid-summer the tent cloth becomes a sun shade (Roaf, 1979).

THE SWALLOW

Just as swallows move south in winter, so many nomadic families around the world pack up their homes and move towards the sun in autumn and away from it in summer. An excellent example of an adaptable building form is the nomadic tent. Not only are they physically moved from the warmer, lower winter quarters up to cooler, higher pastures in the summer, but the actual form of the tent changes over the year (Figure 1.7). In winter the tent is closed right down to keep out the wind and rain but, as spring turns to summer, its cloth opens up, like wings, to form little more than a sun shade for the people inside. By making the envelope of the tent so adaptable, the range of climates in which its occupants can be comfortable, are considerably extended and tents of various shapes and materials are occupied from the Arctic Circle to the Sahara.

THE IGLOO

An important feature of building design in cold climates is the use of stratification of room air. Hot air rises while cold air sinks. This is taken advantage of in igloos, which provide shelter in perhaps the most extreme climates on Earth. The occupants of igloos live on a high shelf, to take advantage of the warmest air in the space, while the cold air sinks down and is contained in the lower entrance area of the building (Figure 1.8).

THE BUILDING AS A BUCKET

Conversely, in hot climates tall rooms mean that the heat and the hot ceiling are far away from the room's occupants. High-level windows can allow the heat to escape from the top of the rooms, thus stimulating air flow even on the stillest days that is driven by the stack effect alone. The stack effect is powered by the buoyancy of air, which depends on the pressure difference between cool and warm air (see Chapter 5). This effect (in an upside-down orientation) has been compared to water: if the building is a bucket with holes in, filled with water, the water will drain out of the holes, as will heat out of a building. The greater the temperature difference, the greater the buoyancy effect.

This property of warm air, which can be thought of, almost, as upside-down water flowing around a building, can be used to thermally landscape the ceilings of rooms. Hot air can be channelled around ceilings, in 'banks' or walls, to form rivers or lakes of heat that can move between areas or rooms within a building. This is well illustrated in Figure 1.9.

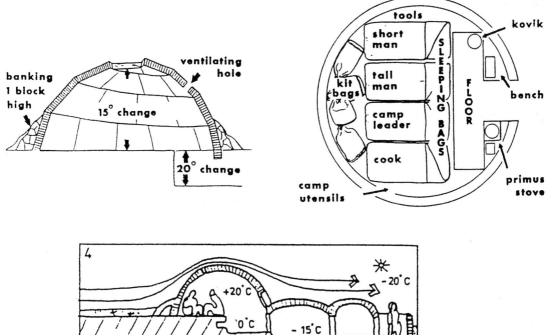

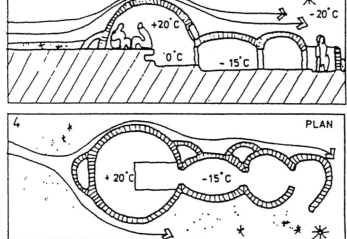

1.8.
Section through an igloo showing the thermal stratification above the raised platform on which people live (Cook, 1994).

A BRICK IN A STORAGE RADIATOR

In very cold climates the rooms of buildings, just like people, huddle together to keep warm, often around a central 'hot core', a heat source such as a fire place. Figure 1.10 shows a classic hot-core building from Lativa where an extended warm wall into the communal room is always a favourite place to sit in winter. The principle is similar to that of a brick in a storage radiator. The heat comes from perhaps a fire or the sun, and is absorbed in the thermal mass of the building, as it is in a radiator brick. Then,

1.9.
This Kakkleoven is the high mass wood-burning stove at the Oxford Ecohouse. Above it is a cloth skirt, 60 cm deep, which has been attached to form walls for the hot air that rises above the stove. This air is channelled in these walls to the ceiling of the room next door where it warms the concrete floor above. This warm floor then acts as a warm radiator, heating the rooms above and below. Equally, the heat could then be taken to an outside wall and would flow out of the building through windows above the hem of the skirt, just as water would flow out of the holes in a bucket, but only below the level of the water (Nat Rea).

gradually, that heat is emitted back into the room over time. If a material is highly conductive, such as the copper or steel shown in Figure 1.1, it will not store the heat. If the Kakkleoven in Figure 1.9 was made of steel or iron it would cool down rapidly when the fire had gone out, unlike the high density concrete stove that actually stores the heat and will stay warm for up to 14 hours after the fire has gone out.

The performance of the thermal mass in a building is dependent on many different factors, including its composition, location in relation to the other building elements and related ventilation strategies, issues dealt with in later chapters of the book.

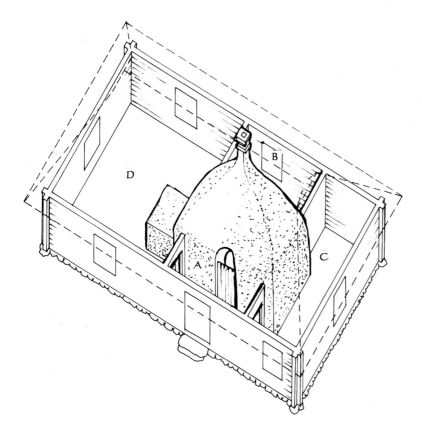

1.10.
The traditional Nam house of Latvia. The Nam is the central masonry room with the kitchen fire and chimney around which are located A, the hall; B, the small chamber; C, the master chamber; and D, the communal and servants room. The outer walls of the house are made of horizontal untrimmed logs (after a drawing by Guntis Plesums in Oliver, 1997, Vol. 2, p. 1263).

THE BUILDING AS A ROMAN BATH HOUSE

In Roman bath houses the floors were warmed by an under-floor heating system called a hypocaust. A fire would be lit under the great basins used to heat the water for the hot baths and the excess heat from the fire would be ducted under solid floors to heat the bath house itself. So, in such systems, there is a heat source, thermal mass to store the heat in and regulate its dissipation into a space, and a system of heat distribution. This idea uses a convective heat transfer medium, air or water, to a radiator that is part of the building. It can be a horizontal hypocaust under a floor or a vertical hypocaust such as a warm wall, column or Kakkleoven.

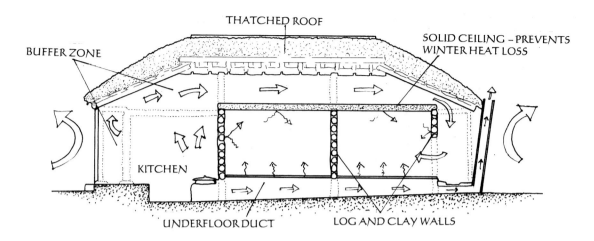

Even in simple village houses there are some very sophisticated design systems that make our modern Western houses look very ordinary. One of these interesting house forms is found on the isolated island of Ullungdo, in Korea (Figure 1.11). It has a double outer-wall construction with the removable outer buffer zone wall, the 'u-de-gi' (a thatched wall), added to provide protection against the driving winds of the island. The two central winter rooms are made of log and clay with high thermal performance and good

1.11.
Tu-mak-gyp house on the remote Korean island of Ullungdo with a horizontal hypocaust under the floor of the central room.

OPTIMIZING THE USE OF WARMTH AND COOL

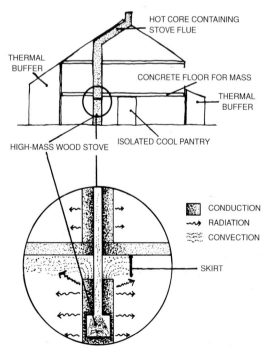

1.12.
Sketch section of the Kakkleoven illustrated in Figure 1.1.f that acts like a vertical hypocaust. The oven not only heats the surfaces it can 'see' radiantly but the hot air rising convectively around it collects under the ceiling, so heating the concrete floor above. The flue passes up through the concrete wall above and heats the adjacent sections of the wall by conduction.

humidity control. The thick thatched roof provides protection against the winter snow and summer sun. The really clever trick is the kitchen flue, which is funnelled under the winter living room to optimize the value of the scarce fuel resources to the inhabitants by being used both for the cooking and the heating. While the mean external temperature measured was 1.2°C, the mean temperature in the Chukdam buffer space was 1.1°C and in the internal room it was a comfortable 15.6°C, with a mean relative humidity (RH) of 44.9 per cent against the external RH of 71.2 per cent. The average floor-surface temperature was 22°C. This demonstrates the excellent ability of the earth walls to control the RH in a space, in a 'breathing wall' (Lee et al., 1994).

THE BUILDING AS A PERISCOPE

Buildings can be periscopes, trained to catch the light, a view, the wind or the sun. If you design them for any of these functions they must face in the correct direction. One of the pioneers of passive building design said that there are three important factors for passive buildings: 1. orientation, 2. orientation and 3. orientation (Docherty and Szokolay, 1999, p. 39).

Outside the tropics the best orientation for solar gain, for light and heat, is towards the equator. In the tropics it is best to hide from the sun under a large hat or a roof. If a building faces 15° to the east or west of the solar orientation it will make very little difference to the amount of energy that can be garnered from the sun. Simply by facing the living rooms of a house towards the sun it is possible to save up to 30 per cent on the annual heating bills of a typical house in a temperate climate. Passive solar design is dealt with in Chapter 7 and is often described in terms of ideal sites. Even in the most difficult sites, with careful thought and sometimes inspired design, as we see in Figure 1.13, it is possible to capture the light and heat of the sun. Even if the site has a difficult orientation it is possible to catch the sun with the use of periscopes projecting from the building in the form of upper-floor clerestory windows, bay and dormer windows and roof lights.

The most difficult orientation is west, because the low western sun coincides with the hottest time of day (mid-afternoon), making overheating of west-facing spaces a probability in summer, except in the high latitudes. A western orientation should be avoided if possible, particularly with sun spaces, because of their potential for overheating. Care should be taken to think about what each room in a house will be used for and what type of light and heat it will require from the sun. For instance, it would be best to give a breakfast room access to eastern, morning, sun. Perhaps proper dining

rooms may be good rooms for evening sun. A little well-designed light will give more pleasure to the building users than too much.

A TREE IN THE BREEZE

How lovely, on a warm day to sit beneath a shady tree, in a gentle breeze. A building can be like a tree. When the temperature of the air is close enough to local comfort temperatures then, simply by opening up the walls of a building, its occupants can be adequately warmed or cooled in a cross-draught. This is well demonstrated in the Queensland case study where, in the tropical climate, set within the rustling eucalyptus trees, being indoors is as comfortable on a hot day as sitting under a tree in the breeze. In some climates the breeze may be comfortable day and night. In most climates the air temperatures at night are too low for comfort. Many people around the world sleep out at night, in the garden, on the roof or in open-sided buildings or tents, in sight of the stars.

1.13.
Professor Georg Reinberg's solar development in Sagedergasse, Vienna, making imaginative use of the building form to optimize the solar potential of the site (Reinberg, 1996).

A COOL-CORE BUILDING

Just as the ice-houses used to store cold from the winter months for use in the 'salad' days of summer, the thermal mass of a building can be used to store the cool of the night winds to lower internal temperatures during the day. This is well demonstrated in Jimmy Lim's case study where he has built a modern version of a traditional Malaysian house, with its verandas and balconies around the high-mass core of a pre-existing building. The thermal mass of the inner walls is completely shaded all year and cooled by the air movement over them at night (Figure 1.14). This is a good example of a cool-core building. It is simple and works well and, in fact, could be compared to the old colonial bungalows with their surrounding verandas.

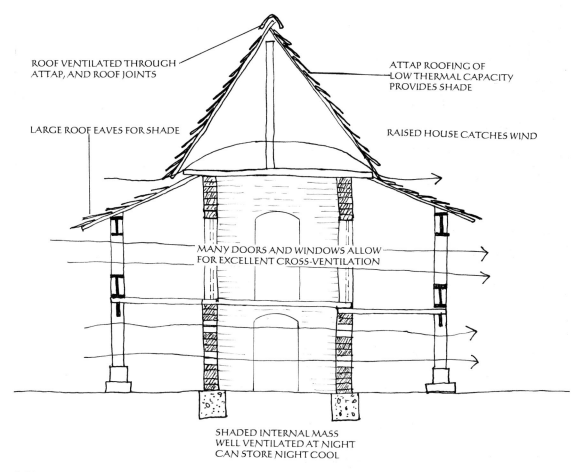

ROOF VENTILATED THROUGH ATTAP, AND ROOF JOINTS

ATTAP ROOFING OF LOW THERMAL CAPACITY PROVIDES SHADE

LARGE ROOF EAVES FOR SHADE

RAISED HOUSE CATCHES WIND

MANY DOORS AND WINDOWS ALLOW FOR EXCELLENT CROSS-VENTILATION

SHADED INTERNAL MASS WELL VENTILATED AT NIGHT CAN STORE NIGHT COOL

1.14.
The introduction of a cool core of well-ventilated, shaded, masonry into a traditional Malay house would have advantages in keeping people in the centre of the house cooler on the hottest days.

AN AIR LOCK IN A SPACE SHIP TO KEEP THE COLD OUT

In temperate or cold regions all outer doors should have a buffer space, or air lock. This acts in five ways:

1 to keep the wind away from the door and the biting draughts out of the house;
2 to modify the air temperature, rather as in an air lock, where the air in the buffer space is usually somewhere half way between inside and outside temperature. This is excellent air to use to ventilate the house inside in winter as it is not freezing. Small, openable, windows should be built between the buffer porch or sunspace and the house to provide natural pre-heat ventilation;
3 as a place to leave wet clothes outside the house so removing moisture from inside;
4 as a security and privacy feature so people can be heard or seen before they enter the house;
5 to protect the floor construction around the inside of the main house door from becoming too cold. In houses without buffer spaces, every time the door opens and cold air comes into the house, heat is drawn out of the floor and walls next to the door. The floor is often constructed with a slab of concrete, making the floor area around the door much cooler than it would be if the door had a porch (Thomas and Rees,1999).

THE COST OF 'FORM' IN SITE PLANNING

An interesting case study of a new ecohousing development in Hungary demonstrates that there are very real financial advantages of adopting solar strategies in housing layout. The developers, Aldino Ltd of Budapest, bought a 64-ha site at Veresegyhaz some 30 minutes from the centre of Budapest, in April 1993. The land had few trees and sloped gently to the south. The first design (Figure 1.15A) using conventional housing layouts planned for a maximum density of 380 houses on 1000 m^2 plots, but was found to be of too high density and not suitable, both for social reasons and for the unfavourable economic returns offered by the development. The second plan for 330 houses was developed along similar lines but the cost of the infrastructure and services, which had to be brought from the nearby village half a kilometre away, was found to be double the price of the land acquisition, and therefore that plan was also not feasible.

Some three years later it was decided to re-evaluate the development potential of the site and a third scheme for 300 houses

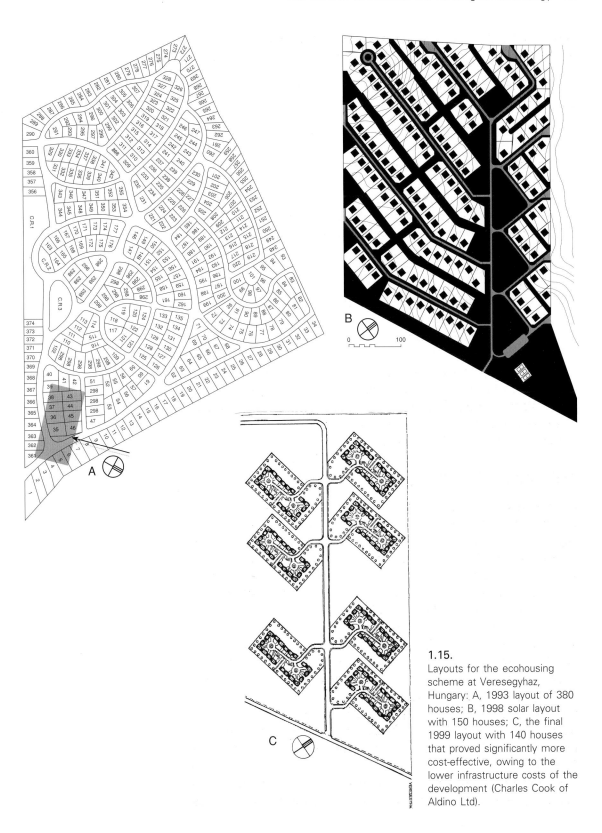

1.15.
Layouts for the ecohousing scheme at Veresegyhaz, Hungary: A, 1993 layout of 380 houses; B, 1998 solar layout with 150 houses; C, the final 1999 layout with 140 houses that proved significantly more cost-effective, owing to the lower infrastructure costs of the development (Charles Cook of Aldino Ltd).

was developed for middle/up-market houses, again with a conventional layout. Again it proved uneconomic using conventional planning. At that time the chief developer, Charles Cook, visited the Oxford Ecohouse and became convinced that a healthy, environmentally friendly development would be a real benefit to the site and region. It would be an important demonstration of what can be achieved for the improved environmental performance of the houses, the quality of life of the householders and the development of solar technologies in Hungary.

It was necessary to create a new site layout that reduced the road area and service lines, provided a green ambience, a secure environment and oriented the houses to the south. After many attempts at site planning he devised a layout of cul-de-sacs of groups of 20 houses that could provide all of the requirements of the brief and a good social atmosphere for the area. The cul-de-sac layouts are served by a single main road that has speed restraining features, so lowering local noise and risks for pedestrians. In so doing, the cost of roads, pavements and lighting has been substantially reduced, as has the cost of the drainage infra-

1.16.
Computer image of the new Hungarian ecohouse development at Veresegyhaz, Hungary. Each house has a solar hot water system, 1 kWp of photovoltaics and is built to the same high construction standards of the Oxford Ecohouse (Matthias Steege, BP Solar, Germany).

structure beneath the site. As a result of this experience he is convinced that developers should look very seriously at re-evaluating how they develop because, by putting new ingredients into the planning equation, such as solar access, security, the quality of the environment and social ambience he has not only come up with a far more pleasant solution for the people who will live in the houses but has also increased profits. The local council is delighted by the new 'green' agenda and has been very supportive of the project. Surprisingly the council have identified a key benefit of this scheme as being that better housing such as this will put less pressure on their local hospitals beds, because many local hospital admissions are of people whose health has suffered from poor housing. So everyone benefits, including the environment, particularly when such a development is serviced by good public transport connections to the city.

CHOOSING WHICH FORM TO USE IN A DESIGN

The first step when approaching a design in a new climate should always be to try to understand the overall climate of the site in relation to how much protection the house will need to provide against it. A simple way of doing this is to use a Nicol graph, named after Fergus Nicol who devised it. First of all a graph is drawn with 10°C intervals on the x axis and the 12 months of the year on the y axis. Then, the mean maximum and mean minimum outdoor temperatures for each month are plotted, showing a double curve for the year. The thermal comfort (TC) line for the year is then calculated. This is done using the equation devised by Michael Humphreys:

$$TC = 0.534 \ (T_{mean}) + 11.9$$

where T_{mean} is monthly mean outdoor temperature: $T_{mean} = (T_{max} + T_{min}) \ / \ 2$, where T_{max} is monthly mean daily outdoor maximum temperature and T_{min} is monthly mean daily outdoor minimum temperature. T_{min} and T_{max} are usually available from Meteorological Office data.

This equation, strictly speaking, applies to summer conditions in freely running buildings (not air-conditioned ones) but gives a general idea of the comfort conditions required by building occupants who have adapted to the local climate. People can adapt to the most remarkable range of temperatures. One person can be very happy sitting in a pleasant breeze in the warm sunshine and then go inside and feel deliciously cool indoors at 7°C cooler climate. A graphic illustration of the complexity of what makes one comfortable is the poor man who was building a hut in the

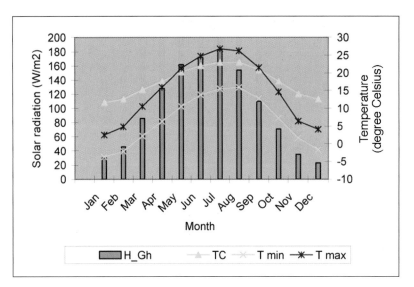

1.17.
A Nicol graph of Budapest, Hungary, showing the indoor temperature line and the convective cooling line at 32°C. Above this line the body begins to lose most of its heat by evaporation.

Antarctic. The bright sunshine was warm on his skin as he tapped the nails into the timber shed but, in an automatic gesture, he put a few nails in his mouth to hold for later and ended up having part of his lower lip removed. This was because, although his skin temperature was high from the sunshine, the air temperature was 20°C below freezing and the steel nails, being excellent conductors of heat, were frozen and in turn instantly froze every part of his skin that they touched.

The TC line does not represent a single temperature but a running mean of the sort of temperatures that an indigenous person would feel comfortable in. In summer they show that people in Scotland would be happy at 18°C while in Malaysia, Japan, Indonesia and the Caribbean the TC is around 27°C.

What the Nicol graph does show is a rough idea of the amount of heating and cooling the building will require in each month. In a good passive, high-mass building the indoor air will tend to revert, without the aid of heating and cooling, to a temperature half way between the mean outdoor maximum and minimum temperature. So a line can be drawn half way between the two to indicate the free running indoor air temperature. If this is below the TC, then the building will need heating up to make the occupants warm. If the air temperature line is above the TC then the building will need to be cooled to make the occupants comfortable.

If a large amount of heat is required it can be partly supplied by passive systems, such as the rock store in the Bariloche house. If a great deal of cooling is required it may be possible to gain it through ventilation, by simply opening a wall of a house, as in the Queensland house. Convective cooling is effective up to average skin temperature (around 32–34°C). Thus, with a simple graph we can tell much about to what extent we want to welcome in or keep out the external climate at different times of the year. The graph also gives a very rough idea of how much extra energy will have to be found in the form of supplementary heating or cooling systems to reach the TC. This is an effective way of looking at the passive potential of a building in a particular climate and using this knowledge to pick an appropriate building form to optimize this passive potential.

When reviewing the case study buildings in the second section of the book it is worth noting that in no climate shown is the difference between the mean maximum and mean minimum outdoor temperature less than 6°C. This means that a well-designed passive building should be able to give up to 3°C free cooling or heating even in a hot humid climate, as shown for Malaysia or Indonesia. 3°C could well be the difference between discomfort and delight.

Having decided how much shelter from the climate a building has to provide, and roughly what form would be best suited to the task, it is then time to start thinking about what materials you would like to use to build it and how to construct the building. These subjects are covered in Chapters 2 and 3.

2 THE ENVIRONMENTAL IMPACT OF BUILDING MATERIALS

Andre Viljoen and Katrin Bohn

The choice of building materials affects the environmental impact of a house. All building materials are processed in some way before they can be incorporated into a building. The processing may be minimal, as in the case of a traditional cottage constructed from materials found locally, or it may be extensive, as in the case of prefabricated construction. This processing of materials inevitably requires the use of energy and results in waste generation.

In the UK it is estimated that the production of building materials is responsible for about one-tenth of energy consumption and CO_2 emissions.

We can calculate the overall environmental impact of a house if we know the impacts that result from its day-to-day use and the manufacture and delivery of its construction materials and components. We can, with this information, see how the choice of materials affects its impact on the environment.

It will become clear that calculations to determine the exact impact of each and every dwelling are, at present, not feasible. This chapter will therefore refer to a very detailed study of the Oxford Ecohouse, which took account of the impact of material selection. It will also refer to other research in this field and will aim to draw some practical conclusions of use to the prospective house builder or renovator.

MEASURING THE ENVIRONMENTAL IMPACT OF BUILDING MATERIALS

When choosing materials several factors have to be considered, and it is unlikely that absolute rules can be given for all situations. The first question is how environmental impact should be assessed. This can be thought of as factors determined by the material's inherent qualities and as factors affected by the way materials are incorporated into a design.

2.1.
Living space within a yacht. How much space does one require? The quantity of materials used will have a direct effect on the environmental impact of a dwelling.

Factors determined by a material's qualities are, for example:

- energy required to produce the material;
- CO_2 emissions resulting from the material's manufacture;
- impact on the local environment resulting from the extraction of the material (e.g. quarry pit, wood taken from a forest, oil spills from an oil well, etc.);
- toxicity of the material;

- transportation of the material during its manufacture and delivery to site;
- degree of pollution resulting from the material at the end of its useful life.

Factors affected by material choice and design decisions include:

- location and detailing of an architectural element;
- maintenance required and the materials necessary for that maintenance;
- contribution that the material makes to reducing the building's environmental impact (e.g., insulation);
- flexibility of a design to accommodate changing uses over time;
- lifetime of the material and its potential for reuse if the building is demolished.

The following headings for comparing the environmental impact of materials, used in the *Green Building Handbook* (Woolley et al., 1997), provide a good checklist.

- Environmental impact owing to production:
  - energy use;
  - resource depletion;
  - global warming;
  - acid rain;
  - toxins.
- Environmental impact owing to use:
  - potential for reuse/recycling and disposal;
  - health hazard.

Perhaps the single most important measure of an object's environmental impact is provided by the concept of 'embodied energy'. 'Embodied energy' describes the amount of energy used to produce an object. We can refer to the embodied energy of a brick, a window or of an entire house. The following sections discuss embodied energy and embodied emissions in some detail. As figures for the embodied energy of materials are not yet widely available, it is hoped that understanding the factors affecting it will help the reader to 'ask the right questions' when considering material selection.

Embodied energy is an important measure because the use of non-renewable energy sources is the principal reason for environmental degradation. Degradation is caused in two main ways: 1) resulting from atmospheric emissions, principally CO_2, contributing to global warming; 2) resulting from the effects other emissions have on the atmosphere, such as acid rain. We can be fairly certain that other effects are taking place that, as yet, remain unidentified.

The concept of embodied emissions is similar to that of embodied energy and refers to the emissions associated with the production of an object, for example the electricity used to produce a window will result in CO_2 emissions associated with that window. In addition, the production of materials, particularly those requiring chemical treatment, can result in the emission of toxins. If accurate embodied emissions figures are to be calculated, the types of fuels used in any manufacturing process must be known, as each fuel gives a different mix of emissions.

Several different methods exist for calculating embodied energy, and this results in a range of figures published for similar materials. Published data should be treated with some caution, unless it is clearly stated how the figures have been calculated.

CALCULATING EMBODIED ENERGY

The following section will help one research the embodied energy of a particular material or to make some educated guesses.

How has the energy been measured?

When reading figures for the embodied energy of a material or house type, the first question to ask is how has the energy been measured? Energy is measured as either delivered or primary energy. Delivered energy refers to the actual quantity of energy delivered for use to a particular site or building, for example the amount of electricity used and recorded on a bill. Primary energy refers to the amount of energy used to produce a quantity of delivered energy. For example, to create electricity, gas will have been burnt to drive the turbines in a power station. The generators will not be 100 per cent efficient, so the energy content of the gas burnt is greater than the energy content of the electricity generated. Also, the electricity has to be transported from the power station to the consumer, a process that is not 100 per cent efficient. All of these inefficiencies mean that for every one unit of electricity delivered to a consumer, a larger amount of primary energy will have been consumed in its creation.

In the UK, the ratio between primary and delivered energy is greatest for electricity: roughly three units of primary energy are used to produce one unit of delivered electricity. For oil and gas used in the home, the ratios are closer to one.

It is still the case that embodied energy figures are often quoted without stating if they have been calculated using primary or delivered energy. Where there is uncertainty over the embodied energy figures quoted, it is better to compare materials using embodied

2.2.
Farm building in Maharashtra State, India. How far have materials travelled and how much energy has been used to process them?

emissions figures, as these should take into account the mix of primary fuels used to produce the goods.

What has been considered when calculating embodied energy?

Once one is clear about the energy measurement, it is important to know where the boundary has been drawn in calculating the energy inputs. For example, consider the embodied energy of a steel-framed window. If the energy inputs are calculated only for the energy used in the factory that assembled the window, figures will differ from calculations that include also the energy used in the steel works to make the steel or the energy used in the mine to gather the iron ore.

In order to calculate accurately the embodied energy of a material, all stages at which energy is used should be accounted for. An accurate figure will be derived if we consider the energy used for extraction of raw materials, transportation to processing plants, energy used in factories, transportation to site and energy used on site to install the product.

RECYCLING AND EMBODIED ENERGY

To achieve a low energy house, is it best to construct a new dwelling or refurbish an existing one?

In most cases, refurbishment would be the preferred option, provided that the core of the building can be reused without extensive demolition. Refurbishment is essentially the recycling of a building.

Recycling is an issue that needs careful thought in relation to environmental impact. It only makes environmental sense to recycle if it can be done easily; that is, without requiring the input of a lot of energy, if the building can be thermally upgraded and if such recycling is not repeated too frequently.

As an example, we consider a typical situation found in a nineteenth-century house. Often, internal walls will be constructed using lime plaster on wooden laths fixed to vertical timber posts. After 100 years or so, the lime plaster can begin to separate from the laths, which typically occurs locally. The best solution would be to remove all of the loose plaster. However, once a loose piece is removed, it is difficult both to prevent a larger area coming away and to replace with new lime-based plaster. Typically, this will be expensive, and it maybe difficult to find a knowledgeable contractor. If you ask a general building contractor they will probably propose to remove all the plaster and replace it with plaster board (which requires a relatively large amount of energy to manufacture). But if you speak to a plasterer, they will often recommend leaving the original lime plaster in place and reinforcing it with a scrim (fine mesh) and a thin coat of plaster over that. The last option will have the minimum environmental impact, because so little new material is used, even though it uses a modern plaster that will require more energy to produce per unit volume than a replacement lime plaster.

PROCESSING AND EMBODIED ENERGY

The greater the number of processes a material or set of components have to go through, the higher will be their embodied energy and the number of associated waste products. Materials such as metal require very large energy inputs for their production, but so will equipment that requires complex manufacturing, for example a modern gas boiler.

2.3.
External table, Le Corbusier's mother's house at Vevey, Switzerland. An object with minimal use of materials, external spaces allow dwellings to expand seasonally and visually.

Within reason, one should aim to choose materials and components that are as close to their natural state as possible. So, a high-performance window with a softwood frame will be preferable to the same window with an aluminium frame. Or, as another example, organic paints or those that are water-based, particularly if using natural pigments, or waxes are preferable finishes to highly manufactured synthetic paints.

TRANSPORTATION AND EMBODIED ENERGY

Transportation is one of the often forgotten factors affecting embodied energy. The further a material has to travel, the greater the energy that is used in its transport. The weight of a material will also affect the energy needed to move it. Some natural products may have travelled great distances, for example polished granite from overseas quarries, the finishing of which may even take place in a second country before delivery to the final point of sale. This kind of information is not always freely available, but asking suppliers about transportation can help you to make decisions while also alerting suppliers to a concern in the market place.

In some situations transportation will have to be weighed against durability. In the UK, natural slate is now available from quarries in Spain. This slate is much cheaper than English or Welsh slate and, though not as durable, the Spanish slate is apparently more durable than artificial slate. On grounds of durability, an imported natural material may be preferable to a local artificial one.

Similar issues arise when considering the purchase of white goods, e.g., fridges and washing machines. Surveys by the consumer organization Which? have indicated that imported washing machines from Germany are far less likely to break down than machines manufactured in the UK. Therefore, we can assume that they will last longer. This longer life has to be weighed against energy used in transport.

TIME AND EMBODIED ENERGY

Studies conducted in New Zealand suggest that the energy used in a typical (i.e. non-low energy) residential building, over a 50-year life, is equal to approximately four times the embodied energy of its structure (Williamson, 1997).

This kind of direct comparison between energy in use and embodied energy is not very useful, unless we know how long the dwelling is expected to last. It will always be the case that, as energy-in-use requirements reduce, the longer this will take to

equal the embodied energy of the structure. When considering the embodied energy of a building, we need to take account of the building's expected lifespan, the maintenance requirements of the various building elements and the building's state at the end of its life.

This cradle-to-grave approach is called 'life cycle analysis'. It is used as a way of assessing the total impact of any building and shows the importance of the building's lifespan. The longer a house can last, the lower the impact of the energy and pollution resulting from the manufacture of its materials will be. A simple way to think about this is to consider the initial embodied energy of an entire building and divide this figure over its lifetime, making an allowance for maintenance.

2.4.
Recycled buildings, mixed-use housing, Ilot 13, Quartier des Grottes, Geneva, Switzerland. If existing buildings can be reused and upgraded in an energy-efficient manner, they will have a smaller environmental impact owing to a lower material use compared with new buildings. Architects: P. Bonhote, O. Calame and I. Vuarambon.

EMBODIED ENERGY AND THE MATERIALS USED IN HOUSES

As noted above, it is difficult to find accurate published figures for the embodied energy of materials. Generally, if an up-to-date database has been assembled, it will be used commercially. The Building Research Establishment (BRE) has set up an

Table 2.1. Embodied energy of building materials. Range of published figures

Material	Density	Low value		High value	
	(kg m^{-3})	GJ tonne^{-1}	GJ m^{-3}	GJ tonne^{-1}	GJ m^{-3}
Natural aggregates	1500	0.030	0.05	0.12	0.93
Cement	1500	4.3	6.5	7.8	11.7
Bricks	~1700	1.0	1.7	9.4	16.0
Timber (prepared softwood)	~500	0.52	0.26	7.1	3.6
Glass	2600	13.0	34.0	31.0	81.0
Steel (steel sections)	7800	24.0	190.0	59.0	460.0
Plaster	~1200	1.1	1.3	6.7	8.0

GJ = giga joule, a unit of energy, 1 GJ = 278 kWh.
Source: Building Research Establishment, 1994.

Environmental Profiles web site (http://www.bre.co.uk), access to which requires registration. The web site 'EcoSite – Worldwide resource for life cycle analysis' (http://www.ecosite.co.uk) publishes the list of embodied energy figures, credited to the BRE, shown in Table 2.1.

Table 2.1 illustrates the range of published figures, but it does not state if the figures are for primary or delivered energy. However, previous research (West et al., 1994) has indicated that, for most building types, the following materials will contribute significantly to the embodied energy of a building:

• steel;
• concrete;
• timber;
• bricks;
• cement;
• aggregates;
• glass;
• plaster.

These materials account for a large proportion of the volume or mass of most buildings, and the designer can significantly affect a building's embodied energy by paying close attention to their specification. Selecting materials from local sources will reduce their embodied energy and emissions because of reduced transport. The range of values for timber shown in Table 2.1 provides an indication of the impact of transport, amongst other factors.

In a typical house with walls built from brick and concrete blocks and with timber floors, these three materials could account for about 50 per cent of the dwelling's embodied energy, with brick and concrete accounting for about 30 per cent of the total. Sheet materials, for example plasterboards or lining boards to timber-framed walls, can also have a significant impact.

THE EMBODIED ENERGY OF DIFFERENT BUILDING MATERIALS

At present, the few published figures available for embodied energy usually refer to individual materials, e.g. brick, concrete, timber or glass. These figures are useful for making strategic decisions regarding a house, i.e. should it be built using a timber frame or concrete blocks, but they are less useful when trying to decide if a particular energy-saving feature should be used, for example mechanical ventilation with heat recovery. This is where cradle-to-grave or life cycle analysis becomes important and this will be considered later in the chapter.

As embodied energy is usually quoted per unit weight or per unit volume of a material, one needs to know the weight or volume of the particular material actually used in a building. Certain materials, such as plastics or metals, have very high embodied energies per unit weight but, if used in small quantities, may have an overall benefit by, for example, providing an elegant joint between materials

2.5.
Equipment used on a building site for pumping 'Warmcell' insulation, made from recycled newspapers, into a wall. At almost every stage in the production and construction process, energy is used. The sum of the energy from each stage, including the energy used for transport, is called the product's embodied energy.

or by increasing the distance a material, such as timber, can span or by increasing the lifetime of an element.

Plastics, timber and metals are materials about which there is much debate over their environmental impact. There is no consensus as to the advisability of the use of plastics or synthetic materials but, in our view, they are best avoided.

Plastics

The embodied energy of plastics is extremely high. They are, on the other hand, waste products from the production of petroleum. So, it can be argued that by using plastics we reduce the accumulation of waste material. But it can also be said that the use of plastics helps to support the very industry that is responsible for a large amount of CO_2 emissions and for over half of all toxic emissions to the environment. After their production, plastics tend to release gases into the atmosphere, these are referred to as volatile organic compounds (VOCs), which can be harmful if breathed in any quantity. They are found in synthetic compounds in carpets and modern paints, especially oil-based paints such as those with an eggshell finish. The effect of VOCs is usually greatest soon after installation.

One plastic generally thought best to avoid is polyvinyl chloride (PVC). It is particularly difficult to dispose of in an ecologically safe manner but it can be recycled and, in its recycled form, is beginning to appear on the market, generally for low-grade products.

Metals

Metals are another group of materials with a high embodied energy for which the manufacturing process results in local environmental degradation from waste products. Owing to the high price of metals, most waste metal is recycled, although this process is not without its own detrimental environmental cost; the smelting process requires large energy inputs and generates highly toxic dioxin emissions because of the chlorine found in most metals. Until such time when the large-scale use of renewable energies makes their production more environmentally friendly, it is best to minimize the use of metals in construction. Metals should only be used in small quantities or for particular purposes, e.g. for the jointing and fixing of materials.

Stainless steel and aluminium are both very likely to be recycled, but have very high environmental impacts as a result of their initial manufacture. Their extensive use in buildings cannot be considered ecological.

Lead, because of its toxic nature and associated pollution resulting from the manufacturing process, is best avoided. Currently, it is mainly used for roof flashings, where it forms a long-lasting waterproofing element between walls and roof coverings or at junctions between roof coverings. Water collected off roofs with lead flashings is best not used for watering edible fruits or vegetables as these may absorb lead as they grow. Lead may prove a hazard when renovating older properties as paint older than 30 years may contain the metal, which was used as a drying agent. Care must be taken to avoid inhaling dust or fumes. It is therefore not a good idea to burn off old lead paint.

Timber

Timber is a material that is generally considered to have excellent environmental credentials. As a renewable resource, its main attributes are that it reduces the amount of CO_2 in the atmosphere until it decays or is burnt and it is easily worked. There are, however, possible disadvantages associated with timber, the principal one resulting from imported timber. This may have been transported over long distances, for example from Canada to the UK. Another potential problem has to do with the way the timber is grown and if trees are replanted when mature ones are cut. Most commercial softwood comes from forests that will be replanted, however these commercial softwood forests are often planted with very few species of trees and provide little potential for bio-diversity. In the case of imported non-European hardwoods, there is a high probability that these come from tropical rainforests and will not be replaced. The Forestry Stewardship Council, based in the UK, does run a scheme for certifying that timber comes from sustainable forests. Currently, only a small percentage of wood commercially available is certified as sustainable and, practically, this can be difficult to obtain. Anyone contemplating the construction of a new building using timber would be well advised to research the availability of locally grown timber. There are local forests with associated sawmills that can supply good quality home-grown timber, such as Douglas Fir, Sweet Chestnut and Oak, suitable for load-bearing construction.

If it is necessary to use imported timber in the UK, then one should aim to use wood imported from Scandinavia, as it will have been transported a relatively short distance. Scandinavian forests are generally considered to be sustainable, but not bio-diverse.

Timber, a note of caution
Timber is a good choice as a sustainable material but, if it is used externally, it must be detailed in such a way as to prevent rot.

2.6.
Recycling a building. London Eco House for the environmental charity Conservation and Urban Ecology. An external wall lined with a timber framework, which will hold 150 mm of insulation to achieve 'super insulation' standards. Window frames will be reused but glazed with energy-efficient argon-filled double glazing. To justify the reuse of buildings on environmental grounds will, in most cases, require that their energy efficiency is significantly improved. Architects: K. Bohn and A. Viljoen.

Currently, most timber suppliers will automatically treat external timber to prevent rot but these treatments are highly toxic and should be avoided in ecological buildings. Therefore, some untreated species of timber, particularly much low-grade imported softwood, is not suitable for external use. If one can source durable timber, it may be used untreated externally by detailing it correctly. This generally means making sure that, if the timber does get wet, water will rapidly drain away and the timber is well ventilated. One should check the durability of any external timber before purchasing it. Oak and Larch, for example, are durable external timbers, whereas much softwood imported into the UK is not and, if used externally, will not have a long life.

As a general rule for materials, choose local materials that have had the minimum processing. But do check that they will be durable and fit for the purpose intended!

See the recommended reading list for publications that provide more detailed information about material selection.

DETAILED STUDIES OF TWO HOUSES IN THE UK

A comparative study between embodied energy and energy in use is a complex task, requiring accurate embodied energy figures and detailed information regarding the construction of the building and its predicted energy requirements. It is not something that every house builder would wish to undertake.

However, detailed study has been undertaken by one of the authors (Viljoen, 1997) of Dr Roaf's Oxford Ecohouse and a similar low-energy house in Suffolk, designed by the architect Roy

2.7.
Green roof from 1924, Le Corbusier's mother's house at Vevey, Switzerland. A building element can have several environmental functions, for example insulating a roof, increasing bio-diversity, extending nature into a building and giving visual pleasure: 'In spring the young grass sprouts up with its wild flowers; in summer it is high and luxuriant. The roof garden lives independently, tended by the sun, the rain, the winds and the birds which bring the seeds' (Le Corbusier, 1924).

Grimwade. Conclusions drawn from the study can be applied generally to housing in the UK and further afield. Figures for the primary embodied energy and associated emissions of construction materials were supplied by Nigel Howard, one of the leading authorities on embodied energy in the UK.

The purpose of the study was to assess the relative importance of embodied energy compared with the energy used by a dwelling on a day-to-day basis. Studies were made using several variations of the Roaf and Grimwade houses. The design of each building was altered from being a low-energy house to one that met the requirements of the current building regulations. Then, in a series of steps, each design was made progressively more energy efficient. In the final case, each house was designed as a 'zero-energy house', a house receiving over 1 year all of its energy requirements for space heating, hot water, cooking and appliances from on-site renewable energy sources. The embodied energy of all materials and components, including solar hot water and photovoltaic systems, were taken account of in a life cycle analysis calculation.

As a zero-energy house will have more materials and technical equipment built into it, the intention of the study was to find out if this extra equipment and its associated embodied energy and

2.8.
Active solar roof from 2000, Centre for Alternative Technology, Wales. Photovoltaic panels used as a roofing material, generating electricity from the sun for use within the building. Systems like this significantly reduce the environmental impact of buildings. Energy used in manufacture is offset by the energy generated while in use.

emissions resulted in a house with a lower total environmental impact over its lifetime than one that used some non-renewable energy sources. Comparisons between different options were made on the basis of the life cycle analysis, which predicted yearly energy and CO_2 emissions per square metre of floor area for each house, resulting from embodied and in-use energy requirements.

RESULTS FROM THE LIFE CYCLE ANALYSIS

Reducing energy-in-use requirements

The results from this study showed very clearly that zero-energy houses had the lowest environmental impact. The first priority of any design should be to reduce energy-in-use requirements as far as possible using energy conservation techniques and then use active and passive solar systems to supply energy needs. The impact of materials is generally of secondary importance.

Building for a long life

Apart from the embodied energy of individual materials, the study showed how important a building's life expectancy is. The longer the low-energy dwelling can last, the lower the environmental impact of the materials that have gone into its construction.

Choosing materials for walls and floors

Both the Roaf and the Grimwade houses were built to low-energy standards and were similar in form. The one major difference between them lies in the materials used for construction. The Roaf house uses traditional building materials, e.g. concrete blocks and brick with precast concrete floors. The Grimwade house was designed to be built with rammed earth walls, using locally grown timber for a structural frame and wooden floors to the first floor. Also, its section minimizes the height of walls and thus the quantity of material required to construct them.

The study showed that, using a life cycle analysis including embodied energy and emissions, one could expect a house built from rammed earth and local timber to have a lifetime energy impact in the order of 20 per cent lower than a house built using medium-density concrete blocks. CO_2 reductions are much greater, at about 50 per cent; see the section below on thermal mass.

While it is almost certainly the case that timber-framed buildings, built using a local source of timber, will have a lower embodied energy than similar houses built using bricks and concrete, this

2.9.
Wooden cladding and colonnade at mixed-use housing, Ilot 13, Quartier des Grottes, Geneva, Switzerland. Timber, from local sustainable forests, has a low environmental impact. Care should be taken when detailing it to ensure it will not rot. Here, a roof overhang provides protection from rain. The raised timber walkway in the foreground has gaps between the planks to ensure good drainage and ventilation. Architects: P. Bonhote, O. Calame and I. Vuarambon.

comparison does not take account of the thermal benefits that may arise from using high-mass materials.

Choosing thermal mass

Bricks, concrete and rammed earth have high thermal capacities, which means they can absorb heat over time and release it relatively slowly as the surroundings cool down. The theoretical

2.10.
Internal view of a bookshop under construction, Centre for Alternative Technology, Wales. Materials with a high thermal capacity, capable of absorbing and storing heat, are placed below south facing windows. During the heating season they help to store heat, reducing the need for space heating. In summer, they help to prevent overheating during the day by absorbing excessive solar gain. The embodied energy of this building is extremely low. The timber comes from local forests, thus minimizing the embodied energy resulting from transport. Internal walls (here with sunlight on one of them) are constructed using rammed earth and act, with their high thermal mass, as heat stores. Architect: Pat Borer.

benefit of high thermal mass is often exaggerated but, for a building continuously occupied, thermal mass can be of some benefit if positioned so as to absorb direct sunlight.

The most environmentally sensitive material for thermal mass is rammed earth. If this is not feasible, concrete blocks will most likely be used. Concrete blocks are available in a range of densities from low-density insulating blocks (0.6 tons m^{-3}), to medium-density (1.1 tons m^{-3}) and high-density blocks (2.2 tons m^{-3}). The embodied energy and CO_2 of concrete blocks varies considerably and unexpectedly with their density. Owing to the manufacturing process and the materials used, high-density blocks have the lowest and medium-density blocks the highest embodied energy and CO_2 emissions by weight and volume.

The life cycle analysis study showed that a low-energy rammed-earth house would result in CO_2 emissions on the order of 10.3 kg m^{-2} year^{-1}, compared with 12.9 kg m^{-2} year^{-1} for a building using dense blocks (2.2 tonnes m^{-3}) or 20.9 kg m^{-2} year^{-1} for a house using medium-density blocks (1.1 tonnes m^{-3}). Compared with using rammed earth, and depending upon the type of block chosen, the CO_2 impact of a concrete house can change by between 25 per cent and 100 per cent!

An interesting strategy for housing is to use a mixture of high thermal mass and lightweight timber-framed construction. Normally, high-mass walls are constructed internally and are surrounded with well-insulated timber-framed external walls. There is a clear analogy with a person wrapped up in a warm coat.

Generally, a well-insulated high-mass house is less likely to overheat in summer than a low-mass one. In lightweight timber dwellings, care is required to prevent summer-time overheating, usually by means of solar shading and ventilation.

Integrating photovoltaic and solar hot water systems

Photovoltaic and solar hot water systems significantly reduce a building's overall environmental impact. The life cycle analysis study showed that a photovoltaic system reduced the total embodied and in-use energy impact of the Roaf house by about 40 per cent and the CO_2 emissions by about 35 per cent.

Integrating whole-house mechanical ventilation with heat recovery

Based on the Roaf and Grimwade house life cycle analysis studies, mechanical ventilation with heat recovery for the whole house makes sense, resulting in energy and CO_2 reductions on the order of 10 per cent. However, recent studies of low-energy houses by the International Energy Agency (Hestnes et al., 1997) have noted that the electricity used by fans in mechanical ventilation systems can be significant. If larger amounts of electricity are used, the energy advantages of a mechanical ventilation system with heat recovery will be less than suggested above, and perhaps these systems have an overall negative impact. Within the UK, the jury remains out on this point. Notwithstanding energy and CO_2 considerations, there is a question regarding the internal air quality delivered by such systems. Whole-house mechanical systems require horizontal pipe runs connecting inlet and outlet points that are generally not cleaned and can, over time, build up deposits of dirt and dust, which may lead to poor air quality.

Comparison with current Building Regulations

The total embodied and in-use energy impact of the Roaf house, as built, is about half that of the equivalent house built to current Building Regulations. CO_2 emissions are reduced by about 60 per cent.

Where to find building materials with a low environmental impact?

Germany appears to manufacture the greatest range of ecological building materials. As the market expands, variety and availability increase. Currently, in the UK the quantity of ecological building materials available is increasing, but many are imported. Although import adds to the material's embodied energy, it seems a good idea to use these products as, apart from their environmental benefits, using them will demonstrate that a market exists. This should stimulate local manufacture, which in the long term would result in significant environmental benefit.

Solar hot water and photovoltaic systems are available in most countries; both systems can significantly reduce the environmental impact of a dwelling. The cost of photovoltaics remains relatively high, but is dropping all the time. Solar hot water systems are considerably cheaper and, given their environmental benefits, should if possible be used.

Other building materials with a low environmental impact, which are generally available in the UK, include paints and stains (water-based), plasters (clay-based), thermal insulation (using recycled paper, flax, wool or cork), local sustainable timber (often

2.11.
Small theatre building built of straw, Centre for Alternative Technology, Wales. A timber frame supports the roof. External walls are constructed using straw bales, which provide high levels of insulation. A render protects the straw bales from moisture. This is a building with low thermal mass; it will cool down and warm up quickly. For a building used intermittently, this can be a good strategy but care needs to be taken to prevent summertime overheating by providing effective ventilation and shading. Architect: Pat Borer.

available if researched), earth wall construction (local soil types need to be tested to see if suitable) and straw bale construction (if space permits and finishes are acceptable, it can be quite rough).

Materials that will save energy (mainly double or triple glazing with low emissivity coatings or insulation) almost always make sense. Low-impact window frames with different glazing types are relatively easy to obtain in the UK.

Windows should be considered in relation to daylight and thermal insulation. A poorly daylit room will require the use of electric lighting with its associated negative environmental impact. One should also remember that double or triple glazing will reduce the amount of light passing through a window as each pane of glass will absorb some of it. Nineteenth-century houses give a good idea of window sizes required for adequate day lighting. Insulation materials with low environmental impact, as well as skilled contractors, are beginning to appear on the British market. Within the UK, as a rule of thumb, 150 mm of insulation in walls, 250 mm in roofs and, say, 100 mm expanded polystyrene under a concrete ground floor are considered to result in a 'super-insulated' house (Olivier, 1992). Synthetic insulations should be avoided, unless water proof qualities are necessary (see reference list for further reading).

Ventilation and insulation must be considered together. There is no point in heavily insulating a dwelling if it is not also airtight. Too much background ventilation results in great heat loss in the winter, too little leads to a risk of condensation and stale air or, at worse, excess CO_2. Adequate background ventilation, usually through 'trickle ventilators' built into window frames, is essential for health and condensation avoidance in most houses. Trickle ventilators for all types of window frames are easily available in the UK, as well as more complex whole-house natural ventilation systems.

CONCLUSION

As a first priority, a design should aim for a dwelling that uses the minimum amount of energy to run. This can be supported by, for example, applying conservation techniques and passive solar design principles. Where possible, the use of solar hot water and photovoltaic systems is highly advisable to generate on-site energy (wind or water power may be appropriate in some situations).

Once the design strategy is clear, local building materials and those requiring the minimum processing should be selected in preference to highly processed materials and those from further afield. Non-toxic products should replace chemically treated materials and those containing toxins. The durability of materials is also very significant as it will affect the lifespan of a building and, the longer a low-energy house lasts, the less relative impact its materials will have. Ideally, all building materials should be easily recyclable. Finally, the potential for flexible occupancy will help to extend the useful lifetime of a building.

ACKNOWLEDGEMENT

Embodied energy and embodied emissions figures used to perform the life cycle analysis calculations for the Roaf and Grimwade houses were supplied by Nigel Howard, currently of the Building Research Establishment's Centre for Sustainable Construction.

RECOMMENDED READING LIST

Anink, D., Boonstra, C. and Mak, J. (1996). *Handbook of Sustainable Building, An Environmental Preference Method for Selection of Materials for Use in Construction and Refurbishment.* James and James, London, ISBN 1-873936-38-9.

Association for Environment Conscious Building (2000). *The Real Green Building Book, Yearbook of the Association for Environment Conscious Building.* AECB, Nant-y-Garreg, Saron, Llandysul, Carmarthenshire, SA44 5EJ (http://www.aecb.net).

2.12.
A chair at the Tipu Sultan's Summer Palace in Bangalore, India. Avoiding artificial finishes in interiors is a good strategy for reducing environmental impact. Modern synthetic paints and carpets generally have high embodied energies and are often environmentally unfriendly. Their frequent replacement also contributes to the negative environmental impact of finishes and fittings.

Borer, P. and Harris, C. (1998). *The Whole House Book, Ecological Building Design and Materials*. The Centre for Alternative Technology, Machynlleth, ISBN 1 898049 21 1.

Talbott, J. (1993). *Simply Build Green, A Technical Guide to the Ecological Houses at the Findhorn Foundation*. The Findhorn Press, Findhorn, ISBN 1 899171 90 8.

Woolley, T., Kimmins, S., Harrison, P. and Harrison, R. (1997). *The Green Building Handbook*. E & FN Spon, London, ISBN 0 419 22690 7.

3 DETAILING THE ENVELOPE

In this chapter we give some rather detailed information on the thermal performance of specific elements used in the construction of a house. These include the insulation, cold bridging in windows and walls, infiltration and a few more general points on window design. This material, very detailed in places, is included in this book because it is so important in the jigsaw puzzle of low-energy house design.

INSULATION

The colder the climate, the more insulation is needed. The Inuit people of the Arctic get most of their insulation from the skin and fur clothes they wear that keep them warm even when living in houses made of ice.

In a similar climate, in the Antarctic, a Mantainer (container for people) was designed for Robert Swan's expedition, in which the wall of the capsule provides most of the necessary insulation. The structure (Figure 3.1) is made of a timber fibre honeycomb base panel (12 mm thick), compressible wool insulation to the exterior of the panel, all contained in a waterproof cotton skin. The double floor panels are of polyamide honeycomb. Similar pods are used in remote regions of the world, such as the Swiss Alps (Figure 3.2), and their success depends on choosing exactly the right insulation that is light and highly efficient, regardless, in this case, of cost. The specification of insulation in many of our own homes may be quite different. The trick with insulation is to choose the right insulation for the job.

But there is a wide range of insulation products on the market at a wide range of prices. How does one choose the right type for the job? The properties of each insulation product should be evaluated and, if necessary, checked with the manufacturer. A clear specification for the insulation should be drawn up. Does the insulation

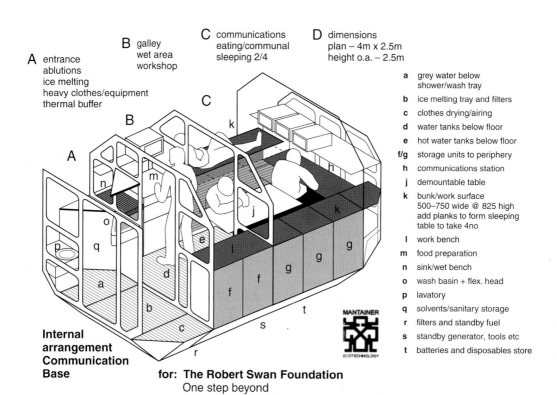

A entrance
ablutions
ice melting
heavy clothes/equipment
thermal buffer

B galley
wet area
workshop

C communications
eating/communal
sleeping 2/4

D dimensions
plan – 4m x 2.5m
height o.a. – 2.5m

a   grey water below
     shower/wash tray

b   ice melting tray and filters

c   clothes drying/airing

d   water tanks below floor

e   hot water tanks below floor

f/g   storage units to periphery

h   communications station

j   demountable table

k   bunk/work surface
     500–750 wide @ 825 high
     add planks to form sleeping
     table to take 4no

l   work bench

m   food preparation

n   sink/wet bench

o   wash basin + flex. head

p   lavatory

q   solvents/sanitary storage

r   filters and standby fuel

s   standby generator, tools etc

t   batteries and disposables store

**Internal
arrangement
Communication
Base**

for: The Robert Swan Foundation
One step beyond
Antarctic Expedition

MANTAINER
ECOTECHNOLOGY

3.1.

The Mantainer pod designed for Robert Swan's Antarctic Expedition. The pod uses photovoltaics to generate electricity and a gas microwave cooker. A multifuel cooker is included where waste can be burnt. Water comes from snow melt. The WC is compositing, and those wastes not compostible or combustible are removed at the end of the habitation (Ian Guilani, Mantainer, Ecotechnology, Henley, UK. Email: giu@mantainer.demon.co.uk).

have to be waterproof? Is it best to use a reflective board, a high mass wall or a bulky insulation product (see below)? How much room in the construction is available for it? How toxic is the product and does it matter? Is it to be put on the exposed side of a house where there is driving rain or on the sheltered solar elevation? How fire-resistant does it have to be? For instance, if the insulation is to be used internally, then a fire-resistant type is essential; this subject is covered under the section 'Fire' in Chapter 6. Where the insulation is to be placed in well-sealed cavity walls this may not be such an issue. The usual basic rules for materials choice should apply: use materials that are as natural as possible and as local as possible. However, in some cases, such as the Mantainer pod, it is possible to justify the transport energy costs of moving insulation long distances because of the amount of energy saved when it is used on location. Who wants to lug a Calor Gas bottle up a Swiss Alp? Here, as always, common sense is essential.

3.2.
A Mantainer pod placed by helicopter in the Swiss Alps for all-season use (Ian Guilani, Mantainer, Ecotechnology, Henley, UK. Email: giu@mantainer.demon.co.uk).

Table 3.1. Some properties of insulation materials

	Type of insulation				
	Expanded polystyrene insulation	Rock mineral wool	Cellular glass	Cellulose	Phenolic foam
Thermal performance	0.033 W mK^{-1}	0.034–0.036 W mK^{-1}	0.042 W mK^{-1}	0.033 W mK^{-1}	0.018 W mK^{-4}
Moisture resistance	NOT considered a vapour barrier. Low water vapour transmission, no capillary action, and high resistance to moisture absorption.	Does not absorb moisture. At 95% RH, hygroscopic water content is only 0.02% by volume, 2% by weight. No capillary action.	0.2% by volume. No capillary action.	Not given (presumed low moisture resistance).	High moisture resistance, low vapour permeability, 90% closed cell structure.
Mechanical performance	10% compression strength of 110–150 kPa.	10% compression strength of 120–180 kPa.	10% compression strength of 230–500 kPa. Average compressive strength is 600 kPa (87 p.s.i.).	Not given (presumed poor mechanical strength).	'Good compressive strength'.
Chemical properties	Resistant to diluted acids and alkalis. Not resistant to organic solvents. Can chemically interact with polymeric single-ply membranes such as PVC.	May need isolating board under asphalt.	Pure glass without binders or fillers. Totally inorganic, impervious to common acids except hydrofluoric acid. May release hydrogen sulphide and CO in a fire.	Treated with inorganic salts for fire protection.	Low corrosion, pH approx. 6.5. Pre-1980s foam corrosive to metal deck surfaces and fasteners in dry conditions and aggressively corrosive when wet.
Fire behaviour	Melts and shrinks away from small heat source. Ignites with severe flames and heavy smoke when exposed to a large heat source.	Non-combustible to 2000°C. Practical limit is 1000°C owing to the additives.	Non-combustible.	Withstands direct heat from a blowlamp.	Class O fire rating.
Toxicity	Thermal decomposition products are no more toxic than those of wood.	None.	None.	None, fully biodegradable.	Formaldehyde used in manufacture.
Embodied energy	120.0 GJ t^{-1}	25.0 GJ t^{-1}	27.0 GJ t^{-1}	0.63–1.25 GJ t^{-1}	27.78 kW kg^{-1}
CFC emissions	Does not use CFCs, HCFCs or CO_2.	Does not use CFCs, HCFCs.	Does not use CFCs, HCFCs.	Does not use CFCs, HCFCs or VOCs.	Does not use CFCs. Uses chemical blowing agents instead of a physical one.
Effects of age	None reported. See Chapter 4.	None (batt). Settling (loose fill).	See Chapter 4.	None reported.	See Chapter 4.
New buildings	On or below sub-floor slab, between timber floor joists. Partial or full fill wallboards. Flat or pitched roofs. Granular and bead forms of EPS can be injected into existing cavity.	Roof or ceiling, walls, floor or foundation.	Roof or ceiling, walls, floor or foundation.	Roof or ceiling, walls, floor or foundation.	Factory engineered panels. Particularly suited for HVAC pipework and ducting.
Existing buildings					Not mentioned.
Prices	Range £1.23–6.50 per m^2. Board: 50 mm £4.95, 100 mm £4.64. Cavity fill: 65 mm £2.75 (including labour).	£1.50–3.00 per m^2	'Expensive'	None given.	'Ballpark' £5.81 per m^2
Lifetime	None given.	60+ years.	None given.	None given.	'Long' – usually exceeds building life.
Recycling	Easily melted and reformed. Low density precludes long-distance transport.	Recycling programs in place in the UK.	Reclaimable on demolition.	100% recycled and recyclable.	Is possible. No programs in UK as reported.

Microporous silicia	Sheep's wool	Flexible melamine foam	Cork	Polyurethane foam	Polyisocyanurate foam
0.020 W mK^{-1}	0.037 W mK^{-1}	0.035 W mK^{-4}	0.037 W mK^{-1}	0.017 W mK^{-1}	R-value/inch: 2.8–5.5
Moisture content of 1–3% by weight.	40% water absorption (by dry weight) at 100% RH.	Undergoes significant dimensional changes with increased moisture content owing to its open cell structure.	Water repellent with zero capillarity. Relatively high rate of vapour transmission.	Closed cell structure forms monolithic, self-flashing surfaces. Can be sprayed with elastomeric coating for further weather resistance.	Low water absorption and vapour transmission.
Tensile strength is low. 5% compression can be fully recovered.	Not given (presumed poor mechanical strength).	'Foam does not have a particularly high strength'.	Compressive strength up to 20 kN m^{-2} without deformation. Bending strength 140 kN m^{-2}.	10% compression strength of 114 kPa. Tensile strength of 120 kPa. Shear strength 80 kPa.	High strength to weight ratio.
Leachable chloride content is low, less than 50 ppm. Leachable silicate content is high, greater than 1500 ppm.	Not mentioned.	Resists hydrolysis, alcohols, hydrocarbons, most organic solvents and dilute acids and bases.	Unaffected by water, alkalis and organic solvents.	Not mentioned. See Chapter 4.	Can be used with asphalt. See Chapter 4.
Non-combustible with zero flame spread.	Ignition point 560°C. Fire resistance B2.	Can withstand up to 150°C with no reduction in performance. Rated as Class 1.	No cyanides, chlorides or other toxic gases are produced. Rated as Class 1.	Interior building applications may be covered with a fire resistive thermal barrier. Do not use welding and cutting torches on or near such foams.	Can withstand high temperatures and when finally burnt forms a surface char, which helps to insulate the underlying foam from the fire.
Safe to handle. Avoid breathing dust from cutting or machining.	None, fully biodegradable.	Non-carcinogenic.	None mentioned.	May cause irritation to skin, respiratory system, and eyes.	None mentioned.
Not given.	30 kWh m^{-3} energy consumption in manufacture.	Not given.	Can be harvested every 9–12 years during the tree's 160–200 year productive lifetime.	Not given.	Low when made from recycled materials.
Not mentioned.	None reported.	CFC-free.	None reported.	Uses HCFCs.	CFC-free.
None.	Will degrade if left exposed to sunlight or water for extended periods.	See Chapter 4.	None reported.	Can be renewed with the application of the elastomeric top coating.	See Chapter 4.
Mostly industrial applications.	Roof or ceiling, walls or floor.	HVAC pipes, ducts, plant. Plant rooms, offices and conference suites, theatres, cinema auditoria, and recording studios.	Single layer system or as part of a composite board.	Can be blown or sprayed into a cavity. Adheres to most surfaces. Conforms to irregular shapes and penetrations. Tanks, pipes, cold storage rooms, etc.	Solid floor, suspended timber floors, partial fill of cavity walls, steel stud-framed walls, timber-framed walls, and roofs.
None given.	Twice the cost of mineral wool products.	£3.72–£29.07 per m^2 depending on thickness.	None given.	None given.	£6.00 per m^2 with 50 mm thickness.
None given.	None given.	None given.	None given.	None given.	None given.
Not mentioned.	Can be fully recycled.	Cannot be melted and reused.	Not mentioned.	Can be renewed with the reapplication of the elastomeric top coating. Not recyclable upon removal.	Can be manufactured from the waste stream of other polyester-derived materials such as PET bottles.

The next question is how much insulation to put into the roof, walls and floors of a building? This decision should be made early on in the design as it determines how thick the house envelope will be and, in turn, what is the most suitable construction detailing for the house. This choice is often made on the basis of cost.

In a recent article Peter Warm explained some calculations to evaluate the optimal thickness of insulation. He based the first equation on a semi-detached house in the UK, with space heating, over a 60-year lifetime with fuel costing £0.164 kWh⁻¹ (Warm, 1997). Normal mineral wool batts at current costs are the cheapest air-based insulation available in the UK at present, and the results showed that actually the most economical thickness is around 200 mm. However this, and many other calculations are based on present fuel prices and insulation costs. We also know that over the next 20 years the price of energy must go up, though by how much is not known. What happens to the cost of insulation materials if the cost of oil and gas doubles or triples over the next 20 years? Warm also redid the calculations independently of prices. He looked at how much energy it takes to manufacture the insulation in comparison with how much energy the insulation saves over a 60-year life. It does suppose that the fuel types are equivalent but it gives a rough tool for answering the question. This changes the picture completely and the most economical thickness of insulation becomes around 650 mm! So the limitations on how much insulation we put in our homes are possibly the practical details of the mounting and fixing systems we use, rather than economic ones.

Already we have introduced a number of variables into the process of choosing the right insulation for a job, including type, fire resistance, time, local material availability, cost, and microlocation, i.e. is it an exposed or sheltered wall. Each of these factors will vary around the world because the amount of insulation required to ameliorate the climate inside a building depends also on the climate of the location (for instance maritime or continental), latitude and also altitude.

In his Doctoral study on energy-saving guidelines in South Africa, Piani (1998) calculated the amount of heating energy needed by each person to keep warm in the different geographical regions of South Africa. He recommended that wherever the heating demand was 2.20 kWh m⁻² or less insulation in the roof for winter heating was not required, but in those areas where more heating was needed roof insulation would be necessary as standard. This, however, does not cover the need for insulation in the roof to keep the heat out in summer. Many readers will have suffered from the 'hot top-floor' problem caused by un-insulated roofs that act as

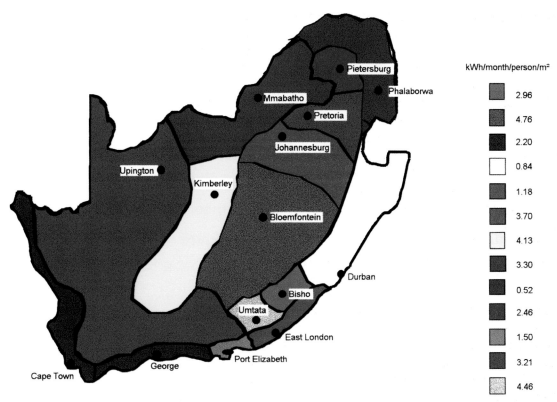

3.3.
Proposed maximum required heating energy for different South African climatic regions in kWh m⁻² per person (Piani, 1998, p. 123).

heat collectors during the day. It is late at night before the upstairs bedrooms are sufficiently cool to sleep in. This is especially true in countries such as India and Pakistan, where the high costs of electricity mean that only the very rich can afford air-conditioning.

Insulation is put around buildings to keep the heat in. Heat is a form of energy that is measured in the same units as any other type of energy, in Joules. Heat always flows from a hotter to a colder state, and it cannot be created or destroyed. In our homes we merely change the state of energy, or degrade it, when we burn wood or heat a kettle. The Celsius scale, with which we most commonly measure temperature, takes the freezing point of water, the beginning point, as 0°C and the boiling point at 100°C. When writing about temperature we describe a particular temperature as being X°C but the temperature difference between two temperatures we confusingly call Kelvin (K). This is named after the man who established the absolute temperature scale that starts at 'absolute zero', which is –273.15°C. Thus, the difference between 30°C and 25°C is called 5 K, not 5°C.

The specific heat capacity of a substance is a measure of how much energy it can store. For different materials, it can be described as how much heat energy is required to raise the temperature of a kilogram of the material by one degree Kelvin. Materials can store very different amounts of heat, have very different densities and be better or worse conductors of heat (Table 3.2).

Table 3.2. The relative density, conductivity and thermal capacity of a range of materials. Note the excellent thermal capacity of water. This makes it an excellent storage medium for heat

Type of material	Thermal capacity $(J\,kg^{-1}K^{-1})$	Density $(kg\,m^{-3})$	Conductivity $(W\,m^{-1}\,K^{-1})$
Lead	126	11 300	37
Expanded polystyrene slab	340	25	0.035
Polyurethane	450	24	0.016
Steel	480	7800	47
Mineral fibre batts	920	35–150	0.035–0.044
Brick	800	1700	620–840
Glass	840	2500	1.100
Plasterboard	840	950	0.16
Marble stone	900	2500	2.0
Adobe	1000	2050	1.250
Concrete	840–1000	600–2300	0.190–1.630
Wood wool slab	1000	500	0.100
Dry air	1005		
Strawboard	1050	250	0.037
Timber hardwood	1200	660	0.120
Chipboard	1300	660	0.120
Timber softwood	1420	610	0.130
Urea formaldehyde foam	1450	10	0.040
Phenolic foam	1400	30	0.040
Cork	1800	144	0.038
Water	4176	1000	

There are three different ways in which a wall can be insulated:

- Resistive insulation. This is what most of us think of as insulation. These are the 'bulk' insulation products, which include mineral wools, strawboard, wood-wool slabs, glass fibre products, kapok, wool and cellulose fibre. They also include expanded and extruded polystyrene, polyurethane, urea-formaldehyde, vemiculite and perlite.
- Reflective insulation. This requires a highly reflective material, aluminium foil, to face a cavity across which high levels of radiant heat are being transmitted. The foil reflects the radiant energy back across the cavity, rather than absorbing it. This type of insulation will not work if the face of the foil is touching the opposite wall.

- Capacitive insulation. This is often described as 'thermal mass' and is found in buildings in the form of 'heavy walls'.

While resistive and reflective insulation work instantaneously, capacitive insulations affect the timing of the heat flows. The difference is best illustrated by the comparison of:

1 10 mm polystyrene slab (U-value = 2.17 W m^{-2} K^{-1})
2 400 mm of dense concrete slab (also U-value = 2.17 W m^{-2} K^{-1}).

Under steady-state conditions there will be no difference in heat flow through the two slabs (Zold and Szokolay, 1997). A significant difference will, however, occur if these slabs are exposed to a periodically changing set of conditions. Figure 3.4 shows the variation of the heat flow rate over 24 hours at the inside face of the two slabs, exposed to the same external temperature variation whilst the indoor temperature is kept constant. The daily mean heat flow is the same but the two sinusoidal curves differ in two ways:

1 The heavy slab's heat flow is delayed: the term 'time lag' is defined as the difference (in hours or days) between the peaks of the two curves.
2 The amplitude (mean to peak) of the heavy slab's curve is reduced well below that of the lightweight material. The ratio of the two amplitudes is called the decrement factor.

A simple rule of thumb to use when sizing mass in a very passive building, designed to minimize heating and cooling loads, is that the optimal depth of mass for diurnal use is 100 mm for each exposed surface. So, if rooms back onto each other the walls should be 150–200 mm thick. In more extreme climates the time lag can be increased, or the decrement factor decreased, by altering the width of the mass wall.

3.4.
The periodic heat flow through a light and heavy wall of the same U value.

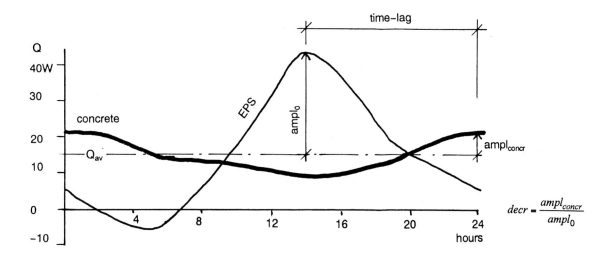

In a colder climate, for instance in Glasgow, a heavyweight building ensures more even and comfortable conditions than the lightweight building and uses slightly less energy to do so if the heating and occupation are regular on a daily basis. If a house is left unoccupied and then has to be reheated, the lightweight version uses less energy than the heavyweight building. During the heating OFF period the house will cool down considerably. However, with intermittent heating (e.g. night shut-down) but continuous occupancy, as in most residential buildings, the heavyweight version would maintain acceptable conditions during the OFF period (Szokolay, 1997). This is why so many of the older houses in Britain, and many other countries, had such thick walls: to keep the warmth in during winter when they were continuously occupied, and the heat out in summer. This does not work when they are used as weekend cottages.

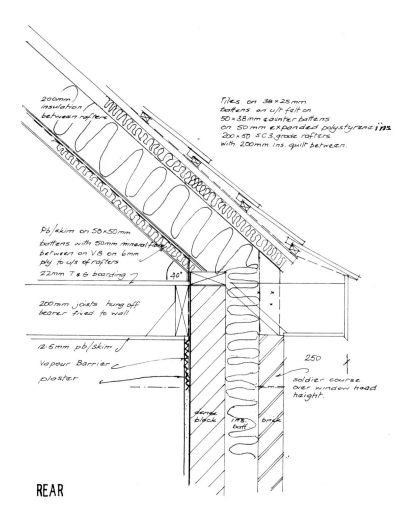

3.5.
Constructional section through the roof/wall junction of the Oxford Ecohouse (David Woods).

200mm insulation between rafters

Tiles on 38 × 25mm battens on u/f felt on 50 × 38mm counter battens on 50mm expanded polystyrene ins. 200 × 50 SC3 grade rafters with 200mm ins. quilt between.

Pb/skim on 50 × 50mm battens with 50mm mineral fibre between on VB on 6mm ply to u/s of rafters 22mm T & G boarding

40°

200mm joists hung off bearer fixed to wall

12.5mm pb/skim
Vapour Barrier
plaster

250

soldier course over window head height.

dense block   175. batt   brick

REAR

A. INTERNAL STRUCTURAL WALL/GROUND FLOOR

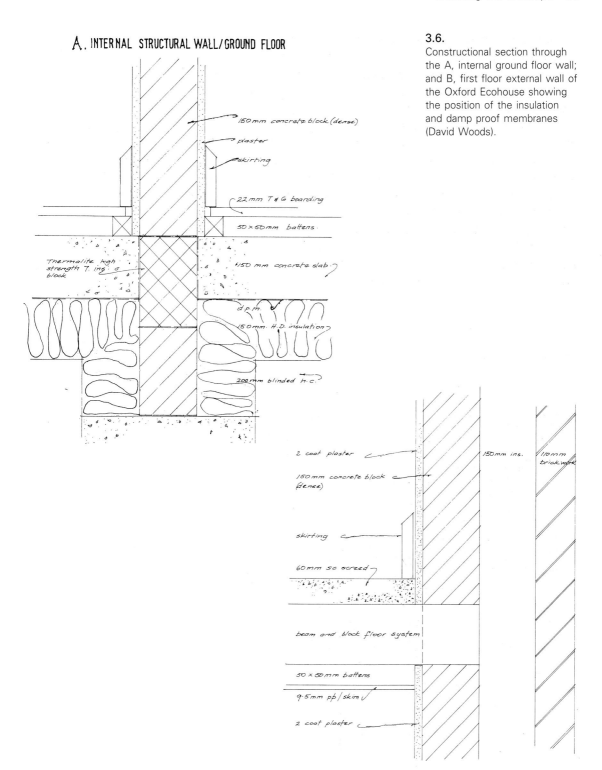

150 mm concrete block (dense)

plaster

skirting

22 mm T & G boarding

50 × 50 mm battens.

Thermalite high strength T. ins. block

150 mm concrete slab

d.p.m.

150 mm. H.D. insulation

200 mm blinded h.c.

3.6.
Constructional section through the A, internal ground floor wall; and B, first floor external wall of the Oxford Ecohouse showing the position of the insulation and damp proof membranes (David Woods).

2 coat plaster

150 mm concrete block (dense)

skirting

60 mm sc screed

beam and block floor system

50 × 50 mm battens

9.5 mm pb/skim

2 coat plaster

150 mm ins.

110 mm brickwork

B. FIRST FLOOR/EXTERNAL WALL

A more flippant rule of thumb for the optimal thickness of insulation could be 'Think of a number and double it'. Insulation will pay dividends for many years when the price of heating energy rises and the price of insulation materials with it. It is not uncommon in some countries such as Switzerland to use up to 500 mm of bulk insulation in the roof and 300 mm in walls. For these thicknesses traditional rafters are difficult to detail and new materials, such as pre-formed masonite beams, are often used that can be specified to such depths (Vale and Vale, 1999). Nylon wall ties up to 300 mm wide are available for cavity walls from K. G. Kristiansen of Denmark (Fax: +45 755 08716).

It is very important to get the construction details correct, and to build correctly on site. Very close site supervision is needed to ensure that the insulated cavities are not filled with dabs of mortar from the walls that will then form cold bridges across the cavity. When sprayed insulation is used great care must be taken that corners are properly filled. Wall batts must be fixed so they do not sag in cavities or in the roof space and insulation must be properly cut to fit snugly against surfaces. In cold climates the water tanks must be included within the insulation envelope to prevent them freezing.

Corners are particularly difficult to get right and their filling should be supervised to ensure that the most vulnerable elements in the building are not exposed by poorly fitting insulation. In areas subject to driving rain care should be taken to place a cavity between the insulation and the outer skin of the building down which water can run without soaking the insulation. If only one side of a cavity has insulation then proper wall ties must be used to hold the insulation in place to maintain the cavity in its right location in the wall.

It is no use putting in very high levels of insulation when the windows have a much lower thermal performance, so very good walls should have very good windows. Check with local window manufacturers about the performance data for available ranges of windows and choose the best windows you can afford, because these will pay dividends over the years.

For a more detailed account of how to calculate insulation thicknesses see Zold and Szokolay (1997). For an excellent guide to detailing insulation into different building types see BRE (1994).

COLD BRIDGES

Cold bridges are the most invidious of all problems that are designed into a building. They are invisible and yet can cause enormous damage to the building and the health of people in it.

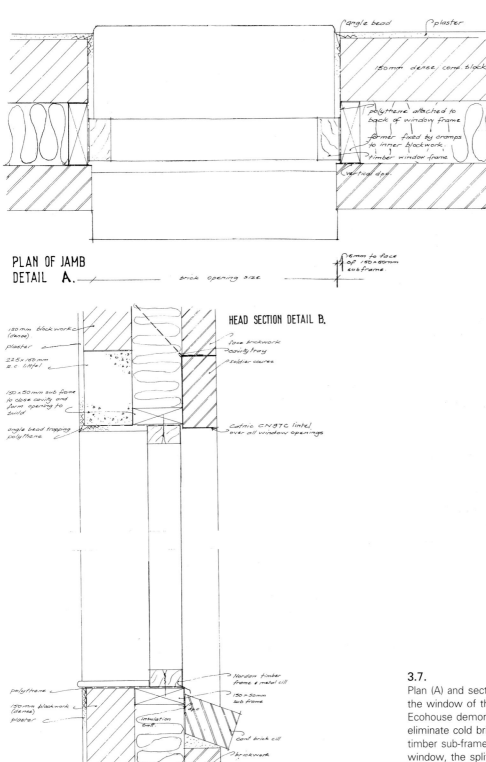

PLAN OF JAMB
DETAIL A.

- angle bead
- plaster
- 150mm dense conc. block.
- polythene attached to back of window frame
- former fixed by cramps to inner blockwork.
- timber window frame
- vertical d.p.c.
- brick opening size
- 16mm to face of 150×50mm subframe.

HEAD SECTION DETAIL B.

- 150mm blockwork (dense)
- plaster
- 225×160mm R.C. lintel
- 150×50mm sub frame to close cavity and form opening to build
- angle bead trapping polythene
- face brickwork
- cavity tray
- soldier course
- Catnic CN97C lintel over all window openings

- polythene
- 150mm blockwork (dense)
- plaster
- Insulation batt.
- Nordan timber frame & metal cill
- 150×50mm sub frame
- conc. brick cill
- brickwork

CILL SECTION DETAIL B.

3.7.
Plan (A) and section (B) through the window of the Oxford Ecohouse demonstrating how to eliminate cold bridging with timber sub-frames around the window, the splitting of the lintels and the elimination of the brick returns (David Woods).

Cold bridges have been, along with too much glazing, the thermal nemesis of 'modern architecture'. A cold bridge is a pathway between the outside cold surface of a building and the internal warm air of the room. A cold bridge, most usually made of metal, conducts the heat out through the wall so cooling the internal wall surface of the building. A wall can be a cold bridge if it is built of solid masonry. Studies have shown that in, say, a 100 mm solid brick wall the internal surface temperature can be very similar to the external temperature. Walls are particularly vulnerable to cold bridging on corners, where they have more than one surface exposed to the elements, as shown in Figure 3.8. Cavity insulation can significantly improve the thermal performance of a wall. The most common cold bridges in buildings are metal lintels, wall ties, window frames and concrete and metal columns and beams that link the internal and external leaves of walls.

The effectiveness of the cold bridge is dependent on the conductivity of the material of which it is made. Figure 1.1 shows that while copper and steel are very good conductors of heat, timber and glass are not. To demonstrate the difference in conductivity of materials, aluminium conducts heat four times better than steel, 200 times better than glass, 1200 times better than timber and PVC, and 8000 times better than air.

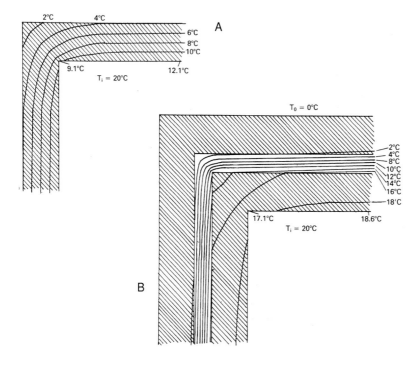

3.8.
Corners of walls lose heat very rapidly as they are exposed on two sides. Isotherms and Temperature Difference Ratios (TDR) at the corner of an insulated and un-insulated wall. A, 100 mm brick, $U = 3.3\ \mathrm{W\ m^{-2}\ K}$, TDR – 0.54. B, 100 mm brick–50 mm insulation –100 mm brick, $U = 0.6\ \mathrm{W\ m^{-2}\ K}$, TDR – 0.14 (Oreszczyn, 1992).

There are a number of reasons why cold bridges should be avoided:

1 They cost the building owner money because they are an effective path for heat out of the building or, in hot countries, heat into the building, so requiring more money to be spent on the heating or cooling of buildings.
2 They can cause serious discomfort in buildings by creating cold (or hot) walls, windows or areas in a room.
3 They cause condensation. Because, when the outdoor air temperature is lower than that indoors, the cold bridges are colder than the internal surrounding wall and room air. So, they cause the adjacent wall and air to cool rapidly. As cooler air can hold less moisture than warm air, so moisture condenses out on the surface of the cooler wall. This moisture can damage the structure of a building and provide a substrate for the growth of mould. This is why mould is typically found on the edges of metal window frames or at wall corners and in patches on the wall in front of a cold bridge. Mould is very bad for health, as described in Chapter 6.

In order to prevent cold bridging in new buildings care should be taken to ensure there are no metal or concrete elements that span from the inside to the outside leaves of walls:

• Replace metal wall ties with nylon ones.
• Do not return the brick work around doors and windows but use a timber sub-frame detail as shown in Figure 3.7 (see also Vale and Vale, 2000, pp. 162–166).
• Eliminate the need for through-wall metal ducts by sensible design of opening windows and vents, and the use of passive stack ventilation systems.
• Split lintels so there is an external lintel for the outer leaf of a wall, a timber sub-frame for the insulation and a separate internal lintel for the inner leaf of a wall. Single metal lintels across the wall should be avoided.
• Choose the windows carefully to have a U (or R) value in keeping with that of the walls. If there is a single glazed window in a very well-insulated wall it will attract condensation owing to its internal surface temperature being much lower than that of the wall. Try to avoid metal window frames.

One method of characterizing the severity of a cold bridge is the temperature difference ratio (TDR). This is a coefficient that specifies how cold a surface is relative to the inside and outside temperature (Oreszczyn and Littler, 1989; Oreszczyn, 1992). The TDR is calculated with the following equation:

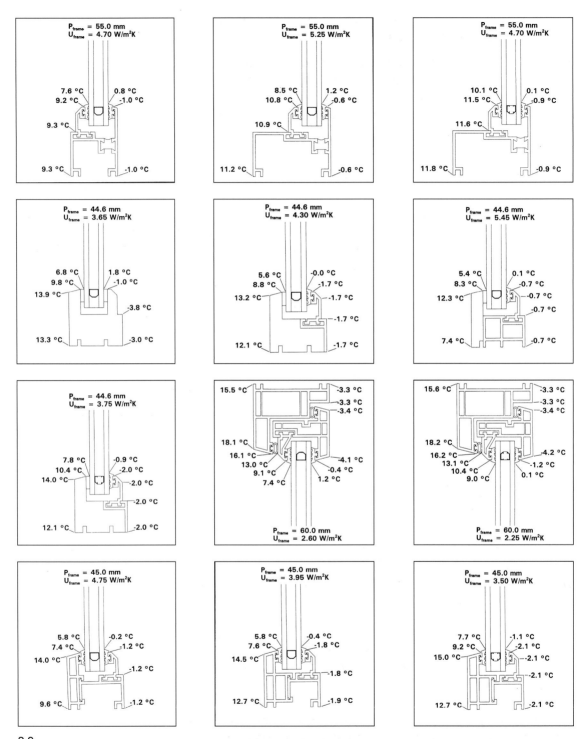

3.9.
A window is often the largest cold bridge in a wall. The top row are aluminium frames. Second row left is simple timber. The next three are timber/aluminium combinations. Centre in the third row down is all PVCu and the last 4 frames are PVCu/aluminium combinations. Thermally broken spacers (with 4 internal lines) improve performance. (Richard Harris, 1995 and the Centre for Window and Cladding Technology, Bath).

TDR = Internal air temperature – cold bridge temperature

Internal air temperature – external air temperature

The more severe the cold bridge the greater the TDR. Cold bridges with a TDR of greater than 0.3 are unacceptable because the cold bridge will be cooler than the surface temperature of adjacent double glazing, hence condensation will appear on the wall before it forms on the window.

Table 3.3. Classification of cold bridges

Cold bridge type	TDR	Examples
Negligible	less than 0.15	Plain walls – U-value less than 1.2 W m^{-2} K External corners U-value less than 0.6 W m^{-2} K. Insulated lintels.
Moderate	0.15–0.2	Plain walls U-value greater than 1.2 W m^{-2} K 3D corner U-value greater than 0.6 W m^{-2} K
Severe	0.2–0.3	External corners U-value 0.9–1.5 W m^{-2} K. Uninsulated lintels. Concrete party wall or floor.
Unacceptable	greater than 0.3	2D corners U-value greater than 1.5 W m^{-2} K 3D corners U-value greater than 1.0 W m^{-2} K Party floor and wall of drylined wall. Window reveal of drylined wall.

INFILTRATION

It is apparently normal for up to 50 per cent of the heat loss from new buildings in the UK to come from uncontrolled ventilation (Olivier, 2000). Rather than continue with the tradition of leaky building more countries should adopt the Canadian practice of 'Build tight and Ventilate right'. Great care should be taken that every time a hole is put through the structure the remaining air gaps are sealed tightly. Watch out for holes that appear around timber beams in masonry walls and pipe inlets and outlets through walls.

In addition care must be taken to ensure that the vapour and wind barriers around the house are kept intact throughout the building process to ensure that walls and poorly built masonry or timber joints do not leak (Mould, 1992). Beware, in particular, of the poor brick layer who does not fill the mortar joints properly but uses dabs of mortar that will leak air around them into the cavity.

Where ventilation is needed, a range of different-sized vents, and windows, can be included to enable residents to easily control the amount of air movement in a range of different ways. This is much

	Description	TDR$_{cb}$	
	Uninsulated solid wall	0.265	
	25 mm drylined solid wall	0.325	✗
	Solid wall plus 187 cm floor and ceiling drylining	0.145	✓
	Solid wall only ceiling and wall drylined	0.315	✗
	Solid wall external insulation	0.115	✓
	Solid wall partial external insulation	0.175	✓
	Uninsulated cavity wall	0.240	
	Insulated cavity wall	0.210	✓
	Insulated cavity wall with floor and ceiling insulated	0.250	✗

3.10.
The TDR for various insulated and un-insulated constructions consisting of a brick wall penetrated by a concrete floor slab. The cavity wall is built of: 105 mm brick–50 mm cavity–105 mm brick. The solid wall is 260 mm brick, the floor is 150 mm dense cast concrete and the insulation is 25 mm drylining or external (Oreszczyn, 1992).

more thermally efficient than having the heat pour out of the house like water from a leaky bucket through holes in the envelopes and across metal ventilation ducts that act as very effective cold bridges across the external wall. Air leakage from buildings is even more of a problem in areas where there is driving wind and rain and special care should be taken in these areas to seal the building tightly and to use buffer spaces, such as porches and sunspaces, for the external doors of the house. Chapter 5 outlines

	Description	TDR_{cb} No fin	TDR_{cb} Plus fin
	Uninsulated cavity wall	0.240	0.235
	Insulated cavity wall	0.210	0.205
	Solid wall	0.265	0.260
	Drylined solid wall	0.325	0.320
	External cladding solid wall	0.175	0.170
	(insulation over edge of floor)	0.115	

3.11.
The TDR for a concrete floor slab both with and without fins or balconies. The cavity wall is 105 mm brick–50 mm cavity–105 mm brick, the solid wall is 260 mm brick, the floor is 150 mm dense cast concrete and the insulation is 25 mm drylining or external.

how moisture problems can be avoided by proper ventilation, house form and the use of correct materials in the house.

GETTING LIGHT INTO THE HOUSE SAFELY

A window is an important element in the building envelope. As with insulation, the greater the difference in temperature between the outside and the inside of a house, the better the windows will have to be. Look carefully to see the relative performance of the windows that are used in the different case study buildings around the world. For details of different windows there are a number of excellent sites on the Internet, listed under 'window performance'. The key things with window design are:

- To ensure windows are similar in thermal performance to the adjacent walls so they do not become too attractive to condensation.
- In temperate or colder climates, the side of the building facing the sun should have more windows and the polar orientation

very few to prevent excessive heat loss from the cold side of the building.

- To design the window for a specific purpose. Look at Dick Levine's case study house in Kentucky where he has separate windows for solar gain, light, wind and view.
- To illuminate the centre of the house as well as its peripheral rooms. This can be done with internal windows, skylights, light tubes through the roof and other clever ideas. One idea that was very popular in the 1930s was to use glass ceilings in the upper floor that took the light from the sunny side of the building to the ceilings on the dark side of the house, often above stair wells.
- To not make unshaded windows too large. It is important to prevent overheating in a house. With global warming the sun will get stronger and rooms that are exposed to the direct sun in summer will have a problem. Shade all windows in summer. Only in the colder climates should the sun be allowed to penetrate into the house in summer. It is very important to design for solar control through windows but also in their external surroundings. Take into account highly reflective pavements outside the window that will bounce light back into a room, as will glass walls next to or opposite the window.
- A window can have many layers. A sunspace, with its second layer of glass, will keep the cold away from the internal windows. Light can result in heat and, in very hot climates, dark interiors will keep rooms cooler. Shutters can be used externally to control solar gain in hot climates at different times of the day and year. Shutters can be used internally in cool and temperate climates to keep excessive sunlight out but some warmth in. Shutters can be wind-permeable but keep the sun out. Once the light has passed through the glass the heat it contains is trapped inside the room and will not escape back out through the glass. Heavy curtains can be used to keep light out in summer (but not heat for the same reason) and warmth inside in winter.
- Consider the problem of glare in rooms. In particular high glare levels will make it difficult to read computer screens and view the TV. Glare is also an indication of very high day lighting levels that may indicate that rooms will also overheat in summer.
- Capture the view. Careful consideration should enable the designer to make maximum advantage of the views on offer from the site. If there are particular features of interest ensure that they are captured in the centre of the window frame rather than the foreground in front of them or the sky above them (Lynes, 1992).

3.12.
Krister Wiberg sitting at his kitchen table in Sweden. Light is a powerful design issue and very important in creating the 'spirit' of a place.

- Make sure that the windows are placed in rooms to enable you to use the furniture you want in the house. If you have low chests of drawers to be placed against the outer wall make sure the window sill is above them.
- If you want to get light deep into a room use high windows.
- Think about the psychological effect of a window or door in a room. What will a window do for the degree of privacy you require? Do you want everyone in the street to be able to see

you in a particular room? Will a large patio door window turn a room into a corridor?

- Think about light as a sculptural medium that changes every daylight hour of the year. You can create dynamic sculptures in shade and light to great effect on floors and forms within the house. Grade light through the house with darker and lighter areas to create visual interest.

All the techniques above provide ways in which we can understand, and design for, the invisible workings of a building. There are, however, also issues that cannot be calculated, that are very important in creating that other invisible factor: the spirit of a place, and these are dealt with, by Christopher Day, in the following chapter.

4 BUILDING-IN SOUL

Christopher Day

Building is expensive – though not half, perhaps not one-fifth, so expensive as having something built for you. It also takes a lot of energy. But most importantly, you invest your soul in what you build, which is why self-built homes are so soul-rich to live in.

It is just this – the soul in buildings – that makes all the effort worthwhile, much more than just a cut-price roof. And self-built homes have infinitely more soul-potential than contractor-built houses. If we cannot build a house ourselves, how can we build-in soul through design and, once constructed, how do we introduce 'soul' into the way we live in buildings? But to have a self-built house or to be built-for, does this issue conflict with ecological concerns?

Buildings are substantive – what they are made of is very much part of their character. Wood, earth, brick, concrete, steel, glass or plastic buildings are totally different from each other to see, to live in, to build and in the forms their construction logically and characterfully demands. Their influence on microclimate, air quality, physical health and psychological state is also very different. So, very important in terms of their pollution and environmental costs, are their manufacturing biographies and how they end their life – do they return to nature or become refuse?

Buildings are primarily made of bulk materials. Though some, such as concrete foundations, are invisible, most are in daily view. Secondary materials range from drainage pipes and windows to small bits and pieces such as draught seals, light fittings and so on. While environmental cost is something to consider in every material choice, there is a need to be pragmatic; it is obvious that there is a lot more PVC in floor tiles or wallpaper than in electric cabling so the relative impacts of choosing tiles/wallpaper and the electric cabling will be very different. Fortunately, alternatives to both exist, though they are not always easy to obtain.

A building's furnishings also need serious thought as they are replaced many times in the life of the building. They tend to be newer, and also are often in warm places. So, as well as seeing and touching them, we breathe them: as materials get warmer they tend to give off more of their chemicals.

How do building (and furnishing, maintenance and cleaning) materials affect us, and the wider world? Every material has some environmental cost; some have compensating environmental benefits, as has been shown in Chapter 2. These can be measured in terms of embodied energy or, more meaningfully, embodied CO_2. This, however, is an imprecise science and values are seldom transferable from country to country. Timber in Britain comes mostly from the pacific side of Canada; in Central Europe from managed forests only a few kilometres away. Whatever its source, and however cruelly the forests are raped, building timber locks up carbon as do other carbon-rich materials such as straw and cellulose fibre, so diminishing the CO_2 emissions from the building.

Contrast this with steel, the cost of which is equivalent to that of 300 times its weight of water and five times its weight of coal – multiplied again by some nine times as much soil excavated as both coal and iron ore. But this is nothing compared with plastic, made at the price of 5000 times its weight in raw materials.

In terms of how we relate to these materials, wood is approachable, easy to work with, absorbs airborne toxins and moderates temperature and humidity. It is sensitive to environment and needs to be maintained and protected from sustained moisture by careful design. Aging adds character. It is easily repairable. It can be recycled or allowed to compost back to earth. Steel is hard, can be worked with hand-scale, semi-industrial tools (such as welding apparatus) and is neutral in health terms. It needs protection from water, but is unaffected by light, insects or aging. It can, with suitable tools, be repaired and recycled. Abandoned, it will rust back into ore – though this does not apply to its (usually toxic) paints and platings. Plastic is generally unappealing to touch and emits toxins. It is unaffected by the environment (except abrasion, UV light and organic solvents) and appears ageless except for scratching, cracking and crazing, which compromise both appearance and performance. It is effectively unrepairable. Little is recycled, some types cannot be, and most types effectively are never broken down – beyond breaking up and slow toxin release.

Not coincidentally, wood is a material from life. Iron is from the earth, but by way of intense heat and heavy industrial rolling. Plastic is from oil and coal deep beneath its surface, after so numerous chemical synthesis operations that it is totally removed from life. These materials connect us to the world from whence

4.1.
The interior of Christopher Day's house in Crymbch, Wales, with its locally made windows and hand plastered walls (Christopher Day).

they came: living and life-cycle bound by nature, or lifeless, dead industrial processes. Whereas plastic needs industrial equipment suited to mass production to form, wood needs only a pocket knife. It is more appealing, accessible and healthy to work with. Indeed, you can put your heart into what you make out of it.

We use thousands of materials in modern building, but a general rule is that the nearer something is to life, the more compatible it is: the healthier to live with, the more recyclable back to earth, thence living matter again. It also needs more care for longevity –

but this care, like the care given to its making, is imprinted into its substance and emanates from it, to nourish those who live next to it. Mass-produced products can never do this; the imprint of care given by an individual maker is, by definition, absent. So the materials of which a building is built, and the extent to which they are imprinted by care and love through hand-work, imprints spirit – or the lack of it – into buildings, even before occupation. This care is something self-builders can easily afford, while those sufficiently well off to get others to build for them rarely can.

One technique I use often is hand-finished rendering. Lime-rich mortar (9:2:1) applied unevenly to walls, preferably with a round-nosed tool so it is a little mounded, but then smoothed by (gloved) hand as soon as it is firm, removing all tool marks and contrived form. This forms a gentle, undulating and sand-textured surface. But more: it has been shaped by the hand. On one hand-plastering course I taught, a massage therapist told me, 'There is no part of the human body that a part of the hand is not shaped to fit'. So this technique imprints our hands into our physical surroundings. And it is impossible to work for long engaging the hands (not just repetitively using them) without the heart becoming involved. Thus, in a hand-plastered room you are surrounded by hand-imprinted heart forces. This works on us in the same way as food prepared with love – as distinct from mass-produced, routinely, institutionally cooked meals.

Another technique I enjoy is repair – inserting a patch of new wood into old. Working with second-hand materials you have to do this quite often. Of course, we use our hands to some extent for everything we make, but the fewer devices between hand and work, the more direct the link between hand and heart.

However, buildings are only part of places. Even 'home' is only part house. It is also entry, gateway and garden – and is enmeshed in street and neighbourhood. Every place has a unique spirit. Part of that spirit comes from how the place is used – the actions, thoughts and values of those who inhabit it. And part comes from how it was formed – the geology, weathering, forces of living nature, the elements and human interaction. Part also comes from how we meet it, the concept of place we then form and how this then influences our thoughts and actions.

How do we meet places? What do they say to us? And how can we transform the negative – all too common in our decrepit cities and their compromised fringes – into the positive, spirit-uplifting?

First impressions tend to influence what we subsequently see, feel and think. The welcome or fortified defensiveness of an entry door colours our expectations – and meaningfully so, for we gain an intuition of the essence of a place. And this impression is

4.2.
The inside of the sunspace of David's house in Wales (Andrew Yeats).

repeated every time we re-arrive there. Whether or not we are commencing a new building or altering an old one, there is some kind of place already there. We are converting a place. What is already there limits what we can do, so how can we ensure the first impressions reflect the spirit we wish to establish there?

There is a technique for this that works with the connections with spirit and matter. To overcome the tendency of individuals to be led by their own ideas, it is a listening technique, so it is easier to do this as a group. We identify and work along the arrival route, from the point that you first meet a building. The first walk is for first impressions if you don't know the place, consciousness of the journey as an entity in its own right if you do. We walk in silence, without judgement, meeting at the final destination, say the kitchen, to reconstruct the journey. This we do at the end of each walk. We then repeat this walk, recording only what is physically there – no feelings, judgements, causes or suggestions. Next, we re-walk the route, focusing only on sequential space: how the space and light expands, contracts, breathes and turns, the gestures of forms and flow of our movements. Our next walk focuses on the moods and the feelings they induce along the journey. Now we can ask how the place would describe itself. What is its essential message? As this message, this spirit of place, is central to why we build, how we wish to live in a place and the nourishment we hope it will feed us will colour our individual ideas of what this message should be. With existing buildings, used for new purposes, there can be harsh discrepancy between the spirit that is and what it should be. A school building, for instance, may well speak of controlling little vandals, not loving and inspiring children on their journey to independent adulthood.

But when we know what a place should say, we can re-walk our route asking: what moods would support this? And then, on our next walk: what journey sequences, qualities of flow, would support these moods? And finally, re-walking to ask: what physical changes would support these qualities of flow?

Invariably these changes are small: pruning trees to form an archway, re-aligning an entry path, pivoting past a bush, easing an abrupt corner with furniture or a plant, flowing ceilings into each other, unifying colour and such like. Small, affordable, material changes that have major impact on what a place says and how it reflects and reinforces the spirit we wish to grow within it.

But what if there is as yet no building? Where should it go? What place should it help make? How can it contribute to, rather than compromise, what is already there?

We use a similar process, starting with silent first impressions and then the physical here and now. But then, instead of looking at time experiences through space (its flow), concentrate on space through time (its biography). How was this place formed in geological process? How was it before the agricultural, then industrial, revolutions, last century, last generation, a decade, a year ago? And continuing into the future, what will it be like next season, year, decade and century? We can thus enter into the flow of time through a place and ask what changes are set in motion when we intervene, postulating various actions and imagining their chain of consequences unfold. We then return to moods and spirit-of-place as before.

We now ask what spirit stands at the heart of what we are about to establish. What activities will this manifest in – and where, in the light of what we know about the place, should these be located? These 'zones of activity' we peg and string on the ground, then record on a site plan. We need now to identify the moods appropriate to each area, and to modify the layout for both this and for appropriate relationships between places, paths, gateways and views. We can next lay paper rectangles representing room areas onto this drawing, confirming its layout more meaningfully. The next step is to replace paper shapes with clay rectanguloid volumes – which rapidly become moulded into more living forms. All this is group work, just one family and myself, or 20 or 30 people. It can be a very strong experience as shared imagination of the future becomes almost substantial amongst the group.

For a single house this is simple (except that small, simple things tend to end up as being the most complicated!) but this process especially suits something larger or a group of buildings. Few larger projects, however, are built all at once. Nor should they be. Disruption to the spirit-of-place is excessive and the greater this is, the more are buildings imposed, not grown. And anyway, cash flow is rarely as predictable as we hope at the outset, so often only half a project gets built. We need to unravel the design to find a sequence so that every phase of building seems perfect – but the next stage makes it even better!

Space need doesn't only grow. In houses, for instance, it also contracts as children grow up and leave home. This doesn't just leave parents with mortgages still to pay, but also with big, lonely empty nests to rattle around in. From working with a Swedish eco-village group, I learnt to design homes that can expand – for instance, into garages, workshops and stores – and contract by division into house and disabled-accessible flat.

Growth is a key to how to blend the new (such as buildings) into the old – be it rural landscape or urban street. Anything that doesn't grow has a different spirit to its surroundings. If they don't talk to each other, can we expect social or ecological harmony, not to mention soul harmony?

With or without human intervention, no place is static. It is changing in response to the living and elemental forces of nature. Socially and economically, it waxes and wanes under these interacting forces; and grows or withers from nodes of growth activity or blight. New buildings feel right in place if they grow in accord with these forces. We can learn from the place study method just described how places want to grow – how they would do so without our intervention. Also what qualities of a place need enhancement and what need balance – so how this growth is asking to be steered.

We also learn about the arrival journey – of central importance to every building, whether home, hospital or work place. 'Home' has an active meaning: 'arriving home' – and a passive one: the state of 'being at home'. Haven and oasis roles. Different parts of the journey: front gate, entry hall, social rooms, bedrooms need different moods, need to meet us with different gestures – which we can gesture with our bodies – and link into different patterns of relationship: front door with street community and socially outward-looking, back garden to neighbour community, yet protectively private and linked into local wildlife habitat.

All these parts of the whole have time- and season-related needs. Bedrooms to wake up in, bathed with optimism for the day ahead. Evening rooms to unwind in. Winter hearth and summer breeze-freshened openness. Sunlight when children return from school or adults from work, not to mention orientations for view, skyscapes, sunsets and qualities of weather.

Rooms within the house range from family to individual realms, each different. Once we start to think of small children's needs as distinct from just practical space planning, new things come up: 'secret' spaces under stairs, in lofts or all the 'lost' spaces architects prefer to hide. With moods of privacy, enchantment, mystery, but also warm security. Then, teenagers need their own 'realms' that they themselves can, to some extent, form. An older person's needs for stability and an anchoring lifespan of memorabilia – along with warmth and sun and the life invigoration of nature's moods, which they can less and less actively partake in. One thing these rooms are not is just rectanguloid volumes – appropriate soul mood is the primary reason they are there.

But no building or garden is just an interior. It links into a wider community, economy and ecology. It links into the infrastructural system of a place. Yet drains and pipes and wires aren't place-related but transporters to and from invisibly distant sources and destinations. Composting, on-site grey-water treatment and autonomous energy link us to ecology, water flow patterns and microclimates. As these have aesthetic implications from water gardens to shelter planting and conservatories, they are also soul links to the forces of nature, interactions unique to every place.

Linkage to place also demands meaning in why we live somewhere and what we do. But our lifestyle and activities relate to where we are – unlike picturesquely preserved holiday cottages, appropriate only in visual appearance but otherwise alien, unrelated and dissociated from place-responsibility.

It also requires local materials. At first sight, many materials – such as stone and brick – don't seem sufficiently energy-efficient – but they can be made more so. Almost certainly, however, local traditional materials are durable in local climatic conditions and have a local skill-base familiar with local, climatically appropriate construction detailing.

The more local and unprocessed materials are, the less the transport and manufacturing energy and pollution, the more health-benign, the better for local employment. Also, the more localized within the community does the money cycle. Local traditional materials also connect us with the cultural continuum of the past and enable us to connect it to a future inspired by different ideals. New technologies and forms can blend harmoniously with the old if given substance in traditional materials and bound by the constructional limitations inherent in them. Giving value to that which has formed the character of a place is also to value its culture, the keystone of community and individual self-esteem. So local materials have energy, minimum pollution, social, economic, cultural, self-esteem and spiritual benefits – and shape, of course, the character of a place – its identity.

Materials connect us to a place. Traditionally taken from the ground, its vegetation and even animals, they are raised into human habitation – connecting those who live there with our roots in place. This is still so, even when we use these materials in less traditional forms: straw as building blocks, timber as round poles tensioned into unfamiliar curves, earth as free-formed cob.

However soul warm are vernacular forms, we should not gloss over the restrictive, narrow conventionality that comes with unnat-urally prolonged past ways of life. Turning our back on them, however, merely dissociates us from where we have come from and in so doing blinds us to all we can learn and obscures where we are going to.

The traditional way was to raise the physical materials of a place to be a home for the human spirit. Largely unconsciously, totemic and elemental echoes remained in stone, earth, tree, straw and hide. Matter, in vernacular times, could not be divorced from spirit. Nor can it be today – however widespread its apparent negation. In every aspect of buildings matter and spirit are cyclically linked.

The materials of which a place – land, town, building, room – is made have effects in multiple directions unified, however, by the 'essence' at their heart. They used to, and still can, link us with locality at several levels, give substance to a spirit-of-place growing out of that locality. We can develop these places in accord with the life-generating energies latent within it. And colour its moods to be appropriate to our soul needs, increasingly individualized and different from a generation ago. We can imprint human energy and care – a gift of spirit – into the material substance of buildings. So inspiriting matter and building-in soul.

4.3.
The hall of Christopher Day's house in Crymbch, Wales (Christopher Day).

5 VENTILATION

Ventilation is the movement of air within a building and between the building and the outdoors. The control of ventilation is one of the most subtle and yet the most important concerns of the building designer. How to make air move about the building in a way that satisfies, and even delights, the occupant.

There is, of course, a simple solution – to use a fan – but this can be a noisy and expensive business and is not the preferred first option for an ecohouse in which mechanical systems should only be used as a last resort.

So how does air move without a fan? Actually, air moves very easily and always down a pressure gradient. Positive pressure exists on the windward side of a building where the air is pushed with some force against the building. Negative pressure occurs on the leeward side of a building, in the wind shadow, and sucks air from the structure.

The trick is to create that pressure gradient. This can be done in two ways:

1 using pressure differences around the outside of the building caused by wind;
2 using pressure differences caused by the pressure variations within the house. Warm air is less dense than cold air, therefore pressure variations that cause warm bodies of air to rise also cause cold bodies of air to fall. This is called the 'stack' effect and can be used to ventilate a space. It can also be in conflict with wind-driven cross-ventilation.

Using wind pressure to ventilate is common, particularly if the house is in a windy part of the world. There are many challenges in designing properly for ventilation including the variability of the wind, its speed and direction, but if carefully handled and understood it can be of real benefit to the indoor climate of a house, for most of the time.

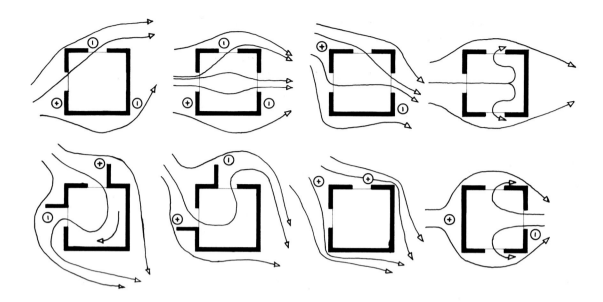

5.1.
Positive (+) and negative (−)
wind pressures around different
building configurations.

Wind and ventilation are not the same thing. Wind is very variable and can present itself in many different guises.

A wailing rushing sound, which shook the walls as though a giant's hand were on them; then a hoarse roar, as if the sea had risen; then such a whirl and tumult that the air seemed mad; and then with a lengthened howl, the waves of wind wept on. *Dickens.*

How different was Dickens' description of the wind from that of Longfellow:

The gentle wind, a sweet and passionate wooer, kisses the blushing leaf.

The wind can be an agent of terror or delight, it can soothe or destroy and it is one of the most important of the invisible building blocks of architecture. This chapter begins by considering the wind, and its usability for a building for a particular site and form. The reasons why and how to use air in buildings for maximum effect are then outlined. Finally, a section is included on how to protect a house from strong winds, such as result from hurricanes and cyclones. A major impact of global warming over the last decade of the twentieth century has been the increase in wind speeds and damage experienced in many countries of the world (Headley, 2000). We cannot predict how badly climate change will affect any of us, but we have taken this opportunity to include design for extreme wind environments, just in case. This section is complemented by two case study buildings, one on a strong wind site in Findhorn, Scotland and the second in cyclone-prone St Maarten in the Caribbean.

To ventilate a house well you first have to develop a relationship with wind. To do this you need to understand the regional and local climate of the site, the form and surroundings of the site and building. Key, also, are the building's occupants and their comfort requirements.

STEP 1 – CHOOSE YOUR WIND CAREFULLY – AND NAME IT

Every region or location in the world has its own winds. In the old days, builders knew the name of every wind, its personality and its potential for benefit or harm. In fact, a single wind would probably have two or three names. One name may denote the direction from which the wind comes, the part of the day in which it arrives or the name of the town, region or country from whence it hails. Another may refer to the quality of the wind, such as cold, hot or wet. If it is a very important wind regionally, it may have its own grand name like Mistral or Sirocco, words that in many countries conjure images of the unique aeolian character of that particular wind. For instance in the Naples region of Italy wind names include:

```
                    Tramontana
                  (three mountains)
                        N

     Maestrale            Grecale (Greek)
       NW                    NE

Ponente (West)                   Levante (Levantine)
     W                                  E

     Libeccio (sweet)       Scirocco
        SW                    SE

                  Mezzogiorno
                   (midday)
                      S
```

Local geographical conditions will have a large influence on local winds. In Naples the cool Tramontana wind sinks down from the hills to the north and east of the city, flushing the heat out of the long streets running down to the sea. As the land and city warm up on summer afternoons they draw the cool sea breeze up the same streets to replace the warm air in them as it rises.

5.2.
Windcatchers on the skyline of Yazd, staggered to catch the prevailing winds (Roaf).

For every site and area designers should get a clear idea what winds exist, which they would like to use in order to heat or cool their buildings and which they wish to exclude as too hot or cold. This can be done by looking at a wind-rose that shows how much wind comes from different directions every month or year. However, it will not tell you the properties of that wind; this can be worked out by looking at the geography of a region. An easier way is to ask a local builder about the winds around the site.

Traditional settlement patterns can reveal a great deal about the wind. The ways in which buildings are arranged in a settlement will indicate if the wind is welcome inside or not. A staggered arrangement means that buildings are spread out to ensure each house can capture some of the wind, as are the great wind catchers of Yazd in the Central desert of Iran, shown in Figure 5.2. Linear patterns indicate that one building is used to shelter the next from unwelcome winds and will show from which direction the unwanted winds come.

WINDSCAPING BUILDINGS

There are many ways to sculpt a building into the landscape and the wind.

- Nestle the building into the landscape. This simple device of hiding a building behind a feature of the landscape is very effective. However, bear in mind that if the wind is needed to cool the building, siting it behind a spur in the landscape may cut it off from the breezes. In some cases people take bulldozers to the landscape to ensure that the winds from the refreshing directions are channelled around their houses and the hot winds are excluded by features in the landscape.
- Split the winds. A single flagpole 20 m from a building in the direction of a strong prevailing wind can split the wind vertically before it arrives at the building and considerably lessen its impact on the structure. In the St Maarten house an open porch has recently been placed in front of the house with vertical columns supporting it to split the winds before they reach the building. In the Findhorn house the architect, Johann Vorster, has nestled the house into the existing settlement, used trees to protect it, and has also angled the window corner into the strong prevailing wind from across Findhorn Bay to split it and reduce its impact on the building structure. Wind can be split

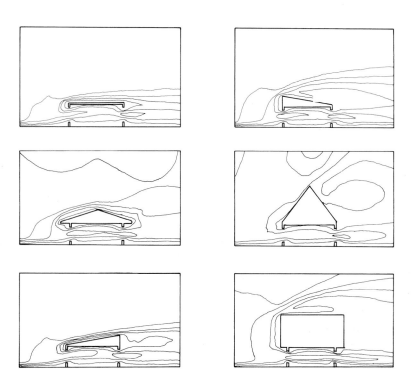

5.3.
The influence of roof shape on the air pressure around the house (Kindangen et al., 1997). The higher the roof the greater the positive pressure on its windward side and the greater the negative pressure on its leeward side.

vertically to reduce wind speeds and turbulence on the face of the building; in the wind towers of the Iranian Desert the wind is very neatly sliced horizontally to throw some wind over the top of a tower while forcing some air down the wind catcher shaft. Beneath the vent the wind is again split cleanly to force wind below the shaft down the face of the tower.

- Shape the roof carefully. Figure 5.3 shows how much difference there is between different roof shapes in the negative pressure they generate. It is this negative pressure that typically rips roofs off buildings (Kindangen et al., 1997).
- Mould the wind impact of wind pressure on facades with features such as balconies. The use of features on building facades will cause an increase or decrease in pressure at different heights on the building facade as shown in Figure 5.3. Note the lack of pressure variation on the leeward side of the building (Chand et al., 1998).
- Use planting as wind breaks.

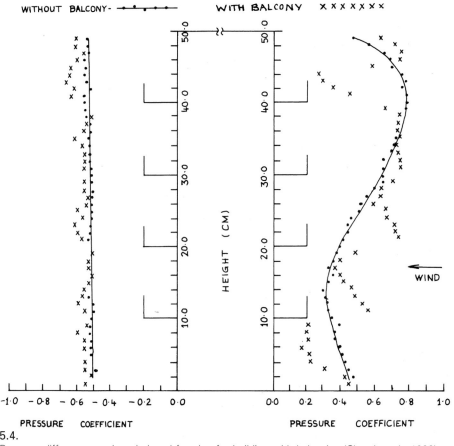

5.4.
Pressure difference on the windward facade of a building with balconies (Chand et al., 1998).

WHY VENTILATE A BUILDING?

For each room of a house you should ask: why is ventilation needed in this space? Three possible reasons are:

- for fresh air supply;
- for direct comfort ventilation to cool or heat the occupants of the space by convection;
- for indirect comfort ventilation, for heating and cooling the actual structure of a building to indirectly enhance the comfort of the room's occupants and to use 'free energy' more efficiently. In this way, day-time solar warmth can be stored in the structure and used at night, or coolth from night air can be stored to cool the people indoors during the day.

FRESH AIR

The need for fresh air ranges from the nominal amounts needed for breathing $(2 \, \mathrm{l \, s^{-1}})$ to the much higher ventilation rates necessary to control odours (up to $16\text{--}32 \, \mathrm{l \, s^{-1}}$ is a commonly quoted figure for fresh air needed to mitigate the effects of smoking smells). In houses, care can be taken to provide zones for smokers where the smell of a cigarette can be dealt with by opening a window. This may be more easily said than done. Studies have shown that homes with smokers use significantly more energy to heat or cool because the windows are continually opened to get rid of the smell. This should be taken into account and the problem designed out by sensible zoning of spaces.

How the room is furnished will affect lingering odours, with smells collecting more easily in the soft fabrics of curtains and carpets. Different activities in the house may be associated with different smell levels, so finishes can be chosen appropriately. The need for fresh air can be influenced very much by the chosen room finishes. It should be noted that building regulations are typically not designed to mitigate against the impact of smells or the transmission of diseases. It is not possible to regulate against air-borne diseases, although many indoor air quality regulations have evolved to deal with condensation risks in buildings that do have indirect health implications.

Fresh air is also needed to prevent the build up of moisture in a room. This is obvious for kitchens, bathrooms and utility rooms but there can be a real build up of moisture in bedrooms as well. There are six ways to design out moisture as a problem in housing.

1 Provide wet zones in the house outside the main envelope of living rooms. Build a front porch/lobby/air lock in which the

temperature of the outside air can be modified to be warmer or cooler before it enters the house. All wet clothing, coats and shoes can be left there, so keeping a great deal of moisture outside the house on wet days.

2 Build an outdoor drying space where clothes and bath towels can be left outside the main body of the house in winter. Wet clothes are a main source of excessive moisture in winter.

3 Build a high-level vent window above the kitchen stove that can be easily opened to immediately remove the hot, wet air generated by cooking. A good, non-cold-bridging, window is much better than a mechanical vent above the stove as metal vents across a wall act as one large cold bridge and will cause condensation to collect in the wall at one of the wettest points in the house.

4 Bathrooms should either have a window that can be opened after a bath or shower or a very good passive stack outlet that will carry the moist air out of the room, which may, or may not, have a small fan to assist its draw.

5 Design out cold bridges from the walls of the house.

6 The wall-surface finishes of rooms should be chosen to be capable of absorbing some moisture. Where possible use an organic water-based paint on walls. These can range from the traditional white-washed walls and natural wood products to the use of modern, sophisticated, water-based paint products. The room finishes can play a significant part in controlling moisture build up in the room as well as smell.

A common-sense approach is needed to estimate the best ventilation strategy for a particular building. For example, a high-volume low-occupancy house with all the above features and wet-plastered high-mass walls or exposed timber walls with a natural finish could, on some days, get all the fresh air necessary from people intermittently opening doors. However, a low-mass, small-volume, high-occupancy room with hard finishes may need significantly more. For a well-designed house, even with low mass, hard finishes and normal occupancy but where the moisture problem has been removed from the interior of the house to a wet zone, most problems of air-quality will disappear when the air-change (ac) rate is 0.2 ac h^{-1}. That means that one-fifth of the air of a room is changed every hour. Humidity control can be achieved with a rate of 0.3 ac h^{-1} or more (Marshall and Argue, 1981). Actually, this level of air change can be achieved almost with door-opening air intake only. In many houses the air leakage rate through the structure will be of this order. Robert and Brenda Vale recommend an air change rate of around 0.45 ac h^{-1} as acceptable but, again, there is little reason not to design to the lower levels (Vale and Vale, 2000). Attention should be paid to houses where radon or carbon monoxide problems from open fires may exist, see Chapter 6.

DIRECT COMFORT VENTILATION

The comfort and thermal delight of the occupant is what makes a great house (Hershong, 1997). Issues of comfort should certainly dictate how to ventilate a building. If you think about times when you have been blissfully comfortable in a house, the feeling is probably either associated in winter with being near a warm radiant heat source, perhaps a fire, or in summer being in a cooling breeze. Sue Roaf remembers a summer's evening in Baghdad, coming out onto the freshly watered veranda at around 7 p.m., with an iced drink, wearing a cool cotton dress, sitting chatting in the early evening breeze and thinking that 'this is bliss'. Only on looking at the thermometer was it seen to be 42°C! It had been almost 50°C all that day.

People acclimatize to ambient temperatures. How warm or cold they feel depends on what the temperature has been over the last three or four days. It can take two to three weeks to adapt to a whole new climate.

5.5.
The cool, shaded, naturally ventilated living room of Jimmy Lim's house in Malaysia, giving thermal delight (Jimmy Lim).

If it is too hot or cold people do something about it. They may put on or take off clothes, they may change places within a room or move from one room to another. They may open a window, close a door or take a cold or hot drink. In extremes they may change buildings or even move to a different region with a more pleasing climate. They adapt their circumstances. It is only at the very extremes that people die of heat or cold. One of the key strategies they adopt in adapting the building to improve the indoor climate is to open a window to let in warm or cool air, another is to go to sleep.

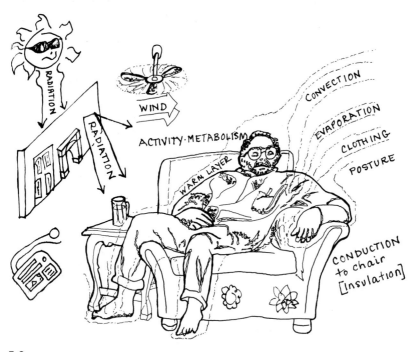

5.6.
Environment and attitude of a person on a hot day (Sab Ventris).

Passive building design is driven by the relationship between the outside and the inside air temperatures. Michael Humphreys demonstrated this over 20 years ago with his classic diagram (Figure 5.7) showing that people who live in hotter climates are comfortable at higher temperatures. In this book we adopt his simple, but effective, equation to show, very roughly, at what temperatures locally adapted people are comfortable:

TC = 0.534 (T_{mean}) + 11.9

Where T_{mean} = (T_{max} + T_{min}) / 2 and is monthly mean outdoor temperature; TC is comfort temperature; T_{max} is monthly mean

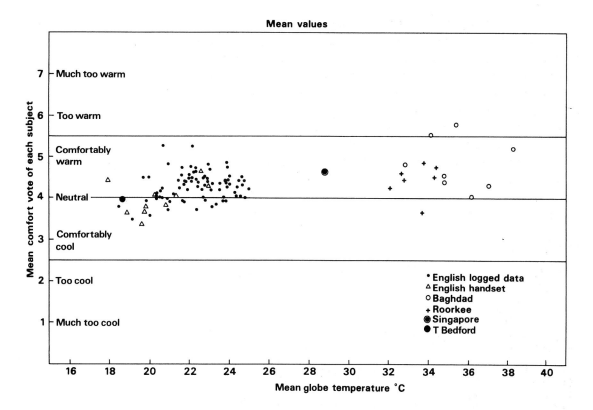

5.7.
People who live in hotter climates are comfortable at higher temperatures (Michael Humphreys).

daily outdoor maximum temperature; and T_{min} is monthly mean daily outdoor minimum temperature. T_{min} and T_{max} are usually available from Meteorological Office data.

This equation, strictly speaking, applies to summer conditions in free-running buildings (not air-conditioned ones) but gives a general idea of the comfort conditions required indoors by locally adapted populations.

Where the comfort temperature lies somewhere between T_{max} and T_{min} in a well-designed passive building with good levels of thermal mass and no excessive solar gain it should be possible to open windows for comfort cooling where T_{max} is 35°C or below. Comfort warming from the window breeze should be achievable in a good passive building when T_{max} is over 22°C and T_{min} is over 15°C.

In temperate or hotter regions, a well-designed passive building should keep out direct solar gain (or too much indirect gain re-reflected from pavements and adjacent buildings) in summer. If it is necessary to reduce summer peak temperatures, or shift them to later in the day, then more thermal mass is necessary.

As the air temperature increases more air movement is necessary, as can be seen from Figure 5.8. This shows the effect of air

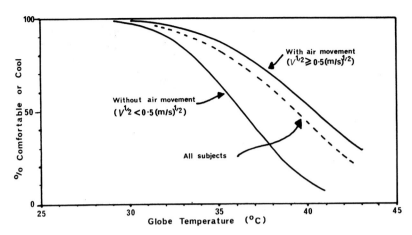

5.8.
The probability of being comfortable with and without air movement at higher temperatures (Fergus Nicol).

movement on the probability of being comfortable. With air movement almost 100 per cent of people will be comfortable at 30°C and around 80 per cent at 35°C (this is only true for people who have adapted to the local climate. You could not really take Inuits to the Sahara and expect them to be happy at such high temperatures).

Convective cooling only works when the air temperature is below skin temperature and an average mean maximum skin temperature is around 35°C. In fact, at temperatures above 32°C the body begins to lose more heat by evaporative cooling, where the moisture on the skin is removed by the air passing over it. As this moisture evaporates off, it cools the skin because the process of turning the moisture into a gas requires heat and draws it from the surrounding air and skin. This is why the most difficult climates to be cool in are very hot humid ones where there is already so much moisture in the air that the only way to remove more from the skin is to pass ever more air over it. More air and higher air speeds are necessary for comfort in hot humid climates, as can be seen in Figure 5.9.

Inhabitants of the Florida Keys who insist on living in naturally ventilated houses find it difficult to understand the fuss, made by their air-conditioning-accustomed friends when they come to dinner, over how hot it is. It is simply that both groups have acclimatized to different temperatures. If the air-conditioning-accustomed group wanted to wean themselves off the 70°F all-night habit they would have to slowly raise the temperatures until the indoor and outdoor air temperatures were the same. In so doing, for much of the year they could kick an expensive habit. In extreme spells of heat, of course, the air-conditioners could go back on but, because the inhabitants had adapted to the ambient outdoor temperatures, the units could be run at much higher temperatures and still give comfortable conditions, so saving lots of money.

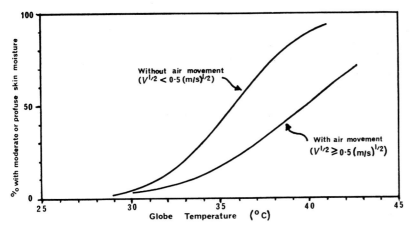

5.9.
The probability of moderate or profuse skin moisture with increasing temperature (Fergus Nicol).

A study some time ago by Terry Williamson and Sue Coldicutt, at Adelaide University, Department of Architecture, showed that people in Darwin, Australia, often have air-conditioners in their houses for use in the hot humid season. However the units were, because of the high cost of running them, typically only used when neighbours came to visit as a sign of status.

If the air coming into the house is too warm to use as a convective cooling medium for people inside then one solution may be to passively air-condition the air before it enters the house.

PASSIVE CONDITIONING OF OUTDOOR AIR

1 Wind breaks. These can be used not only to lessen the impact of strong hot or cold wind but also, if shrubs and trees are used, the air will pick up moisture from the leaves and so increase its humidity, so cooling the air.

2 Dust. Use air that has passed over natural planted groundcover to reduce dust levels. Ensure that land on the windward side of the site or settlement is planted or maintained so that the earth's crust is not broken because, if it is, this produces erodible dust particles that will be carried on the wind to the house. Avoid exposed land and replant natural vegetation if possible, even on unused plots in the centre of towns. Adopt compact plans for groups of houses in hot dry areas to avoid the formation of dust. In addition, a small plot size will increase the likelihood of more of the site being landscaped, so reducing dust. Compact plans also provide more shade (Erell and Tsoar, 1997).

3 Natural air-conditioning. Use air that has travelled over water or vegetation, for coolth. If you are lucky enough to find a site downwind of a body of clean water this will cool it

evaporatively and provide little resistance to the wind, so ensuring that the house gets a breeze that cannot be eliminated by other buildings. Do not forget that leisure water users can be noisy. Also, because the surface of water is flat, wind speeds can be very high over water because of the lack of surface resistance. Make sure the wind coming in over the water is not uncomfortable because of its high speeds. Trees around a house can lower the air temperature by several degrees.

4 Sound barriers. If the site is noisy build a substantial garden wall to keep the noise out. Sound is very persistent and will slip through any holes in a barrier so make sure the barrier is continuous.

5 Coolth ponds. Sunken gardens are a classic example of a coolth pond into which the cooler air descends. Garden walls can act as pond walls. Cool, moist, well-shaded gardens within such walls around a house (not too large that the intrusive wind above will stir up the cool air) can lower the air temperatures by 2–5°C in hot dry climates.

6 Sun traps. If higher air temperatures inside the house are required, expose the ground surface in a sheltered sun spot facing towards the south or west, and shelter from the incident wind. The actual ground temperature can be significantly increased by doing so and will warm the air above it. Using deciduous planting over such a space means that in winter one could have a sun trap and in summer a coolth trap in the same space.

7 Basement coolers. Use the prevailing wind and the coolth of a basement to lower the temperature of the air around the house before it is taken in to ventilate the building. This is shown in Figure 5.10.

8 Wind catchers or ducts through which air travels before reaching the house can reduce or increase the temperature of the air entering the building, as air issuing from ducts in the wall can be cooler or warmer than the incoming air.

9 Use pavements around the house to condition the air. Hard, light surfaces with a high reflectivity directly adjacent to the building will not only reflect light indoors but will also heat the air directly above this hot pavement convectively before it moves into the house. If the object is to reduce the temperature then ensure that the ground surfaces adjacent to the house are shaded and absorptive, or planted. Shading, such as awnings, verandas or deciduous planting, around the building can be designed to allow sunshine in in winter and to keep it out in summer.

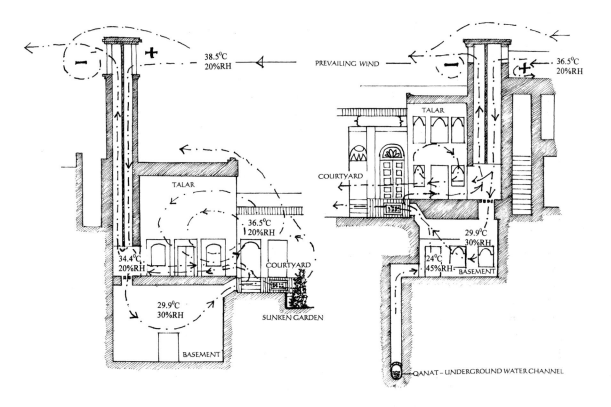

5.10.

Cross-section through a windcatcher showing the temperatures of the external air, the ground-floor living room (the Talar) and the basement air. Air forced down the tower and pushed through the basement cools and humidifies before flowing out into the courtyard, which it cools. In turn, when that courtyard air is drawn back across the ground-floor living room it cools its occupants.

10 Use 'breeze walls' around the garden of the building or on roof parapets. Well placed holes can be placed in the walls to allow the pleasant wind in, while obstructing the view. Walls facing unpleasant winds should have no holes through them.

11 Heat-scape the external envelope of the building (Figure 5.11). People often think that heat only travels into the building via the windows but it can also enter the building through the walls by conduction through the wall. Shade walls to keep them cool in summer if necessary. A wall in the sun will, in still conditions, heat the air adjacent to it, which then rises and can be caught and funnelled into the window above the hot wall. If there is a sun shade above the window, this will trap the rising warmer air in which the pressure will build and so force it in through the window. Vent solar shades to remove this heat if it is unwanted. This may be an excellent thing in winter where the heat will add to the internal comfort of the occupants. Windows can be designed to take advantage of this winter heat if required. A good way of keeping walls cooler is to place planting against the wall that will dissipate the heat before it reaches the wall. If deciduous species are used then the wall can be warming in winter and cooling in summer (Sandifer, 2000).

5.11.
Heat-scaping the outside of a building. The wall temperature of a building will be significantly altered by the use of plants to shade walls, as at the Oxford Ecohouse. The deciduous Wisteria cools and humidifies the air passing into the high-level vent, slightly open in the sun space. Note the washing drying in the sunspace (Susan Roaf).

12 Location, location, location. Choose your location in the street carefully: are you on the sunny side or the shaded side? Are there trees in the street? What alignment is the street in relation to the sun and the prevailing winds? How wide is the street? And so on. All these factors will influence the temperature of air coming in to the house from the street. Extensive work has been done by Isaac Meir and the team at the Institute of Desert Architecture Unit at Sede Boker in the Negev, who are worth contacting for advice on town planning in hot dry climates.

Design strategies for using the breeze have also to fit with the lifestyle of the house occupants. For instance, in Naples there is a traditional window shutter for the full-height French windows that commonly open onto the balconies overlooking the street. These full-height shutters often open in two halves, top and bottom. There are a number of possible functions of the combination of wind access and solar gain that can come into play over the year but one delightful function is as follows. On hot summer afternoons the top pair of external shutters are closed during siesta time, so allowing the sun to fall only on a small patch of the floor adjacent to the balcony, not deeper inside as it would do if the top shutter was open. The afternoon breeze flows in through the open door and open lower shutter, over the people sleeping on the bed, and out through the door opposite. If the top shutter was open the air flow across the room would be above the prone people. This illustrates the need to design for a particular lifestyle to create thermal delight. In many countries where people do not take siestas this particular design strategy would be of no consequence. In many tropical areas of the world windows are louvered and different sections of them can be open to optimize the air flow over a person seated in a particular position in a room (Figure 5.12).

How far into a room the breeze will reach depends on whether there are openings on one or more sides of the room. The most effective system is one where there is a good direct cross-current of air across the room, so preventing the breeze from dissipating. In hot climates single-sided ventilation is not sufficient and more can be effected either by windows in opposite or adjacent walls, by a roof window or skylight, which may also act as a wind catcher (Figure 5.13). In the lower latitudes, such a roof window should be roofed as in a dormer. This would work in the same way as a wind catcher by letting in the air but keeping out the hot sun from the rooms below.

CEILING FANS

In hot areas the ceiling fan is commonly used. A ceiling fan simply moves the air in a room around, so increasing the wind speed over the skin and increasing heat loss from the skin either by convection or conduction. If the walls of the room have some thermal mass and can store heat, then the fan may move the warmer air from the middle of the room and mix it with night-time-cooled air from near the walls. This causes the daytime air temperature to drop by a degree or two. The ceiling fan may also increase the rate of air movement across a room and draw in air from a cooler source so lowering the air temperature a little. It is important in rooms with ceiling fans to avoid creating a pool of hot air directly beneath the ceiling that is then blown down by the fan to heat the room's occupants. Vents near the ceiling would remove this hot air.

PASSIVE CONDITIONING OF INDOOR AIR

Every building has a structural temperature, just as human beings have a body temperature. In the core of the human body the temperature typically stays around 37°C, give or take a degree. At skin level it is a very different picture with very large variations

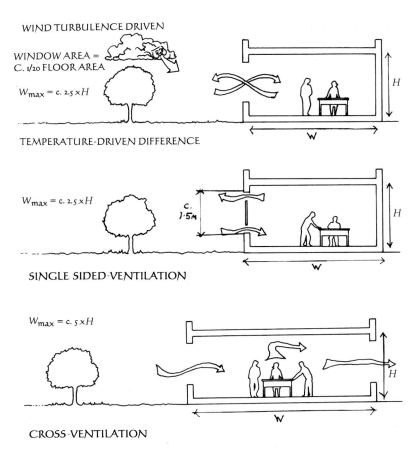

WIND TURBULENCE DRIVEN

WINDOW AREA =
C. 1/20 FLOOR AREA

$W_{max} = c.\ 2.5 \times H$

H

W

TEMPERATURE-DRIVEN DIFFERENCE

$W_{max} = c.\ 2.5 \times H$

C.
1·5M

H

W

SINGLE SIDED-VENTILATION

$W_{max} = c.\ 5 \times H$

H

W

CROSS-VENTILATION

5.13.
Single-sided and cross-ventilation with rules of thumb for their use in different
depths of rooms.

caused by a myriad of reasons (sex, weight, health, exercise, clothing, location and so on). Armpits are very warm and hands and feet
coldest because they are further from the heat pump of the body,
the heart.

Buildings are similar. The core of the building will typically have
temperatures that fluctuate less than those in the spaces around
the edges that are more exposed to the diurnal and seasonal variations in climate. Every room within a building will have its own
metabolism, or internal structural temperature, with daily and
seasonal rhythms. Ventilation in houses can be used at different
times of the day and year to modify the core temperatures of a
building to enhance the comfort of its occupants. The main ways
in which this is done is by warming the building through passive
solar heating (see Chapter 7) and cooling it using night-time
ventilation.

NIGHT-TIME COOLING OF BUILDINGS

This is the process by which heat is removed from the structure of a building by passing cooler night air over the surfaces of the building, thus lowering the temperatures of the walls, floors and ceilings of rooms. For a successful night-time ventilation system it is important that the air inlets and outlets can be left securely open at night.

A good rule of thumb is that for sufficient thermal storage to be built into a house, the walls of each room should be at least 100 mm thick (that is 150–200 mm if rooms are back to back) and made of a high-density building material. Night-time cooling of internal mass is useful where the mean value of the diurnal external temperature range of a building in summer is above the comfort temperature (see Nicol graphs in case studies).

Compartmentalization of a building impedes the free flow of air around it and therefore decouples the building from the outside climate. This is true of buildings with banks of rooms with single-sided ventilation only. Windows in one wall do not evenly distribute heat through the building. In banks of rooms that are not connected, heat builds up unevenly in the room facing the sun and is excluded from the room facing away from the sun. Alternatively, if the rooms are joined, for instance by a door, then the heat can be distributed more evenly across the building, meaning that the sun-facing room may not overheat while the cold room may avoid the need for heating. However, one common problem does still exist and this is the heat pond that builds up beneath the ceilings of both rooms. The air becomes buoyant as it heats and rises, collecting under the ceiling as a heat pond. This is not removed by cross-ventilation as the pressure that keeps it aloft is greater than the pressure of the wind-driven ventilation. The problem is that as the air beneath the ceiling gathers heat during the day it also heats the ceiling above that then becomes warm and begins to radiantly heat the people in the room below. Cool night air flowing along the floor of this space may not affect the hot pool of air on the ceiling. Do note that, in this situation, adding insulation to the ceiling would only exacerbate the problem here.

This case demonstrates the need to look at the thermal design of a building and its ventilation holistically. To solve this problem single-sided ventilation can be replaced with cross-ventilation by making a door between the two rooms. To remove the hot pool beneath the ceiling, either the door should nearly reach to the ceiling or there should be a higher-level window out of which this heat can flow during the day. In so doing it draws the air from the night-cooled floor up over the room occupants, so increasing their comfort. An alternative, not so good, solution is to use angled louvres on the windows that will direct the wind up to the ceiling so disturbing and dissipating the heat pond beneath it. However, the night cooling will not work if the window is improperly shaded and during the day the floor is continually heated, forming a radiant and convective heat source that will make the room occupants even more uncomfortable.

DESIGN OF WINDOW OPENINGS FOR VENTILATION

There are many considerations for the uses of windows for ventilation. Think carefully about the way a window opens in relation to the ventilation needs of the room behind it, its occupants and the small and large wind-flow patterns around the building. Would the room best be served by a sash, side or centre hung, sliding or hopper window? Avoid conflict with opening regimes and furniture, curtains and blinds. Do not forget that one of the most important considerations is the performance of the window over time. The longer it can be kept in good repair the better the life-cycle value of the window will have been. Make sure the window can be cleaned and maintained easily and can be secured. It should be easily accessible and openable by the room occupants and be sized intelligently for the function for which it was designed. There is no use opening a patio door for a little ventilation. The disastrous shift to having huge windows has made buildings much less people-friendly over the last 30 years. Do not design large windows when small ones will do. In many countries, for ventilation requirements in different seasons large windows are not necessary. In other climates, as we can see in the Queensland house, entire walls are not necessary at certain times of year. Lessons can be learnt from Dick Levine's house, where he has 'sundows' for solar gain and windows for ventilation, view and light.

There are many lessons to be learnt from the case studies at the end of this book that show how amazingly rich is the design vocabulary for windows in buildings and how important they are to the metabolism of the home. Do not forget that ventilation in the home should be, above all, about creating delight.

BUILDING HOMES IN CYCLONE AREAS

Stephanie Thomas

If you live in a cyclone belt, ventilation occasionally is less about delight and more about survival. Winds, as they get stronger, begin to do damage to buildings. By the time that wind speeds reach 65 m.p.h. they can become really dangerous. Winds of this speed in a 'closed circulation', meaning they go around in a complete circle, are classified as hurricanes or typhoons. The terms *hurricane* and *typhoon* are regionally specific names for a strong *tropical cyclone*: they are called typhoons to the west of the International Date Line and hurricanes to the east of it (Dommin, 1999).

In the Tropics the cyclone season occurs officially between 1 June and 30 November, yet most hurricanes occur in August, September and October (Galambos, 1990) once the land and water has warmed up over the summer. The hurricanes that originate in the Atlantic basin originate in the area around the Cape Verde Islands and head west towards the Caribbean islands. Their frequency ranges from none up to around five per year, with an average of two. In the last decade the number and intensity of cyclones has increased significantly and in 1999 in the Caribbean there were 12 named tropical cyclones (Headley, 2000), over twice the annual average for the preceding decades.

Hurricanes are classified according to sustained wind speeds, and the Saffir–Simpson scale explains the categories of hurricanes in accordance with their wind speeds (Table 5.1).

Most people who live in hurricane-prone areas can remember at least one major hurricane in their lifetime. When a hurricanes hits land, it can leave a trail of devastation, of fallen power lines and trees, strewn debris, damaged structures and human and animal casualties. For example, in Florida last century, Hurricane Andrew, a Category 4 Cape Verde classified hurricane, is used as the benchmark for comparing hurricanes. On 24 August 1992, southern Florida was directly in the path of Hurricane Andrew, which came

Table 5.1. Saffir–Simpson Scale for Hurricane Classification

Tropical cyclone classification

Tropical depression	20–34 knots (kts)
Tropical storm	35–64 kts
Hurricane	65+ kts or 74+ m.p.h.

Strength	Pressure (inches Hg)	Wind speed (kts)	Storm surge (ft)	Wind speed (m.p.h.)	Pressure (millibars)
Category 1	28.94	65–82	<5	74–95	>980
Category 2	28.50–28.91	83–95	6–8	96–110	965–979
Category 3	27.91–28.47	96–113	9–12	111–130	945–964
Category 4	27.17–27.88	114–135	13–18	131–155	920–944
Category 5	27.16	>135	>19	>155	919

ashore with sustained winds of 145 m.p.h. and gusts of up to 175 m.p.h. By the time the storm moved on into the Gulf of Mexico, 41 people had been killed and hundreds of thousands were homeless. The winds and the 12 foot storm surge caused approximately US$25 billion of damage in Florida alone, and US$26 billion in total, making this storm the most expensive natural disaster in US history to date (Rappaport, 1993).

Another noteworthy storm is Hurricane Luis (August 1995). This storm left behind a pathway of destruction on the island of St Maarten (an island of 37 square miles located about 300 miles southeast of Miami). Luis was a Category 4 Cape Verde hurricane that wreaked harm and havoc on the northeasternmost edge of the Leeward Islands, with an estimated 16 dead and causing US$2.5 billion dollars in damage, US$1.8 billion dollars on St Maarten alone.

Whether you live amongst a population of 14 million (1998 Census for Florida population) or 100 000 (Census from St Maarten Tourist Bureau) hurricanes can devastate both developed and underdeveloped countries in the same proportions. For Caribbean islands such as St Maarten, hurricane-resistant buildings are mandatory because any damage to the island can result in a significant impact on the tourist industry of that island. Hundreds of thousands of tourists visit islands in the Caribbean such as St Maarten every year. But when homes, hotels and restaurants are damaged, the economy can often suffer beyond repair. In Case Study 16 David Morrison describes how he tries to upgrade the defences of his own home against hurricane damage annually.

Table 5.2. Hurricane Damage According to Category

Category 1	Wind damage to unanchored mobile homes and foliage; some coastal flooding.
Category 2	Wind damage to some roofing, doors and windows; significant damage to mobile homes; small craft could break moorings.
Category 3	Extensive hurricane. Structural damage to homes; mobile homes destroyed; flooding at elevations lower than 5 ft above sea level (asl).
Category 4	Extreme hurricane. Major structural damage; extensive beach erosion with flooding at elevations lower than 10 ft asl.
Category 5	Catastrophic hurricane. Massive structural damage; some complete building failures; flooding at elevations lower than 15 ft asl; evacuation necessary.

Following recent hurricane disasters such as Andrew and Luis, the governments, insurance industries and the public have demanded a review of what could be done to minimize the destruction and suffering caused by hurricanes. This has led to a realization that building codes, enforcement and products are seriously in need of improvements. Key elements to hurricane-resistant design are: compliance to the latest code requirements (if applicable); protection of building envelope; and the use of approved missile impact and cyclic windload-tested materials.

The degree of damage to a building will depend on the strength of the hurricane.

When clients rely on architects to design their dream homes in areas of potential hurricane activity, far too often too much money is spent on how the building looks and not enough on protecting it against the threat of hurricanes. To make a house design able to sustain winds of 100 m.p.h. may cost 10–15 per cent extra. To make it safe in winds of 150 m.p.h. will cost another 10–15 per cent on top. It is a false economy in a hurricane zone to think that you may be able to escape the wind. Many people rely on insurance policies to cover the costs of rebuilding, but insurance cannot bring back peoples' lives.

With winds around the globe getting stronger, many house designers would be well advised to take note of the following light-hearted advice for minimizing wind damage on buildings taken from *Design for Tropical Cyclones* (Macks, 1978):

• Avoid roof overhangs	Lose your shade
• Avoid flat roofs	Pitch all roofs 30°
• Avoid large windows	Buy paintings to look at
• Don't use aluminium, asbestos cement and galvanized iron	Build everything in concrete
• Don't use nails or glue	Bolt everything to the floor (which is concrete)
• Avoid wave surges	Build in the hills
• Avoid exposed sites	Don't build in the hills
• Don't build near the sea	Enjoy the desert view
• Don't build near trees	Cut all the trees down
• Don't have roof penetrations	Use invisible vent pipes
• Don't have fancy roof shapes	Live in a box
• Avoid cyclones/hurricanes	Live in Adelaide.

The box gives a task list that may help if you are thinking of building a house in a hurricane area. The list has been compiled from personal experience and a variety of sources that include building code offices, *Design for Tropical Cyclones* (Macks, 1978) and *Tropenbau, Building in the Tropics* (Lippsmeier, 1980).

Site selection
- Identify site, and proximity to the sea.
- Establish flood heights and possible surge levels.
- Is site in a flood plain?
- Is evacuation possible immediately prior to a hurricane arriving (landfall)?
- Is the site in a heavily populated area and susceptible to future growth that may hinder evacuation?
- Check possible effects of damage by debris of both trees and neighbouring properties.
- Where a site is near rivers and open spaces, establish what are the local turbulence effects of wind patterns.
- Study the history of hurricane activity over past 100 years.
- Study the prevailing wind patterns of site.

Landscaping
- Study the topography of the immediate area.
- Can advantage be taken of mounds, etc., to give protection or reduction in wind loads?
- Can trees be planted that are more resistant to fracture and collapse?
- Can tree foliage be easily pruned to reduce wind effects?
- Note any screen walls that can break up wind patterns and act as debris barriers.

Floor levels
- Study the topography and drainage in storm rains to determine flood-free floor levels.
- Evaluate the implications of the number of floor levels needed; one, two or split level (also note local building codes; some regulations may have a first-floor habitable minimum height and a total height maximum).
- Remember that rises in roof heights increase wind loads.
- Ground-level floors can introduce flooding.

Windows and doors
- Check their size and the loads they are to carry.
- Design frames to connect to walls to which wind loads can be transferred.
- Consider the implications of windows breaking in high winds.
- Consider impact-resistant windows.
- Are openings on opposite walls able to funnel the wind through the building without affecting other areas?
- Design shutter fasteners to be part of structural drawings (do not install them after construction is complete).
- Louvre blades leak under pressure and may reduce wind loads.
- Resolve the eternal conflict of wider windows for view and smaller windows for safety.
- Consider balconies and porches for protection – to split the winds.

Structure
- Design for structural integrity.
- Consider a structural grid system of posts and beams to provide stiffness.
- Keep structural systems simple.
- Have generously dimensioned foundations, widening at the base so that the ground pressure can absorb a portion of the forces that arise.
- Extra strong joints between foundations and walls by means of steel reinforcement, bolts, etc.
- Examine large spans and cantilevers.

Shape
- Consider shapes to be adopted and optimize them for wind protection while reducing 'alcoves' in which pressure can build up.
- Can roof profiles be designed to transfer wind loads more evenly over whole roof?
- Design carefully areas where roof projections and shapes cause local turbulence – e.g. chimneys, vent pipes, sharp direction changes, outriggings, roof-mounted solar water heaters, etc.

General planning
- Consider using posted verandas to catch or deflect debris.
- Division of the plan into many smaller rooms increases structural stability.
- Check interior half-height walls and their stiffness.
- Good interior cross-ventilation can be an advantage.
- Stiffen and reinforce the structure around most secure rooms.
- Disposition and planning of internal spaces should fit into a firm structural system or vice versa.

Costs and estimates
- Evaluate costs of alternative solutions (including sustainability and embodied energy).
- Are bolts cheaper than metal fasteners (in areas of high corrosion, evaluate galvanized and stainless steel products for long life performance and lower maintenance)?
- If a post and beam structure is used, size members for optimal safety as well as cost.
- Are grilles on windows cheaper than shutters and do they give adequate protection?
- If impact-resistant windows are chosen, is it cost-effective to include shutters as well?

Selection of finishes
- Are wall and ceiling linings suspect when wet and, if they lose stiffness, can remaining structures maintain stiffness?
- Is it wise to place carpets throughout and up to windows where water damage can ruin carpets?
- Are external walls debris-resistant and to what degree of impact?

- Is there adequate bracing in wall planes, ceiling and roof planes, and in internal partitions for lateral stability?
- Select type of wall cladding appropriate for climate.
- Check higher-pressure areas at walls and roofs near corners and profile changes.
- Check spans and warranty of roof cladding with manufacturers.
- Check type of sheeting, thickness and fixing.
- Are secret fixings to roof sheetings adequate or are screw fixings needed in addition?
- Check that manufacturer's instructions match terrain category of site and verify warranties.
- Check windows selected, and glass size, for the correct thickness to match the pressure to be resisted.

Details
- Check door and window frames, stops, catches and their fixings into walls.
- Check weak joints such as half-height walls with windows above, where joint of vertical cantilevered wall and window needs stiffness to resist breaking or overturning.
- Check flashings to roofs and ensure adequate fixings are provided as loss or damage to flashing often leads to degradation of adjacent material.
- Parapets should be reinforced.
- Tying down of roof members should extend down into foundations in a single element or at least in a straight line.
- There are technical solutions available to fix windows into frames but the actual fixings are seldom made correctly.

Claddings
- When selecting claddings for walls and roofs examine thickness of material for the proposed use.
- Examine manufacturer's instructions and verify that the claddings are suitable for the job.
- Check method of fixing and type and number of fixings used: nails, screws, glue.
- Is the material impact-resistant and to what degree of impact?
- What happens to the material when it breaks? (does it still have strength?).
- Does the material add stiffness to the frame?

Codes
- Designers should use the most up-to-date local design codes available.
- If government does not require code compliance, or code is not sufficient, work to the codes of another country where good codes do exist.
- Do not expect builders and tradesmen to build to a list of codes specified if the specifier does not have the code, has not read it and does not fully understand it.

A building in a hurricane storm area must be able to withstand extreme winds that blow from every direction during a single storm. Good design and workmanship are essential. Rapid and extreme changes in air pressure can be a further cause of damage. For example, if a well-sealed air-conditioned building is hit too quickly by the extremely low-pressure centre of a storm the building can explode (Lippsmeier, 1980).

According to some people in the hurricane regions of the world the most effective line of defence against the winds is to leave a message to the hurricane, often painted on the plywood boards used to protect windows. There are a number of more permanent hurricane shutter types used other than these boards, including the most popular aluminium accordion types, Bahamian wooden shutters and metal rolling doors. The important factor to remember about hurricane shutters is that they are only as good as their installation, and they must be well secured to the wall.

After a hurricane has made landfall, it usually decreases in strength. Although it may seem safe once the hurricane has been downgraded to a thunderstorm, tornadoes often develop and are the most damaging weather patterns to deal with. It is almost impossible to economically build for the shear force of a tornado's direct hit. Sometimes the wind speeds reach 300 m.p.h. During a major tornado hit, wind pressure loads can build up to over 0.5 ton m^{-2} ($P > 100$ p.s.f.). Only reinforced concrete structures are able to withstand these pressure levels. When high-density mobile home areas are subject to a tornado the most inherent danger to people and property is flying debris carried in high winds. In 250-m.p.h. winds, a 2 ft × 4 ft timber can cut right through a building.

As wind speeds increase with climate change, standards for design for the wind will have to improve in many areas. While no building is completely free from hazards, they can be minimized by proper design, good construction, careful selection of materials and homeowner awareness. There are many good books and websites available to learn more about this subject, of which one of the best is the book on *Design for Tropical Cyclones*, by the Department of Civil and Systems Engineering at James Cook University, Queensland Australia (1978). Also try the website http://www.aoml.noaa.gov.

However, we cannot absolutely predict the climate, which no doubt has plenty of surprises in store for us in the twenty-first century.

6 HEALTH AND HAPPINESS IN THE HOME

There are many different health risks in the home. They range from earthquakes and house fires to methane poisoning from a poorly vented gas stove. Many of them can be quite simply designed out, once they have been recognized as a problem.

Think carefully about how to design, not only for the more obvious aspects of health but also for peace of mind, restfulness and delight in your buildings. The mind and body are closely linked; a person at ease, comfortable and peaceful in a house, is likely to be healthier for it. For instance, in Ecolonia at Apeldoorn in the Netherlands, groups of houses in the 1980s and 1990s were constructed, each with a range of different eco-features. The most popular of them all proved to be, surprisingly, the quiet house. This suggests that designing noise out of a building should be near the top of the list of priorities and yet it is a seldom-mentioned item on housing specifications for green buildings.

There can be a global dimension to the impacts of health issues, as well as being about the safety, health and happiness of the people who live in the house. Because the subject is so large we have simply listed alphabetically a number of the most important issues that may concern householders. Some of the issues are touched on in other chapters. Once homeowners are aware that there may be problems in one particular area of their house design many different local and national organizations can be contacted for more information on each area. Local government offices and building research establishments are often good places to start. Many issues will be covered by the local building regulations and can be discussed with the relevant authorities. The Internet is also a great place to search for detailed information on individual hazards and issues. All information from the Web should be thought through to ensure it is backed up by the common-sense intuitions of designers and that it is not simply pushing a certain line of thought in order to sell a particular product.

6.1.
Low-allergen design requires careful thought. Floors are best without carpets, walls of water-based paints and soft furnishings should be made of natural materials that can be easily washed. This view of the balcony at the Oxford Ecohouse shows the French door and vent windows that provide a variety of different ventilation opportunities into the buffer zone of the sunspace, these make dust-collecting ducts unnecessary in this house (Nat Rea).

It is advisable to read through this chapter before starting to design the house as it may significantly affect how you go about the design. In design, as in so many other parts of life, the best decisions are made on the basis of the most information. If you are employing someone else to design your house make sure they can justify, to your satisfaction, the health implications of their design.

ALLERGENS

An allergen is a substance that causes a reaction by the body's immune system against an otherwise harmless foreign protein. People are allergic to many different proteins, from milk to wheat. For allergens that affect breathing the immune reaction occurs when the allergen has been inhaled. Initially the body becomes 'sensitized' against a particular allergen causing the body to generate antibodies against the inhaled protein. These antibodies are Immunoglobulin E (IgE). Certain families are genetically prone to generate more IgE than others and have a tendency to develop more asthma, hay fever or eczema than other groups. The common allergens in houses relate to dust mites and domestic pets.

ASBESTOS

Avoid this material completely. Do not use it in new build and when having it removed employ a registered expert. Asbestos causes lung cancer and mesothelioma (rare tumours) of the lungs, chest and abdomen. Asbestos comes in three forms:

1 White. In board or sheeting products, surface treatments or as thermal and acoustic insulation.
2 Brown. In laminated boards and pipe lagging.
3 Blue. In fire insulation on steel frames or thermal insulation to heating systems. Also mixed with other forms of asbestos in boards or in asbestos cement mixes.

ASTHMA

An increasing number of people around the world are suffering from asthma, a condition with symptoms of chest tightening, coughing, difficulty breathing and wheezing. Symptoms will vary from day to day and place to place. When it is poorly controlled people often wake at night, breathless and distressed. Many different things can cause a narrowing of the airways and asthma, including exercise, cold air, exhaust fumes, cigarette smoke, aerosol sprays, chemicals and strong smells. It is important that sufferers identify what makes their asthma worse so they can deal with its causes. In the home dust mites, organic solvent vapours, wood preservatives, formaldehyde and even certain garden plants are key triggers.

Step by step guide to asthma avoidance in the home

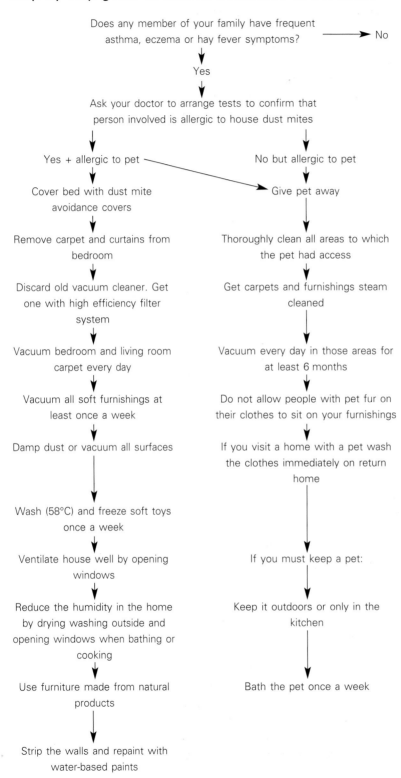

Does any member of your family have frequent asthma, eczema or hay fever symptoms? ⟶ No

↓

Yes

↓

Ask your doctor to arrange tests to confirm that person involved is allergic to house dust mites

Yes + allergic to pet

No but allergic to pet

Give pet away

Cover bed with dust mite avoidance covers

Remove carpet and curtains from bedroom

Thoroughly clean all areas to which the pet had access

Discard old vacuum cleaner. Get one with high efficiency filter system

Get carpets and furnishings steam cleaned

Vacuum bedroom and living room carpet every day

Vacuum every day in those areas for at least 6 months

Vacuum all soft furnishings at least once a week

Do not allow people with pet fur on their clothes to sit on your furnishings

Damp dust or vacuum all surfaces

If you visit a home with a pet wash the clothes immediately on return home

Wash (58°C) and freeze soft toys once a week

Ventilate house well by opening windows

If you must keep a pet:

Reduce the humidity in the home by drying washing outside and opening windows when bathing or cooking

Keep it outdoors or only in the kitchen

Use furniture made from natural products

Strip the walls and repaint with water-based paints

Bath the pet once a week

Choose plants for the garden that are pollinated by insects and exclude those pollinated by the wind, such as ash, birch, hazel and oak trees. Some insect-pollinated plants can cause problems because of their scent, such as geraniums, or because they produce large quantities of pollen, such as the daisy family, or for both reasons, such as Buddleias and honeysuckle. Other plants to watch are those that cause skin allergies; some people find that by gardening in gloves they can avoid the problem. Large areas of grass may cause problems and avoid mulches that may harbour mould spores.

CANCER OF THE SKIN

Ozone depletion has already resulted in an enormous increase in the incidence of skin cancer in the Southern Hemisphere. In Queensland, Australia, where the most damaging UV-B radiation is highest, three out of every four people can expect to get some form of skin cancer during their lives. With the rapidly thinning ozone layer over the Northern Hemisphere, ozone depletion is expected to account for a 10–20 per cent increase in skin cancer in the Pacific Northwest in the next few decades. In the USA in 1935 the chances of developing the most serious form of skin cancer (malignant melanoma) was 1 in 1500. In 2000 it is now 1 in 75 (http://www.geocities.com/RainForest/Vines/4030/impacts.html).

So do people sitting beside large areas of glass or even under glass roofs in buildings have an increased risk of developing skin cancer? The situation here is as follows. There are two different types of wavelength that have been identified as causal in the development of skin cancer. These are UV-A and UV-B. UV-B is ten times stronger than UV-A as a cancer trigger. UV-B is almost totally eliminated by most glass currently on the market. UV-A does penetrate glass but one would need to sit next to large areas of glass for considerable periods to be exposed to significant amounts of UV-A. Because UV-A has around one-tenth the effect of UV-B, sitting near a large glass window could be considered equivalent to being outside all the time with a Sun Protection Factor 10 sunscreen on. In other words, the effects would gradually build up but would probably not be noticeable during the lifetime of the person exposed, particularly in higher latitudes. It is possible that UV-A has special effects that have not yet been investigated. While UV-A has not been identified as a potential carcinogen it is responsible for the ageing of the skin. UV-A would largely enter the building from the exposed, visible, blue sky, so if a person is seated away from a window and receives only reflected light then there is no possible problem. The basic research into this issue has not yet been done but it is not perceived to be a problem by the medical profession (personal correspondence with Professor J.L. Hawk at the Department of Photobiology, Guy's, King's and St. Thomas' School of Medicine, London and Dr James Slusser, Research Scientist Director, UVB Monitoring Network, Natural Resource Ecology Laboratory, Colorado State University, USA).

CARBON DIOXIDE – INDOORS IN HOUSES

In breathing we expire carbon dioxide (CO_2). This can build up in the air of a room. In the home, in rooms where there are several people and consequently very high levels of CO_2, simply opening a window or door is the most effective way of purging the room of CO_2 in a short time, no more than 15 minutes or so.

CARBON MONOXIDE

Carbon monoxide (CO) is a colourless, odourless, deadly gas. When CO is present it rapidly accumulates in the blood displacing the oxygen needed for the cells to function. Inhaled in sufficiently large quantities its effects are rather like suffocation. CO is a common by-product of appliances run on flammable fuels such as gas, oil, wood and coal. CO poisoning often results from blocked chimneys or flues, or improper venting of rooms. Symptoms of CO poisoning include, headaches, giddiness, drowsiness and nausea. If these symptoms are experienced a doctor should be asked to carry out a carboxyhaemoglobin test.

To ensure that CO poisoning does not occur in your home:

- have all stoves, fires and appliances that burn fuel such as gas, coal, wood, etc., properly and regularly maintained;
- avoid using flueless gas or paraffin heaters.

CHLOROFLUOROCARBONS (CFCS)

CFCs are a group of man-made gases that are largely responsible for destroying the ozone layer above the Earth that shields the planet from incoming radiation. CFCs are used in buildings in insulants, aerosols, refrigerants and fire extinguishers. The main CFCs are CFC11 and CFC12. In addition to their role in the destruction of the ozone layer they are 17 500 and 20 000 times, respectively, more potent as 'greenhouse' gases than CO_2. Because they are in a stable form they will take many decades to break down and so the impacts of CFC pollution today will only be felt later on in this century. This is what makes them so dangerous. In 1987 the world's prime consumers and manufacturers of CFCs signed the Montreal Protocol written to reduce and phase out emissions of CFCs into the atmosphere. CFC production had ostensibly stopped by 2000 but the black market in CFCs is still buoyant, largely because of the huge cost of replacing them in refrigeration systems. Their main uses in buildings were in roof and wall insulations, dry linings and pipe sections and, above all, in air-conditioning and refrigeration systems. Do not use any building materials or systems that are made with CFCs, HCFCs, R11, R12 and, if possible, use only R22 products as this is considered a less hazardous material. In temperate and cold climates air-conditioning should not be used and, if specifying a cooling system for a warm or hot climate insist on minimal ozone impacts for the system you choose.

The seriousness of the ozone problem cannot be over-emphasized. Not only are the potential health hazards enormous (see p127), but the occurrence of the ozone holes over the Arctic and the Antarctic – where the freezing atmospheric air is necessary for the breakdown of CFCs into chlorine which destroys the ozone layer – means that below the holes radiation levels are higher, thus escalating the rate at which the ice caps are melting.

CONTAMINATED LAND

With increasing pressure on building land many new housing developments are sited on contaminated land. The first task is to find out how the land was contaminated and with what. Local government offices should have records of the history of sites and, if necessary, hire a specialist consultant to determine the hazards posed by the land. The land may then be treated in situ with neutralizing chemicals, removed altogether and replaced with clean top soil or by sealing the base of sites with horizontal and vertical barriers to prevent the movement of contaminated groundwater into the adjacent land. Seek specialist advice.

DISABLED ACCESS

All houses should be capable of easy access by wheelchair users and ground-floor toilets should be provided. A good way of approaching this particular design challenge is to imagine oneself becoming unexpectedly disabled and still wanting to live in the house. Also, you may still want to live in the house at the age of 95! If it is a proper ecohouse you will not want to leave it before then because its annual energy bills will be so low. The price of conventional fossil fuels and insulation materials may be so high you will not be able to afford the bills in a non-ecohouse alternative anyway.

DUST MITES

Dust mites contain a leading allergen that causes and worsens asthma. Many studies around the world have been done on how to reduce dust mite populations because of the high increase in the incidence of asthma worldwide. Dust mites are found particularly in bedding, furniture and at the base of carpets where the humidity is higher and the temperature more stable. They are very small and up to 2 million of them can live in one mattress.

The best conditions for mite growth are temperatures of around 25°C with 80 per cent humidity. How to avoid them:

1 move to high alpine pastures as they cannot survive in the cold, dry air up there;
2 lower the humidity in a room until it becomes too dry for the dust mites to survive. This can be done by removing wet objects such as washing, raincoats and wet towels from the house; and putting a good ventilation window above and/or beside the cooker;
3 the first line of attack should be to remove their habitat, so out go the wall to wall carpets and curtains, and special asthma covers can be bought for bedding. Barrier covers can be placed beneath the sheets and inside pillow covers. Modern covers are made of materials that are permeable to water but impermeable to dust mites;
4 beat rugs thoroughly.

EARTHQUAKES

The basic rectangular, single-storey, wood-frame house is one of the safest structures in an earthquake. The amount of damage incurred should be minimal if the house is properly engineered and built. The key to a well-designed building is the ability of the structure to withstand an earthquake as a single unit.

Houses built on steep hillsides, or with split-levels, second storeys over garages, or pole foundation systems, cripple walls higher than 1 m; too many windows or irregular features can represent even greater risks. In such situations, a structural engineer should be consulted. Avoid sites with high groundwater tables and/or Lacustrine clay soils that tend to turn liquid during earthquakes. Get advice on the geology of your site before purchase.

The shaking and lateral forces of an earthquake will separate building components at their weakest points. Therefore, all structural elements must be securely tied together:

- the structure must be tied to the foundation with anchor bolts to keep it from sliding;
- the wall studs must be sheathed (tied) with plywood or some other material to reduce deflection and provide strength;
- the floors and roof must be fastened securely to the walls to tie the structure together.

Almost all existing structures can be strengthened to be more earthquake-resistant (but not earthquake-proof). Masonry chimneys should be reinforced with steel and tied to the roof and upper-floor framing with steel straps. Un-reinforced masonry chimneys should either be removed and replaced with a properly braced metal flue and enclosure system (e.g. a wood-frame), or measures should be taken to mitigate the effects of potential damage.

Clay and concrete tile roofs can weigh five to ten times as much as lighter roof systems, such as composition shingles. The increased weight results in significantly larger earthquake loads for the roof and walls. Heavy new roofing should not be added to existing structures without consulting a structural engineer.

Boilers should be strapped to walls. Tall furniture should be fixed to walls with L-shaped brackets. Keep heavy objects on lower shelves. Install shelf guards to hold objects on shelves. Install strong latches to all doors and windows. Ensure that all gas pipelines in the home are flexible. Have very clearly located meter points for turning off gas, water and electricity into the property. Have a clear point in the house for the storage of a medical kit. Have well-serviced fire extinguishers in the home. Have a post-earthquake plan ready for all members of the family. If you live in an earthquake area contact local authorities for advice of making your own house safe in earthquakes. They will have lots of experience.

EARTH SHELTERING

In earth-sheltered structures all or part of the building is sunk into the ground. They are typically built to keep buildings warm or cool, with their internal temperatures modified by the surrounding ground temperature, and to minimize the impact of a building on the landscape. In addition they provide excellent fireproof qualities in high fire-risk areas. Because of their low energy demands for heating and cooling they are buildings that very much promote the health of the global atmosphere by their very low emissions of greenhouse gases. An excellent introduction to the principals of earth sheltering is *Sod It*, by Peter Carpenter.

EPOXY RESINS AND GLUES

These can lead to various forms of dermatitis. A no-touch policy should be employed when using them.

FIRE

This is one of the worst health risks that any house should be designed against. With global warming the risk of houses being engulfed by external fires is increasing year by year. Around the world there have been unprecedented numbers of major bush and forest fires in recent years. If you are in a high-risk area for such fires great care will have to be taken to protect the house as best you can. In some areas it has been shown that judicious placing of earth banks around houses can cause fires to jump buildings. If the site is in a really high-risk area, where annually fires lick up the sides of hills, then an extreme measure would be to earth-shelter the house and sink it completely or partially below ground.

In terms of the envelope of the building there will be very different fire implications if one is building in masonry or timber, and the various pros and cons of each material type will have to be weighed by designers. The roof is often the first element of the house to ignite. Contact local authorities for advice on fireproofing houses.

Care should be taken to consider the fire risks of any design. All local regulations for fire compartments and escapes in buildings should be noted before the design begins. It is difficult to overemphasize the need to design out fire risks from buildings. A major source of fire risk in buildings is insulation materials; the following advice can be offered on the fire implications of different types.

In cavity walls airflow is often limited or prevented by cavity barriers, so lowering the risk of spread of flame in the cavity. This may cause fire to then burst out and ignite adjacent rooms. Please note that this is another good reason to make sure that cracks and holes between the cavity and the room are well sealed. Where the cavity is not capped, air can enter the combustion zone and it has been found that the performance of different materials here depends more on their form, i.e. board, granules or infill, than their basic composition. It is advisable to cap all cavities filled with bead or granular materials but it is essential to do so where a board insulant is fixed into the cavity adjacent to a continuous air gap, as fire can spread quickly up such voids. The use of in-situ foamed materials, particularly thermosetting plastics such as polyurethane and urea formaldehyde, reduces the risk of airflow and keeps smoke or flame spread to a minimum. The flow of bead or granular materials into the fire area, following the breaching of a masonry wall, will increase the heat potential of the fire and the release of smoke and toxins into the room. However, the risk arising from infill materials in cavities is unlikely to occur until the fire has reached major proportions.

Some foamed plastic insulants, once ignited, will burn with considerably greater intensity than cellulose products and will require a thicker protective cover between the insulant and the room that restricts the flow of air to the product or prevents rapid emission of flammable volatiles (e.g. volatile organic carbons, VOCs). Even composite products should be investigated; recent tests in the UK have shown that composite sandwich panels with a polyurethane core can burn very rapidly and cause flashover, achieving very high temperatures.

Materials made of loose fibre granules can be either used as poured or blown insulation in cavities, as a blown foam, or as boards or rigid sheets. The combustible types are often not difficult to ignite and can cause fires when ignited even by a cigarette. Organic materials often produce toxic combustion products, frequently accompanied by thick smoke. Particular care is needed where insulating materials are used as room finishes. Such finishes can create ideal conditions for the spread of surface fire, irrespective of whether the insulating low-density substrate is combustible or not. Plastic materials will usually ignite or decompose when subjected to heat or fire and, as a result, produce heat, smoke and combustion gases. Thermoplastic materials will soften and flow on heating, often before ignition takes place. This can then collapse and ignite. Examples are polystyrene, polypropylene, PVC and acrylics. Thermosetting materials do not soften but undergo localized charring, possibly flaming with combustion. Examples are urea formaldehyde, polyurethane and polyisocyanurate.

With few exceptions no insulation material should be left exposed directly in the habitable areas of a building. It should be protected at all times from sources of heat that could be likely to cause ignition. Many foamed plastics, for instance, can be separated from the room by a layer of plasterboard. Any protection over insulating materials that soften at low temperatures should be independently fixed (e.g. nailing and battening) so that softening of the insulation does not result in premature collapse of the protective material (BRE Digest 233).

Before wet-pumped insulations are added to cavities the house electrics should be checked as faults in the system could cause major fire risks. PVC and electric cables are also best left apart. Electric wiring should be kept above the level of loft insulation to reduce the risk of overheating. Painting the surface of an insulating material such as polystyrene can increase its fire risk and gloss-painted ceiling tiles should be removed; matt-finish flame-retardant paints or water-based emulsion paints should be used.

Mineral wool and glass fibre materials with a low resin binder content can be rated as non-combustible. However, products such as canvas are combustible and, although the addition of a fire-retardant may improve its performance, it may still be a hazard. The same is true of a finishing film of PVC or polythene or any thin film supported on an insulating substrate. If plastic-finished wallpapers are used ask about their fire ratings. Also take care where combustible materials, for instance around ducts, penetrate into room spaces as they could carry fire with them.

Before choosing any material think carefully about its behaviour in fire. If you do not have information on how it performs, ask for it or look it up on the Internet. Non-combustible materials are safer. Be careful of electric wiring, equipment, candles and blowtorches and, if in doubt, ask the local building inspector for advice. Do not underestimate the health risks of fire (BRE Digest 233).

FLOORS

One of the three largest surfaces in the home is its floors. The choice of flooring material is very important. There are many ways of judging which is the best choice for the environment but really the main question is which is best for your house. If there is an asthmatic in the house avoid wall-to-wall carpets. If you do want a wall-to-wall floor covering follow the two main rules for choosing materials:

1 choose the most natural material possible;
2 choose the most local material possible.

These could be pure wool carpets or rugs, or sisal or hemp matting. If you want a heat-absorbing passive solar floor choose ceramic tiles or natural stone floors. If you want to use a renewable material choose cork or reused timber or solid timber from a local sustainable source, with an oil-based finish. If you need a durable flooring choose Linoleum, made from renewable raw materials such as wood and cork powder and linseed; its degradability is also good. Vinyl flooring is less good as it contains harmful substances, asbestos and mercury that are released during its manufacture and chlorine that involves risks of accidents in transport. Vinyl flooring is a petroleum-based product and, as such, is using a finite and scarce resource (Jonsson, 2000). Choices are difficult but think the alternatives through carefully.

FORMALDEHYDE

Many wood-based panel products, such as chipboard, are made with glues that give off formaldehyde, especially when new. In addition, urea-formaldehyde foam (UFF) insulation in the wall cavities may be a source of formaldehyde vapour. This is a colourless gas with a pungent odour. Low concentrations of the gas may irritate eyes, nose and throat, possibly causing running eyes, sneezing and coughing. These products are widely used in the home for flooring, shelving and kit furniture. Some types of foam-backed carpets may also release formaldehyde. The amount of this gas released from these products will decrease over time.

Ways of avoiding this substance include:

1 use blown mineral fibres or expanded polystyrene beads for cavity-fill insulation rather than UFF;
2 if you are exposing UFF in building works plan to expose it for a short time only and cover it up again promptly;
3 make sure there is no possible air leakage through cracks or holes into the house from cavities filled with UFF;
4 repair any damp patches in walls adjacent to UFF-filled cavity or materials.

LEAD

Lead is a poison. Avoid it. Remove all lead pipes from the home. Most house paints and primers dating from before World War I are likely to contain lead. Lead paint is most dangerous when it is broken and flaking. Either paint over it with modern non-lead-based paint to seal it or strip it completely. Do not dry sand it as inhaled dust can be poisonous. Do not burn strip it as this releases fumes. Hot air tools that soften the paint so it can be scraped off may be used but avoid overheating the paint as it will then give off fumes. Wet sanding is the least dangerous but the slowest and messiest method to strip it. Chemical strippers are costly, give off hazardous fumes and are caustic to the skin.

Always use lead-free solder. Older putty contains lead so be careful when removing it. Avoid dry sanding of old lead putty. Avoid lead flashings if the rainwater is collected for drinking purposes.

LEGIONELLA

Legionella pneumophila is a bacterium found in all natural fresh water where it poses little threat to health. In buildings' water systems it grows into high concentrations and can be dangerous when inhaled in droplets of water from sprays, as found in showers, hot and cold taps and ventilation and air-conditioning systems. When inhaled it gives rise to Legionnaires' Disease, which is a type of pneumonia that typically causes death in one in ten of those who contract it. Legionella grows best in stagnant water at temperatures between 20 and 50°C with an optimum of 30–40°C. Organic material in the system also enhances growth rates. Thermostats in water tanks should be set to 55°C or be regularly flushed with water above this temperature. The bacterium will not grow significantly at temperatures below 20°C. Lipped, fitted lids should be placed securely over water tanks. Domestic systems are less of a problem as they have a regular turnover of water. Spa baths and jacuzzis should be drained and cleaned daily, with the strainer removed and cleaned at the same time.

MINERAL WOOL

A wide range of man-made mineral fibres is now used in the construction industry for insulation and reinforcement. These typically look like glassy fibres and are made from molten blast-furnace slag, rock or glass by a combination of blowing and spinning processes to fiberize the melts. The normal diameter of mineral wool fibres being manufactured today is around 6 µm. The main health effects of working with this material are skin and eye irritation; protective goggles can be used if irritation persists. A high degree of exposure to mineral wool can lead to irritation of the upper respiratory tract but this is not considered to be a long-term health risk, although many countries have legislation that specifies maximum permitted exposure levels. There is ongoing research to establish if there is a link with cancer from these fibres. If there is, it has not been proved to be a strong one.

In the home, rock and glass wools are used for insulating loft and wall cavities. Mineral fibres are also compressed into bats or boards, pipe insulation and roof tiles. The main thing to avoid is the inhalation of the mineral wool fibres and this can be achieved with a little common sense, not allowing cracks in the construction where the fibres can infiltrate a room, such as through down-lighters or around pipes. Care should be taken not to disturb the fibres during maintenance. Also, ensure that any water tank exposed to possible pollution by fibres has a firm lid. Simple protective measures, such as the use of suitable clothing, gloves, glasses or disposable respirators, can be used while working with mineral wool if skin, eye or respiratory tract irritations occur.

MOULDS

Moulds present a real health hazard in the home to those who are allergic to their spores or droppings. Moulds also shorten the life of many products in the home.

Moulds require the following to grow:

- Mould spores. Normal air contains several hundred spores per cubic metre, so it is difficult to avoid them. Concentrations increase in summer.
- Nutrients, such as the layer of grease that is found on most buildings' surfaces.
- Temperature. Most moulds survive in temperatures between 0 and 40°C and they thrive at the warmer end of this band.
- Moisture. This is the critical factor in mould growth. Moulds extract moisture from the substrate on which they are growing, so local relative humidity factors are important. Any cold spot on a wall in a house will make the moisture condense because cold air can hold less moisture than warm air. This creates condensation on which moulds thrive. For common wall finishes, such as wall paper, the critical relative humidity is around 80 per cent (Oreszczyn, 2000).

The key challenges of reducing mould growth in homes are to:

- eliminate cold bridges in the external envelope (Chapter 2);
- remove moisture in the home (Chapter 5) with good zoning of wet activities and a range of good opening windows and vents; and
- have breathing surfaces for the walls in the home that will absorb moisture.

NOISE

Sound is generated by creating a disturbance of the air, which sets up a series of pressure waves fluctuating above and below the air's normal atmospheric pressure, much as a stone that falls in water generates expanding ripples on the surface. Unlike the water waves, however, these pressure waves propagate in all directions from the source of the sound. Our ears sense these pressure fluctuations, convert them to electrical impulses and send them to our brain, where they are interpreted as sound.

There are many sources of sound in buildings: voices, human activities, external noises such as traffic, entertainment devices and machinery. They all generate small rapid variations in pressure about the static atmospheric pressure; these propagate through the air as sound waves. Sound is usually measured in decibels (dBs)

Table 6.1. Typical sound levels

	dB
Jet takeoff, artillery fire, riveting	120 or more
Rock band or very loud orchestra	100–120
Unmuffled truck, police whistle	80–100
Average radio or TV	70–90
Human voice at 1 m	55–60
Background in private office	35–40
Quiet home	25–35
Threshold of hearing	20

Decibels are related to the response of the human ear, which responds logarithmically to sound. For example, a 10 dB increase in sound pressure level would be perceived as a doubling of the loudness. In practical situations, level changes of about 3 dB are just noticeable. It is very important to remember that decibels and similar acoustical quantities have properties different from more conventional units. Sound pressure levels, for example, cannot be added together as can kilogrammes. The combination of two noises with average levels of 60 dB does not give a sound pressure level of 120 dB, but 63 dB. In building acoustics, it is important to know the frequencies that make up a sound because different frequencies behave differently.

For most noise control work in buildings, the two most important acoustical properties of the materials and systems used are sound-absorption and sound transmission loss.

Noise from footsteps and other impacts is a common source of annoyance in buildings. Sound carries easily through the structural components of a building. If noise is a problem in the design then some quiet spaces can be zoned into the house by isolating them from areas of most activity, which may be the stairs or front hall.

One method for controlling the sound level within a room is through dissipation of the sound energy in absorptive materials. Sound is absorbed when a portion of the sound energy striking a surface is not reflected, but passes into the material and is converted into heat energy. Generally, higher frequencies are more easily absorbed than low frequencies. Materials that are good absorbers permit sound to pass through them relatively easily; this is why sound absorbers are generally not good sound barriers. They reduce the level of noise inside an enclosure. However, it requires large thicknesses or many passes for the sound energy to be significantly reduced. It is important to understand the difference between sound absorption and sound transmission loss. Materials that prevent the passage of sound are usually solid, fairly heavy and non-porous. A good sound absorber is 15 mm of glass fibre; a good sound barrier is 150 mm of poured concrete. Sound barrier materials are used to reduce the level of steady sound in a room, from a machine for example, and to reduce the reverberance. A solid concrete wall would be used to keep traffic noise out of a room. Solid masonry construction is quieter than timber frame. Make sure that having a quiet peaceful home is high on your wish list at the briefing stage and if you have further questions seek expert advice on sound-proofing your home.

PAINTS

Paints affect health in two main ways: they can be toxic and they can exacerbate humidity problems in a room. A good paint breathes and allows the wall to breathe. It is permeable to air and moisture movement and it allows moisture in the wall, plaster, render and/or joints behind it to evaporate out. The great advantage of a breathing paint is that it reduces the build up of moisture in a room that can be a major source of health problems. Many modern acrylic paints trap moisture in the walls and also impede the movement of heat between the room air and the wall. Traditional paints with a lime base allow the wall to breathe. Be careful when applying lime washes because lime is a caustic substance.

Some of the new water-based eco-paints also perform very well. They are made from substances such as resins, water, pigments, opacifiers, waxes and water. They should not contain solvents, white spirits, turpentine, VOCs, heavy metals such as lead, cadmium or mercury, or formaldehyde. Check the contents of the paints you are offered and if they contain such substances think again. Avoid all paints with any chromium in them, it can cause dermatitis, ulceration and cancer. One of the most polluting products in paints is titanium dioxide, excavated largely in Australia and processed often in China. Its production processes use chlorine and sulphuric acids, which produce greenhouse and ozone-depleting emissions. However, it is the most common of all paint colourings and it is very difficult to find a paint without it.

Also be aware of the fire risk of different paint types. Gloss paints, for instance, can perform badly in fires, exacerbating the ignition times of various products, while water-based paints present less fire risk. If in doubt make enquiries from manufacturers on the ignition times for different paints.

PETS

Around 40 per cent of children with asthma are sensitized to cat allergens. Only 1–15 per cent are sensitized to dog allergens. No pets should be acquired if children in the home have either asthma, eczema or hay fever. If a much-loved pet predates the child's arrival some doctors recommend that the pet be kept out of the bedroom or the house. Pets should be washed regularly, as should the house, to remove their allergens. Do not resort to strong drugs to make life with the pet tolerable. Find your pet a new, loving home and allow occasional visits.

PLANTS IN BUILDINGS

Plants modify the environment in buildings by three processes:

1 photosynthesis, during which a green plant converts CO_2 and water to sugars and oxygen for growth;
2 respiration, the reverse process to photosynthesis. This releases CO_2 back into the atmosphere and in so doing makes energy available for cell metabolism;
3 transpiration, which is the evaporative loss of water from a plant, a process that turns large amounts of energy into latent heat, so producing a net cooling effect from the plant.

Studies have found that plants can indeed not only reduce the CO_2 and the relative humidity of a room but also they can lower the temperature of the room. However, different plants perform very differently and their ability to modify the environment in a room will be affected by the amounts of solar radiation being intercepted by the plant. These properties of plants have already been tested in office environments where, particularly in air-conditioned offices, people often suffer from symptoms of 'Sick Building Syndrome', such as headaches, dry throats and eyes, lethargy, skin irritation and respiratory problems (thanks to Gaynor Coltman for much of this information). Pearson et al. (1994) conducted a range of studies of the impacts of plants in non-domestic buildings and found that there was great difference in the impacts of different plants. For instance, Yucca plants and, best of all, Ficus Benjamina produced significant drops in CO_2 levels in the offices. Hibiscus and Cordyline plants reduced the internal temperature of the space by several degrees centigrade and also increased the relative humidities in the spaces by 5–10 per cent during the middle of the working day. These effects were most significant when the plants were placed on the windowsills, so ensuring that the plants could take advantage of the most sunshine during the day. It is rather nice to think of putting a living machine in the form of plants into buildings to clean up the internal air quality. Any good horticulturalist should be able to help choose the best plants for a particular indoor air quality problem.

PLASTER

Gypsum plaster applied wet or dry has excellent absorption and diffusion properties for heat and moisture. It must be natural gypsum, not phosphogypsum, which is radioactive. When using plasterboard check that it does not contain adverse chemicals. Sand and lime plaster may also be used, possibly with a final coat of gypsum. Do not use cheaper cement-based plaster if possible as it is a poor insulator and is less permeable to heat and moisture. Mud plaster is also excellent and can be made more waterproof by mixing well-fired wood ash into the wet mix before kneading. It should be left for soaking and kneading for several days. Over all plasters an eco-paint should be used.

POLYURETHANE RESIN AND FOAM

When this is applied in situ high-efficiency personal respiratory protection is required – not just simple muslin pads. The problems of this material are for the construction worker and casual DIY person rather than the householder.

POLYVINYL CHLORIDE (PVC)

This polymer is widely used in construction and is known to be a carcinogen for animals and humans. In its early use, high levels of monomers were measured when the material was stored but more recent development of the technology has reduced their emissions substantially. The main concern is for the householder exposed to high levels of newly installed PVC in an airtight home for a long period of time. A number of fairly toxic substances are also combined with the PVC in the manufacture stage. Use timber windows if possible rather than PVC ones and avoid PVC furniture.

RADON

In 1985 an engineer at a Pennsylvania nuclear power plant under-went a routine radiation check at the plant entrance and set off the radiation alarm. The remarkable thing was that he did so upon entering the plant, not leaving it. After an investigation the Environmental Protection Agency recorded very high levels of the radioactive gas called Radon in the air in his home.

Radon is a naturally occurring radioactive gas that is tasteless, colourless and odourless. After its discovery in 1900 by the German chemist Ernest Dorn it became a popular health fad and was marketed in products such as chocolate, bread and toothpaste as a really healthy substance. As late as 1953 it was used in contraceptive jellies, blasting away at all those sperm in the cervix! Today its cell-killing properties are used in cancer treatment. Unfortunately it is also linked to many deaths from lung cancer, myeloid leukaemia, melanoma and DNA breakdown.

The amount of radon emitted into a home depends on the rocks on which the home is built and how much soil or other material covers the radon-emitting rocks. Sedimentary rocks, except for black shales and phosphate-rich rocks, are generally low in the uranium that emits the radon, and metamorphic rocks such as gneiss and schist are richer in uranium than marble, slate or quartz.

Radon has three main routes into the house:

1 groundwater pumped into wells;
2 construction materials such as blocks that emit radon;
3 gas that emanates up from the soil and rocks into basements and lower floors of houses.

Radon levels vary also with altitude (increasing radon with increasing altitude, owing to the thinner atmosphere and higher radiation levels) and with the time of year, readings usually being lower in summer when house windows are open.

In risk areas (check with your local council) radon concentrations can be reduced by placing an unperforated, impermeable membrane between the concrete lower floor slab and the ground, or a well-ventilated crawl space beneath the floor. Sealing all cracks and openings into the basement will prevent the entry of radon into the house and the use of exhaust ventilation can remove any that does. The warm air in a house will tend to draw radon into the home and care should be taken to avoid a build up of the gas in the house.

Radon is measured in grays or sieverts (Sv) and impacts on human health at the following levels:

- 5000 mSv – lethal to all exposed;
- 1000 mSv – vomiting, fatigue, induced abortions, sterility;
- 500 mSv – physiological damage;
- 5 mSv – US maximum permissible annual dose. Natural background radiation averages around 1.0–2.5 mSv per year. See U.S. Protection Agency, A Citizen's Guide to Radon and BRE (1999).

RUBBER

Historically, natural rubber has been used extensively in roofing sheeting, flooring materials and underlays. While in position they pose no threat to occupants. During fires their fumes are very toxic in confined spaces. The use of latex-based adhesives does require considerable care, the solvents in them may cause skin irritation and are dangerous; they should not be used in unventilated spaces and may cause serious health problems. Synthetic rubbers contain more carcinogens and their fumes are lethal in fires.

SECURITY AND PRIVACY

A sense of peace in a home is very important to the quality of life of the people who live there. It is awful to live in a house where you lie awake at night listening for the sound of the door or window being forced or of intruders in the house. A very important part of feeling peaceful is to feel secure at home. As with many aspects of design it may simply require a little thought at the design stage and the house, or housing estate, can be made much more secure through good design and perhaps a little extra investment. A number of websites deal with such issues, including http://www.securedbydesign.com.

6.2.
A, sketch axonometrics of the Oxford Ecohouse showing the wide variety of considerations that have to be taken into account at the outset of a building design, including considerations of A, storage of passive solar gain.

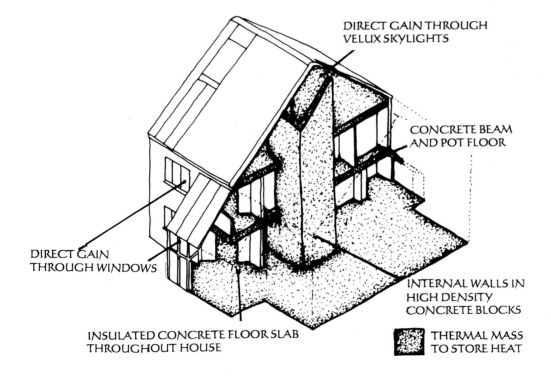

DIRECT GAIN THROUGH
VELUX SKYLIGHTS

CONCRETE BEAM
AND POT FLOOR

DIRECT GAIN
THROUGH WINDOWS

INTERNAL WALLS IN
HIGH DENSITY
CONCRETE BLOCKS

INSULATED CONCRETE FLOOR SLAB
THROUGHOUT HOUSE

THERMAL MASS
TO STORE HEAT

6.2.
B, natural light

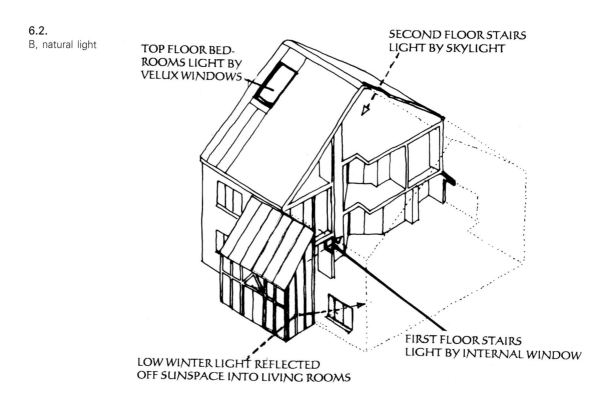

TOP FLOOR BED-
ROOMS LIGHT BY
VELUX WINDOWS

SECOND FLOOR STAIRS
LIGHT BY SKYLIGHT

FIRST FLOOR STAIRS
LIGHT BY INTERNAL WINDOW

LOW WINTER LIGHT REFLECTED
OFF SUNSPACE INTO LIVING ROOMS

6.2.
C, solar gain

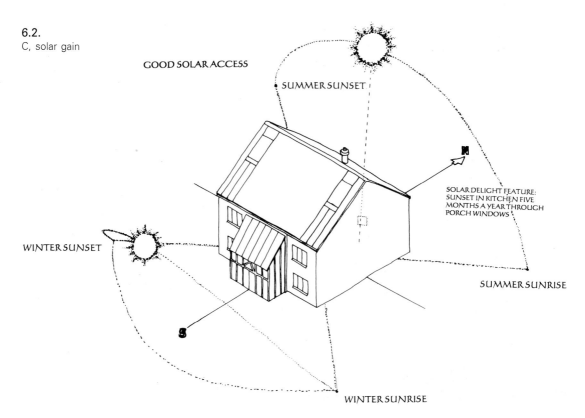

GOOD SOLAR ACCESS

SUMMER SUNSET

SOLAR DELIGHT FEATURE:
SUNSET IN KITCHEN FIVE
MONTHS A YEAR THROUGH
PORCH WINDOWS

WINTER SUNSET

SUMMER SUNRISE

WINTER SUNRISE

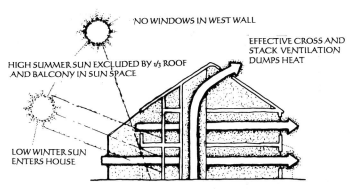

NO WINDOWS IN WEST WALL

EFFECTIVE CROSS AND STACK VENTILATION DUMPS HEAT

HIGH SUMMER SUN EXCLUDED BY 1/3 ROOF AND BALCONY IN SUN SPACE

LOW WINTER SUN ENTERS HOUSE

GARDEN WINDOWS OPENED WHEN WARM

SUNSPACE WINDOWS OPEN WHEN COOL

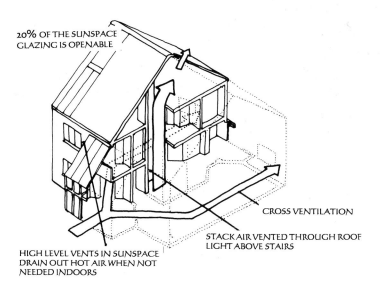

20% OF THE SUNSPACE GLAZING IS OPENABLE

CROSS VENTILATION

STACK AIR VENTED THROUGH ROOF LIGHT ABOVE STAIRS

HIGH LEVEL VENTS IN SUNSPACE DRAIN OUT HOT AIR WHEN NOT NEEDED INDOORS

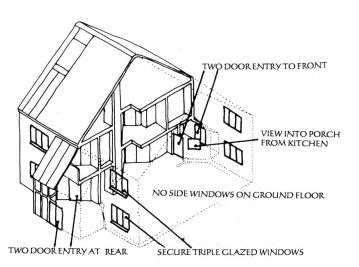

TWO DOOR ENTRY TO FRONT

VIEW INTO PORCH FROM KITCHEN

NO SIDE WINDOWS ON GROUND FLOOR

TWO DOOR ENTRY AT REAR

SECURE TRIPLE GLAZED WINDOWS

6.2.
D, avoiding overheating

6.2.
E, ventilation

6.2.
F, security.

Add to this the challenge of choosing safe, healthy and environmentally benign materials, and one begins to see what an amazing job the ordinary practising architect undertakes every day, without even having a brick laid on site.

Most robberies involve a rear-door entry and escapes are made easier when houses have pathways that are not overlooked. A first step is to design the whole housing development so that everyone in it feels a sense of ownership and responsibility for every part of the development. Clear and direct routes through an area are desirable but should not undermine the defensible space of neighbourhoods. Underused and lonely routes should be avoided. Crime is always easier to commit where offenders cannot be recognized so properties are usually entered from a door that is not overlooked. Communal areas should be designed to allow natural supervision. A sense of defensible space around a house is effective using real or symbolic barriers, i.e. change of road surface texture or colour, to encourage a feeling of territoriality among the residents. Houses can be sited in small clusters or interacting with each other. The front boundaries of properties should be well defined as private property. Strong, lockable gates should be included on the front build-line of a house in the worst areas. Avoid design features that allow climbing and access points. Utility meter cupboards should be located externally, as close as possible to the front building line and should be overlooked. Car parking should be located within view of residents and road users.

For front doors glazed panels, which should be laminated glass, will enable residents to see who is at the door and entries with two doors give added protection. Good locks should be specified on outer doors with entry by key only. Doors should have three hinges and, if the occupants still feel vulnerable, a chain latch device can be installed. Special care should be taken to protect French doors with adequate security devices and do not forget to put a good lock on the door between a house and garage too.

The position of ground-floor windows and those easily accessible above ground-floor level should be carefully thought out to get a balance between security and privacy. Opaque glass can be used to prevent view into some windows that are overlooked. Frames should be securely fixed into the wall. Double- and triple-glazed windows provide a much greater deterrent to intruders than single-glazed ones.

Security alarm systems come in two forms; they can either be tripped by motion in the house or be designed to go off when the perimeter of the house is broken into, with movement sensors by doors and windows. The problem with internal motion-sensor systems is that they only trigger once someone is already in the house, so perimeter systems are safer. It is better to consider security issues right at the outset of the design because the design of the building form can have a significant impact on how safe you feel in the house once it is built.

VOLATILE ORGANIC COMPOUNDS (VOCS) AND ORGANIC SOLVENTS

VOCs are found in many everyday materials in the home, including carpets, underlays, adhesives, caulks, sealants, thermal insulation materials, paints, coatings, varnishes, vinyl flooring, plywood, wallpaper, bituminous emulsions and water-proof membranes.

A wide range of VOCs can be emitted, including solvents or plasticizers used in the manufacture of building products. As the weather gets hotter so the rates of emission of VOCs increase. They can cause discomfort because of their smell and, worse, provide health hazards in the home and initiate symptoms of sick building syndrome.

Organic solvents include white spirit, which is found in many household products such as cleaning fluids, varnishes, glues and paints. Dry cleaned clothes also contain very high levels of solvent residue, so air them outside if possible before wearing and keep them in a nylon cover bag in the wardrobe. In large quantities organic solvents can cause dizziness and in smaller quantities they can exacerbate asthma problems. Avoid them by:

- using water-based eco-paints and varnishes that do not contain ammonia (see the section Paints);
- if you are using glue, paint strippers or varnishes, open the windows wide and ventilate the rooms really well;
- keep only small quantities of them in the house;
- if you have bedding dry cleaned, air it thoroughly before using.

WALLPAPERS

If you must use them, choose wallpaper that is made of paper and not a synthetic material such as vinyl. If you paint over it make sure you choose an eco-paint that does not contain solvents, vinyls or fungicides.

WOOD PRESERVATIVES

Many different chemicals are used to protect wood from insect or fungal decay and many are potentially very harmful. They should be handled with care and contact with skin should be avoided. Any product for protecting buildings from woodworm should be applied only by an expert. Avoid their use in enclosed spaces and do not use rooms where a smell of the chemical product lingers. Avoid storing these chemicals in rooms in the house.

7 PASSIVE SOLAR DESIGN

DESIGNING WITH THE SUN

The first step in creating comfort and thermal delight in buildings is to understand the relationship between the climate and our need for shelter. There is an enormous variation in climates that buildings experience. These can be at the scale of global climates, from the Arctic to the Sahara. They can be regional climates in the centre of a continent or on the seashore. They can be local climates on the sunny or the shady side of a hill or street. All will influence the way in which a building should be designed in relation to the sun.

The sun can be a friend or an enemy in buildings. Poor climatic design of buildings, all too often seen in 'modern' architecture, causes many buildings to overheat, even in temperate or cold climates where such problems traditionally never existed. The power of the sun should be understood and respected by good designers of well-designed, passive solar buildings in which the free energy of the sun is used to power the building but not allowed to interfere with the comfort and economy of the building's occupants.

The five things a designer needs to know for a good passive solar design are:

1 how strong the sun at the site is at different times of the year;
2 where the sun will be at different times of the year in relation to the site;
3 how much of the sun's heat a building will need, or not need, at different times of the year to enable the building occupants to be comfortable;
4 how much storage capacity the building should have in relation to the available solar gain at the site to meet those needs;
5 what the additional requirements are for controlling the heat gain from direct solar radiation, convection or conduction in a design and how they can be met by envelope performance, building form and ventilation.

There are a number of factors that influence the incidence, or strength, of solar radiation at the site including:

- the latitude of the site;
- the altitude and azimuth of the site;
- how much shade will be given by any obstacles that exist between the building and the site;
- the weather above the site.

AZIMUTH AND ALTITUDE OF THE SUN AT A SITE

The angle with which the sun strikes at a location is represented by the terms 'altitude' and 'azimuth'. Altitude is the vertical angle in the sky (sometimes referred to as height); azimuth is the horizontal direction from which it comes (also referred to as bearing). Altitude angles range from 0° (horizontal) to 90° (vertical: directly overhead). Azimuth is generally measured clockwise from north so that due east is 90°, south 180° and west 270° (or –90°).

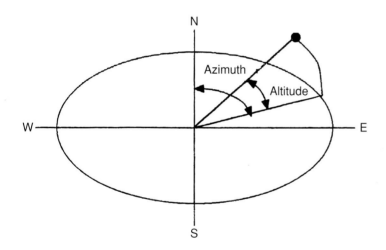

7.1.
The altitude and azimuth of the sun at a site (Andrew Bairstow).

Because the Earth revolves around the sun once a year, we have four seasons. The Earth's axis remains in a constant alignment in its rotation so twice a year the incoming solar radiation is perpendicular to the latitude of the equator and only once a year is it perpendicular to the tropics of Cancer and Capricorn, as shown in Figure 7.2.

The changing values of azimuth and altitude angles are predominantly a reflection of the changes in the relative positions of Earth and sun. These are governed by:

- the rotation of the Earth around the sun;
- the rotation of the Earth about its axis.

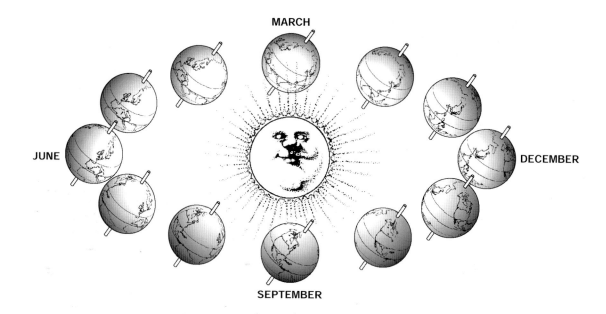

One of the simplest tools we can use for the derivation of altitude and azimuth angles is a graph using Cartesian coordinates (Figure 7.3). Figure 7.3 incorporates two types of line. Firstly, those representing the variation in altitude and azimuth over the period of a day (given for the 21st or 22nd day of each month). Secondly, those joining the points on the altitude–azimuth lines for a specific hour. Thus the solar angles for 11 a.m. on 21 March may be read off on the horizontal and vertical axes where these two lines meet (altitude 36°, azimuth 19°). Values for other days may be read by interpolating between these lines.

7.2.
The Earth revolves around the sun once a year, as well as around its own axis once a day (Mazria, 1979).

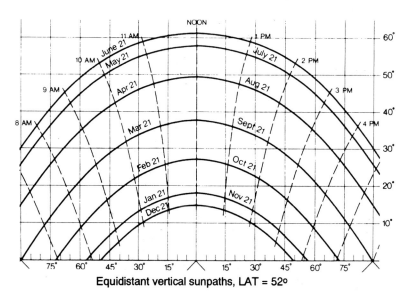

Equidistant vertical sunpaths, LAT = 52°

7.3.
Sunpath diagram for 52°N on cartesian axes (Andrew Bairstow).

It may appear that these are the only determinants of angular position, however we are actually concerned with the direction of the sun's radiation rather than the Earth–sun position. Also, radiation does not travel in an entirely straight line but is bent slightly by the Earth's atmosphere.

The distance between the Earth and the sun is approximately 150 million km, varying slightly through the year with the variation of the azimuth and altitude angles with time.

7.4.
The sun emits solar radiation that arrives at the Earth in the form of a number of different wavelengths ranging from infrared, the hot end, through the visible light spectrum to ultraviolet light (http://www.fridge.arch.uwa.edu.au/).

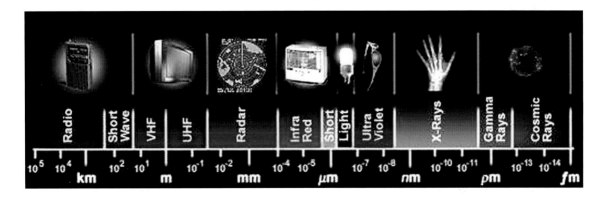

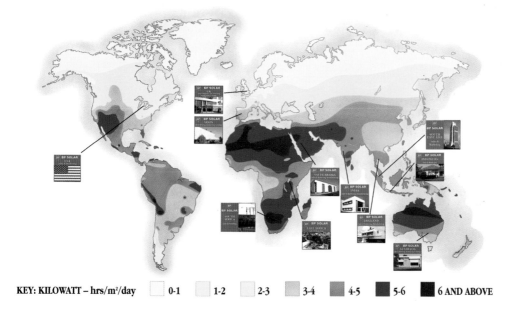

KEY: KILOWATT – hrs/m²/day   0-1   1-2   2-3   3-4   4-5   5-6   6 AND ABOVE

7.5.
Solar incidence at different latitudes. Closer to the equator, where the sun is more directly overhead, the sun is 'hotter' because the energy density is determined by the angle of incidence (Mazria, 1979).

All passive solar features involve the transmission of solar radiation through a protective glazing layer(s) on the sun side of a building, into a building space where it is absorbed and stored by thermal mass (for example thick masonry walls and floors or water-filled containers). The typical processes involved are:

- **collection** – to collect solar energy, double-glazed windows are used on the south-facing side of the house;
- **storage** – after the sun's energy has been collected, some heat is immediately used in the living spaces and some is stored for later use. The storage, called thermal mass, is usually built into the floors and/or interior walls. Mass is characterized by its ability to absorb heat, store it and release it slowly as the temperature inside the house falls. Concrete, stone, brick and water can be used as mass;
- **distribution** – heat stored in floors and walls is slowly released by radiation, convection and conduction. In a hybrid system, fans, vents and blowers may be used to distribute the heat.

There are several types of passive solar system that can be used in homes. The most common are direct gain, indirect gain and isolated gain.

SYSTEM COMPONENTS

There are three key components to all passive solar systems for heating:

- collector;
- mass;
- heated space.

DIRECT GAIN SYSTEMS

Direct gain systems are most commonly used in passive solar architecture. The roof, walls and floor are insulated to a high level. Solar radiation enters through the windows and is absorbed by the heavy material of the building. The whole building structure gradually collects and stores solar energy during the day. Heavy building materials provide thermal storage. The collected solar energy is gradually released at night when there is no solar gain.

Direct gain systems commonly utilize windows or skylights to allow solar radiation to directly enter zones to be heated. If the building is constructed of lightweight materials, mass may need to be added to the building interior to increase its heat storage capacity. The proportion of a building's heating needs that can be met by solar energy increases as the area of sun-facing glazing increases. Additional mass must therefore be used to reduce interior temperature swings and delay the release of solar energy into occupied spaces. While the mass that is directly illuminated by the incident energy, sunshine, is the most effective for energy storage, long-wave radiation exchanges and convective air currents

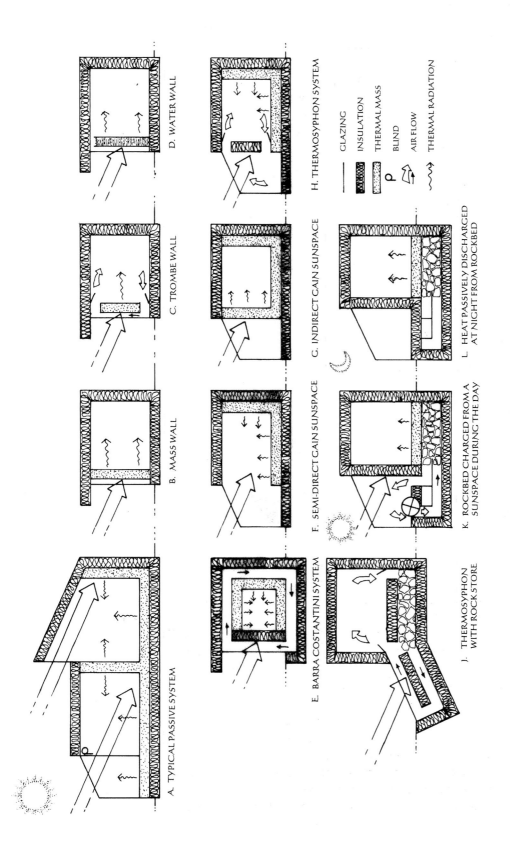

A. TYPICAL PASSIVE SYSTEM

B. MASS WALL

C. TROMBE WALL

D. WATER WALL

E. BARRA COSTANTINI SYSTEM

F. SEMI-DIRECT GAIN SUNSPACE

G. INDIRECT GAIN SUNSPACE

H. THERMOSYPHON SYSTEM

J. THERMOSYPHON WITH ROCK STORE

K. ROCKBED CHARGED FROM A SUNSPACE DURING THE DAY

L. HEAT PASSIVELY DISCHARGED AT NIGHT FROM ROCKBED

GLAZING
INSULATION
THERMAL MASS
BLIND
AIR FLOW
THERMAL RADIATION

7.6.

Passive solar systems: A, a typical passive solar system; B, mass wall system; C, Trombe wall system; D, water wall system; E, Barra Constantini system; F, semi-direct gain sunspace; G, indirect gain sunspace; H, thermosyphon system; J, thermosyphon system with rock bed; K, underfloor rock bed actively charged from a sunspace during the day; L, underfloor rock bed passively discharged by radiation and convection at night.

in the solar heated rooms allow non-illuminated mass to also provide effective energy storage.

THERMAL MASS

Thermal storage mass plays a vital role in the effective performance of direct gain buildings. Thermal mass is needed to store the solar energy for subsequent release into the interior space as heat. It is necessary because the sun's energy is not always emitted in phase with heating requirements. This is why the heat gained must be stored for future use, rather as a brick in a night storage radiator is heated at night using cheap energy and re-radiated as heat out into the space during the day. In passive solar systems the cheap energy comes from the sun.

Thermal mass in a building does two things, it reduces the peaks of the temperature swings (decrement factor) and shifts them to a later time than the air temperature peaks (time lag). The more mass there is, the lower and later the indoor air temperature peaks (see Figure 3.4).

As a general rule, buildings that contain very little thermal mass are unable to store heat for night time use; thus, only the daytime portion of the heat load can be met by solar gains, and overheating can be a serious problem if the solar gains are excessive. Furthermore, heat losses through an aperture whose effectiveness is impaired by insufficient thermal mass can exceed the useful solar gain. Lightly constructed stud-wall buildings with no floor slab (or a carpeted floor slab) are the worst offenders in this category.

The effectiveness of thermal storage mass in direct gain buildings depends on its thickness, surface area and thermal properties (volumetric heat capacity and thermal conductivity). The best materials are those that are capable of storing large quantities of heat (high volumetric heat capacity) and that can readily transport heat from the mass surface to the mass interior for storage and back again to the surface to meet the building's heat load (high thermal conductivity). As a general rule, mass surfaces should be relatively dark in colour compared with non-massive surfaces in order to promote preferential absorption of solar radiation by the thermal storage medium and, for optimal effectiveness, should be located in building zones that experience direct solar gains. Mass located in zones not directly illuminated by solar radiation entering through south-facing windows will be ineffective unless care is taken to ensure adequate free convective exchanges with directly heated zones or unless a forced-air distribution system is employed. In either case, remote thermal storage mass will be less effective than that located in direct gain zones.

Some rules that apply to high-density masonry (roughly 2000–2500 kg m^{-3}:

- Performance variations for mass thickness between 10 and 20 cm are small. The thickness may be reduced to 10 cm without incurring significant performance penalties. This generalization is independent of location, configuration and mass surface area.
- The range of mass thickness between 5 and 10 cm can be considered a transition region. In this region, performance penalties for reduced thickness are becoming significant but, in some cases, may be considered acceptable as design cost trade-offs.
- For mass thickness below 5 cm, performance falls off much more rapidly than in the transition region. Under most conditions it is not advisable to employ mass thickness of less than 5 cm for passive solar building assemblages.
- Lower-density masonry has a lower thermal conductivity and, therefore, has a smaller effective thickness for diurnal heat storage. The same heat storage capacity must, therefore, be achieved with material spread over a larger area.

INDIRECT GAIN SYSTEMS

These are passive thermal systems that collect and store the sun's energy. The storage is directly linked to the comfort of the interior space. In winter, energy is collected and stored to be released later in the day. This allows better control of indoor temperatures and heat distribution. In summer, the systems reverse their operation preventing overheating.

A building component can be heated by absorbing heat radiated from warmer components (walls, floors) or by convection from the surrounding air. The storage is influenced by the component temperature difference, location and emissivity. Indirect gain systems may be characterized by the placing of a sheet of glass in front of, and quite close to, a solid masonry wall or other building element that has a high thermal storage capacity. These systems are designed to capture and store a large fraction of the indirect radiation for subsequent release into the adjoining occupied space. When a wall is used for thermal energy storage in an indirect gain system it is called a Solar Wall or a Mass Wall.

A Mass Wall relies on conduction to transfer heat. For better thermal efficiency mass storage elements are located within a building, taking up some space that could be used for other things. Commonly a large wall is constructed on the sun-orientated face of the building. The sun warms up the mass of the wall during the day. After sunset, the stored heat is emitted for a period of time that depends on the thickness of the wall and its thermal characteristics. The glazing on the external face reduces heat loss to the outside. After sunset, the stored heat is emitted for a period of time that depends on the thickness of the wall and its thermal characteristics. The glazing on the external face reduces heat loss to the outside. There are several variations of the mass wall principle, as follows.

The Trombe-Michel wall

The Trombe-Michel wall (also known simply as the Trombe wall) is a variation of the mass wall principle. Here the mass wall has controllable vents at high and low levels to allow convective heat transfer. Solar radiation heats the wall. The inclusion of vent holes through the heated wall permits some convection to take place, as a means of circulating heat to the building during the day.

The water wall

The water wall is a variation of the mass wall where water replaces the solid wall. This is attractive in situations where a low-mass wall is required. Water-filled containers take the place of a masonry wall. Tall fibreglass tubes are often used. Water has a greater unit heat capacity than brick or cement so, for a given volume, a water wall works more efficiently than a solid wall.

The Barra-Constantini wall

The Barra-Constantini system uses lightweight glazed collectors mounted on a wall. The glazed wall panel acts as a heat collector. Ducts in the building circulate the warm air by natural convection. The heated air warms heavyweight ceilings, walls and floor.

ROOF STORAGE SYSTEMS
Roof storage systems are a variation of the storage wall principle for indirect heat gain. Moveable insulating decks can be situated over the roof (storage medium). These are used to cover the roof during winter nights and summer days.

SUNSPACES, SOLAR GREENHOUSES, CONSERVATORIES

One of the most attractive passive solar features is the use of an attached sunspace (also known as solar greenhouse or conservatory) to gather energy and pre-warm ventilation air for the parent house. An attached sunspace is a solar collector that is also a useful space capable of serving other building functions. Occupants not only have the benefit of lower energy bills but also it can be a most comfortable area of the house on sunny winter days. In winter they make an excellent place to store fire wood or, more importantly, to hang clothes to dry, saving on the need to have an electric clothes dryer. This also removes unhealthy moisture from the house during winter. They also provide a more secure double-door rear-entry to the house.

The sunspace performs its passive solar heating function by transmitting solar radiation through its glazing and absorbing it on its interior surfaces. The solar radiation is converted to heat upon absorption. Some of the heat is rapidly transferred by natural convection to the sunspace air and some of it flows into massive elements in the sunspace (floor, walls and water containers) to be returned later. The sunspace is, thus, a direct gain space in which heat is used directly to maintain a temperature suitable for its intended secondary function, such as occasional living space. But the primary purpose of the sunspace as a solar heating system is to deliver heat to the adjacent building spaces. This may be by conduction through a masonry common wall, by natural convection through openings (doors, windows or special vents) in the common wall. The sunspace system then resembles an indirect gain, thermal storage wall. The common wall may also be insulated so that heat transfer occurs only by natural convection through openings. Then the sunspace system is in the isolated gain category.

Some sunspaces are operated as hybrid systems in which a fan is used to transfer heated air from the sunspace to other building spaces or to storage. Sunspaces have become very popular building features, both for the attractive space they provide and for their ability to deliver solar heat to adjacent spaces. The solar heating performance can indeed be very effective, often exceeding the performance of any other passive solar system occupying the same area of south-facing wall. The sunspace designed in the Bariloche Solar house is a typical case of hybrid sunspace.

The sunspace works in many different ways. On sunny days it collects solar energy that can be transferred into the house. At night and during cold days it acts as a buffer, reducing heat loss. If the sunspace itself is heated or cooled by other means to normal comfort levels with auxiliary energy, the buffering characteristic of this isolated-gain passive solar system is lost. In this case, the benefits of solar heating are lost, and the total energy consumption of such a sunspace may be almost as much as that of the house itself. Sunspaces are popular because of their spatial and architectural qualities.

Semi-direct gain sunspace

This system incorporates a double-glazing system where the sun's rays absorbed by the internal surfaces of the sunspace and living areas are transferred into heat, with a marginal contribution of convective and storage effects.

Adjustment may be critical. Automatic control of openings and screens is expensive and not always reliable. Solar radiation can easily overheat the sunspace and the interiors. This can occur during sunny days of intermediate seasons (spring and autumn). Overheating must be reduced by ventilating the sunspace and, if necessary, part roofing the space.

Indirect gain sunspaces

In this energy storage system a massive wall is placed between the sunspace and the building interior. The wall absorbs solar radiation and converts it into heat, gradually transferring the heat by conduction into the building mass and the interior spaces of the house. This sunspace configuration works well in winter. It can be difficult in summer when radiation levels are high and the collecting surfaces are not sufficiently shaded. Moveable shading devices on the wall's external surface can avoid overheating. Such shading devices can find use throughout the year.

Storage walls have a high thermal capacity and a low conductivity rate. A means of controlling the high winter heat losses of the system, particularly during the night, is by using insulating shading devices on the external surface of the wall. Double glazing further reduces heat losses from the sunspace.

Thermosyphon sunspaces

Thermosyphon sunspaces absorb solar radiation, heat the sunspace air and increase the internal temperature of the sunspace. The sunspace air is transferred to the building interior using automatic shutters or valves at the top of the background wall. Valves at the bottom of the wall recover the cooler interior air. A convective effect is produced, exploiting the thermal stratification in the sunspace and optimizing the heat gain in the house. A regulation system simultaneously controls the sunspace and interior room temperature levels, and allows air to flow from the sunspace to the interior rooms at appropriate temperatures. The main problem with any automatic system is that it presumes that there is one comfort temperature whereas, in reality over the year, people find very different temperatures comfortable. With a manual system that relies on opening top and bottom windows the house occupants can decide for themselves if the sunspace air is sufficiently warm to be used in the house.

Hybrid systems

The term 'hybrid systems' is used to describe ideas and techniques that are not easily described by 'active' or 'passive' systems. Hybrid systems usually contain some active and some passive system characteristics. An example is the thermosyphon system. These passive solar convection systems use the buoyancy effects of heated fluids to transfer solar heat into building spaces or storage by convection. When they use mechanical assistance (pumps, ventilators), they are called hybrid systems. Air or water is the most common heat transfer medium of passive and active solar energy.

One type of hybrid convection system is the thermosyphon air panel. It uses flat-plate collectors mounted on the outside of an exterior sun-facing wall to heat air. Automatic vents located at the top and bottom of the panel allow hot air to flow directly into the space to be heated. The hot vented air is replaced at the bottom of the panel by cooler interior air.

ROCK BEDS

An effective and favourite hybrid application is the use of a rock bed in conjunction with a passive solar building. In many applications the rock bed is located beneath the source of hot air and thus natural convection cannot be used to transfer the heat. In this case a fan is normally employed, resulting in that part of the system technically being an active element. Rock beds can be used effectively in situations where there is an excess of energy in the form of air that is heated above the comfort level. It is desirable to remove this overheated air for three reasons:

1 to reduce the air temperature in the space and improve thermal comfort;
2 to store the heat thus removed for later retrieval; and
3 to redistribute heat from the upper south part of the building where hot air tends to accumulate into the lower north part of the building that normally tends to run colder.

Imbalances in temperature in the building, which might be created by the passive elements operating alone, can be corrected.

It requires very careful design to remove heat from the rock bed in the form of warm air. This air is then blown into the space to be heated. The air temperatures that can be achieved are low, and the flow rates that would be required are therefore high. The effect of a high air-velocity at low temperatures may be cold and unpleasant. A much preferred approach is to remove the heat from the rock beds by means of radiation and convection from the rock bed container surface. In this case the rock bed is thermally coupled to the space that is to be heated, rather than being thermally isolated from it. A convenient approach that is often used is to place the rock bed underneath the floor of the building, although it would also be possible to place it behind one of the walls. Distribution of heat from the rock bed to the space is entirely passive. The floor temperature or wall surface temperature will only be a few degrees above the room temperature. If the installation is properly designed the net result will be a very comfortable situation, heating the house slowly from a large radiant panel.

Experience with under floor rock beds has been very favourable. Comfort is greatly improved by keeping the floor temperatures 3–6°C above what they normally would be. By increasing surface temperatures and thus increasing the mean radiant temperature within the space, the air temperatures can be reduced and energy savings that are even greater than the actual amount of heat released from the rock bed can be realized.

A technique that is suitable for residential applications is to divide the building into two thermal zones and accept fairly large temperature swings in one zone in order to stabilize temperatures in the other. In Zone 1, which is a direct-gain space, large temperature swings can be expected because there is a large excess of heat. Heat storage is in the mass separating the zones and in the floor of Zone 1. Depending on the size of Zone 1, its enclosing mass surface area and the glazing area, temperature swings of 12°C to 17°C can be anticipated. However, such swings can be completely acceptable (and perhaps even advantageous). Uses of such a space could be as a greenhouse, sun room, atrium, conservatory, transit area, vestibule or as an airlock entry. A principal advantage of this approach is the reduced temperature swings in Zone 2. This is a buffered space protected from the extremes of Zone 1 by the time delay and heat capacity effects of the mass wall. With a little care in the design, one can phase the time of heat arrival into Zone 2 so as to maintain an almost constant temperature. An example of the effective use of the two-zone approach is the house in Bariloche.

7.7.
The newly installed rock bed at
Fuentes House in Bariloche,
showing the concrete walls of
the bed and the heat supply and
extract ducts.

TIPS: ROCK BED SIZING

1a The rock bed volume should be 0.6 m^3 m^{-2} of sun-orientated
glazing.

1b The air flow rate through the rock bed should be 0.03 m^3 s^{-1} for
each m^2 of sun-orientated glazing.

2a More than one-third of the net heat should not be transferred
out of the space to the bed rock.

2b The working bed temperature drop should be one-half of the
working air drop.

3 The air velocity should not exceed 3.5 m s^{-1} and 10 ac h^{-1}.

4a The pressure drop across the rock bed should be in the region
40–75 Pa.

4b The pressure drop across the ductwork should be less than
one-fifth of the rock bed pressure drop.

HOW MUCH DOES IT COST TO USE PASSIVE SOLAR SYSTEMS?

Today's passive solar heating systems can typically provide 30–70 per cent of residential heating requirements, depending upon the size of the passive solar system, the level of energy conservation being employed in the building envelope and the local climate. At the upper end of this range the use of specialized components is often required. These performance results are typical for single-family residential buildings, and small commercial and institutional buildings.

The economics of some passive solar techniques are difficult to determine because many features are part of the fabric of the house itself. Take the sunspace for example. The building owner may want to build a sunspace into the house. The capital cost for energy savings would then be zero. Where economic analysis is performed including capital costs, passive solar techniques often offer a good payback.

Passive solar systems have demonstrated their competitiveness with conventional fuels by saving 30 per cent and more of a building's space heating requirements in some climates, though their effectiveness varies from site to site.

7.8.
Graph showing the temperatures in different spaces of the Oxford Ecohouse. These show that the temperatures in the sunspace can fluctuate considerably while the internal rooms maintain a much more steady temperature because of good design and high levels of thermal mass.

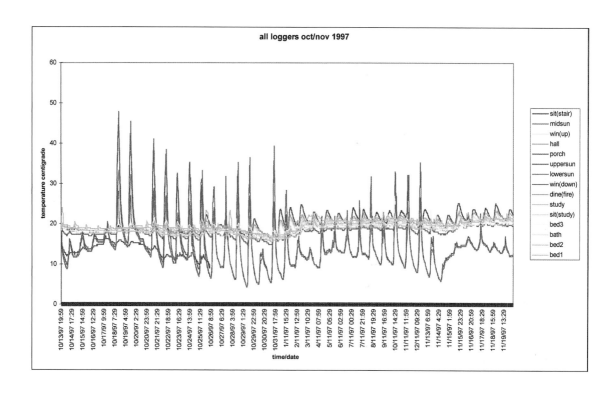

GOOD PUBLICATIONS ON PASSIVE SOLAR DESIGN

Balcomb, J. D. (1979). 'Designing fan forced rock beds'. *Solar Age*, November, p. 44.

Balcomb, J. D. (1980). Passive Solar Design Handbook. Volume I. National Technical Information Service, 5285 Port Royal Road, Springfield, VA 22161, USA.

Balcomb, J. D. (1982). Passive Solar Design Handbook. Volume II. National Technical Information Service, 5285 Port Royal Road, Springfield, VA 22161, USA.

Balcomb, J. D. (1983). Conservation and Passive Solar Guidelines for New Mexico. Los Alamos National Laboratory, Report No. LA-UR-83-1452,USA.

Balcomb, J. D. (1983). Heat Storage and Distribution Inside Passive Solar Buildings. Los Alamos National Laboratory, Report No. LA-9684-MS, USA.

Building Research Station Digest 41 (1970). HMSO, London.

Curtis, E. J. W. (1974). 'Solar energy applications in architecture'. *Low Temperature Solar Collection of Solar Energy in the UK*. UK Branch of the International Solar Energy Society, London.

Duffie, J. A. and Beckman, W. A. (1977). Solar Engineering of Thermal Processes. Wiley Interscience, New York and London.

Hastings, S. R. (ed.) (1995). *Solar Low Energy Houses*. International Energy Agency Task 13. James & James (Science Publishers) Ltd, London.

Hestens, A. G., Hastings, S. R. and Saxhof, B. (eds) (1997). *Solar Energy Houses*, Strategies, Technologies and Examples. IEA, James & James (Science Publishers) Ltd, London.

Kreith, F. and Kreider, J. F. (1975). *Solar Heating and Cooling*. McGraw Hill, Washington, DC.

Lebens, R. (1980). *Passive Solar Heating Design*. Applied Science Publishers.

Lebens, R. (1983). 'Documents of Second European Passive Solar Competition, 1982'. In *Passive Solar Architecture in Europe 2*. The Architectural Press, London.

Littler, J. G. F. and Thomas, R. B. (1984). *Design with Energy, The Conservation and Use of Energy in Buildings*. Cambridge Urban and Architectural Studies, Cambridge University Press, UK.

Mazria, E. (1979). *The Passive Solar Energy Book*. Rodale Press, Emmaus.

McFarland, R. D. and Stromberg, P. (1980). *Passive Solar Design Handbook*. Editors Balcomb, J. D. and Anderson, B., Department of Energy, Washington, DC.

Olgyay, V. (1963). *Design with Climate*. Princeton University Press, Princeton, NJ.

Page, J. K. (1976). *Solar Energy – a UK Assessment*. UK-ISES (International Solar Energy Society).

Wright, D. (1978). *Natural Solar Architecture*. van Nostrand Reinhold.

8 PHOTOVOLTAICS

WHAT ARE PHOTOVOLTAICS?

Photovoltaic cells convert sunlight directly into electrical energy. The electricity they produce is DC (direct current) and can either be:

- used directly as DC power;
- converted to AC (alternating current) power; or
- stored for later use.

The basic element of a photovoltaic system is the solar cell that is made of a semiconductor material, typically silicon. There are no moving parts in a solar cell, its operation is environmentally benign and, if the device is correctly encapsulated against the environment, there is nothing that will wear out.

Because sunlight is universally available, photovoltaic devices have many additional benefits that make them not only usable, but of great value, to people around the world. They are the future and by 2020, when the conventional oil supplies begin to really dry up, they will be everywhere.

Photovoltaic (PV) systems are modular and so their electrical power output can be engineered for virtually any application, from low-powered wristwatches, calculators, remote telecommunications systems and small battery-chargers to huge centralized power stations generating energy only from the sun. PV systems can be incrementally built up with successive additions of panels easily accommodated, unlike more conventional approaches to generating energy such as fossil- or nuclear-fuel stations, which must be multimegawatt plants to be economically feasible.

HOW PV CELLS WORK
Although PV cells come in a variety of forms, the most common structure is a sandwich of semiconductor materials into which a large-area diode, or p-n junction, has been formed. In the presence of light an electric charge is generated across the junction between the two materials to create a charge similar to that between an anode and a cathode. The fabrication processes for making the cells tend to be traditional semiconductor processes, the same as those used to make microchips, by 'doping' the silicon with different elements using diffusion and ion implantation of the elements into the silicon. The electrical current is transferred from the cell through a grid of metal contacts on the front of the cell that does not impede the sunlight from entering the silicon of the cell. A contact on the back of the cell completes the circuit and an antireflection coating minimizes the amount of sunlight reflected back out from the silicon, so maximizing the light used to generate electricity, as shown in Figure 8.1.

Photovoltaic panels have been commercially available since the mid-1970s and were initially used to power some early demonstration buildings, such as those that are still working at the Centre for Alternative Technology in Wales. However, it was the 1990s that saw the first great boom in PV buildings around the world. Germany, the USA and Japan lead the way with Germany already having over 10 000 PV buildings operational and 100 000 planned by 2010. The USA has a Million Solar Roof Programme in place for the same date and Japan, a country that has scarce fossil fuel

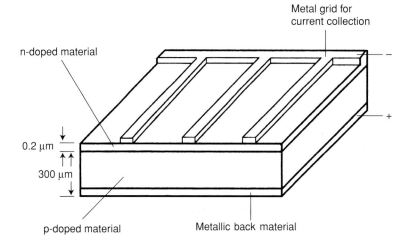

8.1.
Cross-section of a solar cell.

Metal grid for current collection

n-doped material

0.2 μm

300 μm

p-doped material

Metallic back material

reserves, aims to have 70 000 PV buildings installed by 2010. Some countries are way behind in the solar race. Britain had only around ten integrated PV roofs built by 2000.

WHAT IS A PV SYSTEM?

PV cells are typically grouped together in a module for ease of use. A PV system consists of one or more PV modules, which convert sunlight directly into electricity, and a range of other system components that may include an AC/DC inverter, back-up source of energy, battery to store the electricity until it is needed, battery charger, control centre, mounting structures and miscellaneous wires and fuses.

WARNING
Direct current (DC) electricity is much more dangerous to handle than alternating current (AC) electricity, which is typically used for all household appliances. This is because there is no break in the flow of a DC current and, if you grab hold of an exposed DC wire, the muscles in the hand and arm contract and it is very difficult to let the wire go again. Great care should always be taken when dealing with DC electricity.

WHY PV IN BUILDINGS?

Even in cloudy, northern latitudes, PV panels can generate sufficient power to meet all, or part of, the electricity demand of a building. The Oxford Ecohouse, for example, incorporates 48 PV panels on the roof that generate enough energy to lower the household electricity bills by 70 per cent.

The flexibility of PV enables its use in many building products, such as solar roof tiles, curtain walls and decorative screens, which can directly replace conventional materials in the building fabric. These products serve the same structural and weather protection purposes as their traditional alternatives but offer the additional benefit of generating the power to run the house.

WHAT'S GREEN ABOUT PV?

The electricity produced by every square metre of PV can effectively displace emissions of more than two tonnes of CO_2 to the atmosphere over its lifetime. Few now dispute that CO_2 emissions can continue to increase at current rates without dire consequences, such as global warming. Wider use of PV power in buildings can help to reduce such environmental impacts of buildings that are responsible for generating over 50 per cent of all emissions of greenhouse gases globally.

Let us use the Oxford Ecohouse as an example. In order to calculate the environmental impacts of the PV system it is necessary to know the UK energy generation conversion values, the amount of CO_2 released into the atmosphere for every unit of energy delivered to a house. It has been estimated that an average energy conversion efficiency for thermal electricity generation plants in the UK is around 37 per cent. This results from an electricity mix generated from 65 per cent coal, 15 per cent gas, 22 per cent nuclear and 9 per cent oil. For the PV manufacture assumptions see Energy Technology Support Unit (1996).

Based on the monitored data, the PV system produces 3093 kWh per year, that is around 77 000 kWh in its 25-year lifecycle.

The Oxford Ecohouse PV system avoids the release of 1.84 tonnes CO_2 per year. These values can be extrapolated to give the avoided emissions in the case of a massive programme of installing PV on residential building. A system one-eighth of the size of the Oxford Ecohouse would avoid 230 kg CO_2 per annum.

Table 8.1. Environmental impacts of PV manufacture.

Burden	PV (monocrystalline silicon)	UK electricity generation mix
Energy (kWhth kWh^{-1})	0.38	0.61
CO_2 (g kWh^{-1})	74	672
SO_2 (g kWh^{-1})	0.43	4.20
NO_x (g kWh^{-1})	0.21	2.10
Particles (g kWh^{-1})	0.03	0.32

Table 8.2. Environmental benefits of PV systems

Energy and emissions	PV (monocrystalline silicon)	UK electricity generation mix	Total avoided emissions (in 25 years)
Energy (GWhth)	29	47	18
CO_2 (tonnes)	6	52	46
SO_2 (tonnes)	0.03	0.32	0.29
NO_x (tonnes)	0.02	0.16	0.15
Particles (tonnes)	0.002	0.02	0.02

WHAT WILL IT COST TO USE PV IN BUILDINGS?

Solar electric PV systems are now an economic and viable technology in many parts of the world. More than that, they are a sensible economic investment for ordinary householders who want to begin to protect themselves from future changes related to energy and the climate. They should begin to consider the following.

- Climate change is driving the move towards carbon taxes that will make energy more expensive.
- Fossil fuel depletion will push up oil and gas prices. We have around 40 years of conventional oil reserves left and around 60 years of gas left. By 2020 oil and gas scarcity will make future energy prices very unpredictable.
- Climate change may well make heating and cooling our houses more expensive in energy terms as the climate gets warmer or colder.
- Security of energy supply. PV systems can provide electricity during conventionally produced electricity blackouts resulting from poor supply conditions or bad weather. There are already a range of uses for which a secure energy supply should be essential; these include, water pumping, electric garage doors and gates, lift safety systems, smoke and fire alarms, emergency lighting and security systems, computer UPS systems and communications systems.

Investment by people now in their high-earning years in energy efficiency and renewable energy will pay dividends in, say, 10 years when they retire and must inevitably face higher energy bills they are less able to afford. Anyone with a £500-a-year electricity bill would be wise to envisage at least a doubling of electricity costs in 10–15 years time. Will your pension cover £1000 a year for one bill?

Costs of installing PV systems today vary significantly according to the technology used, the application and the efficiency of the system. Capital costs of PV panels are broadly similar to prestige cladding materials, ranging from £350 to £750 per m^2 depending on the technology and its detail. Prices are expected to fall significantly over the next decade as demand grows and the PV industry achieves economies of scale in production. In parts of Germany and the USA (Sacramento municipality) the cost of installing one watt of PV power into a home has already fallen to around £2.75 per watt, which is very low compared with current UK estimates of £9 per watt for an installed system. In those countries, the impact of early investment in the technology by national and local government bodies has paid dividends for consumers while people in countries such as the UK have to suffer because of short-sighted investment policies in this, one of the most important technologies of the twenty-first century.

Your own investment decision should also take account of the marginal cost of the PV system (capital cost minus the cost of the alternative material) and power output. PV systems are not difficult to install and, if maintained properly (annual washing), have an expected lifetime of around 25 years.

What is certain is that today PVs should be an essential feature of a real ecohouse, because ecohouses are setting the agenda for building in a changing climate and helping to prepare society for the 'post-fossil fuel age'. PVs have a very important role to play, like solar hot water systems, in the new agenda for buildings; the earliest PV 'pioneers' in the twentieth century often installed PV systems for ecological reasons rather than economic ones. However, in some farsighted cities, such as Aachen in Germany, a green tariff on every electricity bill enabled the local utility company to pay every householder with a PV roof DM2 per kW exported. This enables householders to pay back the installation costs in around 10 years for systems that will last for 20 years.

But it is no use placing a PV system on an energy-profligate building and expecting it to solve the problems wrought by the building designer. This is just throwing good money after bad. Forget PV for air-conditioned buildings for the foreseeable future. PVs will work well with low-speed fan-assisted passive cooling systems, such as earth-coupling and the night cooling of buildings (see Chapter 5 on ventilation). To use PVs properly the building electricity loads should be as low as possible, and only then should the system be designed to meet part or all of those loads to give you a magic building that generates its own energy.

ADVANTAGES OF PHOTOVOLTAICS AS A DOMESTIC SOURCE OF ENERGY

- It is a clean green energy source. It produces minimal CO_2, NO_x or SO_2 emissions.
- The silicon PV panels are non-toxic in production.
- The energy payback (the time for the PV to produce as much energy as is required for manufacture) is 2–5 years, while the working life of a PV panel can be well over 20 years.
- Energy is generated on site so there are very few losses in transport, unlike remotely generated supplies relying on long supply lines.
- It is reliable. Panel warranties are now typically for 20 years.
- They are silent.

- They are low maintenance. Once installed they will simply require their surfaces cleaning, especially in dusty environments.
- They can provide power in locations remote from the grid.
- PVs are a transportable technology and can be moved between buildings.
- They can provide power during blackouts.

THE PROCESS OF DESIGNING A PV SYSTEM

There are many different types of PV systems available with different features, capabilities and costs. It is important to follow the steps described here to get the PV system that fulfils your own particular needs.

Step 1. Choose your system

What type of system do you require? Do you want batteries? Do you want to power DC or AC equipment? Do you want to grid-connect the system to use the National Grid as a store so you can export the excess during the day when you are out at work and then draw in electricity from the grid when you need it at night? This is called a grid-connected system. Do you want to use PV and wind to cover all your power needs? The different system types are outlined in Figures 8.2 to 8.5.

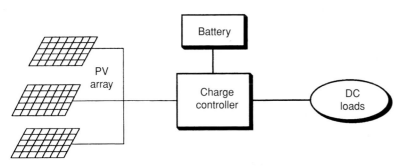

8.2.
Stand-alone DC system.

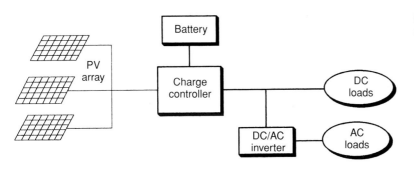

8.3.
Stand-alone DC/AC system.

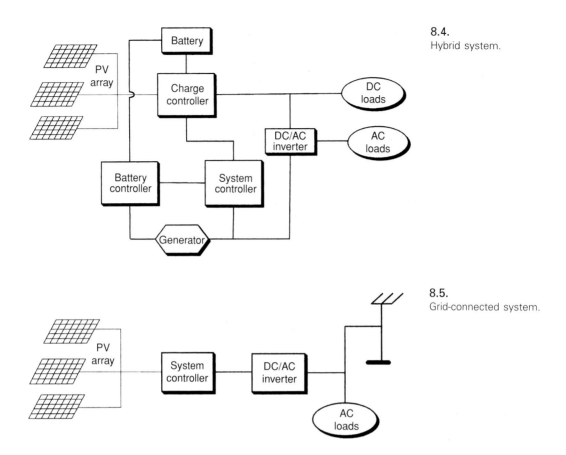

8.4.
Hybrid system.

8.5.
Grid-connected system.

Step 2. Determining the average daily sunlight hours at your site

At the meteorological station closest to your site, look up the average sunlight hours for each month of the year at your site location. Determine the Minimum Monthly Sunlight Hours at your location for the months that you expect to be using the PV system.

The Minimum Monthly Sunlight Hours is the number of sunlight hours for the month with the lowest average number of sunshine hours. It is generally best not to consider the winter months among your months of use when determining Minimum Monthly Sunlight Hours, even if you are installing a PV system in a permanent residence, as the number of sunlight hours in these four months tend to be low. Unless a very large system is purchased, some form of back-up power, such as a generator or a grid supply, will be needed for the four winter months. The most frequently used approach is to design a PV system for a full-time residence to operate optimally for the eight months of the year when the sunlight hours are greatest. The month with the lowest number of sunlight hours out of the eight brightest months is selected as the Minimum Monthly Sunlight Hours month.

If you definitely do not wish to have a back-up source of energy, or the sunlight hours at your location during the four winter months are high, you can use all 12 months to determine your Minimum Monthly Sunlight Hours.

Divide Minimum Monthly Sunlight Hours by 30 to get the Average Daily Sunlight Hours.

> **Note:** Keep in mind that the PV array should be located so that it receives the most hours of sunlight. Avoid obstacles, such as trees or buildings, blocking direct sunlight.

Step 3. Determining your total daily energy load

Make an Energy Budget Chart as shown below. Begin in the 'Electrical loads' column by listing all the devices in your home that consume electricity. Make sure to include everything from the hairdryer to power tools.

Energy Budget Chart sample

Electrical loads	Rated watts	Hours/day	Daily watt hours
Colour television	330	3	990
Microwave oven	1000	0.25	250
Vacuum cleaner	800	0.75	600

The rated wattage of each device can be determined either by using the list of power ratings of common tools and appliances given in Table 8.3 to find the typical power consumption values for common appliances, or by looking at the back panel of each device to determine its specific rated wattage. If the rated wattage is not listed on the device, it can be calculated by multiplying the amps (A) of the device by the voltage (Vac for alternating current and Vdc for direct current).

> Example: if a blender is 2.45 A and 220 Vac, multiply 2.45 A by 220 Vac to get 540 rated watts.

Table 8.3 does not provide rated wattages for refrigerators or freezers. This is because they cycle on and off automatically thus making it difficult to estimate the hours per day they are operated. Instead, the table provides the typical daily consumption in watt-hours. Alternatively, if your refrigerator or freezer has an EnerGuide

Table 8.3. Typical power ratings (in watts) of common tools and appliances*

Blender	700	Lighting (60 watt bulb)	60
Block heater	500	Lighting (fluorescent, 15 cm single ended)	9
Bubble jet computer printer	40	Lighting (fluorescent, 1.2 m double ended)	50
Clock	2	Microwave oven	1000
Coffee maker	900	Radio, solid state	5
Computer/monitor	75	Satellite receiver	25
Deep well pump	1350	Saw, circular	950
Washing machine (automatic)	500	Saw, jig	400
Fan (portable)	115	Vacuum cleaner	800
Stereo	30	Furnace fan motor	350
Television (black and white)	200	Gas clothes dryer	250
Television (colour)	330	Hair dryer	1500
Toaster	1150	Hand drill	300
Iron	1000	VCR	120
Laser printer	700	Dishwasher (excluding hot water)	1300

Typical daily electricity consumption (watt-hours) of refrigerators and freezers (pre-1993 and later)

Freezer (15 cu. ft)	2500	1600
Freezer (15 cu. ft, frost-free)	3600	2500
Refrigerator/freezer (12 cu. ft)	2500	1600
Refrigerator/freezer (12 cu. ft, frost-free)	3100	1700

*Please note these are approximate values only. For exact numbers, consult the appliance, its accompanying instructions or the product supplier.

label on the front indicating the number of kilowatt hours (kWh) the appliance uses per year, or per month, you can use this to calculate Daily Watt Hours. Divide the kWh value by 365, if it provides the yearly number, or by 30 if it provides the monthly number. Multiply the result by 1000 to determine the Daily Watt Hours of the appliance.

> Example: if a refrigerator has an EnerGuide rating of 768 kWh year^{-1}, divide by 365 to get 2.104 kWh day^{-1}. Multiply 2.104 kWh day^{-1} by 1000 to get 2104 Daily Watt Hours.

Add the Daily Watt Hours for all devices to determine Total Daily Watt Hours. Divide the Total Daily Watt Hours by an assumed Inverter Efficiency Factor (see box) of 0.85 to get the Total Daily Load.

> PV cells generate direct current (DC) and the PV system batteries store electricity as DC. Most common appliances, however, require alternating current (AC). As a result, an inverter is needed to convert DC to AC power. Some power will be lost in the conversion, as inverters are on average 75–90 per cent efficient. For the purposes of this calculation, assume that your Inverter Efficiency Factor is 85 per cent.

Total Daily Watt Hours divided by Inverter Efficiency Factor of 0.85 equals Total Daily Load (Watt Hours).

Table 8.4. Typical daily watt hour consumption at hourly intervals in winter

Load type	Watts	Min/hr	6	7	8	9	10	11	12	13	14	15	16	17	18	19	20	21	22	23	24	1	2	3	4	5
Hoover	500	30						250	(once per week only)																	
Bed radio	7	60		7																						
Food mixer	100	10							17																	
Fridge	200	10	33	33	33	33	33	33	33	33	33	33	33	33	33	33	33	33	33	33	33	33	33	33	33	33
Kitchen radio	7	60			7				7					7	7											
Fax	250	4					17				17				17				17							
Game Boy	5	60		5								5														
Stereo	200	0																								
TV	64	60		64								64			64	64	64	64								
Water pump	50	20																								
Fire system	50	60	50	50	50	50	50	50	50	50	50	50	50	50	50	50	50	50	50	50	50	50	50	50	50	50
Boiler	10	60	10	10	10	10	10	10	10	10	10	10	10	10	10	10	10	10	10	10	10	10	10	10	10	10
Dishwash m/c	1200	20									400															
Iron	500	60							500																	
Kettle	0	20			0		0				0		0			0										
Toaster	800	10			133																					
Washing machine	500	20		167																						
1st landing lamp	10	60	10	10	10										10	10	10	10	10	10	10	10	10	10	10	10
Bathroom lamp	10	30			5								5					5								
Main bed lamp	13	60		13											13				13							
Top landing lamp	10	60				10									10	10	10									
WC & wash lamp	10	30				5		5					5					5								
Kitchen/diner lamp	13	60		13							13	13	13	13	13	13	13	13	13							
Study lamp	12	60				12	12	12	12	12	12	12	12	12	12	12	12	12	12							
Totals	4521	790	103	377	270	105	122	360	629	105	505	135	192	130	158	224	202	197	210	128	120	103	103	103	103	103

Step 4. Determining the load profile

Once you have made the calculation for the total load draw up a graph of when those loads will be used. Put hours of the day along the y axis and the loads on the x axis and plot the hours when each piece of equipment will be used and the wattage for that hour. When you have done this, it can be totalled to make a graph of your projected daily electricity use profile. A load profile such as this will have two characteristics that are important when designing your system:

- The typical **peak load** of your house. This is the most electricity you will need at one time.
- The typical **base load** of your house. This is the energy that is needed constantly for items such as your refrigerator and fax machine.

Now you have your first load table sit down and go through it and practice a little of:

- **Load reducing or shaving**. Get rid of all the electric appliances you think you can do without, can replace with lower-energy items or simply have less of them. This may include items such as an extra light in the hall, or four side lamps in the sitting room. Change all the light bulbs to low energy ones and decide if now

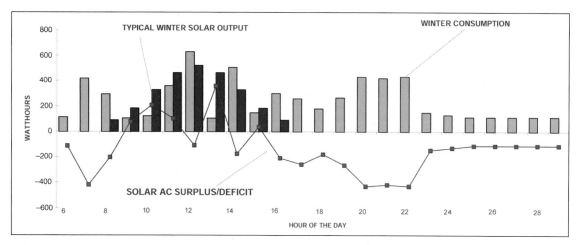

8.6.
Load profile of the Oxford Ecohouse showing the electricity generated in winter.

is the right time to buy a new low-energy washing machine or fridge. These actions will reduce the total load of the system as well as its peaks and base load.

- **Load shifting**. Where previously you had the washing machine and the iron on at the same time start a new habit of doing only one high-energy chore at a time. You will find that your peaks are often significantly reduced, although the base load and the total load will not change. This is why in Germany it has been found that the people who use their PV electricity in homes best are retired people who are at home all day and can manage their chores to reduce peak loads.

REDUCING THE LOADS IN YOUR HOME

Reducing loads by low-energy lighting

- Do not over-light the house. Use a careful selection of background lighting, task lighting and feature lighting to make sure that you are not wasting money and energy. Light the floor where you want to walk, not the ceiling, and the desk top where you want to study, not the walls.
- Use lower general lighting levels.
- Avoid dark lampshades that absorb the light.
- Always use energy-saving fluorescent bulbs that cost more to buy but work out cheaper in the long run. Traditional filament bulbs convert around three-quarters of the energy they consume into heat and not light, which may be good in winter but is silly in summer.

Reducing loads by careful selection of equipment

- **Freezers**. Get rid of the second freezer and use a chest freezer if possible, not an upright one from which the cold air tumbles when opened. Look for low-energy-rated freezers, with thick insulation around them and good door seals; these can be checked with a bit of paper at the shop. If the paper slips easily out of the door when it is cold the door is poorly sealed. Damaged door seals should be replaced in older models. Do not site them next to heat sources such as cookers or tumble dryers. Allow air to circulate freely around the heat exchange element so heat does not build up around it.
- **Fridges**. Check very carefully for the energy rating of the fridge and buy the lowest energy fridge you can afford.
- **Fridges and freezers using CFCs and HCFCs** should be avoided. Look out for hydrocarbon-based models using butane or propane that neither destroy the ozone nor produce greenhouse gasses.
- **Disposal of old fridges** and freezers should be arranged through the local council if possible as they may have schemes to prevent the release of dangerous gases into the atmosphere.
- **Washing machines** should use a hot water supply not heat their own water, which uses a lot of electricity. They should also have a half- or low-load setting to save wasting electricity on a small wash. Side-fill machines use 50–70 per cent of the water used by top-fill machines and are lower in their energy consumption as well. Buy a machine with a high spin-speed of, say, 3000 r.p.m. as these take less time to spin clothes than the 1000/1500 r.p.m. machines.
- **Spin dryers**, where adequate, are much more electrically efficient than tumble dryers, which dry the clothes with electrically generated heat. New EU spin dryers will dry clothes to a 35 per cent moisture content rather than the older models that retained up to 80 per cent moisture content.
- **Tumble dryers**. Gas models dry up to twice as fast as electric models and running costs are around one-third of those for an electric dryer. Good temperature and time controls are essential to prevent overdrying of the clothes. Much better still, build a winter drying space for clothes and save yourself lots of money in the long run.
- **TVs, radios, music players, microwaves, computers**. Check the plated energy rating on the machine before you buy it and choose a low-energy model.
- **Kettles**. Choose gas for your kettle, if possible, because of the lower CO_2 emissions for this fuel, taking into account that the kettle will more often be boiled at night and in winter than in summer so the PV electricity may not be used to heat it.

See Centre for Alternative Technology, 1995 and ECI (Environmental Change Institute), 2000.

Step 5. Sizing the PV system

The optimum size of a system depends on a number of external factors, such as cost of the system, the available budget, government subsidies, the energy payback policy of the local utility company and the amount of PV energy to be used in the building. Here are some options.

- **A base load array**. This generates over the year typically just above your building base load for, in the UK, around 9 out of the 12 months of the year. A base load system will rarely export anything to the grid and can be designed never to do so. However, the base load of the building can work out to be a substantial proportion of your annual electricity consumption and, in countries such as Britain, the price paid for exported electricity is very low. Generating and using as much of your own electricity as possible is currently the most economic way of using PVs in the UK. A typical nominal size for such system is 500 Wp.
- **A Stand-alone system**. For stand-alone systems batteries are used to store the energy from when it is generated until it is needed. The total array output should exceed the domestic loads as calculated previously.
- **Zero energy house grid-connected supply**. The total annual domestic load should be equal to, or less than, the array output over 12 months.

Step 6. Choosing the modules

There are six important considerations when choosing a panel type:

1 power output required of the panel;
2 size of the available roof for panels;
3 what colour you wish the roof to be;
4 the appearance/texture of the panels;
5 what size panels fit into the architectural image of the building;
6 the desired durability of the panels.

The required PV array area (A_{PV} in units of m^2) can be calculated from the chosen nominal PV power using the formula

$$A_{PV} = \frac{P_{PV}}{\eta_{PV}}$$

where P_{PV} (KW) is the nominal power of the PV array and η_{PV} (fraction) is the efficiency of the modules.

The amount of electricity to be generated from your roof as a fraction of the domestic load is dealt with above. If you know the peak wattage required then a review of the panel outputs will determine how many of each of the different types you will need to achieve the necessary wattage for the system. If you choose the lower efficiency, and cheaper, amorphous silicon panels then you will need more roof area to support them. If you want to use the more efficient polycrystalline modules then less roof space is required; the most efficient panels, monocrystalline modules, not only require less space to generate the same wattage but are also more durable.

Table 8.5. Choosing the module type

Module type	Appearance	Colour	Efficiencies (%)	Durability (years)
Monocrystalline	Module composed of circular polygonal shapes	Blue black	10–16	25–30
Polycrystalline	Sparkling crystal chaotic surface	Blue black	8–12	20–25
Amorphous	Matt dull surface	Red, green, orange, blue black, yellow	4–8	15–20

When designing the array, do think carefully about the colour of the cover strips that will link each module. Are the cover strips to be the same colour as the modules or form part of the elevational features of the building with contrasting colours? Panel manufacturers may be able to produce special modules for your building cut to specification. Discuss this with manufacturers. In the development of elevations of new solar buildings the rhythms of the solar panels can form a strong design feature. Use the modules to influence the size of other features in the house, such as doors and windows. Line up, both horizontally and vertically, the proportions of the solar features to introduce balance and harmony into the appearance of the house.

Step 7. Choosing the inverter

An inverter is needed in most residential PV systems to convert the DC power from the array to AC power. The size of inverter needed will depend on whether the system is stand-alone or self-sufficient and on whether base loads will be matched. For the latter option, an inverter that matches the PV and the voltage DC output is needed. In some cases a system with 'AC Modules' may be designed by using the new single-module inverters.

HOW TO CHOOSE AND SIZE AN INVERTER

The optimum power ratio (inverter/PV module power) for a given inverter depends mainly on how much sunshine hits the array at what times of day. This gives the shape of the irradiance distribution, which is determined by local climate and the slope of the PV generator.

The selection of an inverter for a **grid-connected system** generally only takes into account the relative size of the inverter to the PV array. Since PV generators very rarely deliver their full nominal power, results obtained from the monitoring of the German 1000-roof programme show that inverters can be undersized with respect to the PV generator to reduce cost. Output power rating of the inverter for an optimally orientated PV roof generator should be 80–90 per cent of the generator rating. For vertical facades, even values around 50–60 per cent are sufficient.

In **a stand-alone system** the size of the array and the inverter must be matched to the watts required for the largest load that will be operated on the system at one time. To calculate this first determine the device with the largest rated wattage of all of the devices to be operated on the system. This could, for example, be the microwave, which can have a rated wattage of up to 1500 W. If you plan to be very careful about only running one device at a time, then you will need an inverter large enough to handle the largest load. If you think that there is a possibility that you will be running more than one load at a time, then you must have an inverter large enough to handle the largest possible combination of loads.

An example of how to size a stand-alone system is as follows: assume a deep well pump (1350 W) and a washing machine (500 W) are operated at the same time, and there is a possibility that other items, such as the stereo (30 W) and a light (60 W) will also be in use. You will need an inverter that can handle 1350 + 500 + 30 + 60 = 1940 W at once. The larger the inverter needed, the more expensive it will be. You might want to try to schedule certain operations so that you do not have too many devices operating at once. This will reduce the largest potential combined wattage that the inverter is required to handle.

Once you have determined your largest combined potential wattage, select an inverter wattage and find a suitably priced corresponding inverter. Be sure to choose an inverter wattage that exceeds your largest potential combined load. Select a price on the basis of the range given.

IMPORTANT ATTRIBUTES OF INVERTERS
- Maximum output;
- Rated power factor;
- Input/output voltages;
- Number of phases;
- Frequency: 50 Hz
- Protective apparatus:
  - protection against overvoltage and overcurrent;
  - protection against islanding;
  - fulfil local utility company's requirement;
- Performance aptitudes:
  - high efficiency;
  - low harmonic distortion;
  - maximum power point capabilities;
  - low self-consumption.

Step 8. Installing the system

Photovoltaic modules generate the most electricity when they face the sun directly. Integration of PV modules in a building surface may influence the size of the module used, the size of the array, its inclination and its direction.

Several mounting techniques are available with a number of roof structures, styles and designs. Installing the array requires mechanically mounting the modules, attaching the electrical interconnections and checking the performance of the completed array source circuits. All phases of array installation involve working with electrically active components, which can be particularly dangerous with DC supplies. Each option for mounting and wiring an array will present its own special installation requirements.

HOW TO GET THE ANGLE RIGHT FOR YOUR PV ARRAY

This issue depends on the design concept of the particular PV system:

1 If the intention is to maximize the PV output over the year, the PV modules need to be inclined with an angle equal to the site's latitude (from the horizontal).
2 If the intention is to maximize the PV production during winter, the PV modules have to be inclined 10° higher than in case 1 to catch the low winter sun.
3 If the intention is to extend the 'solar' season (where PV production is at its maximum), the PV modules have to be inclined 10° less than in case 1.

Useful design and construction tips for people wanting to install PV

- Make sure everyone is clear who has responsibility for wiring and wire sizing of the:
  - module wires to the string connectors;
  - string connectors to the inverter;
  - inverter to the domestic loads board;
  - electric loads board to the house export and import meters.
- Make sure you comply with the lightening protection requirements of the local utility company. The inverter should always be earthed.
- Ensure that you have a simple way of determining which module on the roof is attached to which wire coming in through the ceiling for later testing in case of module failure.
- Make sure that nowhere in the system does the wiring come into contact with damp or condensation, for instance adjacent to uninsulated cold water pipes.
- Locating the inverter near the DC array minimizes power losses.
- The mains supply should always be disconnected before the PV supply before working on the system and vice versa for reconnection.
- Make sure that the mounting frame is weather sealed.

OTHER WAYS OF USING PHOTOVOLTAICS IN HOUSES

- PV shades;
- PV tiles;
- Translucent PVs, e.g. over sunspaces.

SYSTEM MAINTENANCE AND CHECKS
- Examine the PV array structure for signs of deterioration.
- Check PV modules for cracked cells and glazing.
- Check wiring for rodent damage, indicated by cracking or fraying of wires.
- Check electrical leakage to ground.

CASE STUDY: THE OXFORD ECOHOUSE

In order to take readers through the process of building a PV array on their own house the example of the Oxford Ecohouse will be used to describe from experience what is involved in building a PV array, designed by Energy Equipment Testing Services in Cardiff.

The Oxford Ecohouse is owned by and was designed by Sue Roaf and David Woods, with David Olivier who provided some of the theoretical input into its detailed design.

The design for the PV array on the house was influenced by the following considerations:

- the PV source must be integrated in the house both technically and architecturally;
- the PV array should have a peak power output of 4 kW to ensure that the house generated more electricity than it used over the year, based on the results of the load analysis done by Alan Dichler (1994);
- the system should operate in a normal grid-connected mode, with the grid providing back-up power when needed, for instance at night, in winter or in poor weather.

The house is situated in an area that receives approximately 4.0 peak sun hours in summer, but only 0.6 peak sun hours in winter (Dichler, 1994). The variation in output from winter to summer is therefore significant and the array size was specified to achieve a reasonable level of diurnal autonomy for the house for around nine months of the year.

During the summer months, energy surpluses were predicted to be around 12 kWh per day, which is greater than the house energy deficit in winter. The house is therefore expected to have a positive energy balance. It was known by the time of design of the PV system what the foot print of the house was and the slope of the south-facing back roof was designed to be optimal for the generation of electricity from the PV array at 39° from the horizontal. The project was worked up with Rod Scott from BP Solar who helped in choosing the best panels on the market, the robust, monocrystalline, high-efficiency BP Saturn 585 cells.

The 48 modules required a flat roof size of 6.8 m × 5 m and would be arranged in four vertical rows of 12 modules in each row. Thus, with the optimal angle of tilt and these dimensions now available, we could fix the ridge height of the building just above the top PV panel, so deciding the slope of the north-facing roof.

Description of the system

Electrical power is generated in three strings of BP585 panels. Each string consists of 16 panels, giving nameplate figures as follows:

- open circuit voltage, $V_{oc} = 16 \times 22.03 \text{ V} = 353 \text{ V}$;
- short circuit current, $I_{sc} = 3 \times 5.00 \text{ A} = 15.00 \text{ A}$;
- at maximum power $V = 288 \text{ V}$ and $I = 14.16 \text{ A}$.

The panels are connected in series in the ducting and each string is then linked to its own 6-A miniature circuit breaker (MCB) connector, two of which are in the ducting in the upper bedroom and the third is situated in the small attic space above the stairwell. The three positive and three negative cables then run through the insulated roof space in a conduit and emerge in the small attic room containing the boiler system. The six cables pass through a junction box on the left-hand side of the inverter and then the power flows to a DC power metering box consisting of Hall effect transducers, current shunt and a voltage divider. DC energy is also measured here. From there the DC power flows into the SMA 5 kW inverter and emerges as 240 V AC. It then flows through an AC power metering box where AC current, voltage and energy are measured. It then continues down through the main concrete-block ducting to the house distribution board. A third power metering box, where house power demand, energy and current are monitored, is situated here. This box also contains an MCB for inverter isolation. A simplified block diagram of the PV system is shown in Figure 8.7.

Because DC electricity is dangerous, the DC wiring has to have a series of control switches and fuses so that each string from the modules can either be cut out or turned off if the system fails on the roof or the inverter side of the system. In addition, the main cable to the domestic load board is fused to ensure that if the system fails on its house or grid side the roof will be isolated

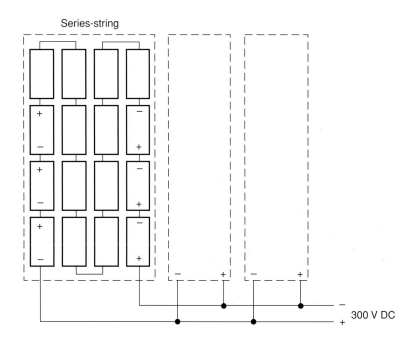

8.7.
Single line schematic of the Oxford PV installation.

immediately. One problem we did suffer is surges in the grid voltage that shut the inverter down temporarily; in countries such as Germany this is not such a problem.

Electricity from the inverter is cabled down to the domestic load board and then either used in the house or exported, via an export meter, to the grid. In Oxford, for each 1 kW of electricity exported the local electricity company pays around £0.02 and for every 1 kW imported to the house via the standard import meter £0.05 approximately is paid to the company. This is not the case in many areas where common practices include:

- **Net metering**. A single meter is employed that either runs backwards or forwards and the same price is paid for imported as well as exported electricity. This practice is widely used in the USA and some European countries, such as Germany and Austria among others.
- **Rate-based incentive schemes** where a premium price is paid for exported PV electricity to help the homeowner pay back the cost of the PV installation. These were pioneered in the German city of Aachen where a nominal percentage increase on every electricity bill helped the local utility company pay back around DM2 for every 1 kW exported. On a house such as the Oxford Ecohouse this would produce an income of around £2000 a year, which would pay off the installation of the 4 kWp system at current prices over 10 years. Not bad for a system that could, and may, last for 30 years before it needs replacing.

However, in the UK there has been no such support for the PV industry. On the contrary, as you will see below, the solar pioneers have had to work hard to stay in business.

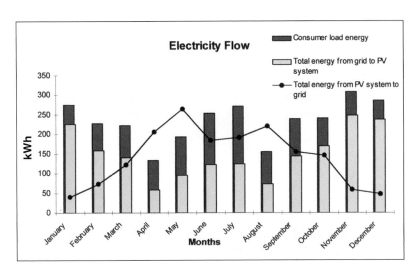

8.8.
Graphs showing PV consumed in the Oxford Ecohouse, exported and imported on different days of each season and the annual inputs and outputs.

Building integration

Aluminium edge frames were incorporated onto the individual panels. To prepare the roof for the mounting of the array a layer of very flat 18-mm marine plywood was laid flat and level over the conventional rafters of the roof. Onto this was laid a layer of good-grade bitumen felt sarking, that could withstand the high temperatures that develop behind the modules. On to this was built a grid work of aluminium extruded profiles designed with a lower foot screwed to the sarking with drip channels on each side to carry any water that penetrates around the sides of the panels down the roof. Some 7.5 mm above this is a lateral shelf onto which the modules are laid, providing an air gap behind the array.

At each module rise a horizontal carrier bar was fixed to the vertical frames to support the lower and upper ends of the panel. Once put into position within this aluminium structure the panels were then secured with aluminium cover strips, screwed onto the centre of the extruded profiles. This is very similar to methods used to construct some conservatory glazing systems.

At the base of the vertical channels up behind the module a strip of plastic netting was placed to prevent birds, vermin and large insects from travelling up behind the modules. At the apex

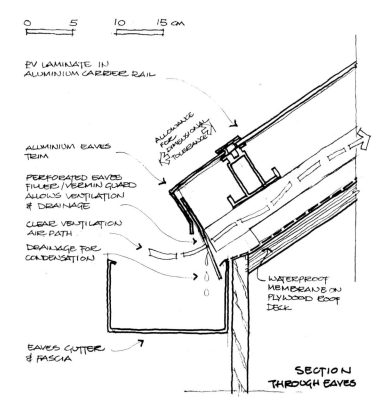

PV LAMINATE IN
ALUMINIUM CARRIER RAIL

ALLOWANCE FOR DIMENSIONAL TOLERANCE

ALUMINIUM EAVES TRIM

PERFORATED EAVES FILLER / VERMIN GUARD ALLOWS VENTILATION & DRAINAGE

CLEAR VENTILATION AIR PATH

DRAINAGE FOR CONDENSATION

WATERPROOF MEMBRANE ON PLYWOOD ROOF DECK

EAVES GUTTER & FASCIA

SECTION THROUGH EAVES

0 5 10 15 cm

8.9.
Section through the eaves of the Oxford Ecohouse PV system (Jeremy Dain).

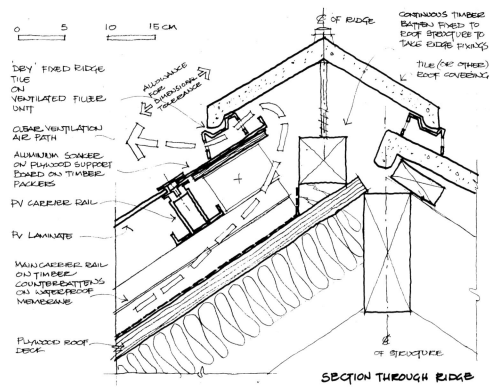

0   5   10   15 CM

CONTINUOUS TIMBER
BATTEN FIXED TO
ROOF STRUCTURE TO
TAKE RIDGE FIXINGS

TILE (OR OTHER)
ROOF COVERING

€ OF RIDGE

'DRY' FIXED RIDGE
TILE
ON
VENTILATED FILLER
UNIT

ALLOWANCE
FOR
DIMENSIONAL
TOLERANCE

CLEAR VENTILATION
AIR PATH

ALUMINIUM SOAKER
ON PLYWOOD SUPPORT
BOARD ON TIMBER
PACKERS

PV CARRIER RAIL

PV LAMINATE

MAIN CARRIER RAIL
ON TIMBER
COUNTER-BATTENS
ON WATERPROOF
MEMBRANE

PLYWOOD ROOF
DECK

€
OF STRUCTURE

SECTION THROUGH RIDGE

8.10.
Section through the ridge of the Oxford Ecohouse PV system (Jeremy Dain).

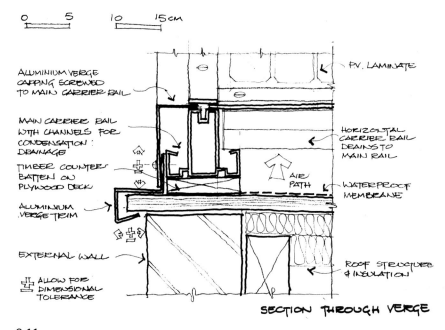

0   5   10   15 CM

ALUMINIUM VERGE
CAPPING SCREWED
TO MAIN CARRIER RAIL

PV. LAMINATE

MAIN CARRIER RAIL
WITH CHANNELS FOR
CONDENSATION
DRAINAGE

HORIZONTAL
CARRIER RAIL
DRAINS TO
MAIN RAIL

TIMBER COUNTER
BATTEN ON
PLYWOOD DECK

AIR
PATH

WATERPROOF
MEMBRANE

ALUMINIUM
VERGE TRIM

EXTERNAL WALL

ALLOW FOR
DIMENSIONAL
TOLERANCE

ROOF STRUCTURE
& INSULATION

SECTION THROUGH VERGE

8.11.
Section through the verge of the Oxford Ecohouse PV system (Jeremy Dain).

of the roof this ventilation channel was vented out through a row of ventilated ridge tiles from Redland Roofing Ltd, which had been tested in their UK laboratories. This ensured that air could enter the space behind the array, move up and be exhausted from the roof ridge. This is important because as the modules get hotter and rise above Standard Test Condition temperature of 25°C, they become less efficient, so moving air behind them is one way to cool them and increase their output. In more recent projects the heat from behind the panels is used as pre-heat air for the heating systems in winter. This can be seen from the OM solar house at Hamamatsu (case study 6) and the Findhorn house (case study 2), where PV heat is used to heat rocks in an interseasonal heat store.

Running between the vertical support bars were plastic conduits through which the wires from each panel were run up to the apex of the roof. The apex of the roof was chosen, rather than the eaves, as the 'higher the drier' rule seems to apply and electricity and water do not mix well. Taking the wires to the apex of the roof also shortens the wire runs from the array to the inverter.

Below the apex of the roof, holes were drilled through the roof structure and plastic conduits placed in them through which the module wires were introduced into a plastic duct beneath the ceiling of the second-floor rooms. Plastic was always used for ducts as it is safer than metal for this purpose.

The modules in the array were wired together in three strings for connection to the inverter. The PV system working voltage was chosen to be nominally 300 V DC for good inverter efficiency (Dichler, 1994). This can present a hazard to installation and maintenance personnel and identifies a training requirement for installers and users.

The inverter is in a closed area on the second floor at the same level as the PV modules. The area has a fire-resistant lining, a smoke detector and is vented. This location ensures that module output cables are kept relatively short with protection devices in place. Standard wiring and wiring installation protocols were used.

During the construction of the array the main building problems encountered concerned the ridge, skylight, verge and eave details. In any PV project the responsibility for the construction of the joining details, where the array meets the building, should be made clear and clarification is required early on as to which contractor should build these and supply the necessary materials. A site manager with day-to-day control of the project would be a valuable asset.

Planning and Building Regulations approval

The local utility company Southern Electric agreed to accept documentation from SMA showing that the inverter had been tested to demonstrate that, in practice under laboratory test conditions, the inverter meets the theoretical performance specified in its attached literature. This was seen as a more practical method of ensuring that the stringent and expensive European G59 requirements are met than site testing the system under variable frequency and voltage conditions.

The Planning Department of Oxford City Council was very interested and helpful during the process of gaining Planning Approval and at no time showed any bias against the use of photovoltaics on the house. This was helped by the fact that the south roof faces away from the road and would only be slightly visible from neighbouring properties. However, the willingness of the Planning Officer to accept a picture of what PVs look like, rather than a sample, demonstrated an open and constructive approach to their use.

Building Control

The Building Control Officer at Oxford City Council requested details of the construction of the photovoltaic roof and a photograph of what the panels would look like. The Officer also requested proof that the PV roof would not be too heavy and that it complied with fire regulations requirements. The BP585 monocrystalline panels weigh 7.5 kg per panel, which is 530 mm × 1138 mm in size. The north-facing roof of the house was covered in Redland Concrete tiles, which weigh 76 kg m^{-2} so the PVs weighed significantly less.

Fire rating

BP Solar had never had their panels fire rated and therefore could not supply any information on the fire rating of their array. A number of fire experts were contacted who helped us demonstrate that the roof did indeed meet the fire requirements in the following way.

Under the relevant UK Fire Test Code BS476, Part 3 (1958) the roof had to achieve an AA, AB or AC rating because the house is less than 6 m away from the adjacent buildings, so qualifying for these ratings under Table 5 of the Approved Documents B, section 14. The first A of the rating relates to fire penetration: A is a one-hour resistance to fire penetration and is mandatory. This is to

HOW TO CATCH THE SUN

Dr Susan Roaf's house faces south so that the
solar panels on the roof get the maximum sun
throughout the year

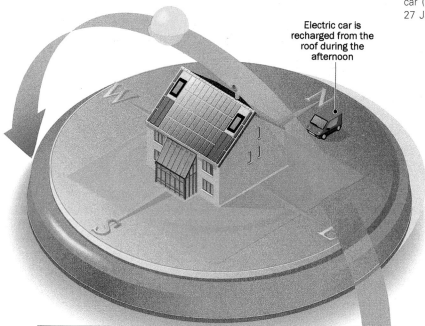

Electric car is
recharged from the
roof during the
afternoon

8.12.
The excess electricity generated
on sunny days is also used to
power a Kewet El Set electric
car (Tony Garrett @ *The Times*,
27 January, 1996).

THE ZERO-ENERGY EQUATION

First six months' results

**Photovoltaic
panels on
roof produce
up to 4kw**

**1,016 units of
gas and
electricity
imported**

**Solar
water-heating
panels**

862 units of
electricity to
top up supply
at night

154 units of
gas for boiler
to top up hot
water in winter

Electricity for
cooking, lighting
and charging the
electric car

Hot water for
washing and
heating

**1,082 units of electricity
exported to the National
Grid**

Careful use of power
means that more
electricity has been
exported than imported
in the first six months

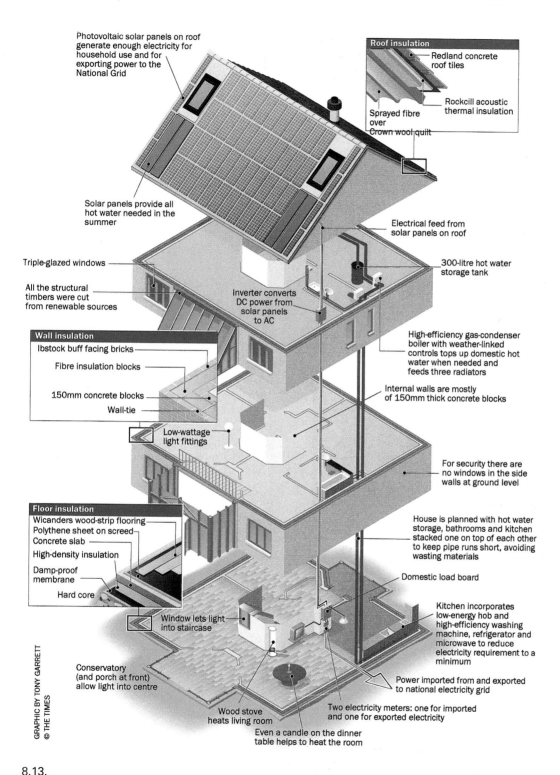

Photovoltaic solar panels on roof generate enough electricity for household use and for exporting power to the National Grid

Roof insulation
Redland concrete roof tiles

Rockcill acoustic thermal insulation

Sprayed fibre over Crown wool quilt

Solar panels provide all hot water needed in the summer

Electrical feed from solar panels on roof

Triple-glazed windows

300-litre hot water storage tank

All the structural timbers were cut from renewable sources

Inverter converts DC power from solar panels to AC

High-efficiency gas-condenser boiler with weather-linked controls tops up domestic hot water when needed and feeds three radiators

Wall insulation
Ibstock buff facing bricks

Fibre insulation blocks

150mm concrete blocks

Wall-tie

Low-wattage light fittings

Internal walls are mostly of 150mm thick concrete blocks

For security there are no windows in the side walls at ground level

Floor insulation
Wicanders wood-strip flooring
Polythene sheet on screed
Concrete slab
High-density insulation
Damp-proof membrane
Hard core

House is planned with hot water storage, bathrooms and kitchen stacked one on top of each other to keep pipe runs short, avoiding wasting materials

Domestic load board

Window lets light into staircase

Kitchen incorporates low-energy hob and high-efficiency washing machine, refrigerator and microwave to reduce electricity requirement to a minimum

Conservatory (and porch at front) allow light into centre

Power imported from and exported to national electricity grid

Wood stove heats living room

Two electricity meters: one for imported and one for exported electricity

Even a candle on the dinner table helps to heat the room

GRAPHIC BY TONY GARRETT
© THE TIMES

8.13.
Axonometric of the Oxford Ecohouse showing the arrangement of the PV integrated roof and system (drawn by Tony Garrett, and published in *The Times* newspaper, London, on 27 January 1996).

mitigate against threat to life of the building inhabitants and protection of the building from burning firebrands landing on the roof. In the case of the roof of the Ecohouse, it is formed of sheer glass between aluminium glazing bars on which a brand would not rest for long enough to cause significant fire penetration. The second letter, A, B or C, relates to fire spread. The Velux windows in the roof achieve AA rating owing to their 4-mm-thick surface glass which, by dint of its thickness, is deemed to have a one-hour rating. The PV modules also meet the A rating fire spread requirement owing to their upper surface being enclosed in 3-mm toughened high-transmission glass (92 per cent), which has a higher fire rating than a single pane of glass and retains its structural integrity in temperatures of up to 1000°C, at which point it becomes friable. The key fire risk to a roof is posed by a burning firebrand from an adjacent building on fire. Wood ignites at around 400–450°C and a softwood firebrand will burn at around 200–250°C, so these temperatures will not significantly damage or ignite the toughened glass. The glass in the PV modules is held in a frame of anodized aluminium in a silicon sealant. The panel has a tedlar backing and is laid on a high-grade sarking on a marine-grade plyboard layer 18-mm thick above the actual structural timbers and insulation. The roof at the Oxford Ecohouse is also insulated with Thermal-Pruf Insulation, which is non-combustible conforming to the British Standard BS476 Pt.4.

The Building Control Officer was satisfied with the information supplied and the roof was deemed to meet the local Fire Regulation Requirements. The PV industry does need to provide designers and regulatory authorities with fire ratings for all products if they are to be used externally on buildings.

Agreement with local electricity company

The requirements of Southern Electricity in terms of protocols required included the following:

- connection agreement;
- parallel running agreement;
- tariff agreement.

CASE STUDY: GRAHAM DUNCAN'S HOUSE IN NEW ZEALAND

Brenda and Robert Vale

It is in its electrical systems that Graham Duncan's house differs substantially from convention. The house is entirely self-contained for its electricity supply, although there is mains electricity available from Mercury's lines directly outside in the road. The electricity is generated by two renewable sources, the sun and the wind. The solar contribution comes from 16 60-W Solarex polycrystalline photovoltaic panels mounted on the north-facing roof at a slope of 42°. The panels are spaced off the roof with 50-mm-thick wooden bearers running down the slope and are carried on aluminium rails fixed across the bearers. This provides a spacing of about 75 mm between the back of the panels and the roof surface, which may help to provide some cooling to the panels that become less efficient at higher temperatures. A recent addition is a further four 50-W panels mounted on the north-facing wall below the roof. The installed capacity for solar power generation was 960 W, but the additional panels have raised this to 1.16 kW. In addition to the solar panels there are three small wind turbines. Two of these are UK-made Marlecs, with a nominal output of 70 W each. The third is an American-made Air Marine turbine, which has a quoted output of 300 W. However, this is at a higher wind speed than the output given by the manufacturers for the Marlecs, so the two different types of turbine cannot be compared directly. Graham estimates that the two Marlecs are notionally 100 W each and the Air Marine is 200 W. The turbines are all supported on galvanized steel poles with guy wires. They are not really mounted high enough in terms of obstruction to the wind from the house and surrounding trees.

The incoming electricity is stored in batteries via a regulator, a solid-state device that ensures the batteries do not become overcharged. The batteries themselves are six Trojan L16s, each with an energy storage of 350 Ah at 6 V. These are lead-acid batteries described as 'the workhorse of the alternative energy industry' (Schaeffer et al., 1994: 181). They have an expected life of 10 years, and each weighs 58 kg. Together, the batteries can hold 12.6 kWh of electricity, about the same power as is provided by just over 1 l of petrol. However, this amount of electricity cannot be drawn from them without shortening their life. Ideally the batteries should not be discharged to more than 50 per cent of their capacity, with an absolute lower limit of 80 per cent discharge. Most renewable energy systems incorporate a cut-off that prevents power being drawn from the batteries when they fall below a pre-set level of discharge. This is achieved by measuring the battery voltage, which drops as the electricity is drawn off.

Batteries store and supply electricity as direct current, but many household appliances use alternating current at 230 V, as supplied by the electricity generating industry. To obtain AC from the batteries Graham uses a transistorized inverter. This was a

Trace 1500 W model, made in the USA. Trace inverters are alleged to be highly reliable and have a good reputation, but Graham's blew up early in 1998 after only about two years of use. For a short time he then used a rotary inverter. This is a very simple mechanical device that uses a DC electric motor to turn an AC alternator. The disadvantage is that it is considerably less efficient than a solid-state inverter, which may provide at the AC output about 90 per cent of the power that goes in from the batteries. The rotary inverter has been replaced temporarily with an Australian Selectronic 350 W inverter. The wattage of the inverter determines what it can operate. Most inverters are described by the load that they can maintain continuously, so a 1500 W inverter will handle more than four times the load of a 350 W model. Most inverters can handle much higher loads for short periods, which enables them to deal with the high starting currents of electric motors. In Graham's house the failure of the Trace inverter means not being able to use the vacuum cleaner or microwave, which worked off the larger inverter but not off the smaller one. The inverters all contain a shut-down mechanism if an attempt is made to draw off too much power by plugging in too large a load for too long. Inverters have other complications that have to do with the type of alternating current that they produce. True alternating current, as produced by the electricity industry or the rotary inverter, has a smooth waveform. A solid-state inverter switches the current on and off very rapidly and creates a version of AC that may be very far from smooth. The better-quality inverters produce a 'modified sine wave', which is a reasonable approximation to mains electricity. The importance of all this is that some devices, such as certain computers or hi-fi equipment, need the smooth sine wave in order to work correctly and may not work at all from a modified sine wave.

Graham has wired his house to make the best use of different kinds of electricity. Since even the best inverter is only 90 per cent efficient it makes sense to use as much electricity as possible as direct current. In Graham's case this means DC lighting, using compact fluorescent lamps in special light fittings that contain the circuitry to run the lamps off DC. The water pumps are DC, as described above, and the refrigerator, which is quite small, has been rebuilt with a DC compressor. There is also a DC television and radio. Low-voltage DC wiring has to be larger in diameter than AC 230 V wiring, as electricity is transmitted more easily at higher voltage. This makes the wiring slightly more expensive. The 230 V inverter runs a larger TV, a video, stereo, computer, fax and washing machine.

8.14.
Sketches of solar panels (either photovoltaic or solar hot water panels) demonstrating that even in the vernacular, with a little thought the panels can be very pleasingly integrated into the architecture of the house.

CHECKLIST – ENSURING YOUR PV SYSTEM WORKS WELL

1 Buy a system display that clearly shows the system output so you can see if the system is working well against predicted outputs per day, month and year. Make sure you have a performance warranty from your installer and, if the system is not performing as expected, call them back to determine if there are any problems.

2 Cleaning. In areas with fairly high rainfall this may not ever be necessary. In hot dusty countries modules may have to be washed every day. The angle of tilt also influences the amount of dust that will settle on a module and those that are horizontally placed will accumulate the most surface dirt. Do not forget that water will lower the panel temperature and, if over 25°C will improve the operational efficiency of the panel. Always ensure there are no exposed electrical connections when cleaning modules as water and electricity do not mix.

3 Insurance companies do not supply standard policies for solar houses. These should have lower premiums because the insurance industry will benefit more than most from low CO_2 buildings. This is because they have to cover the costs of climate damage resulting from increased emissions from buildings that fuel global warming. The first big insurance company that produces a solar house policy for the UK will get a prize from the authors of this book but we do not accept any liability for those crushed in the stampede!

4 Make sure that the contract you sign for the installation, or the exchange of letters, clearly defines the warranty period of the system as installed. Contracts need to be developed that assign clear liability for all work done on site on the PV system and its interface with the building, and warranties need to be drawn up to cover the houseowner in case of failure of any part of the system. For instance, while a PV module company will cover the cost of replacing a panel that fails within 5 or 10 years, who pays for the scaffolding necessary to investigate and replace the module? If the problem was a sheet of glass, the insurance company would pay but what if it is because of faulty wiring on the back of a module by the installation contractor or module manufacturer? It is advised that in the future owners should consider this issue, discuss it with their insurance companies and draw up their own contracts to be agreed and signed before a tender for work is awarded to a sub-contractor.

GOOD PUBLICATIONS ON PVS

Arthur D. Little, Inc. (1995). *Building Integrated Photovoltaics (BIPV): Analysis and U.S. Market Potential*. NREL/TP-472-7850. National Renewable Energy Laboratory, Golden, CO.

Davidson, J. (1987). *The New Solar Electric Home: The Photovoltaics How-to Handbook*. Aatec, Ann Arbor, MI.

Derrick, A., Francis, C., Bokalders, V. (1991). *Solar Photovoltaic Products: A Guide for Development Workers*. Intermediate Technology Publications Ltd, London.

Duffie, J. A., Beckman, W. A. (1991). *Solar Engineering of Thermal Processes*, 2nd edn. John Wiley & Sons, New York.

First International Solar Electric Buildings Conference Proceedings, Volume 1, 4–6 March 1996, Boston, MA. Northeast Sustainable Energy Association, Greenfield, MA.

Forging PV – Building Bridges. A Joint NREL/DOE PV-DSM/PV:BONUS Workshop Proceedings; 19–20 October 1994, Newark, DE. National Renewable Energy Laboratory, Golden, CO.

Fowler, P. J. (1993). *The Solar Electric Independent Home Book*. Rev. edn. Fowler Solar Electric, Inc., Worthington, MA.

Humm, O. and Toggweiler, P. (1993). *Photovoltaics & Architecture: The Integration of Photovoltaic Cells in Building Envelopes*. Birkauser Verlag, Basel, Switzerland.

Kiss, G. and Kinkead, J. (1995). *Optimal Building – Integrated Photovoltaic Applications*. NREL/TP-473-20339. National Renewable Energy Laboratory, Golden, CO.

Kiss, G., Kinkead, J. and Raman, M. (1995). *Building – Integrated Photovoltaics: A Case Study*. NREL/TP-472-7574. National Renewable Energy Laboratory, Golden, CO.

KissCathcart Anders Architects, P. C. (1993). *Building – Integrated Photovoltaics*. NREL/TP-472-7851. National Renewable Energy Laboratory, Golden, CO.

Lasnier, F. and Gan Ang, T. (1990). *Photovoltaic Engineering Handbook*. A. Hilger, Bristol, New York.

Parker, B. F., ed. (1991). *Solar Energy in Agriculture*. Elsevier, Amsterdam.

Mounting Technologies for Building Integrated PV Systems. Proceedings of the IEA International Workshop, 1992. Moenchaltorf, Switzerland.

Roberts, S. (1992). *Solar Electricity: A Practical Guide to Designing and Installing Small Photovoltaic Systems*. Prentice-Hall, Englewood Cliffs, NJ.

Schoen, T. J. N. (1994). *Photovoltaics in Buildings*. IEA Task 16. Ecofys Research and Development Consultancy; Utrecht, The Netherlands.

Sick, F. and Erge, T. (1996). *Photovoltaics in Buildings: A Design Handbook for Architects and Engineers*. IEA. James & James, London, UK.

Strong, S. J. and Scheller, W. G. (1993). *The Solar Electric House: Energy for the Environmentally-Responsive, Energy-Independent Home*. Sustainability Press, Still River, MA.

Thomas, R. and Grainger, G. (1999). *Photovoltaics in Buildings: A design Guide*. Produced by Max Fordham and Partners in Association with Fielden Clegg for the DTI, ETSU Report No: s/p2/00282/REP.

Warfield, G., ed. (1984). *Solar Electric Systems*. Hemisphere Publishing, Washington, DC.

Zweibel, K. and Hersch, P. (1984). *Basic Photovoltaic Principles and Methods*. Van Nostrand Reinhold, New York, NY.

Magazines

Home Power Magazine: A bi-monthly magazine that is information-central for details on working and living with PV and other renewable and sustainable technologies. P.O. Box 520, Ashland, OR 97520, USA. Tel./Fax: 916-475-3179; Subscriptions: 800-707-6585; bbs: 707-822-8640; e-mail: hp@homepower.org; web address: http://www.homepower.com

Solar Today: American Solar Energy Society bi-monthly magazine covering all renewable energy applications, new products and new installations. ASES, 2400 CentralAvenue, Suite G-l, Boulder, CO 80301, USA. Tel.: 303-443-3130; Fax: 303-443-3212; web address: http://www.ases.org/solar

Internet web sites

National Renewable Energy Laboratory: http://www.nrel.gov

Sandia National Laboratories, PV: http://www.sandia.gov/pv

Solar Radiation Data Manual for Buildings: http://rredc.nrel.gov/solar/old_data/nsrdb/bluebook/atlas

DOE Office of Building Technology, State and Community Programs: http://www.eren.doe.gov/buildings

NREL Buildings and Thermal Systems Center:
http://www.nrel.gov/stbt.html

Green Building Information Council: http://greenbuilding.ca

Center for Renewable Energy and Sustainable Technology
(CREST): http://solstice.crest.org

Solar Energy Industries Association: http://www.seia.org

Utility PhotoVoltaic Group: http://www.ttcorp.com/upvg/index.htm

Solar Design Associates: http://www.solardesign.com/~sda

PV Power Resource Site: http://www.pvpower.com

9 SOLAR HOT WATER SYSTEMS

WHAT IS A SOLAR HOT WATER SYSTEM?

Solar hot water systems gather energy from solar radiation and turn it into heat that is then distributed in the form of hot air or water to where it is to be used or stored until needed.

An active solar water heater consists of a *solar collector*(s), a hot water *storage tank*(s), and a *pump*. In addition, a heat exchanger and expansion tank are required in freezing winter climates and an electrical generation device is needed if regular AC grid-connected power is not available. Piping, insulation, valves and fittings are considered installation materials and are normally available at hardware stores and plumbing centres.

A solar collector consists of a translucent cover, an absorption plate and a heat transfer system, involving hot water pipes or hot air.

A good liquid solar collector should have a minimum life expectancy of 20–30 years. Most of the collectors built since about 1980 are manufactured with materials that should give a 30–50 year lifespan with a small amount of periodic maintenance. Good liquid collectors typically have copper water ways (piping and tubing), a tempered glass cover and an insulated metal enclosure.

Although a little of the radiation falling on the translucent cover will be re-reflected away, most will pass through and be absorbed by the absorption plate and heat the water contained in it. As soon as the water begins to get hotter than its surroundings the absorption plate will begin to lose heat to its surroundings, which is why insulation is used under it to avoid excessive heat loss to the roof below by conduction, convection and radiation. In areas where the water is being heated to temperatures over 35°C above air temperature heat losses from the absorber plate could be very high and double-glazing should be used for the translucent cover to conserve this heat. This is despite the fact that the double sheet

9.1.
A solar collector.

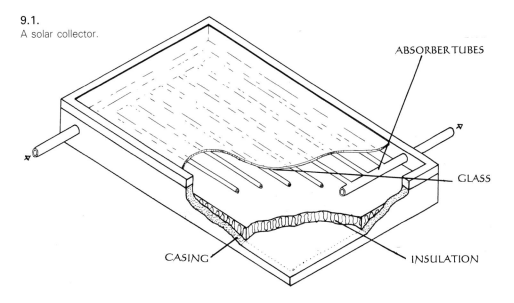

ABSORBER TUBES

GLASS

CASING

INSULATION

of glass may transmit only around 70 per cent of the heat it receives onto the absorber plate. There are a large number of different configurations for collectors, which may range from a simple black hose pipe on the lawn to a very sophisticated evacuated tube collector that is more efficient than a more usual flat plate collector at absorbing heat from an overcast sky. When considering which collector to use on your own building a key consideration is how efficient a particular collector is and how efficient you need it to be.

TIPS FOR CHOOSING A SOLAR COLLECTOR
1 Copper water tubes and headers in the collector are necessary if any water solution is to be used as the heat transfer liquid. A liquid solar collector under no-flow or stagnation conditions can attain boiling temperatures. Plastics other than silicone or PTFE are not suitable materials for liquid collectors.
2 The absorber plate is made of copper, aluminium or steel and bonded to the waterways. The plate surface is approximately equal to the glazing surface and is painted or anodized with a black paint or selective coating. A selective (black nickel or black chrome) surface on the absorber increases the collector output by limiting re-radiated heat (emittence) from the absorber. The method used to bond the plate to the absorber is an important consideration. The better the bonding, the higher the output. Simply wiring or clamping the tubes to the plate will produce discouraging results.

3 The sides and back of the solar collector that do not face the sun should be insulated to prevent heat loss and covered in a weather-tight enclosure. Most collector enclosures manufactured today are made of aluminium owing to its outstanding weatherability. Insulation used is either fibreglass or polyisocyanurate, both of which can withstand very high temperatures. Styrofoams, by comparison, are unsuitable because they begin to degrade at temperatures well below collector stagnation temperatures.

THE HEAT DISTRIBUTION SYSTEM

These are the pipes that circulate hot water from the collector to its storage tank or point of use. It is by circulating water through the solar collectors that the absorbed energy is brought to the point where it will be used. Water can be moved round the system in one of two ways: gravity circulation (thermosyphoning), and forced circulation. The decision to use or not to use a pump is one of the first steps in planning a solar system. Distribution systems can be either direct or indirect.

1 **A direct system** is one where the tap water is circulated directly through the solar collector:

- these systems typically have high efficiencies;
- scaling and corrosion of components often occurs;
- the system is protected from freezing by draining the collectors at night;
- in many hot areas the simple device of putting a black painted metal tank on the roof to absorb the incoming radiation is used to heat the water during the day for domestic use in the evening, being refilled by a simple ball cock valve.

2 **An indirect system** is one that employs a separate fluid circuit to transfer heat from the solar collectors to the preheat tank:

- the separate fluid contains inhibitors and antifreeze, often glycol, that permits a wide range of materials to be employed in the absorber and the pipe work;
- these systems have higher purchase costs and lower efficiencies than direct systems, but lower running costs owing to less damage from corrosion;
- water storage tanks in these systems can either be used as pre-heat tanks or as the main hot water tank into which the solar coil is placed, usually at the base of the tank;

- good controls are needed to ensure that constant water temperatures are maintained in the tank.

CIRCULATION SYSTEMS FOR HOT WATER

1 Natural thermosyphon system:
- heated water naturally rises to the top of the collector and up through the distribution pipes into the upper level of the storage tank;
- cold water is drawn into the bottom of the collector from the bottom of the tank;
- the storage tank should be situated at least 0.6–1.0 m above the collector;
- these systems need careful planning.

2 Pumped system:
This is either in:

2.1 The pumped open system. The pump is fitted on the suction side of the collector, as is the vent and the cistern so that if the collector boils it can vent out directly. When the pump is not running, heat is prevented from rising back to the collector by a valve fitted to the flow pipe of the cylinder. The pump has an electronic control. Remember that the vent is a very important safety feature on these systems and must always have a clear flow path from the collector.

2.2 The pumped, sealed and pressurized solar system. In these systems the open cistern is replaced by an expansion vessel, which is a small metal cylinder about 1 ft high with a rubber diaphragm separating the vessel into two halves. One half contains a compressed gas such as nitrogen while the other half is connected to the system. As water expands on heating it is pushed into the vessel and this extra pressure is relieved by movement in the diaphragm. This vessel need not be at the top of the system. The operating pressure of the vessel is around 2 bar, making summer boiling in the collectors less likely if there is a power failure. Collectors can be placed anywhere on the roof – as high as you like.

THE HOT WATER STORE

Heat storage is a key feature of the solar hot water system. Without it the hot water would be available only when the sun is actually shining. A storage tank allows the solar system to operate

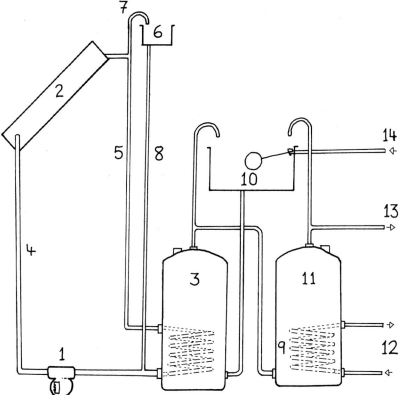

1. CIRCULATOR OR PUMP
2. SOLAR COLLECTOR
3. SOLAR STORAGE TANK
4. RETURN PIPE CARRYING
    COOLED WATER TO
    COLLECTOR
5. FLOW PIPE CARRYING
    HEATED WATER TO
    THE SOLAR TANK
6. SOLAR PRIMARY CIRCUIT
    EXPANSION TANK
7. SOLAR PRIMARY VENT PIPE
8. SOLAR PRIMARY FEED PIPE
9. HEAT EXCHANGER
10. COLD FEED TANK
11. HOT WATER CYLINDER
12. CONNECTIONS TO BOILER
13. TO HOT WATER TAPS
14. MAINS WATER SUPPLY

whenever energy is available and to supply the energy when it is needed.

The storage tank can be sized either to store enough heat for 24 hours, so that the water heated during the day can be used in the evening, or as an interseasonal store with the container of a much larger size. A larger container can be gradually heated up over the hot months and will retain that heat through the autumn and winter. Most domestic systems use only diurnal storage. The hot water store can be used either as a hot water supply tank or as a pre-heat tank for the domestic hot water system.

When an indirect system is chosen, a heat exchanger will be needed in the storage tank. This serves to separate the water

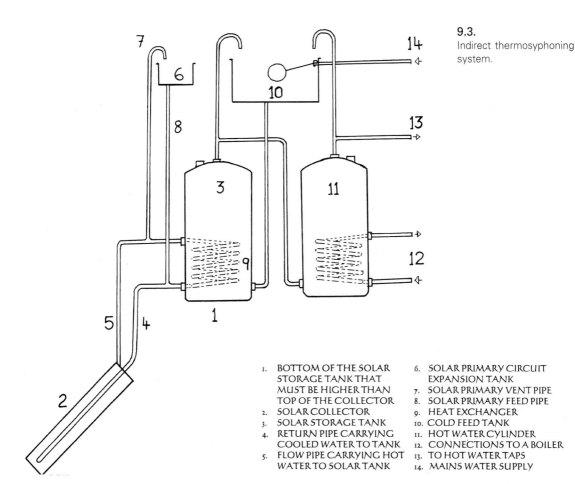

9.3.
Indirect thermosyphoning system.

1.	BOTTOM OF THE SOLAR STORAGE TANK THAT MUST BE HIGHER THAN TOP OF THE COLLECTOR	6.	SOLAR PRIMARY CIRCUIT EXPANSION TANK
2.	SOLAR COLLECTOR	7.	SOLAR PRIMARY VENT PIPE
3.	SOLAR STORAGE TANK	8.	SOLAR PRIMARY FEED PIPE
4.	RETURN PIPE CARRYING COOLED WATER TO TANK	9.	HEAT EXCHANGER
		10.	COLD FEED TANK
5.	FLOW PIPE CARRYING HOT WATER TO SOLAR TANK	11.	HOT WATER CYLINDER
		12.	CONNECTIONS TO A BOILER
		13.	TO HOT WATER TAPS
		14.	MAINS WATER SUPPLY

flowing through the collectors from the water flowing to the tap inside the house. It must allow the heat absorbed in the collectors to pass into the water in the storage tank.

STORING SOLAR ENERGY

- The tank storage should be very well insulated. The equivalent of 75 mm of glass fibre is a reasonable amount.
- Proper sizing of the pre-heat tank is essential for defining the strategy for heat storage to be used and avoiding accidents caused by the water in the collector boiling.

WHY USE A SOLAR HOT WATER SYSTEM?

All Ecohouses should use solar energy to heat their water if possible. This is because solar hot water systems (SHWS) are not only easy to build or buy and install but, above all, they use the free, clean energy of the sun.

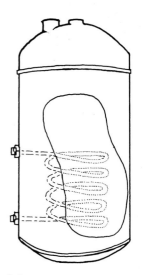

9.4.
Heat exchange coil in the bottom of a hot water cylinder.

HOW GREEN IS A SHWS?

The domestic sector is responsible for around 30 per cent of the carbon emissions of developed countries, mainly owing to the CO_2 emitted as a by-product of power generation and fossil fuel burning. Of this 30 per cent, 25 per cent goes to heating water for use from the taps and to provide pre-heating for space heating systems.

Table 9.1. CO_2 emissions from a typical three-bedroom semi-detached house built in 1995 in the UK

	Emissions (kg CO_2 year^{-1})
Space heating	1506
Hot water	864
Cooking	125
Pumps and fans	96
Lights and appliances	1650
Total	4241

Thus domestic hot water systems are responsible for between 6 and 8 per cent of the total CO_2 emissions in developed countries such as the UK. If every house had a solar hot water system that could produce over half of all the annual hot water requirement using free clean solar electricity then we could save around 3 per cent of all emissions of greenhouse gases from the country simply by adopting a mandatory solar hot water policy. In Israel all new houses have to have SHWS. Of course in a hot tropical country, where SHWS can produce up to 100 per cent of the annual hot water requirement, SHWS could save 6 per cent of greenhouse gas emissions. It is understandable that building owners should more often think about the cost of their purchases rather than the global impacts of their invisible emissions.

WHAT WILL IT COST TO USE SHW?

Clever governments, such as that in the Netherlands, have realized that a little help to an industry at the right time can have a dispro-portionate impact on its success. Hence, in a public–private partnership in the Netherlands the cost of SHW systems has dropped enormously. Even in Britain you can go out and buy a Dutch system now off the shelf, with tank and panels included, for as little £1200. In other parts of the world the production costs of systems are, of course, much less.

An example from the UK
A total solar collector area of around 5 m^2 is recommended for a typical domestic water heating installation. A little maths shows us that it is possible to collect 1500 kWh of energy per year. If the original heating method was an electric heater, that would have cost around £70. Since the 5 m^2 of solar collector will cost around £800, the payback period would be around 11 years. Since the lifespan of solar collectors is around 20 years, one gets 9 years of free hot water. In terms of the modern economy 9 years could be a long time, but we must remember that we do not know what the cost of the energy will be in 9 years' time, though it will not be lower than today, that is for sure.

THE PROCESS OF DESIGNING A SHW SYSTEM

What follows is a step-by-step approach to designing and building a SHW system. There are many different types of SHW systems available with different features, capabilities and costs. It is important to follow the steps described here to get the optimum SHW system.

Step 1. Defining the requirements

Hot water usage
Rules of thumb indicate that 40–60 l of hot water per person per day is often used. This varies from place to place.

Storage capacity
Storage of energy is a key feature of an Ecohouse and for a SHWS the pre-heat water tank should be sized to store hot water for several days.

People use an average of 40–60 l hot water per person per day. A family of three or four will use 160–240 l per day. The storage tank requirements have to satisfy the daily routine of the family. Hot water from the SHWS should be available all day long. A storage strategy of at least two days is a good option.

Step 2. Sizing the system

Two variables of the SHWS have to be sized, the area of the solar collector and the capacity of the storage tank.

- *Pre-heat tank.* A typical size for a family of four might be about 300–350 l.
- *Collector area.* Once an estimate for the amount of water that will be used and the necessary tank size to store that amount of water for a couple of days is determined, the area of the solar collectors can be calculated. The sizing is not exact. Consideration should be given to the fact that owing to a number of variables (usage, climate and system installation) the sizing can be adjusted to increase or decrease the percentage of the total water heating load displaced. Collectors are usually made in modules with fixed areas in the range of 1.5–2.5 m². Hence the choice will usually be between two and six modules.

Tips
- The basic rule of thumb for sizing solar collectors is to use 1 m² of collector for every 50–65 l of hot water needed per day.
- The rule of thumb for relating the solar collector area to the storage size says that 50–65 l of water storage is needed for each 1 m² of solar collector.
- A 5 m² solar collector area provides 60 per cent of the SHW needs for the Oxford Ecohouse in the UK. The same system provides 75 per cent of the SHW system for the Bariloche Ecohouse, Argentina.
- The easy way to measure the contribution of a SHWS to the hot water energy requirements is to look at the energy bills. Exact predictions can be made in cases where weather data and collector performance specifications are available using what is known as the f-chart method.

Step 3. Choosing the system

The three main choices to be made in designing a SHWS are the sizing of the solar collector, the storage tank and finally the choice of a system to circulate the heat between the two. There is considerable variation in the possible systems of distributing the heat within a SHWS. Of the two most common systems, one involves thermosyphoning and the other pumping. For a thermosyphon system the solar collectors have to be placed below and reasonably close to the storage tank to allow the hot-to-cold loop to work best.

In pumped systems, the power to move heat between collector and store is derived from an electrically driven pump. A pumped system:

- does not require the heat store to be above the collector and can be further from it, so giving more freedom in locating the system;

- collects more energy than a comparable thermosyphon system because it will remove the heat from the collector at a higher rate;
- costs more than a thermosyphon system.

Step 4. Protecting the system from the cold

If necessary, decide on a method of protecting the collector from damage by freezing. Key to this is whether you have chosen a direct or indirect system. If the latter is chosen, a storage tank with a heat exchange coil in it has to be installed.

Freezing protection
- An indirect system will not have this problem but a heat exchanger in the storage tank results in a loss of efficiency.
- Insulating covers could be set on top of the collectors on cold nights with the obvious disadvantages.
- A draining system could be implemented.

Step 5. How many tanks?

If there is an existing hot water system in the house, solar pre-heating can take place in the existing hot water tank or in a separate solar storage tank, which then feeds into the existing tank. When considering this question, bear in mind the following:

- If the solar collectors are connected to the existing storage tank there will be saving in both money and space. The conventional heating source has to be connected in the upper half of the tank, above the solar input. This means that the existing plumbing will need to be changed.
- Additional hot water storage capacity and a simpler installation are possible if a separate solar storage tank is chosen. The cold feed from the existing tank is diverted to the bottom of the solar tank, which then feeds from the top of the first tank. This option is more efficient as well.

Step 6. Installing the solar collectors

Key considerations when placing the panels include the following.

Orientation
In higher latitudes it is more important to face the panels either north or south directly towards the sun; 15° either side of south

will make little difference. As one nears the tropics the higher availability of sunshine makes the orientation of the panels less important and they can even face east or west and still provide adequate
heated water for domestic needs, if properly sized. In the tropics
they can operate well even if laid flat, owing to the abundant
sunshine but, of course, if a thermosyphon system is used the
water tank still needs to be above the collectors.

Placing of collectors

Collectors may be placed:

- at ground level;
- as canopies on the outside walls of buildings, above sunspaces
  or as sunshades above flat roofs;
- on a sloping roof;
- on angled collector supports on flat roofs or walls.

Warning! Do not put the collector in a position where it is shaded
from the sun by the building or adjacent trees.

How to get the tilt angle right for the SHW collector

The tilt angle will depend on the design concept of the SWH system.

1 If the intention is to maximize the SHW output over the year,
  the collectors should be inclined at an angle equal to the site's
  latitude, from the horizontal.
2 If the intention is to maximize the SWH production during winter,
  the collectors have to be inclined 10° more than in case 1.
3 If the intention is to extend the 'solar' season then the collectors should be tilted 10° less than in case 1.

Joining the SWH collectors together

Each SHW collector will have an inlet and an outlet pipe. In order
to optimize the flow rate between the panels and the storage tank
ensure that each collector has the hot water outlet pipes
connected to the outflow pipe on the upper side of the panel. The
colder water supply inlets to each collector should all be connected
at their lower ends to the inflow pipe. There are many different
absorber types used in SHW systems but this simple rule applies
to them all.

Proportions

When deciding finally where on a roof a panel will be placed
remember the simple rules of proportion and design. Try to line up

one or more of the sides of the collectors with an existing feature on the roof, such as a roof light or a chimney. Take care to balance the form of the collector pleasingly within the proportions of the roof to minimize the chance of it looking out of place.

How to attach the collector to the roof

When fitting solar collectors to roofs a number of different systems can be used to bolt the collectors to the existing roof beams, using extra timber bearing beams fixed to the inside of the existing rafters where necessary. Panels should be firmly bolted and hung from strong roof timbers, either with metal fixing straps attached to the metal frame of the collector or an aluminium cross-rail support bolted through the tiles to the roof beams. The collector fixings on flat roofs should be very robust. The collectors can be attached in one of three ways:

1 Screwed either directly to the surface of a roof or via a timber frame to the roof in a horizontal plane. Long screws must be used to ensure a good purchase on the roof beams below and the holes in the roof should then be made waterproof, prefer- ably with mastic or pitch.

2 Fixed to triangular supporting frames used at an appropriate angle and orientation to face the collectors towards the sun. These may be made of timber or aluminium L-shaped angles that can then be screwed to the roof.

3 Screwed to a raised frame above the roof, either at a height of at least 50 cm if the system is just to provide shade for the roof below with good through ventilation, or over 2 m above the roof, either on a raised horizontal or an angled frame, in a roof canopy system. The canopy, which may consist of solid elements, photovoltaic and solar hot water panels, is ideal for hot climates where ventilation beneath the solar panels is either beneficial or not detrimental to efficient working of the panels. In addition, the canopy may provide a vital shade for the roof or people on the roof.

Checklist
- Collectors are extremely heavy and timber external fixing members should never be used as it could be extremely dangerous in the event of failure resulting from weather damage over time.
- Space should be left between the collector and the roof tiles beneath to allow free passage to rainwater and melting snow and prevent the build up of debris around the collector that may, over time, cause the roof to leak.

- If the system is left empty cover it with old sheets or blankets to prevent excessive heat build up in the dry metal collector, which may cause damage to it.
- Do not install heavy collectors onto the roof alone.
- Make sure ladders are firmly secured.
- Ensure that there is a pressure release valve at the highest point of the system to prevent air-locking in the system that may reduce its subsequent efficiency.
- Use high-temperature components in the system as the temperature in the pipes and collectors may rise to over 100°C in hot spells. This includes high-temperature piping, valves, sarking, gaskets and insulation.
- Piping should have a minimum of bends.
- Use copper pipes if possible.
- Pipes should be well insulated where possible and, if necessary, using tapers to secure insulation to the bends.
- Fixings should be corrosion-resistant and do not use brass screws with aluminium straps as galvanic action will corrode the alloy.
- On shallow-pitched roofs the safety vent at the highest point of the pipe system may have to go outside the roof, so this must be taken into consideration at the design stage. If external it should be insulated.
- Choose good sunny weather for fitting the SHWS.

Controlling the system?

A reasonable SHWS should be able to control itself and work automatically 100 per cent of the time. The homeowner should never have to be involved in its operation. Sensors are used to monitor the temperature of the water in the system:

- In direct systems, a thermally operated valve, installed at the collector, is used to circulate the warm water into the collector as temperatures approach freezing. The system can be manually drained by closing the isolation valves and opening the drain valves instead of using a thermally operated valve, if desired.
- In indirect and open systems sensors are used to monitor the temperatures of the heat transfer liquid in the system. Above certain temperatures fluid is drained from the collector(s) and piping into the reservoir tank. There is no contact between the heat transfer liquid and the potable water in the system.
- In indirect and pressurized systems sensors are used to monitor the temperatures of the antifreeze solution in the system in such a way that the water in the system is always being heated when the sun is shining. There is no contact between the antifreeze solution and the potable water in the system.

CASE STUDY: THE INTEGRATED SOLAR ROOF AT THE OXFORD ECOHOUSE

The Oxford Ecohouse has a system where the angled roof is built up with a rigid aluminium frame screwed to the roof. Onto this, over parts of the roof photovoltaic panels are fitted and held down by a screw-fixed cover strip. Over other portions of the roof, 5 m² solar hot water panels are screwed down beneath the same cover strips. The solar thermal system consists of a flat plate solar collector manufactured by AES and mounted on the roof co-planar with it. It has two series-connected flat plate collectors with 5 m² surface, connected to a 300 l tank. The solar hot water collectors are used to supplement the energy demand for domestic hot water (DHW) and to pre-heat the tank used for heating the three radiators in the house. At the Oxford Ecohouse the hot water collectors were manufactured to fit into the same aluminium angle grid as the photovoltaic modules and held in place with the same cover strips. This roofing construction has proved completely waterproof.

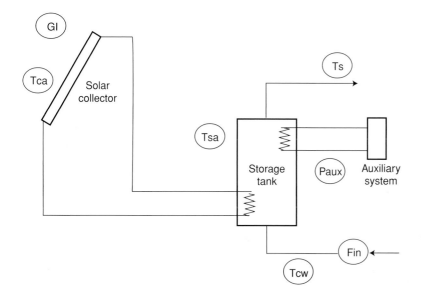

9.5.
A schematic diagram of the DHW system at the Oxford Ecohouse.

The collector feeds directly into a secondary heating coil in the hot water storage tank. The primary coil in the Yorkpark twin coil tank is connected to the gas condensing boiler.

CASE STUDY: THE MADIBA HEAT BARROW FROM SOUTH AFRICA

One of the most innovative SHW systems developed to date, the Madiba Heat Barrow has been developed by the Engineering

Department of the University of Pretoria for use in the poorer communities in South Africa where every drop of water must be carried over vast distances in very primitive containers. The water in many settlements also often contains harmful organisms that would be killed if the water could be heated to certain temperatures for certain periods of time. Wood is scarce in these regions and hot purified water a luxury. The ingenious idea behind the Madiba Heat Barrow was to combine the hot water collector with the hot water store in a moveable water collector/container. An enormous amount of research, largely by Benjamin Rossouw (Rossouw, 1997), went into the development of this product that is now being tested in a number of communities. The amount and location of the insulation were important as were the materials of which it was built that have been designed for mass production and to keep the cost of the barrow below Rand300. The hot water wheel barrow, which also provides the distribution system for the heat, has proved that it can, on sunny winter days, heat water to over 60°C at midday and, by 20:00 h, the water is still piping hot at 40°C. The shape of the barrow and the wheel at the front have been designed for maximum manoeuvrability, for use by children and to prevent erosion furrows in the soil.

9.6.
The Madiba Heat Barrow can be pushed by children and acts not only as a solar hot water collector but also as a water carrier (Edward Matthews, Department of Engineering, Pretoria University).

GOOD PUBLICATIONS ON SOLAR HOT WATER SYSTEM DESIGN

ASHRAE (1977). *Method of Testing to Determine the Thermal Performance of Solar Collectors*. ASHRAE 93-77.

Bectanan, W. A., Klein, S. A. and Duffie, J. A. (1977). *Solar Heating Design by the f-chart Method*. Wiley, New York.

Brinkworth, B. J. (1980). 'The British Standard Code of Practice and its implications for solar hot water system design'. In Solar Energy in the 80s. Conference (M2) Birmingham, UK-ISES Midlands Branch, pp. 79–84.

British Standard Institution Code of Practice (1980). *Solar Heating Systems for Domestic Hot Water*. BS5918: 1980, 17 pp.

Duffie, J. A. and Beckman, W. A. (1980). *Solar Engineering of Thermal Processes*. Wiley, New York.

Gillett, W. B. and Hutchins, M. G. (1981). Heating Water by the Sun. UK-ISES.

Holland, E. (1981). 'Living with the sun'. *Solar Age*, April, p. 22.

Kreider, J. F. and Kreith, F. (1982). *Solar Heating and Cooling*. Hemisphere Press, Washington, DC.

McCartney, K. (1978). *Practical Solar Heating*. Prism Press, Dorchester.

10 USING WATER WISELY

WHY SHOULD WE USE WATER WISELY?

Four things are conspiring to make fresh water one of the most valuable commodities in the twenty-first century:

1 increasing world populations;
2 climate change;
3 man's ever increasing interference with the natural flow of water;
4 pollution.

In 1990 the World Health Organization estimated that 1230 million people did not have access to adequate drinking water. By 2000 this figure was estimated to have risen by 900 million people. Add to this already chronic problem the devastating impacts of climate change and the results can be catastrophic, even in the most developed countries in the world. On top of these issues comes another: the increasing household demand for water around the world. In England and Wales alone household water use is predicted to increase by 10–20 per cent between 1990 and 2021 under a medium-growth scenario without climate change. Per capita demand for domestic water is predicted to rise owing to the projected increase in use of dishwashers and other domestic appliances, with a further increase of 4 per cent with climate change owing to higher use of personal showers and garden watering. Demand for spray irrigation of crops in Britain is predicted to rise by 115 per cent with climate change between 1990 and 2021, with most irrigation water taken from rivers and groundwater.

   This increasing demand for water can be met either by increasing the capacity of supply (e.g. by building new reservoirs), by reducing the consumption of water or by re-using water where we can.

WATER CONSERVATION

Water conservation becomes increasingly important as demand for water increases and shortfalls in supply occur. A number of water conservation measures can be used in the home with little impact on the every day lives of householders. These can involve the following.

Flow restrictors

Flow restrictors are readily available and can be fitted to many appliances, but their use has to be appropriate. Where taps can be left open by careless users and where items are washed under running water they are a cheap way of reducing water wastage. However, a more effective but more expensive solution would be to install taps operated by proximity sensors.

Showers

The average amount of water used by a conventional shower is approximately 30 l, whilst a bath requires about 80 l. Initially, it appears that showering is more energy and water efficient, but the fact is that households with showers use them more frequently than households without showers use their baths. Also, pumped and multihead showers are not so water efficient as conventional showers. Real savings can be made if you choose your products wisely.

Conventional showerheads can discharge water at between 0.3 and 0.5 l s^{-1}. Low-flow showerheads can reduce this to below 0.2 l s^{-1} depending on the supply pressure. Research conducted in the USA has shown that the use of low-flow showerheads can save approximately 27 l per day per person (for a person who mainly showers rather than takes baths). This equates to an energy saving in hot water of 444 kWh per person per year for water heated by gas (or 388 kWh for water heated by electricity). The cheaper alternative to low-flow showerheads is to fit a flow restrictor to the supply to an existing showerhead, although this may increase the showering time.

WCs

WC cistern water displacement devices are available in all countries, albeit only a stone or brick in some cases. More imaginative in the UK, with a typical flush of 6–9 l, is the use of the plastic bags, 'Hippo' and yellow sponges, 'Soggy Doggy', that have been distributed free by water companies to encourage their customers to conserve water. These devices either displace or retain water within the WC cistern to reduce the volume of water that is flushed. Water displacement devices such as dams and bags are very popular in the USA where cisterns are generally much larger and less cluttered than UK cisterns. This is because American cisterns have traditionally flushed over 15 l of water using compact cistern outlet valves: 'flappers'. Unfortunately it has been found that some displacement devices may actually increase the flushing volume if they are fitted such that they obstruct the flush volume limiting aperture in a siphon. If the entire volume of water in the cistern is necessary to clear the WC pan, a reduced flush volume may not be effective, resulting in the repeated flushing of the cistern and hence an increase in the amount of water used, rather than a decrease.

WCs can be flushed with water using compressed air assistance. Some such cisterns use the pressure of the mains water supply to compress a volume of air above the stored water. When the water is released into the bowl it has a much greater velocity than from a conventional gravity-operated cistern. These products are used in parts of France and the USA. To be used efficiently these cisterns need to be matched to WC pans that can use the higher velocity water effectively. Another type of water and compressed air toilet uses water to rinse the bowl and compressed air to evacuate the contents. This type is used in many types of building in the USA.

Composting toilets

Composting toilets use no water for flushing. In its domestic form this toilet is usually electrically powered, heating the waste material to enable composting action to occur. The major problem with this type of toilet is its size; the smallest domestic model is about twice the size of a conventional WC suite. Large (greater than 15 m^3) composting toilets do not usually require the external input of energy for the process, as the aerobic decomposition is sufficiently exothermic to be self-sustaining. Large composting toilets may be environmentally acceptable as they consume only a small volume of water, require no drainage pipe work and produce compost that can be used in the garden. However, the questions of adequate hand washing facilities if there is no available water supply and the safety of children using toilets with open chutes needs to be considered.

Waterless toilets

Waterless toilets that do not compost the waste usually require electricity to operate. Packaging toilets seal the waste into continuous plastic sacks that require subsequent disposal. Incinerating toilets burn the waste to produce a sterile ash that can be disposed of in a garden.

Urinal flushing cistern controllers

Urinal flushing cistern controllers have been widely used in the UK for some time. Water Byelaws for such appliances have to be checked for each area. In the UK such Byelaws state the maximum rate at which cisterns may be filled. Since 1989 new cisterns are required to be refilled only when the urinal is in use. There are various methods of sensing use and operation. Some use changes in water pressure to identify operation of taps and therefore, by association, the use of urinals; others use passive infrared (PIR) detectors to detect movement of persons in the room; some sense the temperature of urine in the urinal traps; and many use various forms of proximity detector. The essence of these devices is they all obviate the flushing of urinals when the premises are not being used and are usually an improvement over the use of the traditional 'pet-cock' that has to be set to drip water at the required rate into the cistern.

Waterless urinals

Waterless urinals are being increasingly used in the UK. Most modern designs feature some form of odour suppressant that requires regular renewal. Claims for large water and maintenance savings are made about these devices but the pipe work must be installed and maintained correctly if prolonged service life is to be achieved. An incinerating urinal is available from the USA, which produces small volumes of ash. However, at a cost of over £1000 considerable water has to be saved to make it economically viable.

Controls

The use of an occupancy detector to isolate the water supply to a washroom when unoccupied is another application of PIR technology. This can minimize the waste in urinal flushing and that caused by taps being left open. Automatic leak detectors are becoming increasingly available in the UK. These devices are fitted into the incoming mains and close when a leak is detected, preventing both the waste of water and damage to property. Some operate by sensing a high flow rate and others use conductivity detectors to activate valves. Automatic closure taps can produce water savings in commercial and public buildings where there is a risk of taps being left open accidentally.

Domestic appliances

Presently, 85 per cent of households in the UK possess a washing machine and 10 per cent a dishwasher. Together, these consume about 12 per cent of domestic drinking water. The ownership of these previously luxury goods is increasing. Water Byelaws govern the maximum permissible volume of water used for a wash: between 150 and 180 l for a washing machine (depending on drum size) and about 196 l for an average dishwasher. Modern high-efficiency washing machines use far less water than this and an AEG washing machine uses as little as 68 l of water for a 5 kg fill and only 1.4 kWh for a hot and cold fill. This is around one-third of the water used in a conventional machine. The Oxford Ecohouse dishwasher is another AEG machine that uses only 15 l of water and 1.2 kWh electricity for a 50°C biowash cycle. That is less than one-tenth of a conventional machine.

WASTEWATER SYSTEMS

Wastewater is used water. Wastewater may contain substances such as human waste, food scraps, oils, soaps and chemicals. In houses, wastewater can include the water from sinks, showers, bathtubs, toilets, washing machines and dishwashers. Businesses and industries also use water for a wide variety of other purposes.

Wastewater can include stormwater (rainfall) runoff. Although many people assume that stormwater runoff is clean, it isn't. Contaminants such as hydrocarbons wash off urban surfaces such as roadways, parking lots and rooftops and can harm our rivers, lakes and marine waters.

We also waste water when we don't use it wisely. For instance, when we fill a glass of water to drink, we may run the water to make sure it's cold. It is perfectly clean but once it disappears down the drain it mixes with sewage and polluted water from other households, businesses and industries.

When we pull the plug in the bathtub or flush the toilet, few of us give much thought to where the wastewater is going but waste-water doesn't just disappear when it leaves our homes and businesses. There are three types of sewer systems:

1 sanitary sewers carry wastewater from sinks, toilets, tubs and industry;
2 storm sewers carry runoff from rainfall, called stormwater;
3 combined sewers carry wastewater and stormwater through the same pipe.

Together, these form our wastewater collection system.

- In the USA each day, the average person produces about 220–450 l of wastewater. That's enough to completely fill a bathtub two times.
- We all produce sludge. An adult is responsible for about 32 kg per year.
- If everyone installed water-saving toilets and showerheads, we could substantially reduce domestic water consumption.
- Each day, in the USA the average person uses 260 l of water for domestic purposes. That's about 7 million l of water in a lifetime.
- A leaky tap will waste in excess of 90 l of water each day.

KEY DIFFERENCES BETWEEN GREY WATER AND BLACK WATER

1 Grey water contains only one-tenth of the nitrogen of black water. Nitrogen (as nitrite and nitrate) is the most serious and difficult-to-remove pollutant affecting our potential drinking water. As grey water contains far less nitrogen, it is unnecessary for it to undergo the same treatment process as black water.

2 The medical and health professionals view black water as the most significant source of human pathogens. Organisms that threaten human health do not grow outside of the body (unless incubated) but are capable of surviving especially if hosted in human faeces. Separating grey water from black water dramatically reduces the danger posed by such pathogens because, in grey water the faeces that carry (and may encapsulate) them are largely absent. However, other bacteria are present in grey water and can cause rapid growth of any faecal contamination present in pipes and septic systems. Care must be taken to ensure that both grey and black water travel rapidly through the pipes in buildings and that there are no points in the system where they can stagnate.

3 The organic content typical of grey water decomposes much faster than the content typical of black water. The amount of oxygen required for the decomposition of the organic content in grey water during the first 5 days (Biological Oxygen Demand over 5 days or BOD5) constitutes 90 per cent of the total or Ultimate Oxygen Demand (UOD) required for complete decomposition. BOD5 for black water is only 40 per cent of the oxygen required. BOD1 for grey water is around 40 per cent of

the UOD; BOD1 for black water is only 8 per cent of the UOD. This means that the decomposing matter in black water will continue to consume oxygen far longer and further away from the point of discharge than it will in grey water. This faster rate of stabilization for grey water is advantageous for the prevention of water pollution as the impact of grey-water discharge generally does not travel as far from the point of discharge when combined with wastewaters. This is especially true for sand and soil infiltration systems. As grey and black waters are so different it is better to separate them and, more specifically, to keep urine and faeces out of the water altogether and to treat them separately for the best protection of health and the environment. Doing so also has significant savings for homeowners.

GREY WATER SYSTEMS

Grey water systems reuse either rainwater or water that has already been used once in the home, such as shower, bath and washing machine water, for secondary, non-potable purposes such as flushing WCs and watering the garden. The concept of domes-

10.1.
Section through the village of Khoranaq, in the Central Persian desert north of Yazd, showing the passage of the water from an underground channel or Qanat through the village, being used from clean to dirty uses. On its path the underground stream is used to: 1. fill the drinking water cistern and 2. the bath house or Hammam; where it emerges it is used for 3. washing of kitchen ware and clothes (without detergents); and 4. drops down a vertical chute to turn the horizontal mill wheel and emerges again to provide drinking water for the animals and water for the fields. Washing of clothes with detergent is done downstream of the animal drinking water pond and the water run to waste (Roaf).

tic water reuse is not new. People have for centuries been reusing water as they go about their daily lives, whether it be throwing the cold contents of a tea pot onto the garden or for surviving in the desert, as shown in Figure 10.1.

In many countries of the world traditional homes had a water cistern incorporated into them to collect rain from the roof for all their domestic needs. As the case study from Mexico City below shows this is still being done in modern ecohouses.

The reuse of grey water and rainwater potentially reduces the need to use potable water for non-potable applications, with the water effectively being used twice before discharge to the sewer. The major reuse potential is for WC flushing, garden watering and, in some parts of the world, car washing, all functions for which the use of pure potable water is unnecessary. Grey water systems would result in the conservation of water resources and reduce demand on both public water supplies and sewage collection and treatment facilities. They could also save the consumer money in the long run. The collection and storage of rainwater also offers potential to reduce runoff flows into the surface-water sewer network.

PLANNING A NEW GREY WATER SYSTEM

1 Make a brief inventory of grey water sources and the number of uses that they get.

Laundry	litres per person per day
Dishwasher	litres per person per day
Bath	litres per person per day
Other sources	litres per person per day
Total grey water	litres per person per day

Try to determine how many litres per cycle your appliances use – or use the short-form sizing estimator given in the box below.

Approximate water use of standard appliances	
US washing machine (top-loading)	120 l
European washing machine (front-loading)	40 l
Dishwasher	10–20 l
Low-flow showerhead (per shower)	10–20 l
Other sink use (shaving, hand washing, etc.)	5–20 l

2 Use the general site data and design considerations in the box below to determine what steps are relevant for your situation. Give special consideration to the final dispersion of the effluent, making sure that the soil can accept the amount of water that will be generated, treated and discharged (your local professional engineer can do a percolation test to determine the ability of the ground to accept water). If water shortage is a particular restriction, note that grey water filtered through a soilbed as described in this text will not become anaerobic and thus can be saved for lawn irrigation, car washing, etc.

DESIGN INFORMATION: EXISTING TREATMENT FACILITIES AND PROCESSES
- Septic tank.
- Leach-field.
- Cesspool.
- Other influent quality and quantity.
- Number of bedrooms.
- Number of persons – normal occupancy.
- Type of appliances and unit flow-rates:
  - Dishwashers,
  - Washing machines,
  - Bathtubs, showers.
- Evaporation rates.
- Temperature data.
- Rainfall data.
- Effluent reuse goals.

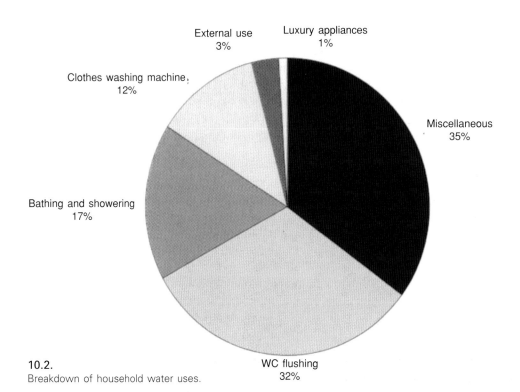

10.2.
Breakdown of household water uses.

3 Check with your local authority regarding any special/local concerns and regulations. Submit your application to the local board of health or consult your local professional engineer for plans and documents needed for your application (usually a topographic site drawing with pertinent information about your site and the proposed solution).

POTENTIAL PROBLEMS WITH GREY WATER

The possible problems of using grey water can be grouped into three categories including those that impact on:

- human health;
- plumbing systems;
- the external environment.

Human health

The first of these is of greatest concern and arises principally as a result of the risk of pathogenic micro-organisms occurring in grey water. Although by definition grey water does not contain faecal contamination, tests have shown that these contaminants can be present. For example, analysis of grey water from the washing machines, showers and bathroom sinks of different families in the USA revealed the presence of micro-organisms of faecal origin (counts were only high in grey water from families with young children, however, where faecal coliforms averaged 1.5×10^3 cfu per 100 ml; Rose et al., 1991). The actual risk to health posed by reusing grey water depends not just on the level of contamination but also on the degree to which humans are exposed to the water and their susceptibility to any pathogens present. Additionally, many systems incorporate a disinfection process.

Plumbing systems

These include the reuse systems themselves. Problems include corrosion, fouling and microbiological growth. These problems may be greater than in potable water supply systems owing to the materials present in grey water, both particulate and dissolved, and the fact that grey water is often warm when first collected. However, risks can be minimized through careful design of systems and the adoption of appropriate maintenance procedures.

The external environment

Problems here include, for example, a risk of groundwater contamination if grey water is used for landscape and garden irrigation and an increase in the concentration of waste discharged to sewers, which could potentially cause blockages and have implications for sewage treatment works. The risk of such effects occurring is only likely to be significant under certain circumstances. The risk might increase, for example, if there were a very high uptake and use of systems in a sensitive area. It is also important to note that in most cases both positive and negative environmental effects can be identified, and that the overall balance is usually positive.

Many countries, such as the UK, at present have no published Grey Water Standard relating to grey water reuse systems. However, depending on the particular circumstances under which the systems are to operate, a number of Regulations and Acts of Parliament may apply. In the UK perhaps the most relevant standard is The Bathing Waters (Classification) Regulations 1991, which have been suggested as possible water quality standards for grey water systems because they are less stringent than the requirements for water for potable use. Additionally they were designed for a situation where there is physical contact with water and in which there may be occasional accidental ingestion. Several Byelaws also affect the use of grey water systems, particularly those related to backflow prevention and accidental cross-connection between potable and non-potable supplies.

TREATING SEWAGE ON THE SITE: SEPTIC SYSTEMS

All modern conventionally designed septic systems are composed of the following four basic components:

1 building sewer;
2 septic tank;
3 distribution box;
4 drainfield (or leachfield).

In a conventionally plumbed home all these combined wastewaters flow out of the house into the septic tank through a single 12-cm-diameter pipe called a building sewer pipe (see Figure 10.3).

The septic tank, usually made of concrete, is designed to be watertight. Tank capacity ranges from 4 m³ for a typical three-bedroom, single-family dwelling to 15 m³, depending on the number of bedrooms in the home. Some large residential or commercial applications may require larger tanks, or more than one tank often arranged in series. Most solids entering the septic tank settle to the bottom and are partially decomposed by anaerobic bacteria to form sludge (Figure 10.4).

10.3.
Diagram of a house, septic tanks and drainfield.

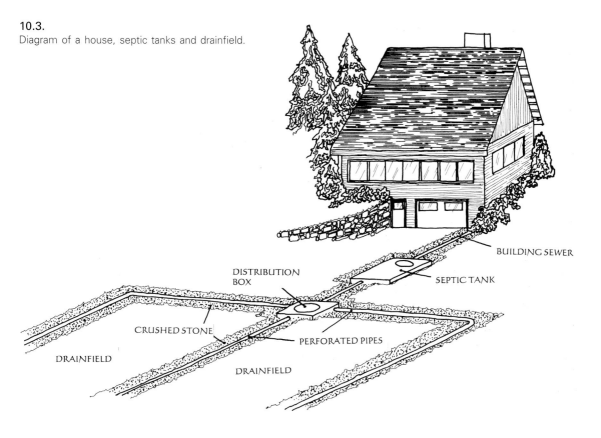

BUILDING SEWER

DISTRIBUTION
BOX

SEPTIC TANK

CRUSHED STONE

PERFORATED PIPES

DRAINFIELD

DRAINFIELD

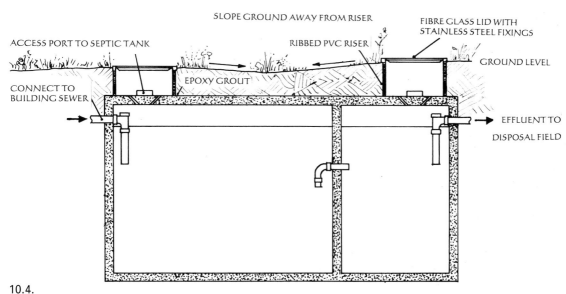

SLOPE GROUND AWAY FROM RISER

FIBRE GLASS LID WITH
STAINLESS STEEL FIXINGS

ACCESS PORT TO SEPTIC TANK

RIBBED PVC RISER

GROUND LEVEL

CONNECT TO
BUILDING SEWER

EPOXY GROUT

EFFLUENT TO

DISPOSAL FIELD

10.4.
Diagram of a conventional two-compartment septic tank.

Some solids float and form a scum mat on top of the wastewater. Little treatment of wastewater occurs in the septic tank, it being mainly a unit for removing solids. A properly maintained septic tank keeps solids and grease from entering and clogging the drainfield, the land into which the tank overflows drain.

The accumulation of sludge at the bottom and scum at the top of a septic tank gradually reduces the wastewater volume storage capacity of the septic tank. When this happens, incoming solids are not settled out efficiently and may be flushed from the tank into the drainfield and cause clogging and premature system failure. Periodic septic tank pumping (every 2–3 years) helps prevent solids from entering the drainfield.

FILLED SYSTEMS

What are they? Most drainfields are installed in the native soil material found on-site. In the case of filled systems, native soil material is removed and the drainfield is constructed above grade in gravel fill material.

When are they used? Filled systems are required at locations where on-site evaluations show that:

- the groundwater table is less than 1 m from the original ground surface;
- the depth to a ledge, or impervious soil layer, is less than 2 m from the original ground surface.

The liquid effluent from the septic tank is discharged via a 12-cm-diameter pipe to a distribution box (D-Box) that separates effluent flow into approximately equal portions to two, or more, pipelines leading to the drainfield (see Figure 10.3). The typical drainfield consists of a network of 12-cm perforated plastic pipes surrounded by crushed stone and installed within native soil material. This type of drainfield configuration is a trench design.

Once in the drainfield, effluent leaving the pipe network percolates through the crushed stone and moves downward into the underlying soil material. Treatment of effluent actually takes place in the adjacent soil. Here nutrients and pathogens may be mechanically filtered out, microbially decomposed or chemically attached to soil particles. The rate at which pollutants are removed and the efficiency of these processes depends on the characteristics of both the soil and wastewater.

HOW DO TRENCHES AND CHAMBERS DIFFER?

Trenches are composed of narrow ditches (0.5–1 m wide) with vertical sides and filled with stone in which a single distribution line is laid. Chambers (either deep or shallow) are hollow (concrete) structures with open bottoms and perforated sidewalls into which septic tank effluent is discharged. Shallow chambers are not permitted in areas where groundwater is less than 1 m from the ground surface. Deep chambers cannot be used in locations where groundwater is less than 2 m. Systems using chambers are easier to design and install and are less subject to damage by heavy equipment during the construction process than are trench-type drainfields.

Large-scale systems are often used in condominia, cluster development, commercial, industrial and institutional situations. With large-scale systems, sewage is collected from each home or building and either gravity fed or pumped to a commonly used septic system installed in an adjacent soil suitable for on-site sewage disposal. Large-scale systems are more complex and difficult to design and tend to be more costly than a single-family system installed under the same site conditions. Failures of large-scale systems can create potential point source pollution problems and serious public health consequences.

SYSTEMS BEYOND THE SEPTIC TANK

These systems are specially engineered and, with the exception of incinerating and composting toilets, are required to discharge to a drainfield.

Nitrogen removal systems

Nitrogen inputs from septic systems can degrade both coastal pond water quality and groundwater supplies beneath densely developed areas. These septic systems are designed to remove nitrogen from the wastestream through biological denitrification. Nitrogen removal systems incorporate an aerobic treatment step, separate anaerobic tanks and carbon sources that supply energy to the bacteria responsible for removing the nitrogen in the wastestream.

Incinerating toilets

Incinerating toilets are designed to handle only the black water component of the household wastestream. In these toilets, urine and faeces combust at high temperatures to produce an inert ash by-product devoid of nutrients, bacteria, viruses and pathogens. Although black water contaminants are totally eliminated from the wastestream, a septic system must still be installed to treat the grey water generated in the household. Water conservation measures can be used to help keep the nutrient and microbial contaminant loadings associated with the grey water wastestream to an absolute minimum.

Composting toilets

In composting toilets, wastewater collects in a tank located beneath a toilet, usually in a basement. The homeowner adds organic material, either sawdust or peat moss to the tank. Micro-organisms break down the mixture into 'compost'. Heat, oxygen, moisture and organic material are needed by the microbes to decompose the waste.

This technology dates as far back as the early 1930s and has recently experienced a surge in popularity. Most composting toilets need neither electricity nor heat to operate, whereas some models require minimal inputs of both. All composting toilets require some care: the owner must periodically add organic material, turn compost to aerate the waste and remove finished compost. The compost is often used around the garden for mulching ornamental plants.

Pumps and siphons

Incorporating pumps into an A&I pressure dosed system utilizing small-diameter pipes in the drainfield has several advantages over the use of pumps with large-diameter drainfield pipes. Pressure dosing small-diameter pipes can create more uniform wastewater distribution throughout the entire drainfield and can eliminate localized saturated flow of effluent. The use of a small-diameter, pressure dosed system can be especially useful in minimizing effluent channelling in sandy soil material with rapid percolation rates.

The use of pumps in a septic system is not without potential problems. Sewage pumps require electric power to operate and can be disabled during power cuts. To compensate, reserve generator power or additional storage volume in the pump tank can be designed into systems involving pumps.

SEPTIC TANK MAINTENANCE

Once built, periodic pumping and inspection of existing septic systems is the key to maximizing the longevity and performance, and reducing the environmental impacts of the system. Tank pumping will prevent solids from overflowing into and prematurely clogging the drainfield. As a rule of thumb, septic tanks should be inspected yearly and pumped every 2–4 years.

As previously mentioned, septic system siting, design and installation are the responsibility of the site evaluator, designer and system installer.

System additives

Many septic system additives are marketed as 'cure-alls' for a variety of system problems. Products sold to 'clean' septic systems generally consist of acids, hydrogen peroxide, biological agents or chemicals containing organic solvents. There is no evidence that any of these additives can correct or prevent failure. Use of chemical cleaners can seriously damage the system, alter soil permeability and contaminate groundwater.

Some biological septic tank additives promise to completely eliminate the need for routine periodic pump outs, claiming solids are removed by enzymatic processes. It appears that biological additives function to disperse and re-suspend solids in the septic tank, which are then flushed into the drainfield, exacerbating the problem of organic-matter clogging.

SEPTIC SYSTEM LONGEVITY

A septic system drainfield that is suitably located, adequately designed, carefully installed and properly maintained still has a certain lifespan. All drainfields accumulate organic slime material at the junction of the drainfield and native soil. This slime layer is referred to as a biological mat (biomat). Biomat formation is an inevitable process, eventually sealing the whole drainfield and restricting wastewater movement into the surrounding soil. Biomats do allow some limited flow through them, but it is considerably less than the percolation rate of the native soil material. Surfacing of effluent can occur when wastewater volume to the drainfield exceeds rate of movement through the biomat and into the surrounding soil.

Biomats are slow to develop in coarse-textured sandy or gravely soils. In finer textured silty or clay soils and in dense compacted soils they develop rapidly. Biomat formation in fine textured or dense soils may produce premature system failure if drainfields are not adequately sized. In contrast, biomat formation in some coarse textured soils may actually improve wastewater treatment by providing an additional step to mechanically and biologically filter out pollutants.

WHY IS DEPTH TO GROUNDWATER TABLE SO IMPORTANT?

The groundwater table is that elevation beneath the ground surface where the soil becomes saturated with water. Determining the depth to the groundwater table (also called water table) at a proposed development site is essential for proper design and function of a septic system. Saturated soils produce anaerobic (very low oxygen) conditions that reduce wastewater treatment and promote pollutant movement. Unsaturated soils are well aerated (aerobic conditions) and encourage wastewater treatment processes. Thick unsaturated zones of soil beneath a drainfield have better wastewater treatment potential and offer more groundwater protection than shallow unsaturated zones. The depth of the groundwater must be measured by a qualified professional in the rainy season when the water table is at its highest.

SITING A SEPTIC SYSTEM IN THE LANDSCAPE

When evaluating a site for on-site sewage disposal, landscape position can give helpful general information about:

- 'lay of the land';
- location within the watershed;
- location relative to wetlands.

Low-lying areas on the natural landscape are often associated with wetlands and floodplains of rivers, streams, ponds and reservoirs. Water tables in these areas are at or near the ground surface. Soils in low-lying areas are wet for long periods of time and are often poorly drained, ponded or flooded. These soils are not suitable for on-site sewage disposal.

Areas located on the sides and tops of hills are called uplands. Upland areas normally have drier soils that are both better suited to and capable of absorbing wastewater loads. Groundwater tables tend to be deeper at hilltop positions and gradually become shallower as one moves down the landscape to low-lying areas. In some cases, however, upland positions may have depressional areas that, owing to local relief and poor soil drainage, are too wet for sewage disposal. Dense basal till soils, often found on the tops and sides of hills, have firm subsoils that restrict water movement. Some dense basal till soils may be suitable for on-site sewage disposal but require large drainfields and careful design.

CASE STUDY: THE GREY WATER SYSTEM AT LINACRE COLLEGE, OXFORD

Linacre College built a great new 'green' building as a hall of residence, gym and restaurant in 1995. Anglian Water decided to use this building as a test bed for their innovative grey water system. This consisted of a two-stage process, in which stored grey water is passed through a sand filter to remove solids, then through a hollow fibre membrane separation process, which removes soap, bacteria and some dissolved organic material. Despite the fact that these filters produced a relatively high quality of water, the design of the system as a whole had serious defects including:

- the underground concrete grey water collection pit was acting as an anaerobic culture vessel, and very quickly rendered the grey water into a condition that was impossible to treat;
- the pipe run from the building was too long and shallow, allowing time for bacterial regrowth;
- the length of time the water was remaining in the tank was too long. Chlorine disinfection upstream was found not to have any effect and was environmentally undesirable;
- the organic material present in grey water changed into a form that was able to pass through the membrane and be assimilated later, in the distribution network. This resulted in the fact that while the treated water was itself clear and sterile, there was sufficient organic material present to allow regrowth later in the system, as the distribution network could never be totally sterile without excessive use of chemicals.

Lessons

- Fast movement to point of treatment, rapid treatment times and avoidance of any possible areas of stagnation will all help to make grey water more readily treatable, by whatever means designers of future systems choose to use.
- Rainwater is usually low in organic material and nutrients, and can be stored in water butts in the home. However, it was found that rainwater can collect material from roofs and down pipes and, when allowed to remain undisturbed for long periods, can become septic. A large amount of black sludge had formed in the rainwater collection tank and analysis showed that anaerobic conditions had developed. Care must be taken at the design stage to allow for complete cleaning of rainwater storage tanks when necessary.

CASE STUDY: GLEDLOW VALLEY ECOHOUSES

The Gledhow Valley Ecohouses are three timber-framed dwellings that are being built to meet high environmental standards. The clients for the scheme are the owners and future occupants of the houses, who undertook their own architectural design, as well as being involved in the actual house construction. An autonomous water system was developed for the houses, without a link to a mains water supply or sewage outlet. The water supply operates off a three-pipe system: drinking water is supplied from rainwater collected off the roof, which is stored and sterilized, whilst hot and cold water for washing and bathing is taken from a storage pond in the communal garden area. Waste water, along with any rainwater run-off, is fed to a reed-bed for treatment and then recycled into the storage pond. Composting toilets are used in all three houses, so the recycling system only treats grey water. Like many self-build schemes, the pace of construction was leisurely, with no fixed 'hand-over' date. Some of the clients started living on the site and using the grey water system on an experimental basis.

A reed bed was constructed in the garden adjacent to the houses, around 8 m^2 in size, planted in a peat/soil base over a plastic membrane. The principle of operation of a reed bed is anoxic and aerobic biological breakdown of organic components in the wastewater. This takes place around the underground stems of the reeds where large populations of common aerobic and anaerobic bacteria grow. The plants will also absorb a certain amount of chemical impurities from wastewater, such as phosphates and nitrates.

Water that has passed through the reed bed is fed to a storage pond, around 12 m^2 in area and 0.5 m deep, which also has a plastic liner. There is no soil medium in this pond, but it does contain oxygenating weeds. The water from the pond is filtered in three stages, with a fine mesh filter at the pond outlet and with cartridge filters between the pump and the tank. The mesh filter has a large surface area and is easily accessible for cleaning, and the second filter has an automatic backwash unit using a stainless steel cartridge The occupiers did not wish to use chlorine or chemical treatment of water, and a Teflon-coated ultraviolet unit is linked to the holding tank to give bacterial sterilization to the incoming water. Water in the tank is recycled through the UV unit at periodic intervals to maintain sterilization during times when little water is being used and to reduce the risk of algae growth in the tank.

Lessons

- Grey water can be mucky stuff! High levels of contaminants and bacteria (including faecal coliforms) can be present, and it needs treating with care. Reed beds can be a successful part of treatment but they require proper design and attention throughout their lives.
- Grey water recycling systems will generally require careful maintenance and monitoring, and control over which detergents, chemicals, etc., are put into the wastewater. This demands acceptance of a high level of responsibility by users of a system.
- Water used for washing and bathing in houses really needs to meet drinking water standards to ensure safety of the occupants. Standards for WC flushing, washing machines, watering vegetables, etc., are often unclear. If you want to put in a grey water system decide what standards you want it to meet, ensure that these standards are included in an agreement with the contractor and test that these standards are maintained over time.
- It is important to minimize water use in designs before adopting recycling schemes. Devices such as those listed at the beginning of the chapter may provide a simpler solution to water conservation.
- Collection and use of rainwater may often be a more appropriate solution to a water conservation problem than grey water recycling.
- The results for control of bacteria were more disappointing. The main reason for this seems to be the failure of the UV treatment, partly caused by a build up of sediment in the UV unit. As UV does not have a residual sterilization effect it was also possible for bacteria to multiply in the pipe work.
- Electrical energy use for the whole water system has been monitored over a three-month period, and showed a total consumption of around 100 kWh (equivalent to a cost of 70 pence). This roughly equates to energy use of 2 kWh per 1000 l of water used.
- The technology of grey water recycling involves a wide spread of disciplines, from microbiology to building services engineering. In these circumstances it is often much more difficult to offer a straightforward 'technical fix' to design problems.

CASE STUDY: NEW ANGLIAN WATER HOUSING PROJECT

The idea of large-scale effluent recycling came from Anglian Water's involvement in household grey water studies, from which it became clear that recycling water on a small scale with existing technology was not practical and could not guarantee a sufficiently high quality of water. The concept was as follows: to collect all wastewater (referred to as black water) from a development of houses via a conventional sewer and treat this using conventional sewage treatment technology. Approximately 60 per cent of this water would then be discharged to the environment, and 40 per cent would be further treated to a standard that could be used for toilet flushing via a separate dedicated main.

The size of development was decided on as 123 homes, giving a population equivalent of 250–280 average. The trial site was chosen as Blackburn, as this was a convenient location, with a watercourse next to the development for discharge and a slope to the site, which allowed for gravity drainage throughout. All new homeowners receive an induction pack, which contains general information on environmental issues, as well as specific instructions on how to maximize water efficiency within their home.

A development of 123 houses would normally use 16 000 m^3 water per year and discharge 90 per cent of this to a sewer, which could run for several miles before reaching a treatment plant. With a water saving system of this sort, the demand is reduced by nearly 5700 m^3 per year on potable water and no sewer services are needed at all, other than the infrastructure on site. This can save millions of pounds.

Treated water standards

The standards needed for the reused water are based on the US Environmental Protection Agency guidelines for non-potable water use, and list BOD as being below 10 mg l^{-1}, turbidity of less than 2 NTU and a disinfection residual of 0.5 mg l^{-1} Cl_2, enough to guarantee zero coliform counts. The Blackburn site currently produces water of BOD <2 mg l^{-1} (the limit of detection), turbidity of 1–1.5 NTU and disinfection residual of 0.4–0.6 mg l^{-1} Br_2. Bromine was chosen as a residual disinfectant as it was found from pilot trials that bromine would last for longer in a network than chlorine and, as it is less reactive, would allow a satisfactory residual to be maintained even at the furthest corners of the distribution network. The use of bromine was found to cause no detrimental effect on the treatment process, or when discharged as bromide in the final effluent.

Environmental impact

The effect on the environment of schemes of this sort are mostly beneficial, although there was initially concern from the Environment

Agency about the possible proliferation of small sewage treatment works, which historically have caused problems with discharge quality. The standards imposed at the Blackburn site are as follows: 40 mg l^{-1} of BOD, 60 mg l^{-1} suspended solids and 10 mg l^{-1} ammonia. These standards are lower than would normally be needed for a site of particular sensitivity such as a marshland area, but were still too strict for the brook that passed the treatment plant. The decision was therefore taken to pump the effluent to the river Darwen, 1 km away. In order to guarantee the quality needed for the brook, a higher degree of treatment would have been needed, increasing the capital cost of the overall process.

The benefit to the river itself is increased flow, although the addition of 30 m^3 per day into a flow as large as the Darwen would be negligible. In future potential sites, the addition of larger quantities of water into small streams and brooks would greatly increase flow and, being relatively constant, would allow a flow to be maintained even in drier weather.

The environmental impact of laying large sewer trunk mains should not be ignored and, as this need is eliminated, damage is reduced to surrounding land, although a development of this sort would of course still need a potable water main to be laid.

RECOMMENDED READING

Jeppesen, B. (1996) Model Guidelines for Domestic Grey water Reuse for Australia. Urban Water Research Association of Australia, Research Report No 107, Melbourne, Vic.

Jeppesen, B. and Solley, D. (1994) Domestic Grey water Reuse: Overseas Practice and its Applicability to Australia. Urban Water Research Association of Australia, Research Report No 73, Melbourne, Vic.

Methods for the Examination of Waters and Associated Materials. Series of monographs, HMSO, London.

Mustow, S., Grey, R., Smerdon, T., Pinney, C. and Waggett, R. (1997). Implications of Using Recycled Grey water and Stored Rainwater in the UK. Report 13034/1, BSRIA, Bracknell.

National Sanitation Foundation Joint Committee on Wastewater Technology (1983) Standard 41: Wastewater Recycle/Reuse and Water Conservation Devices. NSF, Ann Arbor, MI.

Rose, J., Sun, G., Gerba, C. and Sinclair, N. (1991) 'Microbial quality and persistence of enteric pathogens in greywater from various household sources'. Water Research, 25 (1), 37–42.

The Microbiology of Water 1994 – Part 1 – Drinking Water. HMSO, London.

US Environmental Protection Agency (1992) Guidelines for Water Reuse. EPA/625/R-92/004, US EPA Center for Environmental Research Information, Cincinnati, OH.

Water Supply (Water Quality) Regulations 1989 (SI 1989/1147), HMSO, London.

Water Supply (Water Quality) (Amendments) Regulations 1991 (SI 1991/1837), HMSO, London.

World Health Organization (1989) Health Guidelines for the Use of Wastewater in Agriculture and Aquaculture. WHO Technical Report Series 778, Geneva.

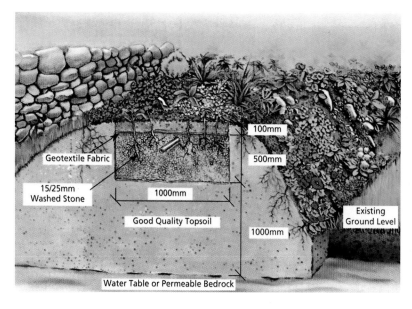

10.5.
Diagram showing how grey water can be incorporated into garden features with the construction of a sub-surface irrigation system (Biocycle Ltd: biocycle@intigo.ie).

CASE STUDY INTRODUCTION: TOWARDS THE NEW VERNACULAR

The following 20 case studies have been collected from friends and colleagues in 14 countries of the world. At the beginning of each case study, a Nicol graph shows the climate at the site. On it are drawn the mean maximum, mean minimum and comfort temperatures for a local adapted population. The comfort temperatures are for naturally ventilated buildings and for indigenous people. They tend to be more accurate for the summer temperatures. The mean solar radiation levels for each month are also given (W m^{-2}). Note that there is often a time lag between the maximum levels of solar radiation and the hottest months, which is caused by the slow heating of the Earth; this also happens in a house. Although the radiation levels are lower at around 3 p.m. than at 12 noon, the air temperature is higher because it is affected not only by radiation but also by the increased temperature of the structure of the building that has been heated earlier in the day. The Nicol graph is included to give a rough idea of what the climate locally is like and so how much work the building itself will have to do to provide indoor comfort temperatures for local people.

Each house is briefly described, its key features listed and elaborated on where appropriate. The key lessons learnt are included to enable the reader to benefit from them regarding what to and, not to do, if they wish to emulate the design ideas described in the case studies. The case studies as a whole do show four things clearly.

1 Time passes. Solar and ecohouse design has progressed steadily from the 1970s until today. We can see the progression from the Matsuoka house in Tokyo built in 1978 to the sophisticated Hamamatsu house built by OM Solar in Japan in 1991. In the later house the solar overheating problem has been solved and the solar technologies appear to be part of the whole building form and appearance, rather than as in the earlier house

where the technology dominated the house form, as it did in the 1970s Levine house in Kentucky.

2 New techologies and issues emerge. The solar house has evolved into the ecohouse as new issues come to the fore and new technologies are devised to deal with them. Materials and their impacts have been the dominant issue of the 1990s. We have now learnt how to count the total energy impacts of buildings, including their embodied energy and energy-in-use costs over the life of the house. These new abilities will be vital as we face the challenges of the next half-century. The next decade will see the rise of real concern about climate change. In the decade following that, society will become obsessed with dwindling fossil fuel reserves and the cost of oil and gas. The pioneering role being played by ecohouses in experimenting with and developing emerging technologies will begin to pay dividends in the near future as they set the agenda for all house design in the following decades. Where the 1970s houses tested the limits of solar hot water technologies, the latest ecohouses are pivotal in establishing photovoltaics in the market place. Architects who cannot incorporate energy and water conservation and reuse, and renewable energy into their buildings, will become dinosaurs, as will their white elephant buildings. Architecture is changing fast.

3 Human beings around the world are ingenious. These case studies are largely about the houses that architects build for themselves. The ingenuity, thought and affection lavished on many of them is apparent. From Bjorn Berge's demountable building to Christopher Day's beautifully sculptured window making a work of art out of a view. Just when one thought there was nothing new to learn about passive buildings a crop of new ideas arises from these examples that will spawn new generations of building forms in the years to come. The use of a hanging radiator in the centre of a space by Ashok Lall, or a cool-core building in the Malaysian vernacular by Jimmy Lim are great ideas. The courage and persistence of individuals is remarkable, as we can see with the house of David Morrison on the island of St Maarten. He displays a Robert the Bruce attitude as he try, try, tries again and again to protect his home from cyclones. Each year the house gets stronger and he learns more about how to grapple with the forces of nature in his search for shelter. Out of that search comes the wisdom that will result in new building forms, new technologies and better buildings.

4 The importance of climate in design. No longer should any client accept a building from an architect that does not deal well with the relationship between the indoor and outdoor climate. The

following case studies demonstrate the importance of climate in shaping buildings and, regardless of money, energy or the environment, in creating that most sought after quality of a building, thermal delight. Comfort can be seen simply as the absence of discomfort but thermal delight makes people happier. Look at the case study buildings and try to imagine what sensations they would create in you as you walked through them: the smells, the warmth, the light. These are the gifts of a good designer who can work the three key ingredients of architecture: the climate, the building and the people who occupy it.

TOWARDS THE NEW VERNACULAR

The analogy of the building as 'a machine for living in' that began this book, is a twentieth-century dream. We start the 21st century in search of the 'organic' house; the natural, healthy, safe, locally appropriate and globally responsible home. These houses should be more animal than machine, shaped by the seasons, the days, the wind and the path of the sun; by local materials, landscapes, culture, economy and of course the people who are to use them. They use technology wisely but are not slaves to it.

In the last half of this century we will probably all have to live in zero fossil fuel energy homes. The seeds of the ideas sown in this book by then will have grown into the New Vernacular of housing for the twenty-first century and beyond. These ecobuildings represent the developing foundations of the New Vernacular movement. Their designers take the best of the old wisdom and combine it with the best of the new technologies. They speak of soul and place. They experiment and they make mistakes, and they evaluate the strengths and weaknesses of each design feature because they want to learn, to change, to make a difference, to lay the foundations for the better houses we urgently need for the twenty-first century. They are the pioneers of the New Vernacular.

1 OXFORD ECOHOUSE

Architects:
Sue Roaf and David Woods

PV:
Energy Equipment Testing:
Cardiff with Jeremy Dain,
Inscape Architects, Bristol

Solar hot water:
George Goudsmit, AES Findhorn

Owner:
Susan Roaf

Location:
Oxford, UK, 51°N, 1°W, 40 m
above sea level

Climate:
Temperate

Area:
232 m², 250 m² including porch
and sun space

CS 1.1.
The Oxford Ecohouse.

CS 1.2.
Nicol graph for Oxford.

ECOFEATURES

• High levels of insulation • High thermal mass • Passive solar sun space with solar shading • Natural lighting • High security form • Air-tight construction • Triple glazing • 4 kW PV roof • 5 m² solar hot water • Energy efficient appliances • Wood burning kakkleoven • Energy efficient lighting • Low embodied energy construction

DESCRIPTION/BRIEF

The Oxford Ecohouse is a three-storey suburban detached house on a north–south alignment. It was built of traditional cavity wall construction. The key elements of the design brief were to have a quiet and healthy house with minimal CO_2 emissions. This was achieved with heavy construction, natural finishes, no carpets and, very importantly, buffer spaces to the front and back of the house in which damp clothes can be kept.

LOW CO_2 EMISSIONS AND FUTURE ASSET PROTECTION

This house has demonstrated that the performance of an ordinary suburban house can be improved substantially yet still be built in the traditional manner. The Oxford Ecohouse produces only around 148 kg CO_2 per annum, compared with the 6500 kg CO_2 of similar houses of the same size. On a number of occasions choices had to be made between putting money into building performance or appearance; the kitchen had only £250 spent on kitchen units. In addition, when Susan retires, it will be possible to run the house on a state pension, so early investment has protected her interests over time.

MATERIALS SELECTION

At the time the house was built there was beginning to be much debate about the materials issues and the manufacturers of products helped greatly in choosing the best energy products. Ibstock wisely suggested Bradgate bricks for the house. Jeffrey Walker and Co. were chosen to supply the timber, at the suggestion of Jewsons, because of the new low-energy timber-drying plant they have and their use of timber only from well-managed sustainable British forests, such as Sherwood Forest. Hepworth Drainage have recently completed a study on the embodied energy of their drainage products. All drainage pipes, WCs, basins and shower trays were of clay or porcelain, with a steel bath for durability, by Armitage Shanks. The tiles for the house came from the award-winning low-energy production line at Marlborough Tiles. Mr Howland ran special tests in the Potterton Myson Laboratories to test the impact of placing an ordinary long radiator vertically on the wall to save wall space; he found it was 25 per cent less efficient but this is of no consequence in a low-energy house. Gordon Grant at Velux developed special roof profiles for the integration of the Velux windows into the PV roof. Chris Thomas at Redland Roof Tiles built a mock up of the ventilated ridge section to see how it would work with the integrated PV roof. Ian Windwood carried out tests to see which adhesive was most appropriate on sunspace balconies for Wicanders floors. From the many people involved in this project came an enormous amount of real, old-fashioned building wisdom, and leading-edge scientific results. A true lesson from this house is that you should ask the company concerned about the product you want to use; they will know more about its performance than anyone else. A final aim for the house was that it should last at least 500 years.

CONSTRUCTION

The roof is constructed of concrete tiles on battens on 50 mm continuous expanded polystyrene over 200-mm-deep cellulose insulation between rafters, with 6 mm ply below. The U-value of the roof's components collectively is $U = 0.19 \, W \, m^{-2} \, C$. In addition the timber attic floor is insulated with 200 mm of mineral wool fibre between joists ($U = 0.24 \, W \, m^{-2} \, C$). The external walls have handmade bricks facing to the outside, 150 mm fill of mineral wool fibre with nylon wall ties behind the brick and 150 mm dense concrete block inner leaf with two coats of plaster finish internally. The U-value of the wall system is $0.22 \, W \, m^{-2} \, C$. The ground floor is a 15 mm floating timber flooring on 60 mm screed, over 150 mm concrete slab, on 150 mm polystyrene floor insulation with a U-value of $0.19 \, W \, m^{-2} \, C$. The Nordan triple-glazed timber windows have a total U-value of $1.3 \, W \, m^{-2} \, C$. In the buffer porch and sun space there are two walls of double-glazed windows, with whole-window U-values of $2.9 \, W \, m^{-2} \, C$ for each glazed wall.

Materials/element	U value (W m^{-2})	Description
Walls	0.22	Brick/block
Floor	0.19	150 mm insulation
Roof	0.14	250 mm insulation
Windows	1.30	Triple-glazed

PERFORMANCE SUMMARIZED

Type	kWh m^{-2} a^{-1}	Electric cost (£)	Gas cost (£)	Total cost (£)	CO$_2$ emissions (kg)	Construction cost (£) (per m^2)*
Oxford Ecohouse	26	8	44	52	148	720
Typical house	90	180	476	566	6500	720
Savings	64	172	432	514	6360	0 extra

*The construction costs have been compared with a similar architect-designed detached house. The finishes in Sue Roaf's house are very basic and the extra cost of the solar heating is probably covered by the savings of not having a fancy kitchen, or a decorator.
£0.66 = US$1.00.

LESSONS LEARNED/PITFALLS

Lessons learned: Sue Roaf

Many of the lessons learned in building the house are included in various chapters of this book. Key lessons learned include:

1 the success of the solution is not dependent on a single grand idea but the aggregation of interacting and correct choices;
2 the use of small vents into the buffer porch and sun space provide a very good quality of natural ventilation even in the coldest periods in the Oxford climate;
3 the stabilization of the indoor climate through the use of high levels of thermal mass provides a safe and comfortable climate throughout the year;
4 the choice of good triple-glazed Nor-Dan windows was very important in the overall building performance, as was the elimination of all cold bridges in the structure with careful detailing by David Woods.

Lesson learned: David Woods

It is not difficult to construct a low-energy house. It requires careful site work. Two important strategies for temperate climates are the reduction of air infiltration and elimination of cold bridges, along with increased passive solar gain and insulation. Having adopted those strategies the design of each individual element in the building takes on more meaning, especially in how each fits into the envelope.

ACKNOWLEDGEMENTS

People who helped with the building of the Oxford Ecohouse include:
AEG, London; AES Ltd, Findhorn; Armitage Shanks, Rugeley, UK; BHS, London; Bill Bordass; Boulton & Paul, Norwich; Richard Burbidge Ltd, Oswestry; Catnic Ltd, Caerphilly, Wales; Loren Butt; Dales Fabrications Ltd (gutters), Ilkeston; Camas Flooring Systems, South Cerney, Gloucestershire; Ecos Paints (now Lakeland Paints, Kendal, Cumbria); Piers Gough; Patti Hopkins; Hepworth Drainage, Sheffield; Ibstock Building Products (bricks), Ibstock, UK; Jewson Ltd, Norwich; K.G. Kristiansen ApS, Kolding, Denmark (nylon wall ties); Marlborough Tiles, Marlborough; Nor-Dan UK Ltd, Tuffley, Gloucestershire; Notcutts, Nuneham Courtney; Philips Lighting, Croydon; Potterton Myson, Gateshead; Redland Roof Tiles Ltd, Reigate; Ritevent, Washington, Tyne and Wear; Siesta Cork Tiles Ltd, Croydon; Smith's Security Services Ltd, Oxford; Stoves, Prescot Merseyside (high-efficiency gas stove and oven); Robert Toland, Sydney; The Velux Company, Glenrothes, Fife; Reinhardt Von Zschock and Nick Hills of the Ceramic Stove Company, Oxford; Jeffrey Walker & Co. Ltd, Harworth, Doncaster; Wicanders Flooring, Horsham; Terry Wyatt; Yorkpark Ltd (condensing boiler), Amersham.

2 FINDHORN HOUSE

Architect:
Johan Vorster

Client:
Inglis & Goudsmit

Location:
Findhorn, Scotland, 57°N, 3°W,
8 m above sea level

Climate:
Temperate

Area:
165 m²

CS 2.1.
Computer-generated photo of the Findhorn house.

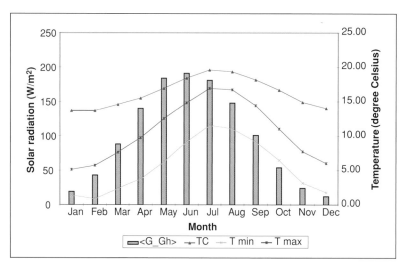

CS 2.2.
Nicol graph for Findhorn house.

ECOFEATURES

• Orientation • Thermal mass • Rock store • Heat re-use from photo-voltaic cells • OM solar system • Thermal solar water heater

DESCRIPTION/BRIEF

This design is a great example of simulation studies directing design decisions. The as-yet unbuilt house will include solar technology, passive design and social spaces with views to the bay and distant mountains. The client wishes to have visual privacy from an adjacent road, which also poses a potential noise problem. An open house plan is designed providing protection from the wind without sacrificing light and natural heat gains during the winter.

LOCATION
FINDHORN SCOTLAND
57 40'N 3 40W
8 m ASL

SITE

The site is at the end of an unused road. The site sits within 275 m (300 yards) of the bay and is blasted by strong, cold southwesterly winds that would force infiltration into the house. However, the site falls within a solar window – a weather condition borne of a series of mountain ranges that encircle the region and reduce cloud formation, resulting in longer annual hours of solar radiation, the benefit of more productive agriculture and a slightly more comfortable climate than surrounding areas. To maximize the full potential of the site the southern façade is optimized.

CS 2.3.
Location of the Findhorn house.

Solar data – sun angles in degrees clockwise from north (for Aberdeen)

	09:00 h		12:00 h		15:00 h		Sunrise	Sunset
	Vertical	Horizontal	Vertical	Horizontal	Vertical	Horizontal		
Winter solstice (22 December)	1	140	9	180	1	220	137	223
Spring/autumn (23 March/23 September)	24	130	33	180	24	230	?	?
Summer solstice (22 July)	43	117	56	180	43	243	43	317

The site demands a design that is narrow in section. High winds from the southwest are to be reduced by surface detailing that offers little resistance to the wind and by the construction of a berm using 'gabions' (mesh baskets that hold aggregate/stone in-fill) adjacent to the house in order to lift the wind onto the roof. This low-maintenance strategy is used along the road as a visual and noise barrier, and around the sub-station to inhibit the potential of electromagnetic radiation. In the summer, for those unusually hot days, the turf roof will enable an evaporative cooling effect, conditioning the air that is fed into the house.

CS 2.4.
UK climatic sketch.

CAUTIONS

- Radon;
- electromagnetic radiation (from nearby sub-station);
- unstable groundfill on site;
- strong, cold winds from the sea (cooling effect and forced infiltration).

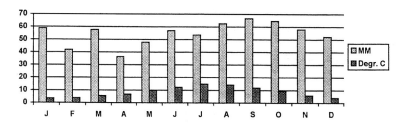

[Rainfall ave. = 656mm/yr . Temp ave. = 8.6 degrees C]

CS 2.5.
Rainfall/temperature averages (climate data for Kinloss from http://www.worldclimate.com).

CS 2.6.
East elevation.

THERMAL MASS

The proposed design incorporates a number of high-mass features, which enable the capture of solar radiation. The sunspace and living room will be constructed of 100 mm of concrete and finished with a low-reflective surface to increase absorption of radiation. The majority of the internal walls will be 200 mm stone, 300 mm polystyrene and finished with 10 mm gypsum plasterboard. External walls will be predominantly constructed of locally available 30 mm softwood with 300 mm fibre insulation and finished with gypsum board. The south and east walls will use TIM (trans-

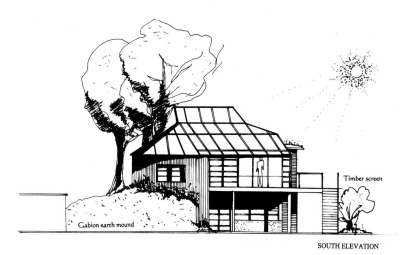

SOUTH ELEVATION

CS 2.7.
South elevation.

parent insulation material) Clad construction, permitting a high degree of solar radiation absorption within the wall, which is more effective than at the surface. It consists of 6 mm glass, 100 mm TIM, 6 mm glass, 200 mm high-density concrete block and 10 mm gypsum plaster board.

ROCK STORE

There will be two rock stores designed to deal with fluctuations in heating demands over a number of days. The primary rock store will be 30 m³ in size and located under the dining room. It will be fed heat from the solar air system. A secondary rock store bed using demolition waste will be located underneath the rooms adjoining the corridor. This secondary rock bed is a short-term subsidiary heat store to the primary rock store. It will be encased by 30 mm softwood, a 50 mm air space, 500 mm of rock, 30 mm plywood and 200 mm expanded polystyrene. It is located around rooms that are some distance from the hotter core of the building and which are deemed to require their own store of heat.

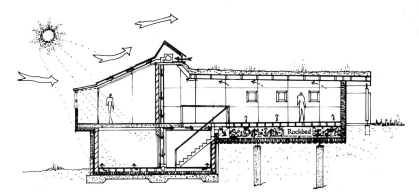

CS 2.8.
Section through the house.

HEAT REUSE FROM PHOTOVOLTAIC CELLS AND THERMAL SOLAR HOT WATER

A heat core is created at the centre of the house comprising the vertical hot air ducts from the solar collectors, the wood burning fireplace and a high-thermal-mass structure. Landscaped ceilings will collect and recover heat via a central distribution/exchange unit (part of OM Solar system, see House at Hamamatsu case study). A strip of photovoltaic panels will be placed at the lower end of the solar air roof. As photovoltaic cells have a tendency to overheat this location will benefit from the cooling effect of the berm-directed wind while utilizing the heat generated to initiate convection in the solar air roof. Waste heat will migrate towards the centre of the house by means of natural convection. A heat exchanger will recover the heat for reuse. A separate thermal solar collector of 4 m² and linked to the dual coil mains pressure AquaSol Duo cylinder will provide some 70 per cent of the annual hot water demand.

LESSONS LEARNED

Planners prefer to work with innovative ideas such as this. However, they have to consider the usually conventionally thinking neighbours. This means that the house needs to be as much hidden from public view as possible. Trees and other vegetation will be used to minimize the visual impact.

ACKNOWLEDGEMENTS/CONTACT INFORMATION

The clients would like to acknowledge the following:

- Sue Roaf's MSc Energy Efficient Building team for producing a wide choice of exciting designs from which to choose;
- Johan Vorster for patiently listening to our requests and requirements;
- Moray Council Planners for not giving up on us;
- Councillor Ronald Gregory for helping to wade through officialdom.

AES Solar, George Goudsmit, Findhorn, Scotland. E-mail: info@aessolar.co.uk

Thanks are also due to Andrew Bairstow and Manuel Fuentes who did the calculations for the house.

3 REUSABLE BUILDING

Architect:
Bjørn Berge, Gaia, Lista AS

Owner:
Økologiske Hus AS, Norges
Forskningstråd, statens
Forurensningstilsyn

Location:
Marnardal, Norway; 58ºN, 8ºW

Climate:
Inland, cold and medium dry

Area:
132 m²

CS 3.1.
Reusable building. Økologiske Hus.

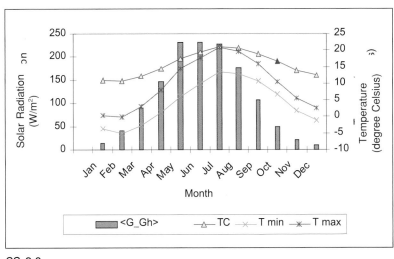

CS 3.2.
Nicol graph for Norway.

ECOFEATURES

• Reusable building materials • Low energy consumption • Excellent
indoor air quality • Avoiding use of poisonous substances during
construction, use or demolition stage

DESCRIPTION/BRIEF

The house is located in a valley 30 miles (48.3 km) from Kristiansand. It is a one-family dwelling that can easily be extended or divided into a two-family building (two flats), a kindergarten, a workshop, small office or similar. The one-family dwelling consists of three bedrooms, one bathroom, kitchen, sitting room and storage for food and others. The interior walls can easily be moved to form other plans.

MATERIALS

The house uses an ADISA (Assembly for Disassembly) building system developed by Gaia. The house is erected on a 3.6-m grid system of concrete pad/pile foundations onto which the timber frame is fixed. The building system consists of 80 different standardized cladding and structural components that are manufactured using a minimum amount of machinery. All components are easy to dismantle. Since the components are prefabricated there is little waste in the building phase, about 0.3 per cent by weight, while for conventionally erected buildings the figure varies from 3 to 5 per cent. The building can be changed, extended or reduced with simple hand tools. Dismantled components and extra parts can be returned to local manufacturers for quality control, and redistributed to new building projects.

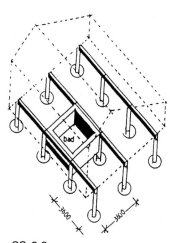

CS 3.3.
3.6 m grid system.

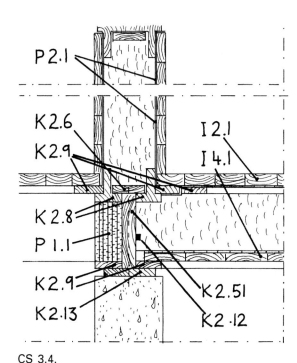

CS 3.4.
Details showing the number of reusable lumber components in the reusable building: ground floor section.

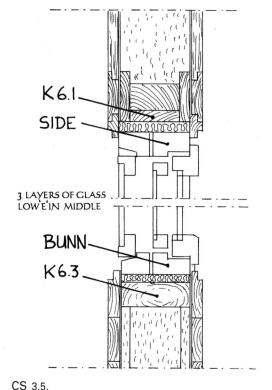

CS 3.5.
Details showing the number of reusable lumber components in the reusable building: window section.

Where only 5 per cent of the materials used in conventional wooden buildings can be reused, the Gaia Lista system achieves a reuse rate of 80 per cent. Of the remaining materials, approximately 13 per cent can be used for material or energy recycling, while approximately 8 per cent is inert and can be used in filling purposes. Only 0.8 per cent has to go to a controlled waste deposit.

Thanks to careful selection of materials and production processes, the components in the ADISA system have a considerably longer lifespan than in other wooden buildings in Scandinavia. Account is taken of such aspects as where the tree comes from, when it was felled, which parts of the trunk are used in which part of the construction, and how they are used. Heavy metal impregnation fluids are not used.

EFFICIENT INSULATION

Dwellings built using this system have high insulation values, keeping the indoor temperature at a comfortable level during even the harshest winters.

Materials/element GL	U value (W m^{-2} K)	Description
Floors	0.176	200 mm cellulose fibre
Walls	0.232	150 mm cellulose fibre
Roof	0.126	350 mm cellulose fibre
Windows	0.16	three layers of glass in a coupled window, low 'E' glass in middle

VENTILATION

Natural basis ventilation. A part of the natural ventilation system is its interior surfaces of wood. These are hygroscopic and form a buffer for humidity in the same way that heavy materials are a buffer for temperature, and this exerts a positive influence on the internal climate. A moderate and stable moisture situation will reduce the chances of mites and microorganisms growing. The disposition and emission cycles of dust on the inside surfaces will also be reduced.

LESSONS LEARNED/PITFALLS

The house is a prototype. The design has to be improved to fit with a broader market. Gaia is currently researching a means of reducing the number of different components from 80 to preferably around 50.

ACKNOWLEDGEMENTS

siv.ark.Dag Roalkvam; Gaia Lista -siv. Ark. Ola Brattset; SINTEF – proff. Hans Granum; SINTEF – proff. Petter Aune; NTNU – siv.ing. Ida Bryn.

The supposed distribution of materials in a demolition phase

	kg	%
Reusable components	38.053	78.4
Recycling materials	987.00	2.0
Recycling energy	5.4	11.1

4 ECOHOUSE WIBERG

Architect:
Krister Wiberg, 1993

Owner:
Krister Wiberg

Location:
Lund, Sweden; 55ºN, 13ºW;
<74 m above sea level

Climate:
Temperate in south with cold,
cloudy winters and cool, partly
cloudy summers

Area:
180 m²

CS 4.1.
Ecohouse Wiberg.

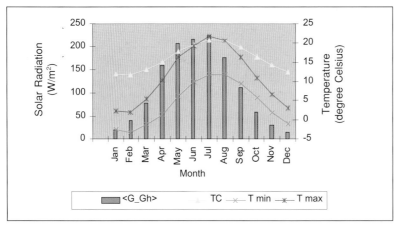

CS 4.2.
Nicol graph for Lund, Sweden.

ECOFEATURES

• Environmentally friendly building materials • Exterior and interior painted with Tempura paints • 250 mm cellulose fibre insulation between two stone walls open to diffusion • Floors of ceramic tiles or solid wood treated with natural oils • Self ventilation • Heating system: active solar heating, bio-fuels and gas • Heavy frame for heat conservation • Greenhouse • Earth cellar • Composting toilets • Solid wood kitchen fixtures

FEATURES BRIEFLY EXPLAINED

Ecohouse Wiberg, located in southern Sweden, is built according to ecological principles. It includes a passive system and a ventilated and easily inspected underfloor creepway. The walls are of lightweight concrete blocks with an intermediate layer of cellulose fibre sheeting, which give the house a heavy, heat-storing frame. The ventilation works on the self-draught system, the heating through a water mantled tile stove and gas. All materials are non-toxic and natural.

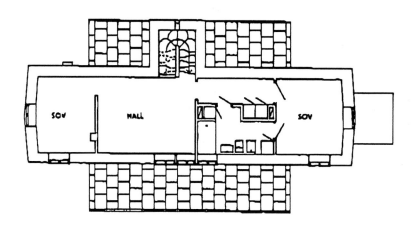

CS 4.3.
Second floor plan.

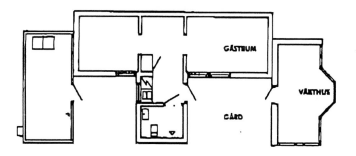

CS 4.4.
First floor plan.

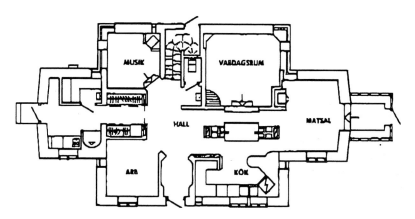

CS 4.5.
Ground floor plan.

5 MONAMA

NORTH ELEVATION

CS 5.1.
Monama, for Dr and Mrs Ramlal.

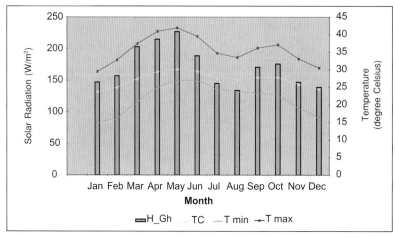

CS 5.2.
Nicol graph for Monama.

Designers:
Prashant Kapoor, Saleem Akhtar

Local Architect:
Arun Prasad

Renewable energy consultant:
Manuel Fuentes

Owners:
Dr and Mrs Ramlal

Location:
Hyderabad, Andra Pradesh, India; 17ºN, 78ºE; 530 m above sea level

Climate:
Inland composite

Area:
234 m²

ECOFEATURES

• Low environmental impact materials • Buried pipes and evaporative cooling • Rainwater harvesting • Renewable energy

DESCRIPTION/BRIEF

Monoma, named after the clients' late daughter, is in the city of Hyderabad. Hyderabad has a history of Moghul invasion and an Islamic character as far as its historical architecture is concerned. It is among the fastest growing cities of India and is becoming extremely attractive to industrial investors. Although there has been a significant increase in the industrial activity of the region, the rate of growth of infrastructure has not been sufficiently significant to keep up with requirements. Hyderabad has deficient power supply, resulting in breakdowns and power cuts almost every day. One of the main objectives for this design was not to rely entirely on the national grid for energy. The house for Dr and Mrs Ramlal relies on energy-efficient design to reduce loads and, where possible, reverts to renewable energy to meet them. Although flexible, the clients

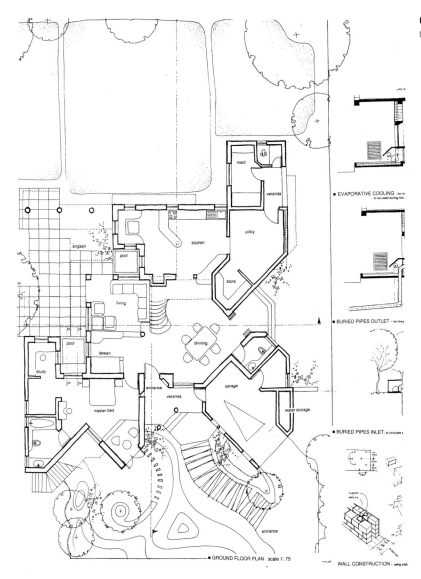

■ EVAPORATIVE COOLING - for m
to be used during hot .

■ BURIED PIPES OUTLET - for living

■ BURIED PIPES INLET - to circulate

■ GROUND FLOOR PLAN scale 1:75

WALL CONSTRUCTION - using slab

Plan labels: maid, veranda, utility, kitchen, ángaan, pool, store, living, pool, dewan, study, entrance, veranda, dinning, master bed, garage, water storage, entrance

require that the master bedroom be located on the ground floor and near the road, that the garage be enclosed, that two bedrooms and a future rental space be located on the first floor with a separate entry from the main entrance to the house. The house is being completed in 2001.

LOW ENVIRONMENTAL IMPACT

The underlying ideology behind the building design was to generate as low an environmental impact as possible, within the limits of site and budget. Environmental impact resulting from both embodied (from materials) and operational (in-use) considerations was assessed.

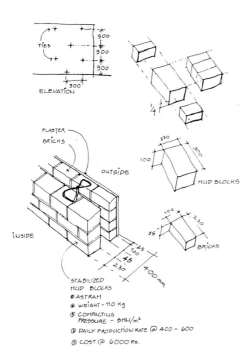

CS 5.4.
Wall construction, using stabilized mud blocks (country bricks).

CS 5.5.
Stairs under construction (master bedroom beyond).

Construction materials

Although the original idea was to use compressed earth blocks, on further investigation the soil quality in the area was found to be unsuitable. It was realized that soil would have to be transported from approximately 400 km away and country bricks that were made within a couple of kilometres of the site would be a better alternative. Country bricks tend to require plaster on the external side as they are not of a quality that can withstand the extreme climate. The solution was to make cavity walls with country bricks on the inside and first-class, wire-cut bricks on the external façade. As a result, the need to use plaster was eliminated. This strategy also provides high thermal mass, which suits the prevailing climatic conditions. The upper floor and roof structure is made with reinforced concrete, which has low environmental impact. Natural materials have been chosen for most internal finishes. Simulations showed that the ground floor would require a high thermal mass to prevent overheating of interior spaces, whereas a high thermal mass had less influence on the top-floor indoor temperature.

WALL ORIENTATION AND FORM

Orientation of the wall openings, combined with their size and angle, modulate solar gains passing through. The south wall orients openings to accept low solar gains in the winter and can easily be shaded in the summer, owing to the sun's high position in the sky. Shading of the west and east windows presents difficulties because of the low position of the sun and, additionally, west-oriented openings are associated with external conditions of high solar radiation and ambient temperature during the summer. Thus, the windows in this orientation were minimized or

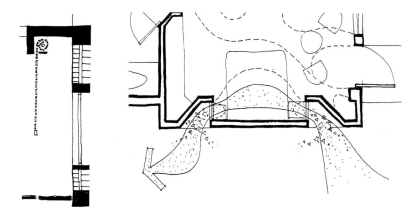

CS 5.6.
South and west windows, designed to avoid direct solar gain.

replaced with other design solutions. Depending on the time of the day, high or low pressure zones form in either east or west directions. This induces air movement from the zone of high pressure to that of low pressure. The windows of the house have been specially oriented such that these pressure differences, in combination with the prevailing wind direction, may be utilized for continuous ventilation. There is also a ventilation shaft to exhaust hot air located in the central part of the house, which is based on the principles of buoyancy and venturi's effect. The difference in pressure between the outside and the inside air results in the drawing up of air through the shaft and inducing further movement through openings such as windows. The open plan design supports this process by eliminating any internal resistance to the full movement of air.

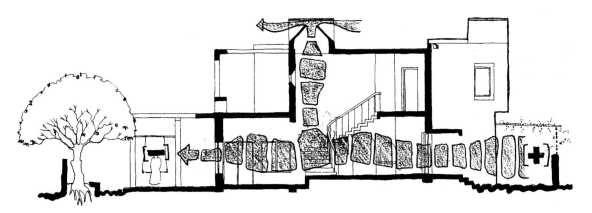

BURIED PIPES AND EVAPORATIVE COOLING

CS 5.7.
Ventilation paths through the house.

Buried pipes function by injecting into the building air that has been previously circulated underground by means of earth-to-air heat exchangers. The air is generally sucked from the ambient air by means of a fan. The temperature drop of the outlet air depends upon the inlet air temperature, the ground temperature at the depth at which the exchanger is situated, the thermal conductivity of the pipes and the thermal diffusivity of the soil, as well as the air velocity and pipe dimensions. Using Summer™ to simulate all the variables, the optimal conditions resulted in:

- length of the exchanger: 26 m;
- radius of the exchanger: 0.125 m;
- air velocity through the pipe: 2 m s^{-1};
- depth of the exchanger: 2 m.

Buried pipes are being utilized for the main living areas of the house, namely the living room and the master bedroom. Since the velocity of the outlet air is low at 2 m s^{-1}, adjustable tubes at the outlet ensure placement as user prefers.

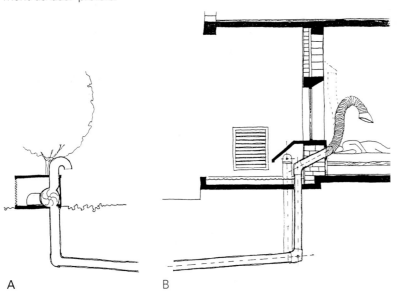

CS 5.8.
Buried pipes. A, inlet – to circulate air 2 m underground at 2 m s^{-1}; B, outlet – for living area, with adjustable 'trunk'.

A   B

Evaporative cooling is the process that uses the effect of evaporation as a natural heat sink. Again, through simulations, results indicated that the indoor temperatures of the room fluctuate between 27.5ºC and 29ºC on a hot, dry day. The peak humidity does not exceed 66 per cent, therefore evaporative cooling would succeed as a low energy cooling strategy for these hot and dry months (March through June). The system used is a water pond along with an air fan. The system provides cooling by consuming just the amount of electricity necessary for the operation of the fans. Since the fans consume far less energy than air-conditioners this proves an energy-efficient design for maintaining human comfort. During the humid months evaporative coolers are rendered inefficient owing to the high humidity levels. The system allows for the ponds to be drained during these months (July through October) and window fans used to forcefully ventilate the house.

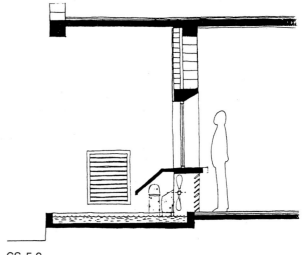

CS 5.9.
Evaporative cooling.

RAINWATER HARVESTING

Hyderabad has a history of water shortages during the dry months. Receiving over 795 mm rain annually justifies storing rain water for inter-seasonal storage. Rainwater harvesting is a method of collecting rainwater and using precipitation from a small catchment area. The water stored will be a valuable supplement for domestic water consumption and irrigation of the garden. As soil from the site is used for building blocks, the resulting pit proves to be an optimal location for the storage tank. The storage tank is located on the northwest corner of the building under the garage for easy maintenance. The outer wall of the garage has a built-in sand filter to process incoming water, as well as temporary storage from which water can be used without the need for a pump.

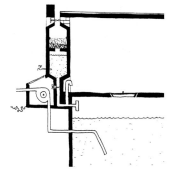

CS 5.10.
Rainwater harvesting. Section showing in situ sand filter.

RENEWABLE ENERGY

The Indian Renewable Energy Development Authority (IREDA) offers a low interest loan that provides soft loans for industrial and commercial projects at 8.3 per cent interest, with 5 per cent for non-profit organizations and 5 per cent for domestic applications (September 1999). This is a substantial subsidy on capital budgets, which clearly proves that as such policy decisions are taken at the level of the government, the fossil fuel situation in India is in a critical state. In Hyderabad there are four hours of power cuts each day. The client specifications were to design a system that works as a photovoltaic stand-alone system during power cuts, and as a regular grid-connected system when the grid is working. The battery chosen for this design allows for four days of autonomy, making it unlikely that the client has to use the utility power to charge the battery. The inverter is multi-functional with 24 V input, 220 V output and a rating power of 800–1000 Wp, and is readily available on the market. The array that is needed to provide the power according to user needs is 850 W. Modules with high-efficiency polycrystalline cells would need a roof area of about 7 m^2.

SOLAR HOT WATER COLLECTOR

There are several systems available but the one chosen for Monama is a free-flow system known as a thermosiphon system. The use of the thermosiphon system is accepted worldwide owing to its simple and reliable characteristics. The system has no pump or controls and is fully automatic in operation.

In the thermosiphon system the tank is positioned above the collector. As the water in the collector is heated by the sun, it rises into the tank mounted above the collector. This causes the cold water in the tank to flow into the collector, where it is heated. In this way, flow is created and the tank is filled with hot water.

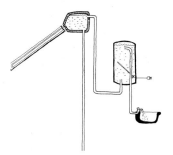

CS 5.11.
The solar water collector works by thermosiphon.

ACKNOWLEDGEMENTS/CONTACT INFORMATION

This project was part of a course-related assignment at Oxford Brookes University. This project has become an example of student solutions generating a real project.

Kapoor Prashant, London, UK. E-mail: designpeople@building.com

6 HOUSE AT HAMAMATSU

Architect:
Touichi Akiyama, Land
Architects Inc., OM Solar, 1991

Owner:
Syounai

Location:
Hamamatsu, Japan; 34ºN,
137ºE; 31.7 m above sea level

Climate:
Tropical • 804 degree
days year^{-1}

Area:
201.6 m^2

CS 6.1.
House at Hamamatsu, by OM Solar.

CS 6.2.
Nicol graph for Hamamatsu.

ECOFEATURES

• OM Solar system • Thermal insulation • Airtight • Heat chimney

DESCRIPTION/BRIEF

Typical Japanese homes have large roofs, deep eaves, wide openings, open room dividers and floors set high above the earth. These are also characteristics of tropical housing systems. These traditions are closely associated with the Japanese climate of high temperatures and high humidity. However, the winter in Japan is not necessarily warm. Even the southern parts of the main island of Japan can encounter snow and temperatures to below 0ºC. The OM Solar system and the house's wooden construction allow it to regulate its indoor climate to a comfortable level between changing seasons.

ECOFEATURES EXPLAINED

OM Solar system

The OM Solar passive system collects solar energy from the roof of the house and utilizes it for space and water heating. This system can provide 300 l of water at 40–60ºC. The system is an air heat collecting system that warms outside air by solar energy. Utilizing air for heat collection is much safer than using water in terms of water leakage or freezing. The use of outside air is the most unique feature of this system, creating a positive room pressure and, as a result, promoting better air ventilation. The system also heats the rooms by transporting the heat collected beneath the roof to be stored under the concrete slab under the floor. At sunset when the temperature decreases, the warm air rises slowly into the room above the wood-finished floor.

Handling box
The OM handling box is the heart of the OM Solar system. The function of moving heat from the roof either to the floor (winter) or to the outside (summer) is done by this mechanical handler.

AIRTIGHT AND THERMALLY INSULATED

The heat balance in the house consists of three elements: heat collection, heat storage and airtight thermal insulation. The means of keeping wooden houses, such as the house at Hamamatsu, from losing heat after collection (wood has poor heat storage capability) is through air tightness and insulation. The house at Hamamatsu has a high degree of air tightness and thermal insulation to reduce air-conditioning loads in the summer, and winter life is made more comfortable with glass wool. Glass wool is one of the most popular thermal insulating materials and is used in the roof and walls in the house at Hamamatsu. The foundations are insulated with polystyrene foam.

ACKNOWLEDGEMENTS

He Jiang, OM Solar Association, Hamamatsu City, Japan. Website http://www.omsolar.co.jp/

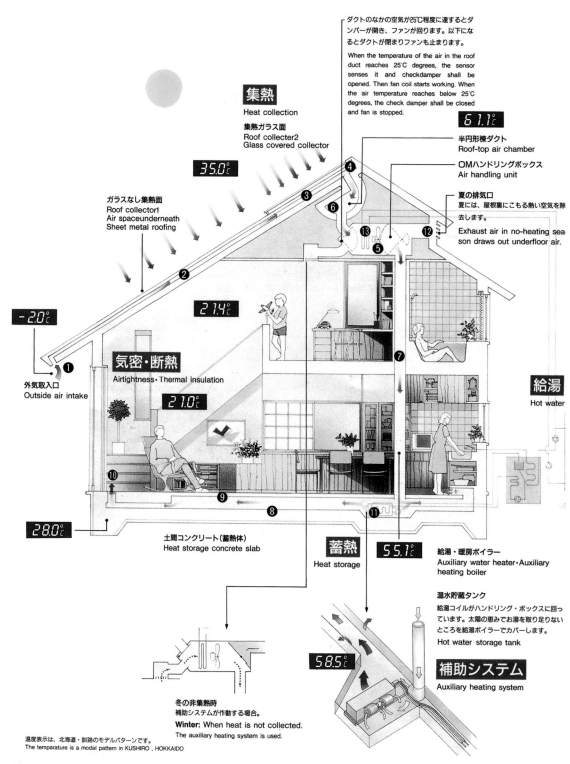

ダクトのなかの空気が25℃程度に達するとダンパーが開き、ファンが回ります。以下になるとダクトが閉まりファンも止まります。

When the temperature of the air in the roof duct reaches 25°C degrees, the sensor senses it and checkdamper shall be opened. Then fan coil starts working. When the air temperature reaches below 25°C degrees, the check damper shall be closed and fan is stopped.

集熱
Heat collection

集熱ガラス面
Roof collecter2
Glass covered collector

ガラスなし集熱面
Roof collector1
Air spaceunderneath
Sheet metal roofing

61.1℃

半円形棟ダクト
Roof-top air chamber

OMハンドリングボックス
Air handling unit

夏の排気口
夏には、屋根裏にこもる熱い空気を除去します。
Exhaust air in no-heating season draws out underfloor air.

35.0℃

21.4℃

−2.0℃

外気取入口
Outside air intake

気密・断熱
Airtightness・Thermal insulation

21.0℃

給湯
Hot water

28.0℃

土間コンクリート(蓄熱体)
Heat storage concrete slab

蓄熱
Heat storage

55.1℃

給湯・暖房ボイラー
Auxiliary water heater・Auxiliary heating boiler

温水貯蔵タンク
給湯コイルがハンドリング・ボックスに回っています。太陽の恵みでお湯を取り足りないところを給湯ボイラーでカバーします。
Hot water storage tank

58.5℃

補助システム
Auxiliary heating system

冬の非集熱時
補助システムが作動する場合。
Winter: When heat is not collected.
The auxiliary heating system is used.

温度表示は、北海道・釧路のモデルパターンです。
The temparature is a model pattern in KUSHIRO , HOKKAIDO

CS 6.3.
Cross-section through Hamamatsu house.

THE MECHANISM OF OM SOLAR SYSTEM

How it works in winter

The OM Solar system uses the roof of the house itself for the purpose of heat collection. The air under the roof is heated by solar energy and used for heating water or is circulated under the floor. At the eaves:

- Fresh air from the opening is heated by the sun radiating on the roof. As it is heated, it rises.
- The glass roof surface (3) is not a special heat collection device, but a simple reinforced glass sheet placed on the metal plate to make heat collection more effective. When the air runs under this, it is heated effectively. At the top of roof there is a thermostat (4).
- The hot air is gathered in the half cylinder duct (6).
- When the air reaches a certain temperature, a small fan (5) starts to operate.
- During the winter, with the help of this fan, this hot air is guided under the floor through the duct (7).
- The concrete slab (8) under the floor is designed to be a heat accumulation body. The heat preserved here is slowly discharged and warms the entire floor.
- The air, heated by conduction from the concrete slab circulates in the room. The release of this fresh air also stimulates the air ventilation (10).

As the OM Solar system utilizes solar energy, auxiliary heating is necessary in case of cloudy or rainy days that would not provide enough sunshine. There are many kinds of auxiliary heating devices. One such is the fan convector (11). The heat generated by the fan convector is also stored under the floor. The characteristic of the OM Solar system is that we can utilize the heating accumulation portion for both summer and winter cases.

How it works in summer

- The heated air is collected in the half cylinder duct (6).
- The air is released to the outside through the exhaust duct (12).
- At the same time, the air under the floor is vented by the air circulation.
- It is discharged outside through the downward duct (7). This can also rid the house of heat in summer.
- But, before it is discharged, it is used to heat water (13). By this means we can achieve two purposes at the same time.

Multifunctional/four seasons-solar

The OM Solar system is multifunctional, which works in all four seasons through floor heating, ventilation, heating water, eliminating heat and cooling the room in the house in summer. This system utilizes the solar energy very effectively and works beneficially for energy saving and creates comfortable living conditions for people.

夏モードと冬モードの空気の流れを、夏・冬切換ダンバーによって、切換えます。

Summer and winter modes can be regulated on and off by the switch of the damper.

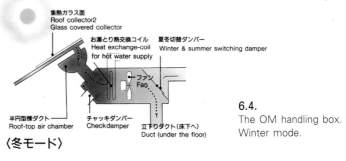

集熱ガラス面
Roof collector2
Glass covered collector

お湯とり熱交換コイル
Heat exchange-coil
for hot water supply

夏冬切替ダンバー
Winter & summer switching damper

ファン
Fan

半円型樋ダクト
Roof-top air chamber

チャッキダンバー
Checkdamper

立下りダクト（床下へ）
Duct (under the floor)

〈冬モード〉

6.4.
The OM handling box. Winter mode.

6.5.
The OM handling box. Winter mode.

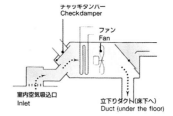

ナッキダンバー
Checkdamper

ファン
Fan

室内空気吸込口
Inlet

立下りダクト（床下へ）
Duct (under the floor)

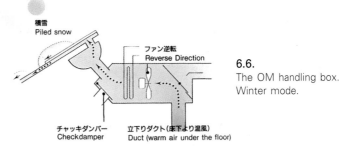

積雪
Piled snow

ファン逆転
Reverse Direction

チャッキダンバー
Checkdamper

立下りダクト（床下より温風）
Duct (warm air under the floor)

6.6.
The OM handling box. Winter mode.

6.7.
The OM handling box. Summer mode.

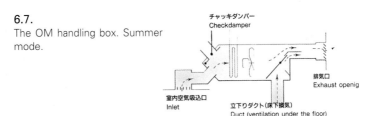

チャッキダンバー
Checkdamper

室内空気吸込口
Inlet

立下りダクト（床下換気）
Duct (ventilation under the floor)

排気口
Exhaust openig

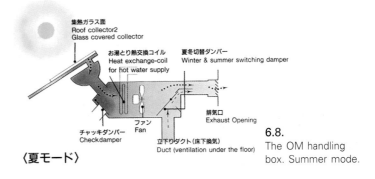

集熱ガラス面
Roof collector2
Glass covered collector

お湯とり熱交換コイル
Heat exchange-coil
for hot water supply

夏冬切替ダンバー
Winter & summer switching damper

チャッキダンバー
Checkdamper

ファン
Fan

立下りダクト（床下換気）
Duct (ventilation under the floor)

排気口
Exhaust Opening

6.8.
The OM handling box. Summer mode.

〈夏モード〉

7 1979 SOLAR HOUSE

Architect:
Professor K. Kimura, Mr H. Matsuoka

Owners:
Mr and Mrs I. Sagara

Location:
Inagi, Tokyo; 35ºN, 139ºE; 50 m above sea level

Climate:
Composite

Area:
120 ms²

CS 7.1.
1979 Solar House by Ken-ichi Kimura.

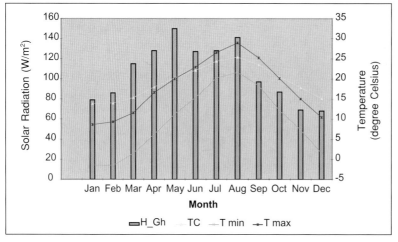

CS 7.2.
Nicol graph for Tokyo.

ECOFEATURES

• Good insulation levels in walls, roof and windows • Passive solar gain • Hybrid solar hot water system for space heating using passive and active circulation to move heat around the building • Buffer spaces • High thermal mass with external insulation • 24 m² solar hot water collector for water and space heating feeding a coil heating system embedded in the concrete slab floor • 950 l stainless steel water tank beneath the stair in the centre of the house for the solar hot water collection system, with pumped pipe system in ground to low tank temperatures in summer • In winter the city water was preheated through the same earth-coupled pipe system

DESCRIPTION/BRIEF

In 1980 the house used only 5020 kWh total electricity consumption, of which 18 per cent was for the hot water supply and space heating. This is 43.5 kWh m^{-2} a^{-1} (Kimura, 1981).

KEY FEATURES BRIEFLY EXPLAINED

The 1979 Solar House in Tokyo was built with good insulation levels in walls, roof and windows, even by the standards of today. This insulation, coupled with passive solar gains, allowed the house to maintain comfortable temperatures through the cold seasons. The hybrid solar hot water system for space heating uses passive and active circulation to move heat around. The roof housed 24 m^2 of solar hot water collectors for water and for space heating, feeding a coil heating system embedded in the concrete slab floor. A 950 l stainless steel water tank beneath the stairs in the centre of the house stored the solar hot water collection system and had a pumped pipe system in the ground to lower the tank temperatures in summer. In the winter the city water was preheated through the same earth-coupled pipe system.

Type	kWh m^{-2} a^{-1}	Cost of electricity (yen)
Case study house	43	32 000
Typical house	290	210 000
Savings	257	178 000

105.52 yen = US$1.00.
The solar system had a build cost of 1 100 000 yen and a payback time of 6.2 years.

LESSONS LEARNED/PITFALLS

- Comfort was achieved in winter when the temperature in the tank sank as low as 20ºC but internal temperatures were maintained between 18 and 22ºC.
- Excess heat dissipation from the storage tank under the stairs in summer needed rectifying.
- The capacity of the auxiliary electric heat of 5 kW could be less.
- Cool tube system should be improved.
- Other passive cooling means should be incorporated.
- Cost reductions on solar system essential if such technologies are to be taken up.
- Heat recovery systems should be incorporated.
- Long-term heat storage system should be improved.

ACKNOWLEDGEMENTS/CONTACT INFORMATION

Mr Matsuoko, Professor Ken-ichi Kimura, Shinbo Construction Company, Chubu Create Company and Showa Aluminium Company are gratefully acknowledged.
Professor Ken-ichi Kimura, Waseda, Japan. E-mail: kimura@kimura.arch.waseda.ac.jp

8 LIM HOUSE

Architect:
Jimmy Lim, CSL Associates

Owner:
Jimmy Lim

Location:
Taman Seputeh, Kuala Lumpur, Malaysia; 3ºN, 101ºE; 17 m above sea level

Climate:
Hot, humid, tropical (the architect describes the climate as having two seasons: 'hot and wet' and 'hot and more wet')

Area:
Site = 1415 m², house = 884 m²

CS 8.1.
Lim House, by Jimmy Lim.

CS 8.2.
Nicol graph for Kuala Lumpur.

ECOFEATURES

• Material reuse • Non-insulation • Natural cross ventilation • Adaptation • Solar shading

DESCRIPTION/BRIEF

A unique feature of the house is that additions are constantly being made experimentally and unpredictably, with gut intuition rather than proper drawing-board planning. Jimmy Lim, resident architect of this progressive hand to material, low-energy, minimum labour and cost habitat, builds for himself to obtain first-hand knowledge of construction methods and the true nature of the materials. No trees were cut down, nor was any part of the slope cut into during the constant renovations that keep this home alive. The heart of the house is the Entertainment Area, which is united with the Living Space. The perimeter spaces of the house are built of timber materials and are semi-open with large windows. Each window has

CS 8.3.
Interior view of living space, by Jimmy Lim.

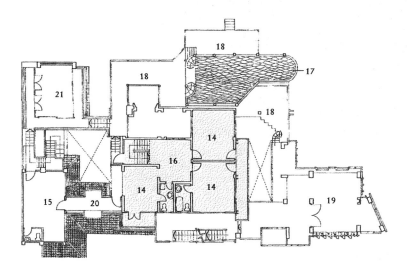

CS 8.4.
Second storey floor plan.

1 garage
2 formal entrance
3 side entrance
4 porch
5 living space
6 dining
7 breakfast area
8 entertainment area
9 kitchen
10 wet kitchen
11 maid
12 bathroom/wc
13 workshop/
    future gallery
14 bedroom
15 guest house
16 hall
17 swimming pool
18 timber deck
19 family area
20 bridge
21 music studio
22 meditation (boat
    house) area

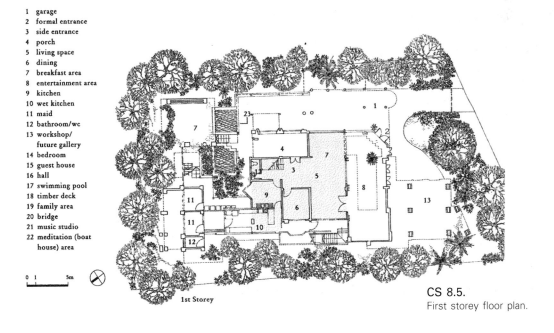

0 1   5m

1st Storey

CS 8.5.
First storey floor plan.

wooden or canvas screens to promote cross-ventilation. All roofs are covered with unglazed tiles and there is no thermal insulation in this house. Endless flights of wooden stairs made from salvaged materials connect a rustic guest house and a music room perched 3.5 m above the ground, to the main house. The elevated music studio for teaching sometimes doubles as a stage with openable side walls of sliding glass on two sides, a back wall made from recycled teak door panels and the bearing wall from the ground. The viewing platform for the audience is on the stage, not unlike a 'Shakespearean Globe' theatre, seating the audience on a timber deck about 5 ft lower. The arena is designed for musical concerts in the tropical heat and under the tropical stars. Jimmy Lim's home is the product of his firm belief that architecture should harmonize with nature.

CS 8.6.
The house has an adaptable envelope that can be altered to suit the time of day and year.

REUSE OF MATERIALS

The house has evolved around a pre-existing home that serves as the central core with the perimeter spaces having been built from recycled materials, such as old timber and bricks salvaged from demolished buildings. The original building form and other prime features are still intact and have been left unaltered. The main living space is about 13.5 m high and naturally lit from the apex of the roof, which is glazed. In the music room the use of old shutters and railings gives a feeling of nostalgia to the space. Jimmy Lim puts seemingly useless materials to good use in his own home as well as in his projects. Discarded Canton tiles, roofing, 80-year-old wood, broken marble and glass, grace his home. The elevated terrace balcony overlooks the garden and the house, once again putting to good use stained glass in a 'juinling' design by CSL Associates.

NON-INSULATED

Jimmy Lim's home is his personal and professional ongoing research project for understanding materials, construction jointing and connections, light penetration through the roof and ventilation. He experiments with moving wall parts and roof panels to promote ventilation while maintaining a comfortable temperature without insulation. Unlike other designers, who insist that insulation is the answer to cooling in the tropics, Jimmy Lim does not use insulation in walls or roofs in his home nor in his projects. He believes insulating a building is like putting a fur coat on a person telling them the fur is the insulation against heat getting to the skin and this will keep them cool. He asks, 'Where and how does the hot air get out?'. Although Jimmy Lim does not insulate his buildings he shades all windows from solar exposure.

VENTILATION

The monthly average wind velocity in Kuala Lumpur is about 1 m s^{-1} throughout the year, except in July when it is about 2 m s^{-1}. According to Jimmy Lim, in this area the wind is caused by the heat island phenomenon of the city. The three ceiling fans in the living space and one in the entertainment area help with the cross-ventilation strategy. This atrium-like space is a central air well, inducing cross-ventilation reminiscent of the old rubber smoke houses of multi-tiered roofs, brick piers and timber

CS 8.7.
'Sails' used for ventilation, by Robert Powell.

trusses. However, the music house and bedroom on the first floor have an air-conditioning system chosen by Jimmy's wife, who teaches music in the adjacent music house. Teaching violin and piano for long periods in the music house, Jimmy's wife finds the air-conditioning system to be indispensable and a necessity for instruments that require a stable humidity level. This highlights the potential problem of adapting to different indoor climates in one's lifestyle.

A number of opening devices on the roof act as 'sails' to catch the wind and assist in cooling the interior. By a strange and fortunate coincidence, Jimmy placed his apertures and openings for ventilation purposes facing west where, in this area of Kuala Lumpur, there is a cool westerly prevailing breeze in the afternoon (from about 4.40 p.m. until about 6.30–7.00 p.m.).

PROBLEMS AND RESOLUTIONS

The influence of the exhaust heat from the air-conditioning system on the naturally ventilated rooms is a problem. This problem is widely experienced in hot countries. It is considered that the exhaust heat should be directed to the top of the house rather than its current location between the veranda of the concrete house and the pool deck at the atrium. A typical problem is water discharged from the dehumidification mechanism. However, in Jimmy Lim's house he has improvised by collecting and routing the discharged water to a large basin irrigating the trees in the centre of the house. The contrast in this house between the air-conditioned and non-air-conditioned rooms highlights the importance of acclimatization to energy consumption in buildings.

When asked about any problems with associated insects, mainly mosquitoes, Jimmy concludes that 'there are actually fewer insects in tropical Malaysia than in, say, the summers of some of the sub-tropical or temperate countries, such as Australia'. As for mosquitoes, Jimmy answers that this is dependent 'on the surrounding area that the house is in and how clean the grounds are'.

ACKNOWLEDGEMENTS/CONTACT INFORMATION

CSL Associates, Kuala Lumpur, Malaysia. E-mail: cslcyy@tm.net.my

9 SURABAYA ECOHOUSE

Architect:
Professor Silas, the Institute of Technology Sephluh Nopember, Indonesia; Dr Y. Kodama, Kobe Design University

Owner:
Ministry of Construction, Indonesia; Infrastructure Development Institute of Japan

Location:
Surabaya, Indonesia; 7ºN, 112ºE

Climate:
Hot, humid

Area:
±294 m²

CS 9.1.
Surabaya Ecohouse, by Ministry of Construction.

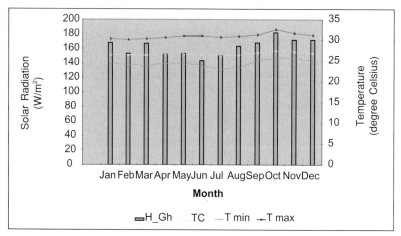

CS 9.2.
Nicol graph for Surabaya.

ECOFEATURES

• Double roof system • Deep eaves • Cross and stack ventilation • Nocturnal cooling • Polypropylene pipe system

DESCRIPTION/BRIEF

In tropical countries, as dependence on energy-consuming cooling systems or air-conditioners increases, growing concern over future global environmental problems and a possible drain on energy resources requires important developments in passive design, especially passive cooling techniques. The Surabaya Ecohouse, with its durable concrete structure and flexible use of partitions and external walls, is an essential design in a sustainable future recycling society to improve thermal performance of buildings.

KEY FEATURES BRIEFLY EXPLAINED

The double roof system consists of a roof of tiles over a waterproof membrane with an air gap and layer of coconut fibre insulation. The roof extends with deep eaves to shade the walls and windows against heat gains. The outer wall system is made of timber to also reduce solar penetration.

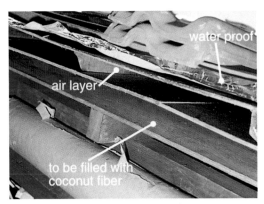

CS 9.3.
Double roof, by Ministry of Construction.

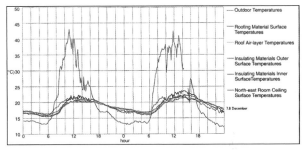

CS 9.4.
Effects of double roof.

Walls are open in communal spaces to promote cross-ventilation. Wind vents through the central roof to promote stack ventilation. Nocturnal cooling is induced by storing the lower-temperature night air in thick concrete floor slabs. A polypropylene pipe system is ducted through the floor slab that circulates water kept in an underground tank via a photo-voltaic-driven pump. This water at a cooler temperature radiates through the slab keeping it cool and is then reused for flushing toilets or irrigation.

LESSONS LEARNED/PITFALLS

The double roof is extremely effective in lowering the internal temperature as shown. Night ventilation, when in use, reduces the daytime temperatures lower than the control room without it. The radiant cooling floor is very effective in lowering the daytime peak temperatures, even when the circulating temperature is 28°C.

CS 9.5.
Plan.

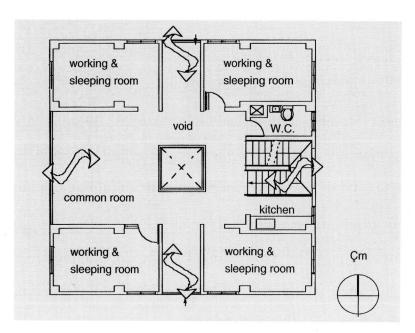

CS 9.6.
Section.

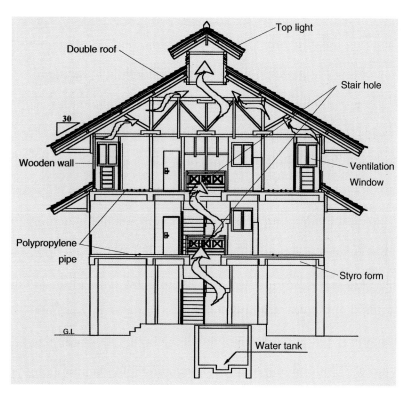

ACKNOWLEDGEMENTS/CONTACT INFORMATION

Infrastructure Development Institute, Japan. http://www.idi.or.jp/

10 HOUSE AT YARRAWONGA

Architect:
Felix Riedweg Architect, RAIA

Owners:
F. and F. Riedweg, 1990

Location:
Townsville, Australia; 19ºS,
147ºE; 300 m above sea level

Climate:
Coastal, tropical humid

Area:
450 m²

CS 10.1.
House at Yarrawonga, by Felix Riedweg.

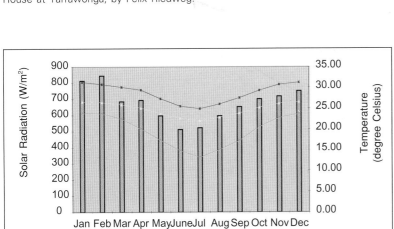

CS 10.2.
Nicol graph for House at Townsville.

ECOFEATURES

• Orientation • Shade • Cross-ventilation • Hurricane resistant

DESCRIPTION/BRIEF

The house was built in 1990 on the steep northern slopes of Castle Hill overlooking the suburb of North Ward and Cleveland Bay, with Magnetic Island in the distance. It is located about 3 km from the central business district of Townsville, the capital of North Queensland. Originally built with four bedrooms, two rooms have been converted into office space for the inhabitants. The upper level is open plan with living, dining, his and her studies and the master bedroom with a bath. It has a front (summer) and back (winter) veranda with views of more than 180º.

The design concept adopts the three key features: orientation, shade and cross-ventilation. The coastal area allows a pleasant outdoor living climate all year round; for comfort the client needs 'a big shading roof'. The building does not touch the ground, enabling the breezes (prevailing north/easterly summer breezes) to circulate in all directions.

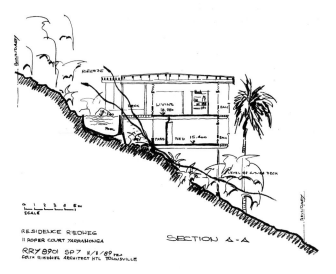

CS 10.3.
Section.

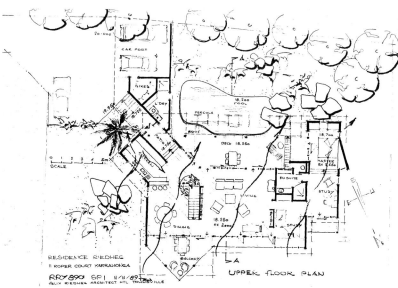

CS 10.4.
Upper floor plan.

ECOFEATURES EXPLAINED

Comfort is achieved by manipulating the temperature, humidity and air movement in the indoor environment. We can improve the temperature and air flow through the appropriate choice of building material (thermal mass), the right orientation, the provision of adequate shading (built or natural grown landscaping) and the selection and placement of windows for cross-ventilation.

Orientation

The house is oriented facing north with its back to the south using the embankment as its mass for keeping the lower level cool. It also orients itself to accept north/easterly prevailing winds to circulate throughout the open plan. The concept of openness and translucency is retained with well-shaded windows and access from every internal space to outdoor areas in front and back and on both levels. The house has both internal and external stairs. The glass in the windows is largely for security purposes.

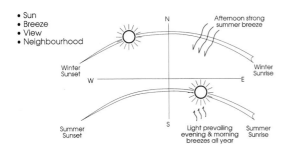

CS 10.5.
Orientation.

Shade

The native growth of the site was retained to enhance air quality as well as to assist in shading. The wide roof overhangs protect the windows and walls as, even in winter, direct sunlight is unwanted (approximate day temperature 25°C). Note that Figure 10.6 is not a direct representation of the House at Yarrawonga, but a diagram showing the strategy used.

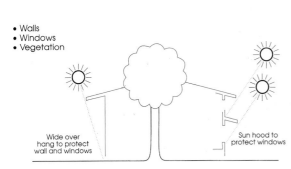

CS 10.6.
Shade.

CS 10.7.
Interior, leading outdoors, by Felix Riedweg.

Cross-ventilation

The open plan design allows optimal cross-ventilation of the north/easterly prevailing winds. The house is not air-conditioned but has some ceiling fans to assist with air movement on very still days. The inhabitants have appreciated the comfort of the house since 1990 and, comparing temperatures and air flow with the houses in the area, they have proved you can live comfortably in a tropical environment without air-conditioning. A number of energy-efficient issues are currently being addressed by the Australian Building Codes Board. It is the intention of the Code to indicate low-energy strategies for construction and equipping low-energy, cost-efficient designs. The house at Yarrawonga is truly an energy-efficient house, for its ventilation strategy utilizing cool breezes uses less than one-fifth of the energy used by a five-star NatHERS (National House Energy Rating Software) rated air-conditioned house.

- Windows (Geometry & size)
  (Location)
- Walls (With gaps)
  (Half height)

Radiation heat removed in draft through high level windows

Ancillary rooms shade wall to living/bedrooms

Cross ventilation

Floor ventilation

CS 10.8.
Cross-ventilation.

Construction

Owing to the difficult nature of the building site (steep and narrow, access between the rocks) prefabrication was an ideal option in order to retain the natural landscape without cut and fill. The steel skeleton is heavy so that it will withstand cyclonic winds of over 200 km h^{-1}. The roof uses insulated sheet metal guaranteeing shade all day throughout the year. Walls are mostly lightweight and the thermal mass is in the suspended concrete slabs of both levels.

LESSONS LEARNED/PITFALLS

Since the windows are well shaded and the house is cross-ventilated, there is no problem with overheating. However, the glare is problematic. At the time and without the expertise and knowledge that the architect has experienced since, he felt he should have spent a little more money and installed tinted glass.

ACKNOWLEDGEMENTS/CONTACT INFORMATION

Professor Dick Aynsley, Director Australian Institute Tropical Architecture, James Cook University, Townsville. E-mail: Richard.Aynsley@jcu.edu.au. Felix Riedweg, Architect RAIA, North Ward, Qld, Australia. E-mail: Riedweg@ultra.net.au

11 DUNCAN HOUSE

Architect:
Graham Duncan, 1998

Owner:
Graham Duncan

Location:
Ostend, Waiheke Island, New
Zealand; 36°S, 174°E; 10 m
above sea level

Climate:
Temperate, 1100 degree-days
per year

Area:
84 m²

CS 11.1.
Duncan House, by Robert Vale.

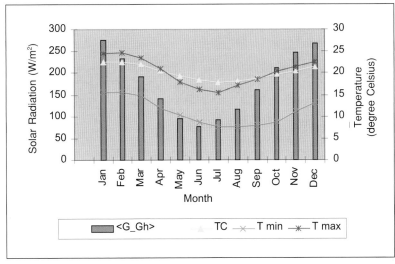

CS 11.2.
Nicol graph for Waiheke Island.

ECOFEATURES

• Solar and wind generated power • Solar water heating • Rainwater
supplies all water needs

DESCRIPTION/BRIEF

This house is a simple two-storey home, rectangular in plan. It is located in the centre of Ostend, the administrative centre of Waiheke Island. This village also contains the island's only supermarket and building supply store. This house was designed by Graham Duncan and intended to be simple and cheap. Its pitched roofs face north and south. The north and south facades are 6 m long and the east and west facades are 7 m. The entry is from the west with the main views from the house directed towards Anzac Bay (south). The north side of the roof is uninterrupted by dormers, giving the full area for solar energy collection systems. The house is conventionally built of New Zealand timber frame construction with R2.2 glass fibre insulation, internal linings of plasterboard on the ground floor and plywood on the first floor. External finish is plywood sheeting and the roof is a typical corrugated iron roof. Windows are locally made with single glazing in aluminium frames (with built-in draught proofing).

ECOFEATURES EXPLAINED

Electricity

Graham's house differs substantially from a typical Waiheke house. The house is entirely self-contained for its electricity supply, although there is mains electricity available from Mercury's lines directly outside in the road. The electricity is generated from two renewable energy sources: wind and sun. The solar contribution comes from 16, 60 W Solarex polycrystalline photovoltaic panels mounted on the north-facing roof at a slope of 42° (from horizontal). The panels are placed above the roof on 50-mm-thick wooden bearers and are carried on aluminium rails fixed across the bearers. This provides spacing of about 75 mm between the panels and the roof's surface to provide an air space to cool the panels, maximizing efficiency. Recently, an additional four 50 W panels were added to the north-facing wall below the roof, increasing the original 960 W capacity to 1.16 kW. In addition to the solar-generated power there are three small wind turbines. According to manufacturer's specifications these turbines have the capacity to output a total of 440 W but Graham estimates that with respect to surrounding obstructions (houses and trees), the turbines are producing about 400 W. Graham has wired his house to make the most efficient use of different sources of electricity. Since inverters tend to reduce efficiency, he uses DC lighting, through compact fluorescent lamps in special fittings; water pumps run off DC power; the refrigerator (although small) has been rebuilt with a DC compressor; and there is a DC television and radio. The 230 V inverter runs a larger television, stereo, computer, fax and washing machine.

Power generation	kWh a^{-1}
Wind power output	100
PV output	1100
Power bought (in)	0
Power sold (out)	0
Net	1200

Water heating

The water is heated by two Solarhart solar panels on the lower part of the north sloping roof and supplied through pipes to a 300 l thermosiphon system located between the ceiling and the roof at the peak. On cloudy days, the water can be heated by a wetback on the wood burner.

Space heating

Owing to the climate, the region does not experience dramatic changes in temperature. The floor is concrete, complimenting the passive solar gains but allowing the house to maintain a comfortable temperature for most of the year. Its main source of heat is retained in the slab and supplemented by a wood burner in the centre of the house, if needed.

Cistern and sewage

Typical of island homes, Graham's house has a 25 000 l cistern that stores rainwater for all domestic water uses. The water is pumped into the house by means of three 12 V pumps with pressure-sensing switches that activate the pumps by turning the tap. One pump is the main supply from the storage tanks and the other two serve hot and cold water supplies. These 12 V pumps are considered more efficient in terms of electric consumption. Sewage is treated by means of a conventional septic tank.

LESSONS LEARNED/PITFALLS

The total non-renewable energy consumption of the house is in the form of gas used for cooking (about 45 kg). Liquefied petroleum gas has a calorific value of 13.9 kWh kg^{-1} for propane, this is equivalent to 626 kWh years^{-1} or 7.4 kWh m^{-2}. Therefore the house uses much less energy than the sophisticated advanced houses of Canada and Europe, although this is achieved largely through simplicity and 'doing without' (lower internal temperatures, few appliances, smaller space and co-ordination of appliance use time).

ACKNOWLEDGEMENTS/CONTACT INFORMATION

Robert Vale, Auckland, New Zealand. E-mail: r.vale@auckland.ac.nz

12 REDEVELOPED PROPERTY AT CIVIL LINES

Architect:
A. B. Lall Architects, 1997–1999

Client:
Ashok and Rajiv Lall, Ratiram Gupta and sons

Location:
Civil Lines, New Delhi, India; 28°N, 77°E; 220 m above sea level

Climate:
Composite

Area:
Total 1687 m²; each house 421.7 m²

CS 12.1.
Façade of Courtyard House, by Ashok Lall.

CS 12.2.
Nicol graph of New Delhi.

ECOFEATURES

• Orientation • Wind-driven evaporative cooling • Courtyard roof •
Insulation materials

DESCRIPTION/BRIEF

This project explores the challenges of designing and building a house in a dense urban setting. This eco-project includes four courtyard houses built on a street. The houses on the north face of the street are courtyard houses leading towards gardens on the south side; whereas the houses on the south side of the street have their gardens on the north side and are linear. These are all large single-family houses, two to three storeys high. This enables the sections of the buildings to be designed integrally for enjoying the winter sun. The passive devices that interact with the external elements are given a central place in the architectural language of the buildings.

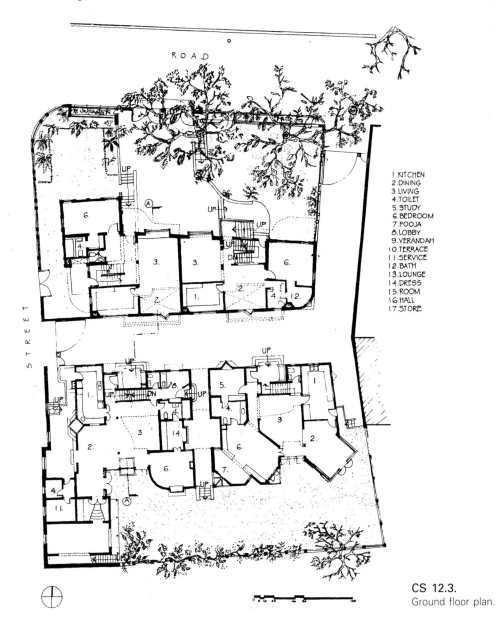

1.KITCHEN
2.DINING
3.LIVING
4.TOILET
5.STUDY
6.BEDROOM
7.POOJA
8.LOBBY
9.VERANDAH
10.TERRACE
11.SERVICE
12.BATH
13.LOUNGE
14.DRESS
15.ROOM
16.HALL
17.STORE

CS 12.3.
Ground floor plan.

ECOFEATURES EXPLAINED

Orientation

The general orientation of the buildings is aligned east–west, with most window openings in the north and south faces. The courtyard houses, because of their square proportions in plan, also face towards the east and west. The windows on these faces look into narrow protected alleys or the small courtyard between the houses. The alley space on the west side is shaded by retaining the wall of the original double-storey building that had previously lined the side street.

For the linear houses on the north side, the width of the driveway that separates the two rows of houses is just sufficient to enable winter sunshine to enter the first-floor windows. The sections of these houses are designed with a cutout such that the winter sun is brought into the living/dining space, the heart of the house, on the ground floor. Terraces on the second floor have skylights that again admit winter sun into the first-floor rooms on the north side of the house.

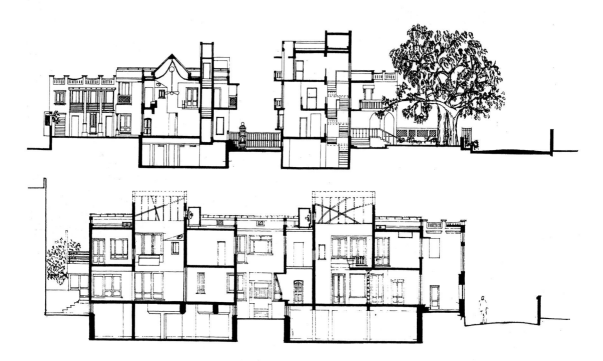

CS 12.4.
Section.

Wind-driven evaporative cooling

The West House takes advantage of the prevailing northwesterly hot winds that blow during the hot-dry seasons. A vertical screen tower is built on the west wall. This tower houses khus evaporative pads on its outer surface, fed by a water pump. The inner side has adjustable windows opening into the adjacent rooms. The natural wind pressure will drive air through the wet khus pads and will then flow into the adjacent rooms. This vertical arrangement would spread the khus fragrance across the two storeys of the house. In the summer, the combination of ceiling fans and the evaporative cooling gives a comfortable environment, except during the season of very high temperatures (38ºC) and high humidity (65 per cent) before the monsoon in mid-June to mid-July. But 'if you wear skimpy cottons and drink cool sherbet – there is a refrigerator lurking somewhere – you could be comfortable enough' (Mr Lall, 19 May 2000). The first test season is taking place as this book goes to print.

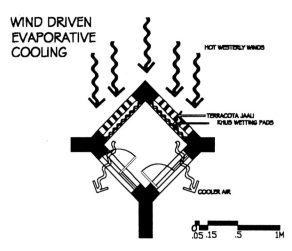

WIND DRIVEN EVAPORATIVE COOLING

HOT WESTERLY WINDS

TERRACOTA JAALI
KHUS WETTING PADS

COOLER AIR

.05 .15   .5   1M

CS 12.5.
Wind-driven evaporative cooling.

CS 12.6.
West wall, 'khus' cooling tower, by Ashok Lall.

Courtyard roof

The roofed courtyard of the two courtyard houses is intended to be the main climate response device. The hipped steel frame roof is clad with a 20 mm glass sandwich with a reflective film and frosted underside for the most part, with a panel of transparent glass on the south slope. This is under-slung by a pair of razais (quilts), which can be pulled across to cover the underside of the roof (for insulation) or allowed to hang down vertically (to allow heat transfer). Above the roof is another frame in chicks (bamboo severs), which can similarly be opened to shade the roof or rolled up to catch the sun.

The ridge of the roof is a water channel from which water overflows on to the thin roofing membrane of stone and glass. Some water evaporates and excess water is collected at the foot of the slope and re-circulated. This makes the roof a large evaporative cooler over the central space of the house. All rooms communicate directly with this central space. This

INTERACTIVE COURTYARD ROOF

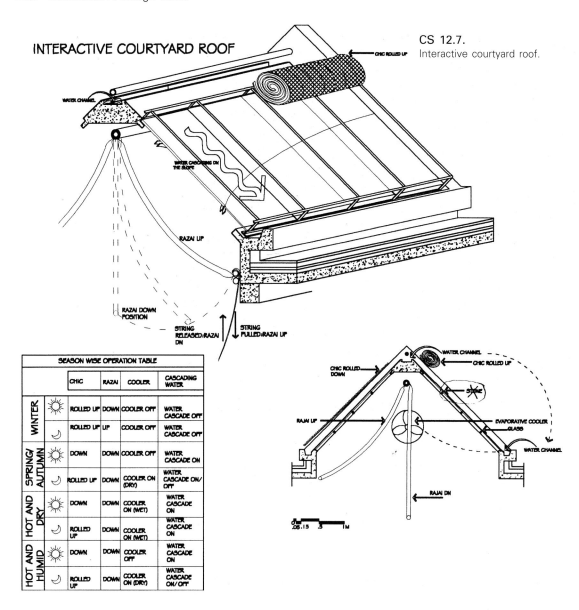

CS 12.7.
Interactive courtyard roof.

SEASON WISE OPERATION TABLE		CHIC	RAZAI	COOLER	CASCADING WATER
WINTER	☀	ROLLED UP	DOWN	COOLER OFF	WATER CASCADE OFF
WINTER	☾	ROLLED UP	UP	COOLER OFF	WATER CASCADE OFF
SPRING/AUTUMN	☀	DOWN	DOWN	COOLER OFF	WATER CASCADE ON
SPRING/AUTUMN	☾	ROLLED UP	DOWN	COOLER ON (DRY)	WATER CASCADE ON/OFF
HOT AND DRY	☀	DOWN	DOWN	COOLER ON (WET)	WATER CASCADE ON
HOT AND DRY	☾	ROLLED UP	DOWN	COOLER ON (WET)	WATER CASCADE ON
HOT AND HUMID	☀	DOWN	DOWN	COOLER OFF	WATER CASCADE ON
HOT AND HUMID	☾	ROLLED UP	DOWN	COOLER ON (DRY)	WATER CASCADE ON/OFF

method of evaporative cooling will supplement a conventional evaporative cooler and, in the hot-humid period of July to August, would give considerable cooling when evaporative cooling is no longer effective. The operation of the roof component: chick, water, razai, is to be adjusted from winter to summer and for day and night. The roof provides for:

1 shading from outside/insulation from inside;
2 roof evaporative cooling;
3 direct radiation.

The dominant portion of the roofed courtyards with their quilts of mirrors and colourful cloth, the chicks and the possibility of visible monsoon and night sky – stars and moon – would become a strong aesthetic experience of the idea of responding to the rhythm of seasonal cycles.

CS 12.8.
Looking up from the Court, by
Ashok Lall.

Insulation/materials

The roofs are finished with broken marble mosaic, which is reflective in nature. The roof construction sandwich contains 30-mm-thick polyurethane board insulation above the concrete slab. For the courtyard houses the western wall of the upper floor, the east and west walls of the courtyard roof and the water tank walls are insulated using an innovative construction sandwich of 115 mm brick + 15 mm plaster + 30 mm polystyrene foam + 50 mm terracotta jalis, whose cavities are rendered with cement sand mortar. Their resultant construction expresses the special nature of the wall as a decorative textured surface. This strategy shifts the performance to the fabric by spending a little on insulation where it makes the most difference. The windows are single glazed (heavy curtains for summer afternoons and winter nights but tight-fitting with double rebates). This proves that an economical solution can in fact be implemented.

LESSONS LEARNED/PITFALLS

Initially the courtyard roof was to be designed with 20-mm-thick stone slab. After revisiting the idea, it was decided to replace the stone with glass sheets sandwiching a reflective film to ensure a crack-free, damp-proof cover for water to stream over.

ACKNOWLEGEMENTS/CONTACT INFORMATION

A.B. Lall Architects, Civil Lines, Delhi. E-mail: ablarch@del13.vsnl.net.in

13 BIDANI HOUSE

Architect:
Arvind Krishan, 1984

Owner:
M. L. Bidani

Location:
Delhi, India; 28°N, 77°E; 216 m
above sea level

Climate:
Composite

Area:
Site = 1000 m², house = 295 m²

CS 13.1.
Bidani House, by Arvind Krishan.

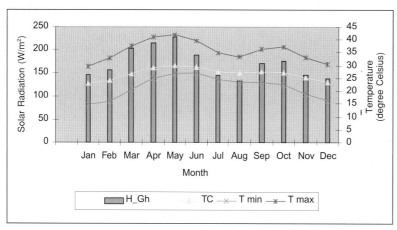

CS 13.2.
Nicol graph for Delhi.

ECOFEATURES

• Architectural design (form) in response to solar geometry •
Northeast courtyard as heat sink • Materials • Thermal mass

DESCRIPTION

Faridabad, located in the 'composite climate' zone near Delhi, is subject to large climatic swings. It has a very hot and dry period of almost two and a half months, where maximum dry bulb temperatures can reach 45°C. It also has a cold period of a shorter duration, in which the minimum dry bulb temperatures can drop as low as 3°C. The hot dry period is followed by a hot humid – monsoon – period where maximum dry bulb temperatures can climb to 38°C combined with 90 per cent relative humidity.

ECOFEATURES EXPLAINED

Northeast courtyard as heat sink

Learning from traditional wisdom, the entire house has been designed around a courtyard facing northeast, developed as a heat sink. Main living spaces are wrapped around it, having a southeast exposure. A large-volume double-height living space wraps around the courtyard. The three-dimensional form of the building is developed in response to solar geometry. In other words, it eliminates or allows solar penetration in response to seasonal changes. Large-volume spaces coupled with a courtyard allow good ventilation and thermal control essential for the hot humid period.

Internal thermal mass as local stone walls

The internal walls are built from local materials incorporating thermal mass, which helps attenuate thermal swings. The walls are stone with a low U value of 1.5 W m^{-2} and the windows are single glazed.

Materials

The materials are locally available and have low embodied energy. The floors are terrazzo with a stone base and the roof is made of RCC slab with 'mud phaska'. This works as an insulation on top, with a brick tile covering.

Figures 13.4 and 13.5 show the key features and explain how the building configuration responds to solar geometry.

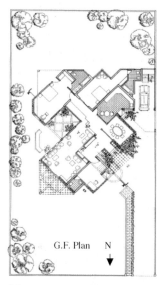

CS 13.3.
Ground floor plan.

- Summer condition eliminates the sun.
- Winter condition allows solar access.
- Courtyard facing northeast designed as a heat sink.
- Large-volume double-height living space wraps around the courtyard.

USER FEEDBACK

- While the building has not been monitored, users have been very satisfied with the thermal conditions prevailing inside the house.
- Large-volume spaces have allowed attenuation of thermal swings and users enjoy the volume and feel very comfortable in all living spaces.
- User installed 'room type' air-conditioning units in bedrooms and then complained that the air-conditioners were tripping off all the time. This is testimony to the fact that the building is not over heating.
- User is satisfied with the air quality of the house.

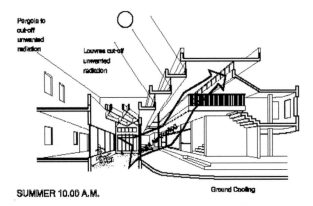

SUMMER 10.00 A.M.

Ground Cooling

Pergola to cut-off unwanted radiation

Louvres cut-off unwanted radiation

CS 13.4.
Key features of Bidani House.

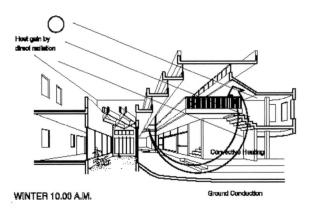

WINTER 10.00 A.M.

Ground Conduction

Heat gain by direct radiation

Convective Heating

CS 13.5.
Key features of Bidani House.

CS 13.6.
Double height living space, by Arvind Krishan.

LESSONS LEARNED

- Architectural design is a very powerful tool for attaining sustainable architecture.
- Could have exploited the building configuration a little more to achieve thermal buffers on overheated facades.

14 MEIR HOUSE

CS 14.1.
Meir House, by Isaac Meir.

Architect:
Isaac A. Meir, 1992–1994

Owners:
Orna and Isaac Meir with their
three children

Location:
Sede Boqer Campus, Negev
Desert Highlands, Israel; 30°N,
34°E; 470 m above sea level

Climate:
Arid, with hot and dry summers;
cold winters; +1017 degree days
per year

Area:
208 m²

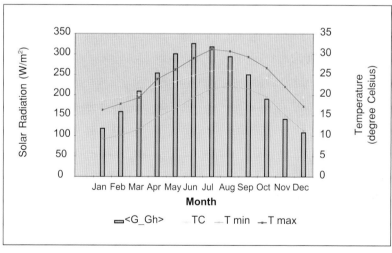

CS 14.2.
Nicol graph for Negev.

ECOFEATURES

• Orientation and plan • Thermal mass • Winter solar heating •
Summer cooling • xeriscape

DESCRIPTION/BRIEF/CONCEPT

The Meir House is located in the first solar neighbourhood in Israel, Newe Zin, and was designed as a prototype towards creating an energy-conserving urban building code. It combines external insulation and internal thermal mass with open plan. Through QUICK simulation prior to construction and monitoring post-construction, the Meir House proves the success of an integrative approach to the design of a bioclimatic desert house.

ECOFEATURES EXPLAINED

Orientation and plan

Considering the site's geometry and climatic constraints, among them solar angles, air temperatures and wind directions, the log axis of the house is east–west, with four bedrooms and the living room to the south.

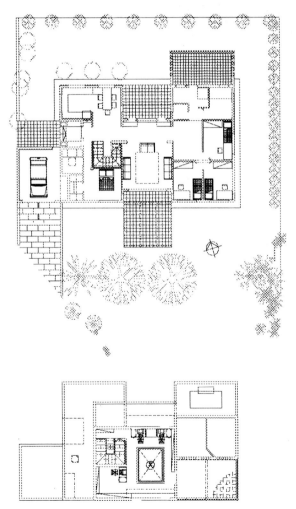

CS 14.3.
Ground floor plan (above) and first floor plan (below).

The ground floor is exposed in all four directions. The kitchen, baths and laundry room are located at the northern part of the plan and the garage serves as a western buffer. All spaces, excluding the garage, are a single thermal zone. The house also includes a number of verandas and balconies facing in different directions. Main fenestration is placed to the south, with smaller openings to the north for cross-ventilation. However, all rooms have openings in two directions to ensure appropriate ventilation. There are only a few, small, recessed openings in the west facade. The second floor is exposed in all four directions.

Winds are north and northwesterly in the early noon and evening hours, whereas at night and early morning they may turn northeast by southeast. Average maximum windspeeds range between 40 km h^{-1} in winter and 30 km h^{-1} in summer. The environmentally responsive open plan layout proved to be successful as far as heat transfer and circulation are concerned.

Another advantage that the Meir House integrates with its form is weather protected adjacent open spaces. The south and north verandas and the southeastern balcony are protected from wind by the mass of the building to the north and west and by the garden wall to the west. These spaces are shaded partly by overhangs, partly by deciduous plants (such as vines and *Prosopis*), and partly by pergolas with agricultural shading fabric that has a 75 per cent shading coefficient.

Thermal mass

The wide diurnal temperature fluctuations characteristic of the Negev Desert climate dictate the use of thermal mass, both for internal temperature damping and for energy storage. Based on simulation results, the construction optimizes thermal performance by using medium-weight exterior walls and heavy-weight interior vertical and horizontal partitions.

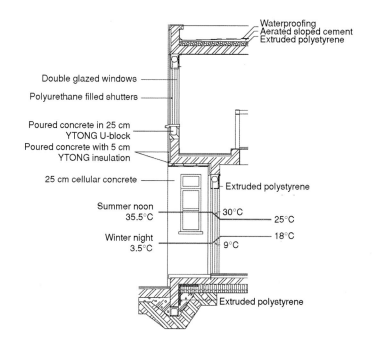

CS 14.4.
Section through wall.

The exterior walls are 250 mm cellular concrete (YTONG) blocks, painted with a high reflectivity ochre-coloured paint. The low conductivity (0.2 W m^{-1} C) of the YTONG blocks eliminates the need for traditional sandwich wall sections or external insulation that demands precise construction. Floors are reinforced concrete poured in place. The roof is cast reinforced concrete, covered by extruded polystyrene, aerated sloped cement and waterproofing.

Climatic conditions and termites exclude the option of wooden frames for windows and doors. Aluminium frames encase double glazing for acoustical considerations and are fitted with mosquito screens. To further reduce solar gains in the summer, external aluminium rolling shutters filled with insulation (expanded polyurethane) and interior venetian horizontal and vertical blinds are fitted.

CS 14.5.
House with shutters lowered, by Isaac Meir.

Winter solar heating and solar water heating

Approximately 24 m^2 (30 per cent of the south facade, or approximately 14.5 per cent of the total floor area) and 8 m^2 of the east facade is glass, achieving a passive approach to heating the house. The addition of a collapsible greenhouse (2.25 m^2) on the balcony, made of polycarbonate sheeting recovered from a dismantled agricultural greenhouse, yielded winter temperatures of 35–36°C during the afternoon (while the ambient temperature was 14–15°C) increasing the room temperatures by 1–2°C with the help of a small fan that pushes the air into the living spaces. Through passive designs, orientation, thermal mass and the collapsible greenhouse, savings of almost 90 per cent on electric back-up bought from the utility company were realized, compared with a typical electrically heated house in the Negev Desert climate. The Meir House includes solar water heating using a high-efficiency solar collector (7000 kcal for a 1.5 m^2 collection area) and 150 l water heater.

Type	Heat only, excluding bathrooms (kWh m^{-2} a^{-1})	Unit cost (NIS)	Cost of electric (NIS)
Meir House	5.5	0.25 kWh	250.00
Typical house	72.2	0.25 kWh	3250.00
Savings	66.7		3000.00

Savings are US$750.

Summer cooling and stack ventilation

Although the higher windows provide solar access to the northern parts of the plan (necessary in the winter), the different height of spaces and operability enhance stack ventilation and exhaust hot air from the upper strata (during the summer). North- and south-facing windows enable cross-

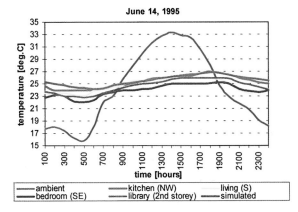

CS 14.6.
A day monitored in the summer.

CS 14.7.
Interior view of two-storey living area, by Isaac Meir.

ventilation during summer nights, when outside temperatures are below thermal comfort. Mesh screens play a definitive role by cutting windspeed down to 20–25 per cent of external windspeeds, but these screens are a necessity, keeping out pests and insects.

Xeriscape

An intense post-occupancy project was carried out to reduce by landscaping the amount of wind-driven dust. By laying stone paving, pebble ground covering, and planting drought and salinity resistant plants, airborne dust is trapped and kept on the ground. Plants are drip-irrigated by a computer, providing a relative humidity sensor by-pass to the automatic operation mode.

LESSONS LEARNED/PITFALLS

Initially a ceiling fan installed over the two-storey living area was thought adequate to create air movement when windows remained sealed at times when ambient temperatures were greater than interior temperatures. This proved insufficient owing to the large volume and complex geometry of the space. To correct this, a smaller fan was added on the ground floor to supplement circulation. The open plan has proved very efficient as a strategy for the creation of a thermally uniform house, but has drawbacks regarding acoustics, privacy and smells transferred from the kitchen.

ACKNOWLEDGEMENTS/INFORMATION

Center for Desert Architecture and Urban Planning, J. Blaustein Institute for Desert Research, Ben-Gurion University of the Negev, Sede Boqer Campus, Israel, 84990, Tel.: 972 7 6596880; http://www.bgu.ac.il/CDAUP; http://www.boker.org.il/davids/nvzin/sakis/housakis.htm. Isaac A. Meir, Negev Desert Highlands. E-mail: sakis@bgumail.bgu.ac.il

15 BARILOCHE ECOHOUSE

Architect:
Research Centre Habitat and Energy (University of Buenos Aires) with Claudio Delbene

Owners:
Manuel Fuentes and Ana Lopez

Location:
Bariloche, Argentina; 41°S, 71°W; 1000 m above sea level

Climate:
Cold mountain area; 3600 heating degree days

Area:
244 m²

CS 15.1.
Rendering of Bariloche Ecohouse, by Evans.

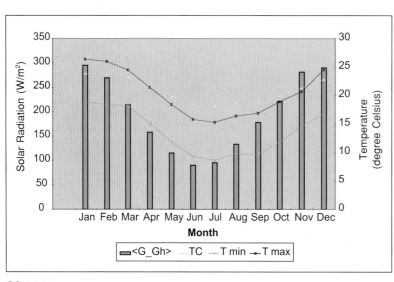

CS 15.2.
Nicol graph for Bariloche.

ECOFEATURES

• Limited site location • Thermal insulation • Greenhouse and rock store integrated into design • Roof integrated photovoltaic system • DHWS • Wastewater reuse for irrigation

DESCRIPTION/BRIEF

The Fuentes–Lopez house is located in Bariloche, an important tourist and ski centre in the cold southwest region of Argentina. The house is built in a low-density, hilly and wooded area, approximately 18 km from the town centre, with attractive views of surrounding mountains and the Nahuel Huapi National Park. Planned for convenient and flexible family living with four children, the house also provides a study and home office for the parents. The large kitchen-living-dining room forms the centre of family life. The main bedrooms are located on the ground floor. The upper floor was originally planned as a large flexible open space with possibilities for later subdivision to form additional bedrooms. The clients, with their

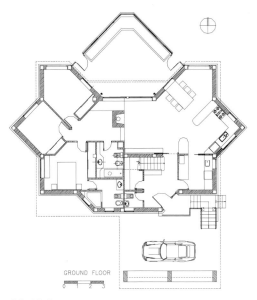

CS 15.3.
Ground floor plan.

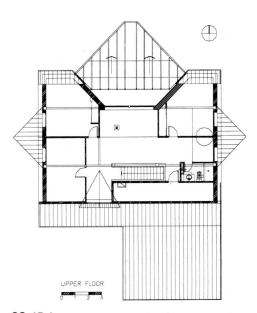

CS 15.4.
Upper floor plan.

CS 15.5.
Section.

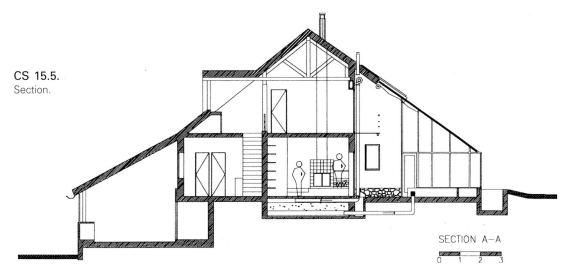

children, were actively involved in all stages of the design process including programme formulation, location, design alternatives, detailing and construction.

ECOFEATURES EXPLAINED

Limited site location form

Local regulations that only allow limited tree felling impacted the design stage. Other 'setback' regulations and site characteristics limit the possibilities for locating vehicular access and siting for good solar access. The location of the house was carefully chosen to take advantage of an existing clearing in the woods and a reasonably level area, although difference of 2 m in height within the 'footprint' of the building still exists. A heliodon (a device that simulates solar angles and measures the number of hours of potential sunshine) was used to select and define a suitable area and to detect those trees that reduced solar exposure in winter. A reasonably clear view of the sky is achieved in orientations between 45° to the east of north to 45° west of north, with maximum obstruction height of 26° to the north (note that the house is located in the southern hemisphere and receives winter sun from the north), falling to 19° to the northeast and northwest. The form combines a compact overall shape to reduce heat losses with a good exposure to the north. This is achieved by superimposing a V shape, with the principal internal sides facing northeast and northwest, on a rectangle with the longer side facing directly north.

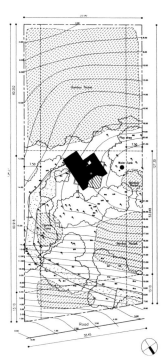

CS 15.6.
Site location and orientation.

Thermal insulation

The volumetric heat loss coefficient of the house is under $0.8\,\text{W m}^{-3}\,\text{K}$, considerably less than the maximum value of $1.4\,\text{W m}^{-3}\,\text{K}$ recommended for a house of this size in Bariloche (National Standards for Thermal Insulation). These low heat losses are a result of the compact form and very low thermal transmittance of both walls and roof. About 40 per cent of these heat losses are due to infiltration, based on a nominal one air

CS 15.7.
Insulation installation, by Manuel Fuentes.

change per hour. However, the quality of the windows will likely reduce this value to approximately 0.5 changes per hour and achieve a heat loss coefficient of less than 0.7 W m^{-3} K, half the recommended maximum value. A factor that increases heat loss is the north-facing glazed area. However, these losses are offset by useful heat gains on sunny days during colder periods of the year. The roof incorporates 150 mm of expanded polystyrene between the roof joists and a further 50 mm above the joists reaching 0.17 W m^{-3} K. This method of incorporating a high standard of thermal insulation has the following advantages:

- no extra timber is needed to form the cavity where insulation is placed;
- the roof timbers are not exposed to indoor spaces, so rough sawn wood can be used, rather than more expensive sanded joists;
- continuous ceiling of tongue and grooved boarding, which is interrupted only by the principal roof trusses, provides an attractive and easy-to-maintain surface;
- two layers of insulation reduce the possible effect of thermal bridging.

The **walls** reach a value of 0.22 W m^{-3} K. This value is achieved with a solid inner brick wall of 125 mm within an earthquake-resistant reinforced concrete structure, 150 mm of thermal insulation and an outer finish of timber boarding. This construction not only has an excellent level of thermal insulation, but also provides the following advantages:

- cold bridges are avoided, as there is negligible thermal connection between the inner brick and concrete structure and the outer finish;
- a thermal time lag of over 8 h is obtained, reducing possible overheating in summer and the cooling effect of sudden cold spells in winter;
- thermal admittance of the indoor side of the external wall is also high, 5.3 W m^{-3} K, allowing effective storage of daily solar heat gains;
- as the inner brick wall, with a dense render, is less permeable than the outer finish of timber boarding, there is no risk of internal condensation, even without a vapour barrier.

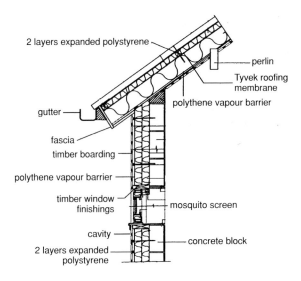

CS 15.8.
Section through wall.

PASSIVE SOLAR SYSTEMS

The northern facade incorporates three passive solar systems:

1 **The sunspace**, a large glazed volume, is thermally coupled to the house by four complimentary heat flow mechanisms: forced convection to a rock bed beneath the living area, natural convection to the living areas through openable windows, radiation through the closed windows, and transmission through mass walls.
2 **Direct solar gains** are obtained through openings with favourable orientations for winter sun. These windows are in the kitchen, dining-living room and ground floor bedrooms, as well as on the upper floor.
3 **Mass storage walls** consists of two dense wall panels with exterior glazing placed on the north facade, with summer shade provided by a roof overhang.
4 **Two Trombe walls** are also placed on the north facade with a combined exposed surface area of 5.5 m^2.

Rockbed system

A rockbed system was built following the recommendations and sizing methods given by Balcomb. It consists of two, 12 m^3 rockbeds with two channels each. Each channel is 6 m long and 0.8 m deep. The rocks used have an average diameter of 150 mm. The solar gains from the upper part of the greenhouse are transferred to the rockbed beneath the living area of the house using ducts with thermostatically controlled fans. After heating the rocks the air returns to the sunspace. The whole system was designed to store 21 kWh day^{-1} with a storage capacity of 1.5 days. The fans provide an airflow rate of 0.7 m^3 s^{-1}. The system is thermally coupled through the slab, acting as an underfloor heating system.

The large glazed sunspace is a key feature of the house and fulfils a series of thermal and functional objectives:

• in addition to the solar gains on sunny days, the volume acts as a thermal buffer, reducing heat losses from the house on cold cloudy and windy days;
• this intermediate buffer area can be used for family activities when the weather is unfavourable, as it is protected from rain, snow, wind and low temperatures. During sunny spells in winter the temperature increase in the sunspace will be favourable;

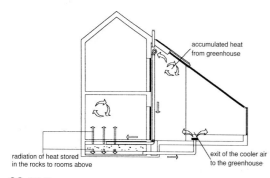

CS 15.9.
Passive solar systems.

CS 15.10.
Rockbed, by Manuel Fuentes.

- the exposure of the sunspace to summer sun may produce overheating owing to the intensity of solar radiation. Five measures were therefore adopted to control this problem:
  - upper floor balcony: provides shade, especially to windows between the sunspace and ground floor. The roof overhang serves a similar purpose on the upper floor;
  - high-level opening windows: designed to allow the exit of hot air to the exterior while allowing ingress of cooler air at a lower level. The stack effect to achieve this is reinforced by the double height;
  - thermal insulation and double-glazed windows: reduce the thermal transmission to indoor spaces in summer.

Domestic solar hot water (DSHW) system

The house has a flat plate solar collector manufactured by AES and mounted on the roof co-planar with the photovoltaic panels. The solar hot water collectors are used to supplement the energy demand for domestic hot water (DHW). The 5 m^2 collector is considered to be cost-effective for a single family in Bariloche. The solar hot water collector was predicted to supply 76 per cent of the household requirements. The domestic hot water system was designed for the highest solar fraction. For this purpose, the roof was tilted 35°. The collector feeds directly into a pre-heated or 'solar' tank (250 l) that feeds into the primary tank, which is a conventional 150-l tank heated by a high-efficiency, Peisa-manufactured gas boiler. The principle for choosing this two-tank, preheated system was to have the best technology available in Argentina that could be quickly adapted to produce a high solar fraction system with a gas boiler back-up.

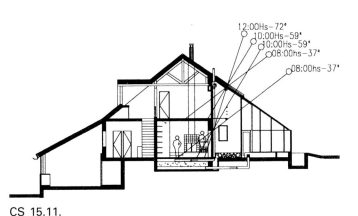

CS 15.11.
Internal morning temperatures.

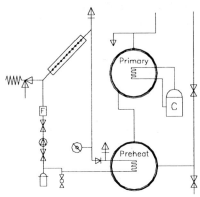

CS 15.12.
DSHW system.

PHOTOVOLTAIC SYSTEM

The house is situated in an area that receives approximately 7.8 peak sun hours in summer, but only 1.7 peak sun hours in winter. The variation in output from winter to summer is therefore significant and the array size has been specified in order to achieve a maximum level of solar input in spring and autumn. Power has to be drawn from the utility company during winter days and also at night-time. The system was sized in order to provide around one-third of the annual electricity demands for the house. It consists of 16 MST-43MV BP-Solarex thin-film modules with capacity for 700 W peak of electricity, wired to a SMA 7000 W inverter.

The PV system is connected in parallel to the electricity supply. Energy from the solar array will be consumed by the AC loads in the house with any excess energy being exported into the utility supply. Any shortfall in output from the array will be made up by importing from the supply connection. This is a fully automatic process.

The PV modules were mounted on the roof using aluminium frames designed by the architect Marshall from Marshall and Associates. These frames, designed for their simplicity, make fastening to a standard roof structure an uncomplicated procedure.

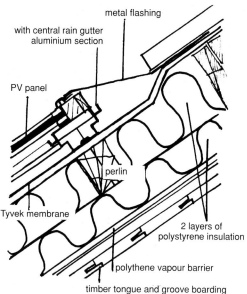

CS 15.13.
Photovoltaic system.

ENERGY BALANCE

Type	kWh m^{-2} a^{-1}	Cost of electricity (US$)	Cost of gas (US$)	Total (US$)	CO_2 emissions (tonnes a^{-1})	Construction cost (US$ m^{-2})
Fuentes–Lopez House	43	256	96	352	5.5	700
Typical house	235	512	575	1087	30	700
Savings	192	256	479	735	24.5	

ACKNOWLEDGEMENTS/CONTACT INFORMATION

This house was designed and built with the help of a group of people and companies that believe in the idea of sustainable architecture. The design team directed by the architects Martin Evans and Silvia de Schiller from the Research Centre Habitat and Energy, University of Buenos Aires, the architect Claudio Delbene and TEVSA SA contributed their knowledge to design and build this house. Marshall developed the structure that integrated the PV and solar collector into the roof, this being the first solar roof in Argentina. Esteban SA provided the double-glazed windows with Rehau technology and detailed the Trombe walls. Peisa provided the best heating technology available in Argentina, building a prototype for a SHW system with the goal of manufacturing and commercializing solar systems. BP Solarex provided photovoltaic modules, believing that the PVIB market is not just a dream but is the market of the future.

Dr Manuel Fuentes, Bariloche, Argentina. E-mail: mfuentes@bariloche.com.ar

16 TAMARIND HILLS NO. 15

CS 16.1.
Tamarind Hills, No. 15, by David Morrison.

Architect:
David Morrison Associates

Owners:
David Morrison and Susan Parson

Location:
Tamarind Hills, Oyster Pond Hill Road, Gibbs Land, St Maarten, Netherlands Antilles; 18°N, 63°W; 60 m above sea level

Climate:
Tropical maritime, cooled by trade winds

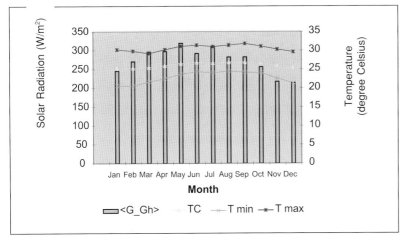

CS 16.2.
Nicol graph for St Maarten.

ECOFEATURES

• Hurricane-resistant roof appurtenances • Solar water heater • Trade wind flow optimized • Fresh and storm water cisterns • Seismic-resistant concrete frame structure

DESCRIPTION/BRIEF

The house on Tamarind Hills cascades down a hill 60 m above the sea on an island of 37 square miles and governed by two governments. It is located 300 miles southeast of Miami and is susceptible to hurricanes annually. With one bedroom and 1–1/2 bath on the main level, a guest bedroom and a one-bedroom apartment located below the main house, its view above Dawn Beach is spectacular, looking towards St Barts. Also at main level are a swimming pool, gazebo and deck, workshop, study and covered car port. The vegetation on the island is classified as dry scrub, acacia, and it receives an annual average rainfall of 400 mm.

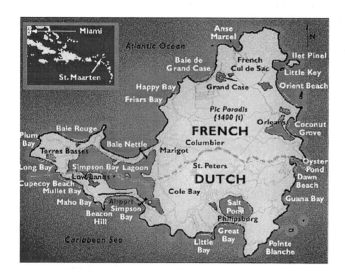

CS 16.3.
Island map, by Interknowledge
© 1996.

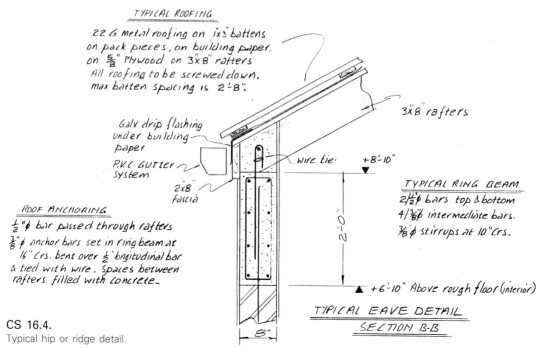

TYPICAL ROOFING

22 G metal roofing on 1"x3" battens
on pack pieces, on building paper,
on ⅝" plywood on 3"x8" rafters
All roofing to be screwed down.
max batten spacing is 2'-8".

Galv. drip flashing
under building
paper

P.V.C GUTTER
system

2x8
fascia

Galv. drip flashing
under building
paper

3"x8" rafters

wire tie.   +8'-10"

TYPICAL RING BEAM
2/½"φ bars top & bottom
4/⅜"φ intermediate bars.
⅜"φ stirrups at 10"crs.

ROOF ANCHORING
½"φ bar passed through rafters
⅜"φ anchor bars set in ring beam at
16"crs. bent over ½"longitudinal bar
& tied with wire. Spaces between
rafters filled with concrete.

2'-0"

▲ +6'-10" Above rough floor (interior)

TYPICAL EAVE DETAIL
SECTION B-B

8"

CS 16.4.
Typical hip or ridge detail.

FEATURES EXPLAINED

Hurricane-resistant structure

Built to withstand 250 kph winds this home has survived hurricanes of Category 4 and 5 more than once without structural damage. However, impact damage from flying objects is always a problem. The house has reinforced concrete tie-beams, roof rafters held down with steel anchors, floor-grade decking screwed to rafters and sealed with heat-applied asphalt (several layers); clay roof tiles are glued, screwed and cemented but are still liable to damage from wind-blown debris. Roofs are also braced internally, either by tie-rafters (exposed) or with a timber matrix and a suspended (false) ceiling. The roof pitch is important: too low a pitch increases upthrust (or uplift) owing to wind pressure and a pitch too steep is vulnerable to downward forces on the windward slope and uplift forces on the leeward slope.

Doors and windows are lagged into hardwood sub-frames and turn bolted into concrete jambs. Glass is covered by storm-shutters (non-permanent) made mainly of steel or hardwood. In less exposed areas, terraces are enclosed in trampoline fabric strung tightly across openings: these allow some air-passage during a storm but protect from flying debris. The trampoline mesh protection is a less expensive and easier installation alternative than the steel and wood shutters, but has had mixed success. If not sufficiently tight, they chafe and can come apart. On the other hand, when used on covered balconies and terraces, they can allow movement to the outdoors during a storm, reducing claustrophobic effects.

Hurricane-resistant natural ventilation

Many windows are hardwood jalousie (louvre) type, promoting the flow of the trade winds through the house, eliminating the need for air-conditioning. These can survive a bad storm in themselves. The rooms are angled to increase the effects of the breeze, but only the experience of residing in the neighbourhood can perfect this

CS 16.5.
Trampoline screen in place, by David Morrison.

CS 16.6.
Bahamian style shutter, by David Morrison.

CS 16.7.
Jalousie window, by David Morrison.

orientation. These design strategies optimize the trade-winds flow and are aided by paddle fans. Artificial air-conditioning is an in-wall unit located in the study. However, the habitants never use this cooling system; it is provided in the event of a visiting guest not acclimatized to the higher temperatures on the island.

Cistern

Water is at a premium with no piped water available. With only 400 mm of rain annually, as much rain as possible is collected from the roof into a fresh-water storage tank in the basement, built of gunned concrete for strength. For irrigation, deck water is also collected into a separate tank, both sources powered by small electric shallow-well pumps.

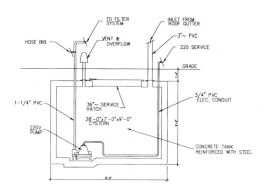

CS 16.8.
Cistern detail.

HURRICANE EXPERIENCES AND LESSONS LEARNED

Even though hurricanes hit the Leeward Islands so frequently, sometimes more than twice a year, Hurricane Luis (August 1995) leaves behind a benchmark for constant comparison. Luis was a Category 4 Cape Verde hurricane that wreaked harm and havoc on the northeasternmost edge of the Leeward Islands, with an estimated 16 people dead and US$2.5 billion in damages, US$1.8 billion to St Maarten alone.

The house on Tamarind Hills is 13 years old and, after Hurricane Luis (with winds gusting up to 325 kph), was partly rebuilt, extended and improved. Although the roof held well in this storm (other than damage caused by the neighbour's rafters) it was strengthened further, doors and windows were upgraded (including frames) and shutters improved. The house withstood Hurricane Lenny in November of 1999 very well with no damage to speak of (like Hurricane Luis, Hurricane Lenny was a Category 4 hurricane with winds gusting to 200 kph and killing three people on St Maarten).

CS 16.9.
Before Hurricane Luis, protected with aluminium shutters, by David Morrison.

CS 16.10.
After Hurricane Luis (back). Winds ripped off shutters and their tracks, while flying debris shattered clay tiles. By David Morrison.

CS 16.11.
After Hurricane Luis (front). High winds and flying debris responsible for downed trees, roof tile damage and solar water heater being ripped off. By David Morrison.

CS 16.12.
Before Hurricane Lenny. Remodelled after Hurricane Luis with a new protected entry and roof tiles glued, screwed and cemented. By David Morrison.

CS 16.13.
Hurricane Lenny. Trampoline screens secure Tamarind Hills No. 15 during Hurricane Lenny. By David Morrison.

ACKNOWLEDGEMENTS/CONTACT INFORMATION

David Morrison Associates, Philipsburg, St Maarten, D.W.I. E-mail: dma@sintmaarten.net

17 LINDAVISTA HOUSE

Architect:
Jose Roberto Garcia-Chavez;
1998

Owner:
Jose Roberto Garcia-Chavez

Location:
Lindavista, Mexico City, Mexico;
19°N, 99°W; 2240 m above sea
level

Climate:
Temperate

Area:
300 m²

CS 17.1.
Lindavista House, by Jose Roberto Garcia-Chavez.

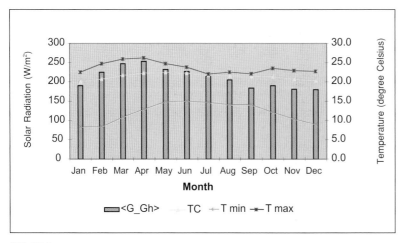

CS 17.2.
Nicol graph for Mexico City.

ECOFEATURES

• Bioclimatic design • Solar water heating and cooking • Optimized natural day lighting • Energy-efficient equipment • Low energy materials and insulation • Rainwater collection and storage with low consumption devices • Sustainable waste treatment recycling • Healthy construction environment • Life-supporting systems: vegetable garden and orchard

DESCRIPTION/BRIEF

This house is three-storey, rectangular in plan and located in the centre of Mexico City. On the ground floor it has a car park area, studio, greenhouse, vegetable and flower garden, inorganic waste material separation, living and dining room, kitchen, studio, bathroom, rainwater collection and storage system, rainwater absorption well and garden. The second floor has three bedrooms and two bathrooms. The third floor has a studio, bedroom, bathroom, laundry room, solar photovoltaics area, terrace and flower growing area. The roof has a storage area, solar collectors area and rainwater collection area.

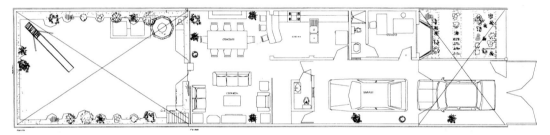

CS 17.3.
Ground floor.

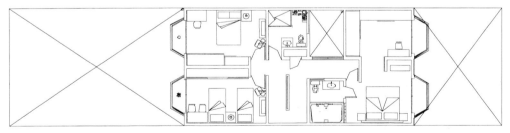

CS 17.4.
Second floor.

ECOFEATURES EXPLAINED

Bioclimatic design

Through the application of passive cooling and heating systems, good orientation, natural ventilation solutions, shading devices and evaporative cooling the entire house is naturally climatized, providing comfort conditions to occupants throughout the year.

Energy efficient

The orientation and site placement of the house provides optimal daylight to enter the house, therefore reducing the amount of energy used for lighting. A stand-alone photovoltaic solar system supplements artificial lighting with the use of energy-efficient fixtures and equipment. Good insulation standards for exterior walls and roof also reduce heating loads when solar heating provides space heat during underheated periods.

Materials

Regional stone, brick, concrete, earth landscaping and glass were the building materials used because they were locally available, builders were familiar with their application and because they have relatively low cost and low embodied energy. This simple and robust solution for building systems requires little user maintenance and is viable for a sustainable design.

Materials/element	U value (W m^{-2} K)	Description
Walls	1.80	Solid brick and plaster
Floor	0.54	Concrete slab and ceramic tile
Roof	1.10	Concrete and polystyrene
Windows	4.50	Glass and aluminium, solar protected

Ventilation

The house is naturally ventilated and windows have 'wing walls' to enhance air movement indoors. The windows are bay widows, with two lateral openings and the central one is fixed. The first opening is located in a high-pressure zone (in the downwind). The wing wall is upwind of the second window, which creates suction in front of it, providing effective natural ventilation into the rooms. Openings are located 30° from prevailing winds, which has been proven to be optimum for better ventilation. The doors have manually controlled upper and lower operable louvres for promoting air movement through the house as desired. During the summer, nocturnal ventilation takes place through the louvres. The east-facing garden and vegetation act as microclimate modulators, increasing the air movement indoors. Building surfaces act as powerful 'heat sinks', providing comfortable temperatures the following day. During the winter the louvres remain closed, reducing heat losses.

	Air changes per hour
Lindavista House	Three average, and ten during overheating season for nocturnal structural cooling
Typical house	One

Water and waste

Water is conserved through rainwater collection and storage systems that supply domestic water for all uses. Devices that save water consumption in water closets, showers and taps, etc. are also used. Used water from the kitchen and bathrooms (black water) is recycled to the water closet tank. Rain water (grey) is collected and stored for gardening.

	Water consumption $(m^3\ a^{-1})$	Water purchase price a^{-1} (US$)
Lindavista House	42	48
Typical house	180	308
Savings		
Total	138	260
%	77	84

Food and waste

At Lindavista House there is: sorting of waste within the home for local collection sites and the possibility for some recycling, compost production used in the garden and excess organic waste for use in intensive gardening, life-supporting systems by means of organic vegetable garden and orchard, reducing solid waste. Therefore, the energy–ecological systems integrated in the house provide high levels of self-sufficiency in energy, water and food and are aimed at providing energy savings, whilst improving economy, the natural environment and the quality of life. It is expected that this design premise eventually will generate a new energy, water and food production culture and that, in turn, will promote a favourable application of sustainable development nationwide.

	Consumption $(kWh\ a^{-1}/ kWh\ m^{-2}\ a^{-1})$	Cost of electricity (US$)	Gas consumption $(l\ a^{-1})$	Cost of gas, annual (US$)	Total cost, annual (US$)	CO_2 emissions (tonnes a^{-1})	Construction cost (US$ m^{-2})
Lindavista House	2760/9.2	180	300	90	270	1880	315
Typical house	4500/15	300	1800	540	840	3065	300
Savings							
Total	1740	120	1500	450	570	1185	−30
%	61	60	83	83	68	61	−5

Total annual savings

- Electricity and gas   US$570
- Water   US$260
- Total   US$830
- Payback period   US$4500/US$830 a^{-1} = 5.4 years

(Food production economic benefits from life-supporting vegetable garden and orchard not considered, but these can also contribute to reduce payback period even further.)

Healthy construction

One of the main design premises was to promote healthy building. This was accomplished by the use of healthy building materials, organic as much as possible, without inducing health hazards. Natural ventilated and moisture-open construction provided a healthy outdoor environment. The use of plant materials and vegetation forms a natural barrier against heavy local pollution and dust. This not only promotes a healthy environment for the workers but also inactive neighbours.

LESSONS LEARNED/PITFALLS

It is difficult to make clients and building occupants aware of the potential economic, health, environmental and quality of life benefits from implementing ecological-bioclimatic-sustainable projects.

ACKNOWLEDGEMENTS/CONTACT INFORMATION

Mr Garcia-Chavez would like to 'thank all persons involved in this project during the whole process and above all thanks to God for granting us the essential serenity and holistic understanding to overcome all difficulties'.

Jose Roberto Garcia-Chavez, Mexico City, Mexico. E-mail: jgc@correo.azc.uam.mx

18 RAVEN RUN

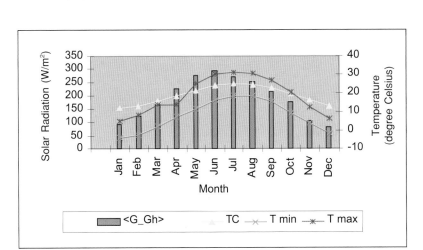

CS 18.1.
Raven Run, by Richard Levine.

Architect:
Richard Levine, 1974

Owners:
Richard Levine and Anne Frye,
daughter Laura Frye-Levine

Location:
Raven Run, Lexington, KT;
38°N, 84°W; 258 m above sea
level

Climate:
Temperate

Area:
344 m²

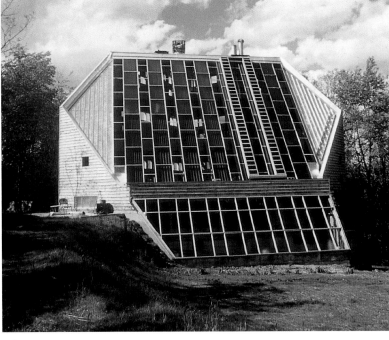

CS 18.2.
Nicol graph for Lexington, KT.

ECOFEATURES

• Diagonally sliced half cube form (no north face) • Single function
windows • Passive/active mechanical system • Rock store

DESCRIPTION/BRIEF

The house was built by the architect and his artist wife, Anne Frye, assisted by architecture students from a number of American universities. The house currently has three bedrooms, a library, large studio, kitchen-dining room, living room, shop, basement and a 37 m^2 greenhouse. The house has eight levels. Three large spaces stacked in the north corner are 3 m floor-to-floor, the living room is more than 6 m high, while the smaller spaces in the east and west corners are 2.3 m floor-to-floor. The house is of a square plan form with its corners oriented to the cardinal points, with the south corner cut diagonally to face the solar facade at an optimal angle of 54°44′ for solar efficiency.

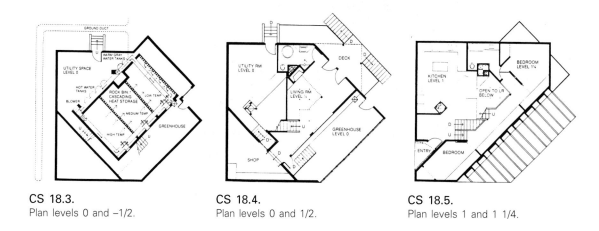

CS 18.3.
Plan levels 0 and −1/2.

CS 18.4.
Plan levels 0 and 1/2.

CS 18.5.
Plan levels 1 and 1 1/4.

ECOFEATURES EXPLAINED

Form

There is a dynamic dialogue between several families of geometries within the 40 ft cube. Organizationally, the design is fairly simple; large tall spaces (kitchen, two studios) are essentially orthogonal and move from the north corner south towards the centre of the house. Small low spaces (bedrooms, library, shop, darkroom, porch) work more with the diagonals and move from the east and west corners toward the centre. At the centre is the living room working orthogonally with its south face lending its space to all the others. As the two geometries approach one another in the centre of the house, the unusual stairs serve to multiply the spatiality of all the adjacent spaces.

Single-function windows

Different windows were designed for particular functions and located where they were needed to work best; they are well insulated and simply but inexpensively built. The windows for letting in light are continuous horizontal clerestories made of six layers of plastic (fibre glass and Tedlar) for insulation and light diffusion, and span continuously across vertical studs. View windows are fixed, double-glazed units with thick insulated

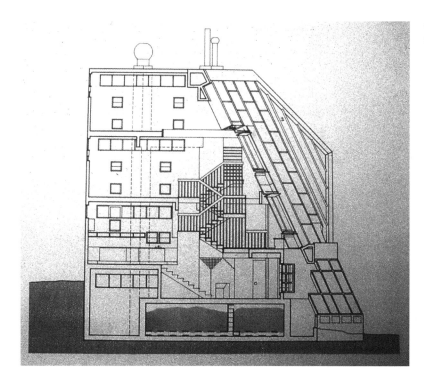

panels that slide up into the wall and out of sight when not in use. They are installed where views are desirable. Ventilation windows have no glass, but are otherwise similar to the view windows, having thick panels of insulation that can slide up and down, out of sight. They are located near the floor in the northeast wall to maximize ventilation effects of the cool summer breezes coming up the hill from the east. Sundows, windows installed between the multistage active hot water collectors, work as passive solar collectors. They are single-glazed to permit the maximum amount of sunlight to enter and have sufficient combined area so that on sunny days they heat the house by themselves. They are fitted with pivoted insulated shutters that open and close automatically, powered by the sun. The sundows close at night and on cloudy days, minimizing heat loss. Most of them are closed during the summer to prevent overheating. During construction, a pair of connected ladders served as a moveable scaffolding; this design feature remains after construction to serve as a washing rig and shades two strips of sundows on warm days.

Passive and active mechanical system

The 9.7 m sloping facade illustrates Levine's integrative strategy, combining passive collectors and active devices. The passive direct gain sundows and greenhouse, accompanied by the active multistage air collector supplying the three-stage rock bin controlled by a computer, were the mechanical means of making sure the comfort temperatures were maintained. The back-up system is a draft-controlled fireplace, but it was never necessary to use this system, coupled with ground tubes for heating and cooling. The south façade is built as a structural element and supported by long plywood box beams running east–west (reinforcing the diagonal grid that influences the organization and form of the spaces). The collectors were built on-site and form the rain screen cladding, structure and insulation for the south face. To maximize heat gains, Levine added layers of glazing and changed the corrugation of the black-coated foil toward the top of the channels, so heat gained was retained at the top.

Rock store

There are three rock bins each approximately 2.7 m wide, 6.1 m long and 1.5 m deep. The idea was that a computer routes the collected hot air to the bin with the lowest temperature above that of the collector output temperature. This gave the system a low-temperature, a medium-temperature and a high-temperature storage bin. This arrangement meant that the system could begin in the morning, collecting when the collector output was only slightly above room temperature and could continue to collect in the evenings even after sunset, when it would draw the residual heat out of the collectors. In house-heating mode the computer would operate the dampers such that heat would be withdrawn from the bin with the lowest useable temperature.

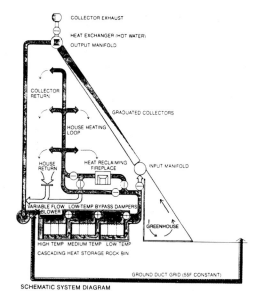

SCHEMATIC SYSTEM DIAGRAM

CS 18.7.
Schematic system diagram.

LESSONS LEARNED/MODIFICATIONS

The computer that controlled the rock bin temperatures has had to be replaced. It was replaced with a simplified system that is not so efficient but proves to be more reliable. An earth-coupled (geothermal) heat pump was installed in the late 1990s, which provides cooling (or mostly dehumidification) as well as auxiliary heating. In addition, the greenhouse was reglazed with triple-paned, heat-mirrored glass. Previously with only single-glazing, an operable curtain was employed to prevent excessive heat gain or heat loss. Now the curtain is no longer necessary. The interior of the sundows have also been glazed by a similar glazing regime, permitting them to be opened most of the time without unwanted heat gain or heat loss. Originally there was a fin-tube heat exchanger installed in the upper hot air manifold to convert the hot air to solar hot water. It worked very well and required no separate collector. One winter the temperatures dropped below –23°C and the heat exchanger was destroyed and never replaced. An electric water heater now heats the water.

ACKNOWLEDGEMENTS/CONTACT INFORMATION

Richard Levine, Lexington, KT. E-mail: rslevine1939@yahoo.com

19 MIDDLETON HOUSE

CS 19.1.
Middleton House in winter, by Charles Middleton.

CS 19.2.
Middleton House in summer, by Charles Middleton.

Architect:
Charles Middleton, 1990

Client:
Charles Middleton and Peggie Beattie

Location:
Gravenhurst, Ontario, Canada; 45°N, 79°W; 270 m above sea level

Climate:
Continental; 4800 heating degree days per year

Area:
152 m²

CS 19.3.
Nicol graph for Ontario.

ECOFEATURES

• Passive design • Materials, local and low embodied energy • Solar systems

DESCRIPTION/BRIEF

The main objective of this designer/occupant project, beyond the immediate issue of getting a house built, was to achieve accepted Canadian levels of comfort and amenity using only renewable-energy technologies, along with conventional, affordable construction. In other words, to show that a life-style based on low and renewable energy could be accessible to ordinary families, without using exotic and expensive technologies, or having unacceptable or unreasonable expectations of the occupants. The house has been in continuous use since 1990. For minimal environmental impact, solar energy was harnessed to the maximum. This entailed design to control energy both passively and

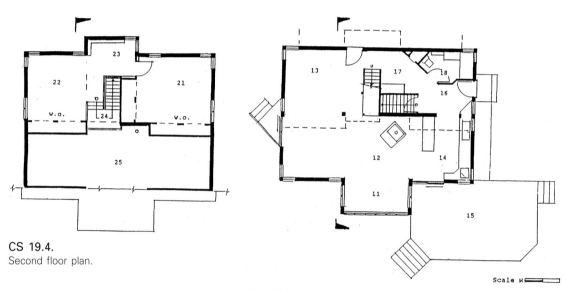

CS 19.4.
Second floor plan.

CS 19.5.
First floor plan.

Scale M

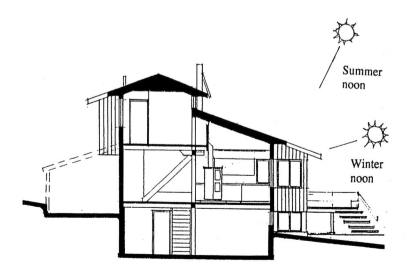

Summer
noon

Winter
noon

CS 19.6.
Section.

actively, winter and summer. It also required construction with low embodied energy and minimum waste. The house is the primary home for a married couple, with visits from the extended family. It is located in Muskoka in Ontario, some 150 km north of Toronto. The Muskoka region is on the Canadian Shield and is noted for landscapes or rock slabs, lakes and windblown trees. It provides outdoor recreation year-round. There are pockets of farmland, generally of marginal quality, but more than acceptable for experiments with 'sustainable' lifestyles such as this. For the idea of sustainability to become more widely accepted it had to be accessible and user-friendly. The house was intended to demonstrate that this is possible using simple design techniques, showing that environmental responsibility does not mean returning to the 'horse and buggy' days, but is a step towards a more desirable and sustainable future.

PASSIVE DESIGN

The passive design strategies respond to seasonal climatic characteristics and include careful selection of site planning and orientation for good solar exposure in the winter. The house is oriented with open plan, living spaces facing south, service spaces and a garage to the north. The north wall, which has few windows, is sheltered by a sloping natural wall of rock with large coniferous trees. South-facing glazing provides solar heat gain in the winter. The eaves provide these widows with protection from the higher-altitude sun in the summer. The windows are side-hung casements. Careful choice of left- or right-hand openings in relation to the prevailing westerly winds allows ventilation without rain penetration. Roughly 30 per cent of the average annual precipitation of 993 mm falls as snow in winter when the windows are shut.

LOCAL AND LOW EMBODIED ENERGY MATERIALS

The compact design of the house was based on a 12 ft module, using standard timber sizes to minimize construction waste. Canadian wood-frame construction is well established, affordable and a means of using a renewable locally available resource efficiently. The concept of highly insulated, airtight design has been well developed through such programmes as Canada Mortgage and Housing Association's (CMHC) R2000 programme. With no need to re-invent the wheel, these practices were adopted for construction of the envelope.

1 Conventional wood-frame construction for low embodied energy and affordability. 5 cm × 15 cm pre-cut wood studs minimize waste, as do roof trusses pre-assembled from 5 cm × 10 cm wood.
2 Conventional fibreglass or rock-wool insulation with careful installation of vapour barrier to achieve a high level of airtightness. Wall insulation, 4.4 rsi; roof, 831 rsi.
3 Conventional concrete block basement with exterior insulation for about 1 rsi.
4 Side-hung casement windows, triple glazed.
5 Supplementary heat source: centrally located airtight wood stove using wood gathered from wood lot, eliminating need for mechanical fossil-fuelled furnace and all ductwork.

SOLAR SYSTEM

The house is powered off-grid with a range of conventional electrical appliances for the kitchen, as well as computers, fax, satellite television and other conveniences. The house is fitted with a 600 W photovoltaic array for electricity and a small generator for backup. The battery stores 1800 Ah, allowing several days' use without recharge. The house has a solar hot-water system with a nominal 200 l storage tank. The system draws water from the well using a 0.5 hp (0.373 kW) pump. Rainwater is collected from the roof for use in the garden, conserving well-water and energy for pumping.

LESSONS LEARNED AND FIXES

1 Passive solar approaches work well, as do R2000 type construction, the photovoltaic and hot water systems. The latter produces more hot water than can be used at present.
2 The exterior insulating sheathing of 4 cm of dense fibreglass was found not to be vermin-proof. The problem was solved by additional sealing at the bottom of the exterior wood siding. It would be better to use uninsulated plywood sheathing in the first place, adding further insulation if desired.
3 Photovoltaics work well but the 'learning-curve' on installation was steep. This installation seems to reflect the current state of development of this technology in North America. Components work well individually, and support is good. The problems arise with integration. Systems are not sold as complete and fully integrated packages. In that case it is all the more essential that systems should be described with clear instructions of how components contribute to a comprehensive installation. Perhaps this will improve as systems become more widely used.
4 The range of 12 V DC appliances widely available for recreational uses is welcome, but they are often expensive, e.g. water pumps or refrigerators. Careful calculation is necessary to balance capital costs versus operating costs, taking into account losses in inverting to 110 V AC. Convenience is also a factor. An increasing variety of time-dependent appliances are available. These should be avoided to eliminate stand-by losses.
5 The biological toilet provided an unexpected advantage in that it drastically reduced the need for water and consequently electrical energy for pumping. However, the particular system used here was not 'user friendly'. Design was poorly developed and materials distorted in use. Manufacturer support has been virtually non-existent. The problems have been resolved by a series of fixes, but this technology cannot be considered sufficiently mature for general use. Much more committed development is needed by the manufacturers.

ACKNOWLEDGEMENTS/CONTACT INFORMATION

Charles Middleton, Gravenhurst, Canada. E-mail: mid.beat@sympatico.ca

20 PEN-Y-LLYN

CS 20.1.
Pen-y-Llyn, by Christopher Day.

Architect:
Christopher Day, retrofit
1975–1977

Owners:
Christopher and Penina Day,
children: Dewi, Michael Taliesen
and Martha

Location:
Pembrokeshire, Wales, UK;
51°N, 4°W; <10 m above sea
level

Climate:
temperate, coastal

Area:
103 m²

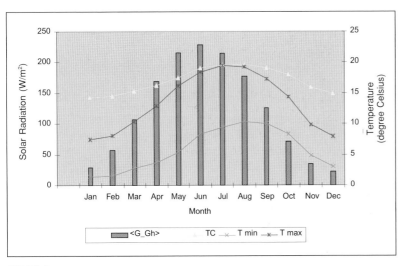

CS 20.2.
Nicol graph for Pembrokeshire.

ECOFEATURES

• Self build • Second-hand materials • Insulation • Solar heating and
wind power

DESCRIPTION/BRIEF

When the architect acquired Pen-y-Llyn in 1975, he was left with little to build from. The structure, a farmhouse occupied by caravan dwellers and vacated 20 years previously, had barely any walls with which to start, what one might call, a renovation. Today this house has been transformed to meet the changing needs of the family existence. The young children are now teenagers and the architect works from his home.

ECOFEATURES EXPLAINED

Self build

Christopher Day has built his career promoting volunteer and self-build structures. Building with volunteers can be cheaper and, on past projects, estimates of 12–14 per cent savings on contract costs have been attributed to volunteers. In addition, there are rich cultural experiences to be gained. In one of his earlier projects, there were volunteers from over 13 nations helping to build. He found when he started rebuilding his home at Pen-y-Llyn that people were always stopping in to help, frequently without any prior warning. At the time the house did not have a phone or accommodation for volunteers. There was a chicken shed in which he and his wife lived during construction. Others had to stay in tents on the site. At times when weather was bad they would all cram into the 9 ft × 5 ft chicken shed. Some of the advantages of self build include:

- it is economical;
- it puts the focus on activity instead of institutionalism;
- it builds communities;
- it offers the opportunity for personal growth for those involved.

Second-hand materials

Second-hand materials are not always inferior and, when you look at a raped rainforest or the hillsides raked from mining, you can begin to value the extra time it may take when using second-hand materials. Second-hand timber is frequently well studded with nails. Christopher would rarely

Materials to look for	Materials to avoid
RSJs (steel beams)	Pressed steel radiators – life probably limited
Structural timbers	
Boards for	Demo hardcore
floors (time consuming to finish)	Electrical wiring (invisibly damaged)
cupboard doors	
shelving, etc.	Timber infected with dry rot (or other rot, insects, etc.)
Floor tiles	
Slates	Timber that has been treated with biocides
Roof tiles	
Handmade bricks (for appearance only)	
Sinks, baths, basins	
Solid fuel heating appliances	

de-nail the studs but would simply knock over protruding points for safety and not fully cinch them down in case they fell in the line of a saw cut. He estimates that when ordering second-hand material 20 per cent more than what is actually needed is a safe order, owing to damaged ends, rotting, etc. In Christopher's book *Building With Heart* he includes a list of those second-hand materials to look for and those to avoid.

Insulation strategies

In the 1970s, when the Building Regulations required that a building's roof be insulated with 50 mm insulation, Christopher tripled this regulation in some rooms and doubled it in all others. Even though the regulations have changed to require 150 mm, it is apparent that his strategy paid off, although he specifies 300 mm of roof insulation in his current projects. The existing south wall of Pen-y-Llyn was approximately 600 mm thick, built of sedimentary stone that had deep capillary cracks. Owing to the climate most gales and the rain drive towards the south elevation of the house, so Christopher insulated the outside of the south wall with 75 mm insulation with 200 mm of stone-rock on top of this. The west wall was extended during reconstruction and the new construction consisted of 150 mm insulation, 50 mm rock wool insulation, a 25 mm cavity space, 100 mm concrete block and an average of 250 mm of stonework. The windows on all sides were site-built by hand and double glazed. Owing to the amount of moisture received by the south side of the house, condensation between these window panes has required the removal of the interior pane. Also, the wooden frames around the doors and windows are constantly swelling and shrinking, causing consistent draught-proofing replacement.

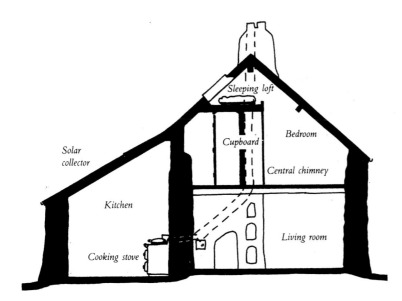

CS 20.3.
Section.

Solar heating (principal heating strategy)

A solid fuel cooking stove and central chimney provide a large area, low-temperature, radiant wall that heats the five rooms around it. South-facing windows mean that life in the house faces south and the architectural studio (converted from the hayloft) can be solar heated even on the cold winter days. A home-made solar water heater is used as a proprietary system integral to the roof; such systems were not commonly used when installed. In the summer the water is heated 100 per cent by the sun and, since there is little rain, there is a low flow setting on the hydrogenerator producing lower electricity for this cause. Between the seasons the sun is used to pre-heat the water, which is then topped up by the 1.5 kW hydrogenerator, warmed by the boiler from the stove. During the winter, the water is heated 100 per cent by the Rayburn cooking stove. The hydrogenerator that diverts any power not drawn directly for use to a ballast circuit, which heats an oil-filled radiator or hot water immersion heater. In the 1980s, when Christopher monitored his electric consumption, he purchased on an average about £25 of electricity per year from the utility company. Pen-y-Llyn consumes an average of about 1.08 tons of anthracite coal per year, supplementing both heating and cooking needs. Natural gas consumption is negligible as its main use is for summer cooking.

LESSONS LEARNED

We all know family patterns change. The children grow into teenagers and technology invents new items for amusement, e.g. computers, compact disc players, etc. Since the re-habitation into Pen-y-Llyn in the 1970s, this family has also acquired new habits. It is important to build with the future in mind. Recently, Christopher has become unable to maintain the generator that was part of an ethical ritual relevant to his philosophy of building. He quotes that 'teenagers and others in the house have a different attitude to electricity and gadgeting resulting in the hydrogenerator being turned off! Hence, electric consumption has soared'.

ACKNOWLEDGEMENTS/CONTACT INFORMATION

Christopher Day, Pen-y-Llyn, Wales, UK. Tel.: +44 1239 891 399.

21 TANDDERWEN

Architect:
Andrew Yeats

Energy Consultant:
Matthew Hill

Renewables Supply:
Steve Wade

Owner:
David Johnson

Location:
Monmouth, Wales, UK; 51°N,
2°W; <600 m above sea level

Climate:
Inland

Area:
223 m²

CS 21.1.
Tandderwen, by Andrew Yeats.

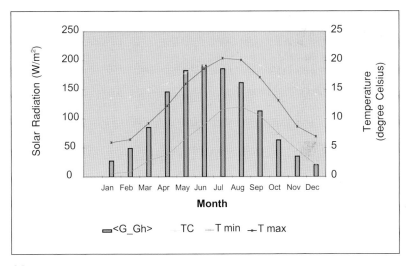

CS 21.2.
Nicol graph for Monmouth.

ECOFEATURES

• Wind/photovoltaic and battery backup power supply • Rainwater reuse

DESCRIPTION/BRIEF

David's house, Tandderwen, implements an environmental design strategy that outlines and establishes a holistic environmental agenda. The brief essentially searched for an architecture that was non-polluting, resource-conserving and as respectful to the environment and people as possible. It was important to give real value to the characteristics of Tandderwen and not list 'optional extras' or 'add ons'. When David moved into the house his intent was to be disconnected from the grid (autonomous) within a year.

WIND/PHOTOVOLTAIC AND BATTERY BACKUP POWER SUPPLY

CS 21.3.
Photovoltaic array, solar water heater and wind turbine, by Steve Wade.

David's house combines wind and solar power to compensate for seasonal variances and to produce a consistent and steady supply of renewable energy. 28 BP Solarex photovoltaic panels, which provide a 2.1 kW peak rating, are mounted on a simple garden timber trellis permitting optimal solar orientation without relying on the house orientation. This also prevents excess heat build-up on the panels and allows them to be cleaned without the need for roof ladders. It also allows the system to be upgraded easily in the future. When the wind is blowing more than the sun is shining, then the 2.5 kW Scottish-made Proven wind turbine provides supplemental power. To ensure a backup electrical supply if the sun is not shining and the wind is not blowing, a battery store is provided.

Both the wind turbine and the photovoltaic array supply to the battery and the power is converted to 230 V AC for running normal domestic appliances in the house. However, all appliances have been carefully considered to eliminate unnecessary demand and to optimize the efficiency of essential items. A low-energy cooker, fridge and washing machine have been installed, along with low-energy mini fluorescent lighting throughout the house.

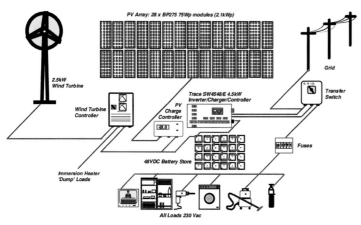

CS 21.4.
Power supply from the wind turbine and photovoltaic array.

RAINWATER REUSE

Whilst most people complain when it rains, David is comforted knowing his water tank is being topped up to provide drinking water. All household drinking and washing requirements are met by the 900 mm of collected precipitation annually. Rainwater is routed from gutters on the roof to an 8 m^3 cistern in the storage undercroft. Water is then plumbed from the tank through a filter and UV sterilizer to a 200 l holding tank in the roof. All outlets simply draw water from the holding tank in the normal way. Excess rainwater collected is drawn off to service the garden pond.

PASSIVE VENTILATION AND INTERNAL AIR QUALITY

The building is constructed in such a way that the vapour barrier is eliminated, which ensures that the permeability and density of the layers within the fabric reduce towards the outside. This layering system eliminates condensation. Natural fabric scatter rugs over waxed reclaimed timber floors, organic paints and stains to walls, avoiding all formaldehyde and equivalents, combined with natural ventilation promise a healthy internal air quality. Energy-consuming mechanical ventilation has been avoided at David's house to promote a healthier vapour-permeable building fabric construction and a natural passivent system. This natural process draws air from intake vents in dry rooms through wet rooms (bathrooms and kitchen) and vents the stale moist air through the roof ridge vents. This system eliminates mechanical or moving parts and is self-regulating, depending on humidity level.

LESSONS LEARNED

- Double height living spaces are very effective heat drains as the hot air from the ground floor rises making the first floor warm but the ground floor much colder.
- The lack of thermal mass in the house means that there is very little thermal capacity for the house itself to store free heat from the sun, cooking, people and equipment. As soon as the heating goes off the house cools down which is not a problem for David but should be noted by those wishing to emulate the design.

ACKNOWLEDGEMENTS/CONTACT INFORMATION

Photos by: Andrew Yeats, Eco Arc. E-mail: ecaarc@cwcan.net. Matthew Hill, LEDA. E-mail: MHillLEDA@aol.com. Steve Wade, Wind & Sun Ltd. E-mail: info@windandsun.co.uk

GLOSSARY

absorber
The blackened surface in a solar collector that absorbs solar radiation and converts it to heat.

absorptance
The ratio of absorbed to incident solar radiation on a surface.

AES
Manufacturer of solar water heaters at Findhorn, UK. aes@findhorn.org

aerobic
Having oxygen as a part of the environment. Growing or occurring only in the presence of oxygen.

air changes
A measure of the air exchange in a building. One air change is an exchange of a volume of air equal to the interior volume of a building.

air mass or AM
A specification for solar spectra; AM 1 is the spectrum for the shortest path through the atmosphere corresponding to the sun directly over head (possible in the tropics); AM 1.5 is used for standard specifications because it represents the more typical condition of the sun at about 45° above the horizon.

altitude angle
The angular distance from the horizon to the sun.

amorphous silicon
A type of silicon in which the atoms have no order, as in glass, so it is not crystalline; also called thin-film silicon.

anaerobic
The absence of oxygen. Growing in the absence of oxygen.

annual specific yield
The actual electrical energy generated over 1 year divided by the peak power of the array; given in units of kWh per kWp (although a more precise notation would be kWh year^{-1} kWp^{-1})

array
An assembly of several PV modules connected in series and/or parallel.

auxiliary heating
The conventional (i.e. non-solar) contribution to the total load (e.g. gas boiler, etc.).

azimuth angle
The angular distance between true south and the point on the horizon directly below the sun (negative before noon, positive after noon).

beam radiation
See 'direct solar radiation'.

berm
A man-made mound or small hill of earth, either abutting a house wall to help stabilize the internal temperature or positioned to deflect wind from the house.

biological dentrification
The biochemical reduction (conversion) of nitrate nitrogen to nitrite nitrogen and to the gaseous molecular nitrogen or an oxide of nitrogen.

black body
A perfect absorber and emitter of radiation. A cavity is a perfect black body. Lampblack is close to a black body, while aluminium (polished) is a poor absorber and emitter of radiation.

black water
Wastewater generated within a household, including toilet wastes.

calorific value
Describes the energy content of a unit mass or volume of a fuel ($kWh\ kg^{-1}$, $J\ kg^{-1}$, $kWh\ m^{-3}$, $J\ m^{-3}$).

carbon source
Carbon used as an energy source by anaerobic bacteria in the denitrification process.

casual gains
See 'internal gains'.

chimney or stack effect
The tendency of air or gas in a duct or other vertical passage to rise when heated owing to its lower density in comparison with that of the surrounding air or gas. In buildings, the tendency towards displacement (caused by the difference in temperature) of internal heated air by unheated outside air, owing to the difference in density of outside and inside air.

collector, flat plate
An assembly containing a panel of metal or other suitable material, usually a flat black colour on its sun side, that absorbs sunlight and converts it into heat. This panel is usually in an insulated box, covered with glass or plastic on the sun side to take advantage of the greenhouse effect. In the collector, this heat transfers to a circulating fluid, such as air, water, oil or antifreeze.

collector, focusing
A collector that has a parabolic or other reflector that focuses sunlight onto a small area for collection. A reflector of this type can obtain considerably higher temperatures but will only work with direct-beam sunlight.

collector, solar
A device for capturing solar energy, ranging from ordinary windows to complex mechanical devices.

conduction
The heat moving from a warmer to a colder region in the same substance without mass transfer; this type of heat transfer depends on the thermal conductivity of the material.

convection
The mechanism of heat transfer between a surface and a fluid.

creepway
Crawlspace beneath the ground floor of a house.

crystalline silicon
A type of silicon in which the atoms have a regular diamond-like structure; also called single crystal or polycrystalline.

declination of sun

The angle of the sun above or below the equatorial plane. It is positive if north of the plane and negative if below and varies day by day through-out the year from 23.47° on 3–21 June to 23.47° on 21 December.

degree days

The product of the number of degrees below a given base temperature and the number of days on which that difference occurs. The base temperature is usually defined between 15.5 and 21°C.

differential thermostat

A thermostat that operates on the basis of the temperature difference between two points. Blowers and pumps turn on or off depending on the magnitude of □t.

diffuse solar radiation

The solar radiation as received on a surface with the exception of the solid angle subtended by the sun's disk (direct solar radiation). Solar radiation reaches the Earth indirectly through scattering in the atmosphere.

diffuse transmission

The type of solar transmission through a diffusing or translucent glazing, namely, transmission that is scattered by interaction with the glazing material. The diffuse transmitted radiation is assumed to be isotropic, that is, equally intense in all directions.

direct solar gains

Direct solar radiation passing through glass areas (mainly south-facing) that contributes to space heating (kWh).

direct solar radiation

The solar radiation from the solid angle of the sun's disk. Solar radiation reaching a surface in a straight line from the sun.

DSHW

Domestic solar hot water.

ecliptic

The great circle cut in the celestial sphere by an extension of the plane of the Earth's orbit. The great circle drawn on a terrestrial globe makes an angle of about 23°27' with the equator.

effluent

Sewage, water or other liquid, partially or completely treated or in its natural state, flowing out of any component of an ISDS or flowing beneath the ground surface in groundwater or over the ground surface.

electrical current

The rate of flow of positive charge in a circuit; units amps or A; symbol I.

emissivity

The ratio of the radiant energy emitted from a surface at a given temperature to the energy emitted by a black body at the same temperature.

extraterrestrial radiation

Solar radiation impinging on the Earth's outer atmosphere.

global irradiance

The sum of direct and diffuse irradiance.

Glasshead Ltd. Email: tv@glasshead.co.uk

grey water

Wastewater generated within a household consisting of sink, tub, shower and laundry wastewater, and excluding toilet wastes.

heat exchanger

A device, usually consisting of a coiled arrangement of metal tubing, used to transfer heat through the tube walls from one fluid to another.

heat load
The total energy required for space heating.

heat loss
Heat flow through building envelope components (walls, windows, roof, etc.).

heat pump
A thermodynamic device that transfers heat from one medium to another. The first medium (the source) cools while the second (the heat sink) warms up.

heating season
The period of the year during which heating the building is required to maintain comfort conditions.

heliodon
Device that simulates solar angles and measures the number of hours of potential sunshine.

hybrid solar heating system
Solar heating system that combines active and passive techniques.

I-V curve
Plot of current versus voltage for a PV cell, module or array as a load is increased from short circuit to open circuit under fixed conditions of irradiance and cell temperature.

incident angle
The angle between the sun's rays and a line perpendicular (normal) to the irradiated surface.

indirect gain
The indirect transfer of solar heat into the space to be heated from a collector that is coupled to the space by an uninsulated, conductive or convective medium (such as a thermal storage wall or roof pond).

infiltration
The uncontrolled movement of outdoor air into the interior of a building through cracks around windows and doors or in walls, roofs and floors. This may work by cold air leaking in during the winter or the reverse in the summer.

infrared radiation
Electromagnetic radiation having wave length above the range of visible light. This is the preponderant form of radiation emitted by bodies with moderate temperatures, such as the elements of a passive solar building.

insolation
A contraction of 'incoming solar radiation' meaning the amount of solar energy incident on a given area over a certain period of time; a common unit of insolation is $kW\,m^{-2}\,day^{-1}$, often referred to as *peak hours per day*.

internal gains
The energy dissipated inside the heated space by people (body heat) and appliances (lighting, cooker, etc.). A proportion of this energy contributes to the space heating requirements (kWh).

irradiance
Rate of incidence of solar energy on a flat surface at a particular angle of tilt ($W\,m^{-2}$).

isolated gain
The transfer of heat into the space to be heated from a collector that is thermally isolated from the space to be heated by physical separation or insulation (such as a convective loop collector or an attached sunspace with an insulated common wall).

juinling
Sun-shaped pattern at the end of a gabled roof.

kakkleoven
A traditional, European, wood-burning stove made of high-mass materials and typically covered with ceramic tiles.

khuh
Fragrant fibrous root that swells or bloats when soaked in water and can be woven into mats. Has been used traditionally as an evaporative cooling curtain, not a new technology.

kilowatt hour
Energy unit equivalent to 1000 W used for 1 hour; also referred as a 'unit' of electricity: 1 kWh = 3.6 MJ.

latent heat of fusion
The amount of heat required to change the state of a substance from solid to liquid at constant temperature (e.g. ice to water at $0°C$ = 335 kJ kg^{-1}). The same amount of heat is liberated with a change of state in the reverse direction.

latitude
The angular distance north (+) or south (–) of the equator, measured in degrees of arc.

longitude
The arc of the equator between the meridian of a place and the Greenwich meridian measured in degrees east or west.

mean radiant temperature
The area weighted mean temperature of all surrounding surfaces, i.e. $(s \times t) / s$, where t is the temperature of each surface of area, s. It is an approximate indication of the effect that the surface temperatures of surrounding objects have on human comfort.

open circuit voltage
The maximum voltage between the terminals of a PV cell or module when only connected by a voltmeter, so no current is flowing. Symbol is V_{OC}; (compare a 'macho body builder' of great strength but poor ability to move carrying a load).

orientation
The orientation of a surface is in degrees of variation away from solar south, towards either the east or west. Solar or true south should not be confused with magnetic south, which can vary owing to magnetic declination.

peak hours per day
An alternative unit to kWh m^{-2} day^{-1} for daily insolation.

peak power
The maximum amount of power a PV module can generate under standard test conditions of irradiance and cell temperature; units of Wp; (compare a 'wagon puller' who has both the strength to pull the load and can do so at speed).

per cent of possible sunshine
The actual number of hours of sunshine divided by the maximum possible number of hours of sunshine, expressed as a percentage for the month.

phase change material (p.c.m.)
A heat-storage medium which relies on the latent heat of phase transition for absorbing and releasing heat.

photovoltaic (PV)
The process of direct conversion of light into electricity within a material.

pyranometer

An instrument for measuring the solar irradiance on a plane surface. When the solar radiation coming from the sun's disk is obscured from the instrument, a pyranometer can be used to determine diffuse solar radiation.

radiant heat transfer

The transfer of heat by heat radiation. Heat radiation is a form of electromagnetic radiation. Radiant heating resulting from infrared radiation is very prevalent in passive systems.

RCC

Radiation control coating.

rebates

Seal used for draught proofing.

reflectance

The ratio or percentage of the amount of light reflected by a surface to the amount incident. Good light reflectors are not necessarily good heat reflectors.

relative humidity

The ratio of the amount of water vapour in the atmosphere to the maximum amount of water vapour that could be held at a given temperature.

rock bed

A container filled with rocks, pebbles or crushed stone, to store energy by raising the temperature of the rocks, etc.

selective surface (absorber)

A surface absorbing essentially all incident solar radiation (short wave – high-temperature source), while emitting a small fraction of thermal radiation (long wave – low-temperature source).

severs

Movable slats (like blinds) that can roll up or down.

short circuit current

The current between the terminals of a PV cell or module when only connected by an ammeter; symbol I_{SC} (compare a 'marathon runner' who is fast but only when not carrying any load).

solar constant

The irradiance of solar radiation beyond the Earth's atmosphere at the average Earth–sun distance on a surface perpendicular to the sun's rays. The value for the solar constant is 1.37 kW m^{-2}.

solar energy, useful

The amount of solar energy contributing to the total heat load. It is expressed in absolute figures (kWh) or per unit collector area (kWh m^{-2}).

solar fraction (or percentage solar)

The percentage of the total heat load supplied by the solar heating system, including useful losses from the storage.

solar radiation

The energy-carrying electromagnetic radiation emitted by the sun. This radiation comprises many frequencies, each relating to a particular class of radiation:

- high-frequency/short-wavelength ultraviolet;
- medium-frequency/medium-wavelength visible light;
- low-frequency/high-wavelength infrared.

This radiation is relatively unimpeded until it reaches the Earth's atmosphere. Here some of it will be reflected back out of the atmosphere, some will be absorbed. That which reaches the Earth's surface unimpeded is referred to as 'direct' solar radiation. That which is scattered by the atmosphere is referred to as 'diffuse' solar radiation. The combination of direct and diffuse is called 'global'.

specific heat capacity
A measure of the amount of energy required to raise a unit mass or volume of a material through a unit temperature change ($kWh\ kg^{-1}\ K$, $J\ kg^{-1}\ K$, $kWh\ m^{-1}\ K$, $J\ m^{-3}\ K$).

specular reflectance
The proportion of incident luminous flux reflected from a polished surface.

standard test conditions
A set of accepted test conditions used by manufacturers of PV modules to specify a module's electrical output; the conditions are an irradiance of $1000\ W\ m^{-2}$ with a light spectrum of AM 1.5 and the PV cells maintained at 25°C.

storage efficiency
The percentage of solar energy input to the heat storage, subsequently used in the heat distribution system (i.e. excludes unwanted heat losses from the storage device) (%).

thermal conductance
The thermal transmittance through $1\ m^2$ of material of a given thickness for each 1 K temperature difference between its surfaces ($W\ m^{-2}\ K$).

thermal conductivity
The thermal transmission through a material 1 m thick for each 1 K temperature difference ($W\ m^{-1}\ K$).

thermal mass
The mass of the building within the insulation, expressed per volume of heated space ($kg\ m^{-3}$). 'Primary thermal mass' receives direct sunlight; 'secondary thermal mass' is in sight of the primary thermal mass and so receives radiative and convective energy from the primary thermal mass; 'remote thermal mass' is hidden from view of both the primary and secondary thermal mass and so receives energy by convection only.

thermal resistance or R-value
The reciprocal of thermal conductance – see above ($m^2.K\ W^{-1}$).

thermal resistivity
The reciprocal of thermal conductivity ($m.K\ W^{-1}$).

thermal transmittance
The thermal transmission through $1\ m^2$ area of a given structure (e.g. a wall consisting of bricks, thermal insulation, cavities, etc.) divided by the difference between the environmental temperature on either side of the structure. Usually called 'U-value' ($W\ m^{-2}\ K$).

thermosiphon
The convective circulation of a fluid that occurs in a closed system where warm fluid rises and is replaced by a cooler fluid in the same system.

tilt
The angle of a plane relative to a horizontal plane.

TIM
Transparent insulation material.

thin-film silicon
A form of silicon as applied to a substrate, usually glass; atomic structure is amorphous.

tracking
The process of altering the tilt of a module throughout the day in order to face the sun and thus maximize the power output.

transmittance
The ratio of the radiant energy transmitted through a substance to the total radiant energy incident on its surface. In solar technology, it is always affected by the thickness and composition of the glass cover plates on a collector or window, and to a major extent by the angle of incidence between the sun's rays and a line normal to the surface.

ultraviolet radiation
Electromagnetic radiation having wavelengths shorter than visible light. This invisible form of radiation is found in solar radiation and plays a part in the deterioration of plastic glazings, paint and furnishing fabrics.

U-value
See 'thermal transmittance'.

vapour barrier
A component of a construction that is impervious to the flow of moisture and air and is used to prevent condensation in walls and other locations of insulation.

ventilation losses
The heat losses associated with the continuous replacement of warm, stale air by fresh cold air.

voltage
The electromotive force or electrical 'umph' that is available or being used in a circuit; units of volts or V; symbol V.

volumetric heat loss coefficient (G-value)
The total heat loss of a dwelling (through the fabric and ventilation), divided by the heated volume and the temperature differential at which the loss occurs ($W\,m^{-1}\,K$).

watershed
The land area that drains to a common outlet, such as the outflow of a lake, the mouth of a river or any point along a stream channel.

watt
Unit of power which is the rate of flow of energy, whether electrical, light or heat; definition is $1\,W = 1\,J\,s^{-1}$; for electrical, also equals 1 VA.

watt hour
Convenient unit of energy corresponding the use of 1 W for 1 hour; 1 Wh = 3600 J, 860 calories or 3.41 Btu.

windspeed
The speed of the air measured in accordance with the recommendations of the World Meteorological Organization, normally measured 10 m above ground level.

wing wall
Vertical projection on one side of a window or wall used to increase or decrease the wind pressure or solar incidence on the wall or window.

zenith angle
The angular distance from the sun to the zenith, the point directly above the observer (at noon = latitude solar declination).

REFERENCES

Allen, P. and Todd, B. (1995). *Off the Grid: Managing Electricity from Renewable Sources*. The Centre for Alternative Technology. E-mail: help@catinfo.demon.co.uk

Andrews, A. (1997). *Nomad Tent Types in the Middle East*, Part 1, Vol. 2. Beihefte Zum Tubinger Atlas Des Vorderen Orients.

Anink, D., Chiel Boonstra, C. and Mak, J. (1996). *Handbook of Sustainable Building: An Environmental Preference Method for Selection of Materials for use in Construction and Refurbishment*. James and James, London.

Association for Environment Conscious Builders (2000). The Real Green Building Book 2000, Yearbook of the Association for Environment Conscious Building. Nant-y-Garreg, Saron, Llandysul, Carmarthenshire SA44 5EJ (http://www.aecb.net).

Auliciems, A. and Szokolay, S. (1997). Thermal Comfort. University of Queensland Printery.

Bartsch, U. and Muller, B. (2000). *Fossil Fuels in a Changing Climate*. Oxford University Press.

Beamon, S. and Roaf, S. (1990). *The Ice-houses of Britain*. Routledge, London.

Beaumont, P., Bonine, M. and McLachlan, K. (1989). *Qanat, Kariz & Khattara Traditional Water Systems in the Middle East and North Africa*. Menas Press Limited.

Berge, B. (2000). *Ecology of building materials*. Architectural Press, Oxford.

Berman, A. J. (2001). *The Healthy Home Design Handbook*. Frances Lincoln, London.

Borer, P. and Harris, C. (1998). *The Whole House Book*. Cambrian Printers.

Building Research Establishment. *Review of Ultra-Low-Energy Homes*. General Information Report 38. A Series of UK and Overseas Profiles.

Building Research Establishment. *Review of Ultra-Low-Energy Homes. Ten UK Profiles in Detail*. General Information Report 39.

Building Research Establishment Digest (1980). Fire Hazards from Insulating Materials.

Building Research Establishment (1992). *Building Your Own Energy Efficient Home*. Good Practice Guide 194.

Building Research Establishment (1994). *Thermal Insulation, Avoiding Risks*. Report C1/SfB(A3j)(M2). HMSO, London. Tel.: +44 0207 8739090, Fax: +44 0207 873 8200, e-mail: brecsuenq@bre.co.uk

Building Research Establishment (1997). *Improving Airtightness in Existing Homes*. Good Practice Guide 224.

Building Research Establishment (1997). *Passive Solar Estate Layout*. General Information Report 27.

Building Research Establishment (1997). *Selecting Energy-Efficient Windows*. Good Practice Guide 227.

Building Research Establishment (1998). *Building a Sustainable Future. Homes for an Autonomous Community*. General Information Report 53.

Building Research Establishment (1998). *Planning for Passive Solar Design*. Available from BRECSU, BRE, Garston, Watford WD2 7JR, UK.

Building Research Establishment (1999). Radon: Guidance on Protective Measures in New Dwellings.

Building Research Establishment (2000). *Energy Efficient Offices*. Energy Consumption Guide 19.

Buono, M. (1998). *Architectura Del Vento*. Clean Edizioni Napoli.

Carpenter, P. (1992). *Sod It*. Coventry University Press.

Centre for Alternative Technology (1995). *Save Energy, Save Money*.

Chand, I. P., Bhargava, K. and Krishak, N. L. V. (1998). Effects of balconies on ventilation inducing aeromotive force on low rise buildings. *Building and Environment*, 33 (6), November, 385–396.

Chartered Institution of Building Services Engineers (1998). *Energy Efficiency in Buildings*. CIBSE Guide. For more information contact CIBSE.

CIBSE (1987). Applications Manual: Window Design.

Cook, J. (1994). *Extreme climates and indigenous architecture*. Proceedings of the PLEA Conference, Dead Sea, published by Desert Architecture Unit, Ben-Gurion University of the Negev, Israel.

Curwell, S. and March, C. (1986). *Hazardous Building Materials*, A Guide to the Selection of Alternatives. E. & F. N. Spon, London.

Curwell, S., Fox, R. and March, C. (1988). *Use of CFCs in Buildings*. Fernsheer Limited.

Curwell, S., March, C. and Venables, R. (1990). *Buildings and Health*. The Rosehaugh Guide. RIBA Publications Limited, UK.

Day, C. (1998). *A Haven for Childhood: The Building of a Steiner Kindergarten*. Starborn Books.

Day, C. (1990). *Places of the Soul: Architecture and Environmental Design as a Healing Art*. Aquarian, Wellingborough.

Day, C. (1990). *Building with Heart: A Practical Approach to Self and Community Building*. Green Books, Bideford.

Department of Civil and Systems Engineering (1978). *Design for Tropical Cyclones*, Volumes 1 and 2. James Cook University of North Queensland.

Dichler, A. (1994). *A review of the Technical merits of a proposed PV house in Oxfordshire*. ETSU S/02/00128/24. Energy Technology Support Unit, Harwell.

Diprose, P. (1999). *Architectural Implications of Sustainability on Built Form*. Ph.D. Thesis, Department of Architecture, University of Auckland, New Zealand.

Docherty, M. and Szokolay, S. (1999). Climate Analysis. PLEA Note 5. University of Queensland Printery.

Dommin, S. (1999). *A Hurricane Hunter's Photo Album*. http://www.members.aol.com/hotelq/page10.html

Dunn, G. E. and Miller, B. I. (1964). *Atlantic Hurricanes*. Louisiana State University Press, Baton Rouge, LA, 326 pp.

ECI (2000). *Lower Carbon Futures*. Environmental Change Institute, Oxford.

Energy Research Group (1999). *A Green Vitruvius*: Principles and Practice of Sustainable Architecture. James and James, London.

Energy Technology Support Unit (1996). S/P2/00240/REP. *A study into lifecycle environmental aspects of photovoltaics.*

Energy Technology Support Unit (2000). *Photovoltaics in Buildings Safety and the CDM Regulations*. ETSU Report No. S/P2/00313/REP. For more information contact BSRIA or e-mail: electrics@bsria.co.uk

Erell, E. and Tsoar, H. (1997). An experimental evaluation of strategies for reducing airborne dust in desert cities. *Building and Environment* 32(3), May, 225–236.

Farmer, J. (1999). *Green Shift*. Architectural Press.

Fawcett, T., Lane, K. and Boardman, B. (2000). *Lower Carbon Futures for European Households*. Environmental Change Institute, University of Oxford.

Fordham, M. and Partners (1999). *Photovoltaics in Buildings: A Design Guide*. Report No. ETSU S/P2/00282/REP. For more information contact The British Photovoltaic Association (PV-UK) at Tel: +44 0118 932 4418 or Fax: +44 0118 973 0820.

Galambos, T.V. (1990). *Making buildings safer for people: during hurricanes, earthquakes and fire*. van Nostrand Reinhold, New York.

Givoni, B. (1994). *Passive and Low Energy Cooling of Buildings*. Van Nostrand, New York.

Givoni, B. (2000). Minimum climatic information needed to predict performance of passive buildings in hot climates. *Proceedings of the PLEA Conference*, Cambridge, Pergamon Press.

Givoni, B. (2000). Building design in hot climates. *Proceedings of the TIA Conference*, Oxford, July. Available from TIA, School of Architecture, Oxford Brookes University, OX3 OBP, e-mail: tia@brookes.ac.uk

Gleick, P. (1993). *Water in Crisis*. Oxford University Press, USA.

Halliday, S. (2000). *Green Guide to the Architect's Job Book*. RIBA Publications, London.

Harris, R. (1995). The Thermal Performance of Timber Window Frames. *21AD: Offices*. Oxford Brookes University, School of Architecture Publication.

Headley, O. (2000). Renewable energy and the Small Island Developing States (SIDS): a case study of the Caribbean. *Proceedings of the TIA Conference*, Oxford. TIA, Oxford Brookes University.

Herschong, L. (1979). *Thermal delight in Architecture*. The MIT Press, Cambridge, Mass.

Hestnes, A., Hastings, R. and Saxhof, B. (1997) *Solar Energy Houses, Strategies, Technologies, Examples*. James and James, London, pp. 31–34.

Holland, G. J. (1993): 'Ready reckoner'. Chapter 9, *Global Guide to Tropical Cyclone Forecasting*. WMO/TC-No. 560, Report No. TCP-31. World Meteorological Organization; Geneva, Switzerland.

Houghton, J., Jenkins, G. and Ephraums, J. (eds) (1990). *Climate Change: The Intergovernmental Panel on Climate Change Assessment*. Cambridge University Press, Cambridge.

Jonsson, A. (2000). Tools and methods for environmental assessment of building products. *Building and Environment* 35(3) 223–238, ed E. Matthews, Pergamon Press.

Kindangen, J., Krauss, G. and Depecker, P. (1997). Effects of windshapes on wind-induced air motion inside buildings. *Building and Environment* 32(1), Jan., 1–14.

King, S., Rudder, D., Prasad, D. and Ballinger, J. (1996). *Site Planning in Australia*. Australian Government Publishing Service, Sydney.

Krishan, A. (1995). *Climatically Responsive Energy Efficient Architecture – a Design Handbook*. 1. Department of Planning at Delhi University, Dehli.

Kukadia, V. (1997). *Ventilation and Air Pollution: Buildings Located in Urban and City Centres*. Building Research Establishment Limited.

Lawson, B. (1996). Building Materials, Energy and the Environment. Royal Australian Institute of Architects, Canberra, Australia.

Le Corbusier (1924). *Une Petite Maison*. Le Corbusier Aux Editions d'Architecture, Zurich.

Lee, K., Han, D. and Lim, H. (1994). Evaluation of the thermal performance of traditional house in Ullungdo, Korea. *Proceedings of the PLEA Conference*, Dead Sea, Israel.

Lippsmeier, G. (1980). *Tropenbau, Building in the Tropics*. Verlag Callwey, Munich.

Lomas, K. J. (1996). The UK applicability study: an evaluation of thermal simulation programs for passive solar house design. *Building and Environment* 34(2), 139–164.

Lynes, J. (1992). Daylight and energy. In *Energy Efficient Building: A Design Guide*. eds S. Roaf and M. Hancock. Blackwells Scientific Publications Ltd.

Macks, (1978). Design for Tropical Cyclones.

Majoros, A. (1998). *Daylighting. PLEA Note 4*. The University of Queensland Printery.

Markham, S. F. (1982). *Climate and the Energy of Nations*. AMS Press, New York. First published in c.1947.

Mathews, E. (1997). *Building and Environment*. 32(1). Pergamon Press Ltd.

Matthews, J. (2000). *The Havelis of Jaiselmer*. Ph.D. Thesis. East London University.

Mazria, E. (1979). *The Passive Solar Energy Book*. Rodale Press, Emmaus, PA, USA.

McCartney, K. and Ford, B. (1978). *Practical Solar Heating*. Unwin Brothers Limited, UK.

McHarg, I. (1971). *Design With Nature*. Doubleday & Company Inc.

Mould, A. (1992). 'Designing effective insulation'. In Roaf, S. and Hancock, M. (eds), *Energy Efficient Building: A Design Guide*. Blackwell Scientific Publications, pp. 145–174.

National Asthma Campaign, UK (1997) *Asthma in Daily Life*. Website: http://www.asthma.org.uk

National House Building Council (1998). *Sustainable Housing – Meeting the Challenge*. NHBC Annual Conference. For more information contact the HSBC or see: http://www.nhbc.co.uk

Neumann, C. J. (1993). Global Overview. *Global Guide to Tropical Cyclone Forecasting*. WMO/TC-No. 560, Report No. TCP-31. World Meteorological Organization, Geneva, Switzerland.

Nowak, A. S. and Galambos, T. V. (eds) (1990). *Making Buildings Safer for People*. Van Norstrand, New York

Observ'ER (1998). *Systemes Solaires*. Special Architecture edition, May–June, No. 125. Available from Observ'ER, 146 Rue de l'Universite, 75007, Paris, France.

Oliver, P. (1997). *Encyclopedia of Vernacular Architecture of the World*. Cambridge University Press, Cambridge.

Olivier, D. (1992) *Energy Efficiency and Renewables: Recent Experience on Mainland Europe.* ISBN 0-9518791-0-3. Energy Advisory Associates.

Olivier, D. (2000). Plugging the air leaks. *Building for a Future,* Journal of the Association for Environment Conscious Builders, 9(4), 16–17. AECB.

Oreszczyn, T. (1992). Insulating the existing housing stock: mould growth and cold bridging. In Roaf, S. and Hancock, M. (eds), *Energy Efficient Building: A Design Guide.* Blackwell Scientific Publications, pp. 174–189.

Oreszczyn, T. (2000). Mould index. In, Rudge, J. and Nicol, F. (eds), *Cutting the Cost of Cold.* E. & F. N. Spon, London, pp. 122–133.

Oreszczyn, T. and Littler, J. (1989). *Cold Bridging and Mould Growth.* Final Report to the Science and Engineering Research Council by the Research in Buildings Group at Westminster University, London.

Pearson, S., Wheldon, A., Hadley, P., Awabi, N. and Parker, A. (1994). The Effects of Plants on the Environment in Non-Domestic Buildings. Report for the Building Research Establishment, Reading University, UK.

Piani, C. B. (1998). *Novel, Easy to Use Energy Saving Guidelines for South Africa.* Ph.D. Thesis, Department of Mechanical Engineering, University of Pretoria, South Africa.

Pitts, G. (1989). *Energy Efficient Housing – A Timber Frame Approach.* TRADA, ISBN, 0-901348-79-1.

Pitts, G. (2000). *Timber Frame: Re-engineering for Affordable Housing.* TRADA Technology Report 2/2000. ISBN 1900510251.

Quirouette, R. L. and Warnock, A. C. C. *Basics of Noise.* Building Science Insight website by the National Research Council of Canada. www.nrc.ca/irc/bsi/85.1_E.html

Rappaport, E. (1993): Preliminary Report 10 December 1993. National Hurricane Centre.

Reinberg, G. W. (1996). About the language of solar architecture. *Proceedings of 4th International Conference on Solar Energy in Architecture and Urban Design.* Berlin, pp. 108–111.

Ricklefs, R. E. and Miller, G. L. (1999). *Ecology.* 4th Edition, W. H. Freeman and Co., New York.

Roaf, S., Yates, A., Brownhill, D. and Howard, N. (2000). *EcoHomes The Environmental Rating for Homes.* Construction Research Communications Limited. A BRE Publication.

Roaf, S. (1979). *A Study of the Architecture of the Black Tents of the Lurs.* Diploma Thesis at the Architectural Association, London.

Roaf, S. and Fuentes, M. (1998). *Demonstration Project for a 4 KW Domestic Photovoltaic Roof in Oxford – Volume 1.* ETSU Report No. S/P2/00236/00/00, School of Architecture, Oxford Brookes University.

Roaf, S. and Hancock, M. (1992). *Energy Efficient Building.* Blackwell Scientific Publications.

Roaf, S. and Walker, V. (1996). *21AD: Photovoltaics.* Architectural Digest for the 21st Century: Photovoltaics. For more information: V. Walker, School of Architecture, Oxford Brookes University, Oxford OX3 OBP, UK.

Roaf, S. and Walker, V. (1997). *21AD: Water.* Architectural Digest for the 21st Century. For more information: V. Walker, School of Architecture, Oxford Brookes University.

Rossouw, B. J. (1997). A new low-cost solar water heater. Thesis for a Master of Engineering, Faculty of Engineering, Department of

Mechanical Engineering, University of Pretoria. Contact e-mail: emath-ews@postino.up.ac.za

Rudge, J. and Nicol, F. (2000). *Cutting the Cost of Cold.* E. & F. N. Spon.

Sandifer, S. (2000). Thermal effects of vines on wall surfaces. *Proceedings of the TIA Conference*, Oxford. Contact e-mail: sandifer@ucla.edu

Santamouris, M. and Asimakopoulos, D. (eds) (1996). *Passive Cooling of Buildings.* James & James Ltd, London.

Schaeffer, J. et al. (1994). *Solar Living Source Book.* Chelsea Green Publishing Company, White River Junction, VT.

Seymour, J. and Girardet, H. (1987). *Blueprint for a Green Planet.* Dorling Kindersley Limited.

Stephens, H. (1996). *Solar Energy in Architecture and Urban Planning.* H. S. Stephens and Associates.

Strong, S. and Scheller, W. (1993). *The Solar Electric House.* Sustainability Press.

Szokolay, S. (1996). The role of thermal mass in warm-humid climates. *PLEA Conference Proceedings*, Louvain le Neuve, Belgium.

Szokolay, S. (1996). *Solar Geometry.* PLEA Note 1. University of Queensland Printery.

Szokolay, S. (1997). The role of thermal mass in cold climates. *PLEA Conference Proceedings*, Kushiro, Japan, pp. 207–212.

Szokolay, S. and Sale, R. (1979). *The Australia and New Zealand Solar Home Book: a Practical Guide.* Australia & New Zealand Book Company Pty Ltd.

Talbott, J. (1993). *Simply Build Green.* Findhorn Press, Scotland.

Thomas, H. R. and Rees, S. W. (1999). The thermal performance of ground floor slabs – a full-scale in-situ experiment. *Building and Environment* 34(2), 139–164.

Trimby, P. (1999). *Solar Water Heating a D-I-Y Guide.* The Centre for Alternative Technology.

U.S. Protection Agency. A Citizen's Guide to Radon. OPA-86-004.

Vale, B. and Vale, R. (2000). *The New Autonomous House.* Thames and Hudson Limited.

Viljoen, A. (1997). *The Environmental Impact of Energy Efficient Dwellings, Taking into Account Embodied Energy and Energy in Use.* European Directory of Sustainable and Energy Efficient Building 1997; James and James, London, pp. 47–52.

Warm, P. (1997). Optimum thickness of insulation. In *Building for a Future*, Journal of the Association for Energy Conscious Builders, 7(3), 11. Tel. and Fax: +44 1559 370908, e-mail: admin@aecb.net, http://www.aecb.net

Warm, P. (1998). 'Reflective, thin insulations'. In *Building for a Future*, Journal of the Association for Energy Conscious Builders, 8(2), 48–49.

Wells, M. (1982). *Gentle Architecture.* McGraw Hill, New York.

Were, J. (1992). Air is stupid (it can't follow the arrows). *Proceedings of the PLEA Conference*, Auckland, 1992 (in press with Steven Szokolay).

West, J., Atkinson, C. and Howard, N. (1994). *Embodied Energy and Carbon Dioxide Emissions for Building Materials.* Paper 2, Materials Session, Proceedings of the First International Conference, Buildings and the Environment, CIB, 16–20 May 1994. BRE, UK.

Williamson, A. G. (1997). *Energy Efficiency in Domestic Buildings, a Literature Review and Commentary.* Ministry of Commerce, New Zealand.

Woolley, T., Kimmins, S., Harrison, P. and Harrison, R. (1997). *Green Building Handbook*. E. & F. N. Spon, London.

Yannas, S. (1994). *Solar Energy and Housing Design*, Volume 1. E. G. Bond Limited.

Yannas, S. (1994). *Solar Energy and Housing Design*, Volume 2. E. G. Bond Limited.

Zold, A. and Szokolay, S. (1997). *Thermal Insulation*. PLEA Note 2. University of Queensland Printery (for a copy, contact: s.szokolay@mailbox.uq.edu.au).

USEFUL WEB ADDRESSES

http://www.interknowledge.com/st-maarten/index.html
http://news.ai/luis.html
http://www.nhc.noaa.gov/1995luis.html
http://www.boker.org.il/davids/nvzin/sakis/housakis.htm
http://www.ecoscape.se
http://www.mapsofindia.com/worldmap/index.html
http://www.findhorn.org/index.html
http://www.cmhc-schl.gc.ca/
http://www.solarcat.co.jp/eomsolar.html
http://www.idi.or.jp/

CONVERSION FACTORS by Andrew Bairstow

$1 \text{ m}^2 = 11 \text{ feet}^2$
$1 \text{ cm} = 0.39 \text{ inches}$
$1 \text{ m}^3 = 35 \text{ feet}^3$
$1 \text{ km h}^{-1} = 0.62 \text{ miles h}^{-1}$
$1°\text{C change} = 1.8°\text{F change}$
$0°\text{C} = 32°\text{F}$
$1 \text{ l} = 0.22 \text{ gal}$

INDEX

Acryllic, 133, 139
Adaptation, 11, 35
Aggregates, 47
Air, 70
Air-conditioning, 8, 9, 122
Air quality, 58, 76
Allergens, 125
Aluminium, 45, 49, 70, 76
Anglian Water housing project, 235–7
Antarctic, 36
Asbestos, 125
Asthma, 125–7

Bariloche Case Study Ecohouse, 36, 157, 161, 296–302
Benefits of Ecohousing, 35
Berge, Bjorn's Ecohouse in Norway, 240, 251–3
Booth, Roger, 9
BP oil company, 10
BP Solar, 34
Breathing wall, 29
Bricks, 47, 48
Building analogies 17–32
Buildings:
    invisible life of, 15, 16
Building Regulations, 58
Building Research Establishment, 46

Cancer of the skin, 7, 127

Carbon dioxide, 128
    emissions from buildings, 49, 50, 57, 58, 78, 86
    emissions from PV systems, 167–8
Carbon monoxide, 103, 128
Centre for Alternative Technology, 53, 56, 59
Chipboard, 70, 135
Chloroflourochlorines (CFCs), 128
Cladding, 55
Climate, 1, 239, 240
Climate Change, 5, 6, 8, 11, 13
Climatic design, 9, 17, 35
    in hot climates, 20–21
Coal, 1, 5
Cold bridging, 63, 74–81, 102
Colonial bungalows, 31
Concrete, 47, 48, 54, 55, 70
Conservatories, 156
Contaminated land, 129
Cool Core buildings, 31
Cooling buildings, see ventilation
Courtyards, 20
Cradle-to-grave, 46, 48
Cross-ventilation, 20
Cyclones, 20

Day, Christopher's house in Wales, 87, 94, 240, 321–4
Design, 90–2

Disabled access, 129
Draughts, 32
Duncan, Graham's house in New Zealand, 279–81
Durability, 45, 60, 93
Dustmites, 130

Earthquake design, 130–1
Earth sheltering, 131–2
Ecohouse:
    what is an, 1–13
    key issues, 10
    projects, 32
Ecological:
    buildings, 13, 51, 92
    concerns, 86
    niche, 13
    watersheds, 1
Ecolonia in Holland, 123
Embodied energy, 40, 47, 52, 53, 54, 56, 58, 61
Energy:
    primary and delivered, 41
    efficiency, 8, 43
    in-use, 45, 52, 54, 58
Envelope of the building, 63
Environmental impacts, 49, 54, 58
    buildings, 13, 49, 54, 58
    materials, 38–48, 86, 93, 134
    PV systems, 168
    solar hot water systems, 205, 206

Epoxy resins and glues, 132

Findhorn house in Scotland, 99, 246–50
Finishes, 102
    Hand rendering, 88
Fire, 132
Floor slab, 32
Floors, 134
Form, 15–18
Forestry Stewardship Council, 50
Formaldehyde, 135, 139
Fossil fuels, 1–5, 13
    depletion of, 5, 11
Fresh air, 88
Furnishings, 101
    carpets, 134–5

Garcia-Chavez, Roberto's Echouse in Mexico city, 308–12
Gas, 1, 2, 4, 5, 13
Glass, 47, 48, 70, 76
    roofs, 9
Glazing, 51
    too much, 76
Gledlow Valley Ecohouses, 234–5
Global warming, 5–7, 10, 11, 22, 23
Goudsmit, George and Mary's Ecohouse at Findhorn, 246–50
Greenhouses, 22, 23, 156
Greenhouse gasses, 5, 7, 8
Green design, 1
Green roof, 52
Ground storage systems, 5

Happiness, 123
Hardwood, 50, 70
Havelli in Jaisalmer, 21
Health, 123–47
Heat recovery, 48, 57
Hot core buildings, 25, 27
Housing layout, 32, 33
Humidity control, 29.102

Humphreys, Michael, 35
Hungarian Ecohouse project, 32, 33, 36
Hurricane 115, 116
Hypocaust, 27, 28

Ice-house, 19, 20, 31
Igloos, 24, 25
Indian Ecohouses:
    Bidani house in Faridabad, 288–90
    Lall house in New Dehli, 282–7
    Monama house in Hyderabad, 256–61
Indonesian Ecohouse in Surabaya, 37, 272–4
Infiltration of air, 79, 80
Innovation and the temptation to innovate, 10
Insulation, 4, 8, 51, 58, 63, 68, 70, 74
    as in a tea cosy
    capacitive, 71
    cavity, 76
    cost of, 68
    fire and, 132–4
    optimal thickness of, 65
    reflective, 70
    resistive, 70
    in windows, 60
Insulation materials:
    cellular glass, 66
    cellulose, 66
    cork, 67, 70
    expanded polystyrene, 66, 70, 133, 135
    glass fibre, 133
    melamine foam, 67
    microporous, 67
    mineral.rock wool, 70
    phenolic foam, 66, 70
    polyisocyanurate foam, 67
    polyurethane foam, 67, 70, 133, 141
    urea formaldehyde foam, 70, 133, 135
    Warmcell, 48

Intergovernmental Panel of Climate Change, 5
Iron, 86

Japanese Ecohouses:
    O.M.Solar house at Hammamatsu, 262–5
    Sagara house in Tokyo, 266–7
Johnson, David's house in Wales, 89, 325–7

Kakkleoven, 28, 29
Kapoor, Prashant's Ecohouse, 256–61
Kimura, Professor K's Ecohouse in Tokyo, 239, 266–8
Korean village house, 28, 29

Lall, Ashok's Ecohouse in New Dehli, 240, 282–7
Lead, 50, 70, 135, 139
Le Corbusier, 15, 17, 44, 52
Legionella, 136
Levine, Richard's Ecohouse in Kentucky, 5, 240, 313–6
Lifecycle analysis, 46–8, 54, 57, 61
Life span, 40, 45, 46
Light, 81, 144
Lightwell, 20
Lim, Jimmy's Ecohouse in Malaysia, 31, 103, 240, 268–71
Lime rich mortar, 88
Linoleum, 134
Linacre College in Oxford, 233
Low carbon lifestyle, 8
Low energy houses, 58

Malaysian house, 31, 37, 268–71
Mantainer, 63–5
Maintenance, 40, 46
Marble, 70
Materials for buildings, 13, 38–48, 51, 58, 88, 93, 134
Mechanical ventilation, 48, 57, 58

Meir, Isaac's Ecohouse in the Negev, 291–5
Metals, 48, 49, 77
Mexican Ecohouse of Roberto Garcia-Chavez, 308–12
Middleton, Charles's Ecohouse in Ontario, 317–20
Moisture, 32
Morrison, David's Ecohouse in St.Maarten, 240, 303–7
Moulds, 137

New Vernacular, 13, 239–41
New Zealand Ecohouse, 192–4
Nicol Graph, 17, 35–7, 114, 239
Nicol, Fergus, 35
Nightime cooling of buildings, 114
Noise, 137–9
Nomadic architecture, 24
Norwegian Ecohouse by Bjorn Berge, 251–3
Nylon wall ties, 77

Oil, 1–5, 13
O.M.Solar Ecohouse in Hammamatsu, 262–5
Orientation, 29
Overheating in buildings, 9, 22, 29, 59, 145, 148
Oxford Ecohouse, 8, 26, 34, 38, 52–4, 61, 72, 73, 75, 110, 124, 143–5, 162, 168, 182–92, 213, 242–5
Ozone, 5, 10

Paints, 45, 58, 139–40
Passive design, 9, 29, 36, 37
Passive solar design, 5, 143, 149–64
Pasive cooling, see Ventilation
Pets, 126, 140
Photovoltaics, 9–11, 34, 53, 57, 58, 165–99
Place, 88–91
Plants, 140

Plaster, 47, 58, 102, 134, 141
Plasterboard, 48, 70
Plastics, 48, 49, 86, 87, 133
Polypropylene, 133
Polythene, 134
Polyvinylchloride (PVC), 49, 85, 133, 134, 141
Population, 1
Porch, 101
Privacy, 32, 143, 145

Queensland Ecohouse by Felix Riedweg 30, 36, 275–9

Radon, 103, 141–2
Rammed earth, 55–57, 59, 70
Recycled materials, 43, 46, 51, 58
Reinberg, Georg, 30
Renewable energy, 9, 54
Renewable resources, 50
Reusable buildings, 251–3
Riedweg, Felix's Ecohouse in Townsville, Queensland, 275–9
Rockbeds, 5, 36, 159, 161
Rot in wood, 50, 51
Rubber, 143

Security, 32, 143, 145, 146
Shell Oil company, 9, 10
Site, 1, 239
Slates, 54
Solar buildings and design, 5, 152, 148–61
Solar hot water systems, 5, 34, 57, 58, 205–14
Solar potential of sites, 30, 32
Solar shading, 57
Soul in buildings, 85–94
St.Maarten Ecohouse by David Morrison, 99, 303–7
Stainless steel, 49
Steel, 43, 47, 70, 76, 86
Stone, 70
Straw, 59

Starwboard, 70
Sunpath diagram, 150

Tents, 21–3
Thermal delight, 15, 103, 148
Thermal comfort, 35, 36, 101–7, 148, 239
Thermal mass, 25, 27, 55–59, 71, 72, 102, 112–14, 143, 155
Timber, 47–52, 54, 57, 58, 76, 86, 87, 102
hardwood, 50, 70
softwood, 45, 50, 51, 70
Time lags between indoor and outdoor temperatures, 21
Toxic materials and emissions, 49, 51, 60
Typhoons, 115–22

Vale, Brenda and Robert, 192
Vapour barrier, 79
Ventilation 20, 21, 32, 36, 57, 60, 79, 95–122, 145, 239
Vinyl, 134, 135
Volatile Organic Compounds (VOCs), 49, 133, 139, 147

Wall paper 134, 147
Water, using it wisely, 216–31
conservation of, 217–20
grey water systems, 221–6, 233–7
septic tanks systems, 226–32
Waxes, 45
WCs, 217–9, 229–30
composting WCs, 64, 92, 230, 218
Wiberg, Krister's Ecohouse, 254–5
Wind, 32, 96–100, 107, 115–22
Windcatchers of Yazd, 98, 109
Windows, 45, 60–3, 78, 81–4, 111, 115
Woodwool slabs, 70
Wood preservatives, 147